Command-Level CICS Programming

Command-Level CICS Programming

Alex Varsegi

FIRST EDITION
FIRST PRINTING

Library of Congress Cataloging-in-Publication Data

Varsegi, Alex.
   Command-level CICS programming / by Alex Varsegi.
     p.   cm.
   Includes index.
   ISBN 0-8306-6705-9 (H)
   1. CICS (Computer system)   2. Systems programming (Computer
science)   I. Title.
QA76.76.T45V37   1991
005.4'3—dc20   91-19586
                                         CIP

For information about other McGraw-Hill materials, call 1-800-2-MCGRAW in the U.S. In other countries call your nearest McGraw-Hill office.

Acquisitions Editor: Jerry Papke
Book Editor: Sally Glover
Production: Katherine G. Brown
Book Design: Jaclyn J. Boone   WP1

Dedication
To my wife, Marie,
and to my children, Mary and George

Acknowledgments

I would like to thank Mary Sullivan and Larry Cheeks for providing vital material and supporting me in this project.

Contents

Introduction

This book focuses on a wealth of conventional and special topics relating to CICS, the Customer Information Control System software developed by IBM. The examples used in this presentation are extensive, and they assume a certain amount of coding skills past the beginner level. Nevertheless, beginners can also use parts of this material because it is built from ground-level up, while systematically introducing topics of additional complexity in later chapters.

One of the many strengths of this book is a thorough explanation of the specific environment necessary to understand and evaluate a problem and write source code. Each chapter is organized into three major sections, supported by numerous tutorial exhibits. These sections are:

1. A case study to familiarize you with a specific problem and the overall working environment.
2. A section containing a list of the source program.
3. Excerpts from a compiler-expanded source code, including all necessary copy statements and the symbolic map.

The tutorials include comprehensive overviews, background studies, control tables, maps, and a glossary that explains technical terms.

In Chapter 1, I describe the operating environment necessary for problem solving. Read this chapter carefully because it will help you understand some of the standard requirements common to all source programs.

Chapter 2 explains how to code simple menu programs, including all the necessary documentation. The book uses two separate menu programs to illustrate how to branch and utilize the COMMUNICATIONS AREA for messages required by the recipient transaction.

In Chapter 3, I show you how to develop an INQUIRY program. INQUIRY programs are those that, unlike BROWSE programs, need to meet exact user-supplied criteria. INQUIRY programs, as a rule, do not require special editing logic, and they are fairly straightforward from the programmer's perspective.

Chapter 4 reviews the mechanics of a DELETE program. The reason I cover a DELETE transaction before familiarizing you with an ADD or CHANGE transaction is simply because of the complexity of ADD and CHANGE transactions. DELETE programs are relatively uncomplicated, and you need not worry about extensive edits. In fact, the only prerequisite is that the particular record that is ear-marked for deletion must be on file. Once you have located that record, you need to reemphasize to your terminal operator that the record flagged for deletion is about to be erased, which requires an additional function key action.

Chapter 5 continues with a more complex set of UPDATE procedures, such as an ADD program. In this chapter, you learn how to use extensive edits and some important methodologies regarding attributes, symbolic map definitions, and the use of tables.

Chapter 6 provides you with the mechanics to develop a CHANGE program and perform all the necessary editing procedures. This chapter also highlights in detail a technique utilized in creating *program shells*. Program shells are useful tools for developing similar programs the easy way. For example, your source code for a CHANGE transaction can be built based on a similar ADD transaction.

Chapters 7 and 8 highlight two BROWSE programs of different complexities. The source code developed in Chapter 7 is simplistic compared to the one reviewed in Chapter 8. The source code in Chapter 7 only performs a forward BROWSE, meaning that back-ward browsing can only be achieved by resetting the search key to a lower value. In contrast, the source program listed in Chapter 8 uses both forward and backward BROWSE capabilities, as well as function key procedures to locate the first and the last record on file. For efficiency, both source programs rely on OCCURS statements in the BMS and when subscripting in the source program.

Chapter 9 introduces the concept of creating tutorial programs that are user-oriented. Exiting and returning to a set of tutorial procedures are both transaction I.D.-oriented, and you will not lose your place on the current panel during your jumping sequence.

In Chapter 10, I describe an environment that uses "transient" or online reporting facilities. In programming for such an environment, I utilize a three-step approach. In step 1, I invoke an online report through menu selection. In step 2, I build a transient data queue using exact print images. This includes headers and other constant information, as well as multiple detail lines. In step 3, I use the previously built transient queue to print the desired report, while depleting the contents of the above temporary dataset.

1

Introduction to a problem-oriented CICS environment

The primary purpose of this chapter is to describe a working environment within the framework of problem-oriented case studies. This is important for the following reasons:

1. Most of the narratives pertaining to a case study do not have to be restated every time a particular environment is described.
2. Some of the technical issues need to be explained in advance so that you fully understand how standards are applied and how files are set up to accommodate a number of different user communities.

This book is designed to highlight a number of practical issues in efficient coding techniques, covering an array of cases on browsing, inquiring, maintaining and reporting on a particular database. The book essentially focuses on three separate applications in describing a working model. The first model deals with a vendor database viable in a typical Billing/Invoicing application, as highlighted in Chapters 3 through 6. These chapters explain in detail the mechanics of an INQUIRY, a DELETE, an ADD and a CHANGE transaction. A second set of applications are prevalent in a typical inventory environment, which is the topic of Chapters 7, 8, and 10. These chapters expand on the role of simple and advanced INQUIRY procedures and the use of online, transient reports. A third set, Chapter 9, is dedicated to the philosophy of preparing advanced tutorials or HELP screens custom-tailored to a user's specific needs.

Applications presented in Chapters 7, 8, and 10 deal with transaction processing using a transportation-industry model, an industry now serving millions of Americans in all major U.S. cities and still gaining in momentum. This customized aspect of problem solving provides a better perspective in dealing with certain situations, including a truly dynamic environment. For example, the customized inventory in the railroad industry would include "rolling stock" equipment that largely encompasses control cars, switch engines and locomotives, in addition to other, more conventional pieces of equipment such as trucks, cars, snowplows, electrical fixtures, office equipment and so on. What's more important is the gradual introduction of added complexity and logic required to develop a CICS-driven working model.

Background review for the case studies

Because of the specialized nature (and complexity) of some of the programs presented in Chapters 7, 8, and 10, let's review and clarify some of the procedures. The commuter system in a major U.S. city is handled by the Metropolitan Commuter Railway Agency or MCRA, which is responsible for the day to day operation of five major commuter railway systems or carriers. For the purpose of consistency, the term carrier will be used throughout this book. The five carriers are: the Central Commuter Railway System (mostly referred to as Central), Southeastern Commuter Railroad, the Southeast Indiana System, Central Michigan and the Northeastern Illinois Railroad Company. MCRA is responsible for the above carriers in terms of printing payroll checks and tickets, maintaining their rolling stock in an operating condition, and assigning work. The agency maintains all five carriers in a number of consolidated files. This means that there is only one Equipment Inventory file for all five carriers, one Equipment Repair file, one Personnel or Employee Roster and so on. To maintain file integrity, and especially file security, each record type on file carries a concatenated key that is organized in the following manner:

- It has a three-position carrier code, which is the highest qualifier of the KSDS or key sequenced data set key. This field is mostly present regardless of the particular record type being accessed.

    The carrier code is essentially the basis for MCRA's file scheme, allowing a single carrier to access only its own logical database, or more precisely, record type. MCRA, on the other hand, is the parent agency and has access to all five of the carriers, depending, of course, on the range of authority of the particular user.

- A second field in the concatenated key is normally dedicated to the carrier's line, which is a two-position long alphanumeric field. A line is simply a subdivision within a carrier. For example, the Northeastern Illinois Railroad Company can be subdivided into two physical lines or regions. The first one is referred to as the "182nd Street Line," since it runs from the city out to 182nd Street based on a regular or holiday schedule. The second line is called the "North Line" because the latter encompasses most of the northern communities on the perimeter of the city.

    Typically, in an inventory situation, a line has little significance, since equipment ownership and equipment use is not restricted to a particular line. So in most inventory records, the line is replaced by an equipment number, which is also incorporated into the concatenated key.

- The third component of the key varies, depending on a specific procedure. In most personnel related applications, for example, the key carries a seven-position long employee identifier, which, for the purpose of uniformity among the carriers, needs to be zero in its high-order positions if the identifier falls short of seven numeric positions. This is accomplished through BMS (Basic Mapping Support) and some programmer edited procedures.

To keep matters in perspective, I used BMS for the screen-mapping process, since this is probably the most standard in the industry. This is coupled with the fact that screen painting productivity tools currently available on the market are so numerous that it would be next to impossible to use any one of them as a prototype.

Structural organization and path definition

The system presented in this book performs a variety of functions, such as inventory, billing, invoicing, and so on. It also introduces some new concepts in developing an extensive, user-maintained tutorial subsystem (Chapter 10) to resolve some of the more complex procedures.

Because of the comprehensive nature of our application, this system is completely menu-driven. The term "menu-driven" enables a specific user or user group to access a small functional area in an otherwise complex application. This method enhances and expedites user training, a learning process that allows users to

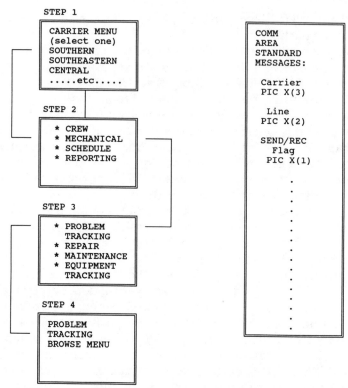

1-1 A hierarchical overview to show how TRE6BRS fits into the overall path

become "experts" in a relatively brief period. Figure 1-1 is an overview of this structural makeup.

As you move "down" from top to bottom on the system path, notice that you are getting more and more involved in specifics. If you only have access to an equipment browse function, for example, steps 1 through 3 will need to be performed only once after you have logged onto the system. With standard security precautions (not necessarily CICS provided), you won't have to worry about getting off track. A security methodology is in place to make sure that selections other than the one you are restricted to are disallowed. This forces you to observe your individual user path. Note that most security packages on the market today provide you with multilevel safeguards such as those pertaining to files or to transactions, some offering restricted access based on data fields, as cumbersome as it may seem.

As you move on from one transaction to another, you need to update the communications area. Since our system utilizes a top down approach, each program in it relies on certain hierarchies expecting carrier information at first, then functional information, and so on. This means that unless you satisfy the first set of requirements, you cannot proceed.

In the sample programs shown in this book, I assume that the programmer has followed a predefined hierarchical path. Thus, each program relies on certain basic information or messages, regardless of what hierarchical level it "tunes" into the system. The first level of this hierarchical dependency assumes that you have entered a valid carrier number. It also assumes that in step 2 you have made the proper functional selection and so on. You will not be able to invoke a program merely by clearing the screen in front of you and entering a transaction identifier, since this would not provide the COMMUNICATIONS AREA with some of the required messages.

Security plays an extended role in the design, as well. If you are a user, for example, from the Central Commuter Railway Company wanting to access information other than your own carrier, the system will simply lock you out of such a transaction. Full access to the entire system (that is to all carriers) is only provided to the parent company, which is the Metropolitan Commuter Railway Agency. An overview of this is shown in FIG. 1-2.

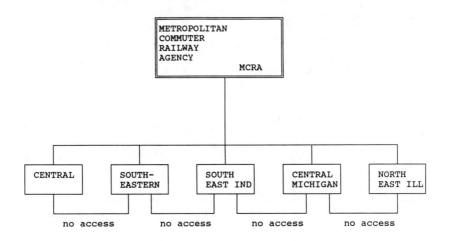

1-2 Security arrangements between carriers

Source code and narrative presentation

Sections with source code listings are arranged to reflect a set of corresponding narratives on a line by line basis, where possible. Thus, source programs are accompanied by an extensive overview on corresponding pages. As you will soon see, it is difficult to keep up with a typical program in a sequential manner, since program logic does not, as a rule, flow in a straight line or in a linear fashion. Subroutines are constantly invoked through the various perform statements, triggering additional procedures that might have as many as six or seven alternate routes available to them. This is reflected in FIG. 1-3. One of the significant features of this book is a comprehensive presentation on the compiled version of each source code that shows you statements, record layouts, etc., expanded from the original copy library, where there is information on record layouts and other CICS blocks.

075	MOVE 'Y' TO CARRIERA	Statement 075 is designed to
076	MOVE CARRIER-CODE TO	intensify the carrier code field.
077	CARRIERO	This is followed by moving the
078	MOVE EMPLOYEE-ID TO	record portion of the carrier
079	EMPLOYO	field (line 076) to the map.
080	MOVE 'Y' TO EMPLOYA.	
081	EXEC CICS HANDLE AID	After these move statements the
082	CLEAR(0100-CLEAR-ROUTINE)	programmer defines a set of
083	PF1(0200-MAIN-MENU)	handle condition which conforms
084	PF2(0300-CANCEL)	with certain shop standards. For
085	PF3(0400-DELETE-RECORD)	example, line 082 sets up a
086	ANYKEY(0500-INVALID-KEY)	procedure in paragraph 0100-CLEAR-
087	END-EXEC.	ROUTINE. Like-wise in lines 084
088	IF PFENTER	through 086 , other function keys
089	MOVE 'X' TO PF-KEYS	are defined. For additional
090	GO TO 800-START-SESSION.	record layout, please refer to
091	0100-RECEIVE-MAP.	lines 334 through 445 in the
092	MOVE '-' TO MSGA.	compiler section of this chapter.
093	MOVE 'A' TO EMPIDA.	
094	MOVE 'Y' TO CARRIERA.	Lines 092 provides the field
095	MOVE ' ' TO MSGO.	with a protected mode displayed
096	EXEC CICS	in blue. The attribute "A" in
097	RECEIVE MAP('TCSB')	line 093 enables you to display
098	MAPSET('TCSBMAP')	the employee identification field
099	END-EXEC.	in an unprotected, low intensity
100	IF EMPIDI = SPACES OR	mode (shown in green) for data
101	EMPIDL = ZEROS	entry by the terminal operator
102	MOVE 'I' TO MSGA	
103	MOVE -1 TO EMPIDL	Once the attributes are set up

1-3 Shows the standard way of presenting source code and associated narratives

Each section in this book has a standardized format to provide clarity and the necessary structure to explain a particular environment, translate such an environment into source code, and show a machine expansion of the source code through compiler processing. Supporting documents are also provided, such as FCT (File Control Table) definitions, DCT's (Destination Control Tables), and symbolic and programmer-developed maps.

As mentioned earlier, there are two types of program listings available in this book. The first listing is a programmer-written source code, which is part of the "Source program listing and narrative" section. The second listing is a compiler-generated version of the original source code, where all the copy statements are expanded from the copy library. This list is shown under "Compiler generated source code: excerpts." Due to the length of the compiler listing, (generally speaking, three to four times the length of the source program), only the DATA DIVISION portion of the compiled program is presented. An exception to this rule is shown in Chapters 2 and 5, where an entire compiler listing is presented. Note that I use the term line and/or statement numbers interchangeably in reference to a particular line of a source code.

Security considerations

In most automated environments, security provided by CICS is greatly enhanced to address certain customized situations. Currently, there are a variety of security packages on the software market, such as ACF2, TOP SECRET, etc., that will give you almost any level of security: read only, read and update, transaction level control, and protection on the file, record and data field levels. In this section, I am going to give you a brief overview of some of the considerations necessary to build a viable security environment to meet your specific needs.

READ ONLY security refers to the user's ability to read a file without being able to change its contents. READ ONLY security normally applies to users with limited file access, such as BROWSE and INQUIRY capabilities. READ ONLY displays a panel showing data fields in a protected mode, usually leaving a single inquiry key available to initiate a predefined search.

READ and UPDATE enables you to ADD, CHANGE, and DELETE both data fields and record types. READ and UPDATE security normally operates in an unrestricted manner, which means it enables you to have full control over a file, regardless of the data-elements contained on that file.

Data field level security is a refinement of the READ and UPDATE mode. With data field security, you would be allowed to change a field, such as a voluntary deduction field for professional or union dues, but you would not be able to alter some of the other fields, such as your gross or your net pay, insurance deduction, and so on. This type of security is normally in place when a particular panel is being accessed by a number of different users. The implementation of this type of security requires substantial work, and it is somewhat painstaking.

TRANSACTION-level security refers to the user's ability to have access to a particular CICS transaction using one of the above situations, (i.e., READ ONLY, READ and UPDATE, Data field-level security, etc.). Suppose you have written two UPDATE programs. One can add a record to a file, while the other one only deletes a record upon request. The ADD program has a transaction identifier of ADD1. The DELETE program, on the other hand, is referred to as DEL1. Thus, you may have full access to ADD1 in the READ and UPDATE mode, while you are locked out of the latter DEL1 transaction.

FILE-level control monitors access based on a particular file. Thus, you might have access to an accounts receivable transaction file, but not to the accounts receivable master. Once you have defined a FILE-level transaction, you can achieve access a number of ways as previously discussed.

RECORD-level security further subcategorizes the contents of a file into various record types. Thus, if your payroll master contains a number of different record types, such as a deduction record, an insurance record, a demographic record, and an employee history record, you might need to have access to the insurance segment of the file, but not to the other record types.

TERMINAL or LOCATION security, in conjunction with some of the earlier mentioned restrictions, enables you to have access to a system only through a particular terminal or terminal location. So, if you work in purchasing, and it has a predefined terminal in that location, you cannot use other terminals elsewhere, for example, to access, enter, or modify any transaction.

Security is normally controlled on a user's logon identifier, which is processed by the system just as soon as it is entered. In sophisticated security packages, such as ACF2 (Computer Associates), you can write individual security rules for just about any number of users in the system. When writing rules in this fashion, it is important to classify the user community into a number of similar groups. Consider as much standardization as practical under the circumstances.

Standard function key assignments

It is necessary to standardize the way you use your function keys in order to simplify some of the procedures frequently used in your system. Thus, if you were to use PF 6 to BROWSE forward in a particular BROWSE program and PF 7 to BROWSE backward, then it only makes sense to repeat the same assignment when using identical procedures in another program. To carry this a step farther, assume you are referring to an ADD or a DELETE program that, as a rule, does not perform any of the above procedures. If you were not concerned with standardization, you might reassign PF 6 and PF 7 to other functions, such as updating a file or deleting a record. But this would be too confusing in a large system. It would be a great deal more efficient not to reassign those command keys. Thus, PF 6 and PF 7 would be unassigned in an update or in a menu program. After all, in a typical IBM 3270 environment, you do have 24 function keys to refine your transaction-oriented procedures.

The problem that comes into play is the variety of different hardware pieces used in a typical system. For example, in our model, we relied extensively on other than "dumb" terminals, such as a number of PC's emulating an IBM 3270 environment. In a typical PC environment, function keys are not used as readily as in most main-frame systems. The keyboard, as a rule, does initially accommodate 12 function keys. Once you need to have access to additional, double-digit function keys, you will simply have to emulate them. This undoubtedly tends to complicate things, especially with the less-sophisticated users. For example, to arrive at function key 13 in an IBM System 2 environment, you need to combine two keys into a single stroke, such as the alternate key and the character Q. Function key 14, on the other hand, uses the alternate key and the character W pressed at the same time.

Figure 1-4 shows a standard assignment used in the various parts of the model. PF 3, which is normally used for updating a record, stands for a DELETE task under one set of conditions, while it might stand for an ADD function under other circumstances. As you can see, PF 1 simply returns you to a menu screen that is one hierarchical level above your current activities. PF 2 cancels a transaction so you can start out from scratch with an empty screen. PF 4 and PF 5 were left open for some specialized assignment. PF 6 and PF 7 enable you to BROWSE forward or backward, as needed. PF 8 will invoke the very first record on file, which comes in handy with voluminous datasets. Likewise, PF 9 will take you down to the last record of a given file.

Attributes and the symbolic map

Once you have developed your BMS code for a particular screen-layout, it will have to be assembled very much like you would assemble a source program written in basic assembler language. Following a successful assembly, the map is placed into a library, defined by shop standards or by the programmer. This map is referred to as the symbolic map.

Maps that are assembled in this book use the copy library so

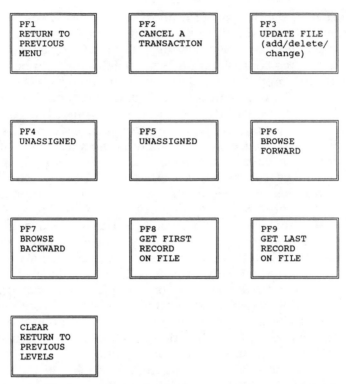

1-4 Shows standard PF key assignments in the system model

that they are available for those programmers who need to have access to them. Referencing the symbolic map is normally done in two stages. In stage 1, all you need to do is to issue a copy statement in your initial source program. Once your code compiles, it brings a copy of your symbolic map into your program, which is stage 2 of this operation.

Symbolic maps are the end product in building and processing a map, which takes the programmer-defined data fields and promptly explodes them into five major component data fields, as depicted in FIG. 1-5. Each of these data fields receives a suffix that is then used by the programmer in referencing the various portions or attribute bytes of the same data field. For example, the field coded as CARRIER in your BMS is shown in the symbolic map as:

- CARRIERA to denote the attribute portion of the field
- CARRIERL to reveal the length of that data
- CARRIERF in case you need to utilize a modified data tag
- CARRIERI for an input and CARRIERO for an output reference.

```
CARRIER    DFHMDF POS=(4,36),ATTRB=(ASKIP),LENGTH=3
LINE       DFHMDF POS=(4,42),ATTRB=(ASKIP),LENGTH=2
           DFHMDF POS=(5,9),ATTRB=(ASKIP),LENGTH=20,
                  INITIAL='EMPLOYEE I.D.       :'
EMPID      DFHMDF POS=(5,36),ATTRB=(NUM,FSET),LENGTH=7
           DFHMDF POS=(5,44),LENGTH=1,ATTRB=(ASKIP)
           DFHMDF POS=(6,9),ATTRB=(ASKIP),LENGTH=20,
                  INITIAL='EMPLOYEE NAME       :'
EMPNAME    DFHMDF POS=(6,36),ATTRB=(UNPROT),LENGTH=25
           DFHMDF POS=(6,62),LENGTH=1,ATTRB=(ASKIP)
           DFHMDF POS=(7,9),ATTRB=(ASKIP),LENGTH=20,

                  INITIAL='OCCUPATION CODE     :'
OCCODE     DFHMDF POS=(7,36),ATTRB=(UNPROT),LENGTH=1
           DFHMDF POS=(7,38),LENGTH=1,ATTRB=(ASKIP)
OCDESC     DFHMDF POS=(7,40),ATTRB=(ASKIP),LENGTH=20
```

```
00143 C    02   CARRIERL   COMP PIC  S9(4).
00144 C    02   CARRIERF        PIC  X.
00145 C    02   FILLER REDEFINES CARRIERF.
00146 C         03   CARRIERA   PIC  X.
00147 C    02   CARRIERI        PIC  X(3).
00148 C    02   LINEL      COMP PIC  S9(4).
00149 C    02   LINEF           PIC  X.
00150 C    02   FILLER REDEFINES LINEF.
00151 C         03   LINEA      PIC  X.
00152 C    02   LINEI           PIC  X(2).
00152 C    02   EMPIDL          PIC  S9(4).
00153 C    02   EMPIDF          PIC  X.
00154 C    02   FILLER REDEFINES EMPIDF.
00155 C         03   EMPIDA     PIC  X.
00156 C    02   EMPIDI          PIC  X(7)
```

1-5 Shows a portion of a programmer-developed BMS (top) and the symbolic map after the assembly process

These suffixes are attached to a data field regardless of the ending character. Thus, the field XDATA would also receive an extra suffix to look like XDATAA, should you decide to reference the attribute portion of that field. Attribute bytes enable you to display a field in different modes and combinations, such as in a protected or unprotected mode, intensified, blinking, underscored, or even in dark or non-display mode, in case you need to enter a password.

The suffix "L" tells you whether you have, or have not entered any data into a specific field. If you have, the length portion of the field will reflect the actual size of that field. If you have not, the above value will simply be zero. In conjunction with the length attribute, the symbolic map also contains the suffix "F" to denote a modified data tag (MDT). The purpose of this MDT is to modify the length component of a field from a value of zero. Let me give you an example. You need to display a screen with five data fields, all having a length attribute that is greater than zero. Assume now that one of the five data fields is in error and needs to be corrected and re-keyed into the system. So when you key in that field and press enter to resend the map, only the recently corrected data field will show a length that is greater than zero. The other four fields, since they have not been referenced in the previous cycle, will subsequently show a length of zero. Data fields containing a zero value in that attribute byte are essentially considered unavailable for programming purposes.

Finally, the "I" and the "O" suffixes enable the programmer to refer to a certain data field either as an input or output type. Note that I have used several methods in referring to multiple line displays. On a simplistic level, I defined every line on the map that got the job done, although it created a great deal of redundancy in the coding process. On a more intermediate level, I used one or several OCCURS statements in the basic mapping (BMS), utilizing subscripting. On a third level, I took the symbolic map and inserted "OCCURS," where OCCURS were applicable, directly into the symbolic map.

2
The essentials of coding menu programs

In learning CICS and classifying your program development in terms of complexity, you'll probably want to first review the menu or directory process. Menu programs are developed to enable you to select a task and then branch to the task to perform it. As a rule, you start out with the main systems directory, through which you can choose your immediate area of interest. This process provides you with a window for viewing and maintaining a file or database with certain security guidelines in mind. You can use a menu screen as a path to a specific set of activities, and once you're locked into such activities, there will be no need for you to continuously refer back to these menus.

From an organizational perspective, it is important to do your work in a logical, transaction-oriented manner. In maintaining the customer database, for example, you'll probably want to do your ADD transactions before switching to a set of DELETE or BROWSE transactions. That way, you won't have to constantly jump back and forth between detail and subdirectory panels.

Figure 2-1 highlights a path required to do maintenance on *recurring customers*. Recurring customers are those who do business with your company on a frequent or periodic basis. As you can see, the menu process is necessary in a state-of-the-art, interactive environment to allow you some flexibility and familiarity in an otherwise intimidating application.

Menu programs are relatively simple to write. Each screen gives the user the opportunity to select a task and then exit the current procedures to perform a requested transaction. In this

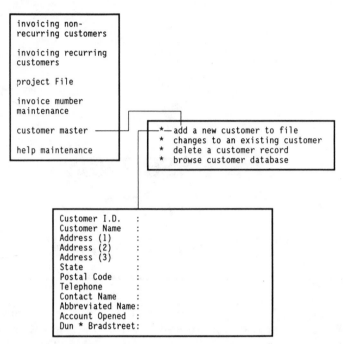

```
 invoicing non-
 recurring customers

 invoicing recurring
 customers

 project File

 invoice mumber
 maintenance

 customer master ─────        ─*─add a new customer to file
                                * changes to an existing customer
 help maintenance              * delete a customer record
                                * browse customer database
```

```
 Customer I.D.      :
 Customer Name      :
 Address (1)        :
 Address (2)        :
 Address (3)        :
 State              :
 Postal Code        :
 Telephone          :
 Contact Name       :
 Abbreviated Name:
 Account Opened     :
 Dun * Bradstreet:
```

2-1 Path through two levels of directory screens to the Customer Master maintenance procedures

process, you might or might not need to transmit a message via
the COMMUNICATIONS AREA. In a CHANGE program it is often necessary to establish an indicator (CUSTOMER-COMPARE) to see if the
user changed the initial record key before updating a particular
record. It is frequently desirable to set up an indicator with a blank
value to select before exiting the current procedures. A blank
might stand for a SEND command or anything else, but preferably
the blank would be an "R" designating a RECEIVE instruction.

Typically, your options are limited in entering data on a menu
screen. One of these options has to do with a single, or in some
cases some multiple, set of selections. If the terminal operator
selects a "legitimate" task, the system will branch to the proper
transaction and start executing it. If the user enters an erroneous
criterion, that is one that is not listed on that panel, the program
responds with an ERROR message that the requested task is either
not in existence or is inactive. An inactive task is one that relies on
other dependent programs for directives that are either incomplete
or simply unavailable. In simple terms, it means that the programmer, instead of issuing an XCTL (exit control) instruction, will now
have to reinvoke the entire transaction and advise the terminal
operator of the current situation via a WARNING message.

Submenus or screens other than the main systems directory normally use a function key (PF), such as PF 1 to "navigate" back to a prior, dependent menu screen. The use of the CLEAR key can also parallel that of the PF key. In reference to a main systems directory, on the other hand, there is no dependency or "precedence," so both CLEAR and PF 1 can result in a sign-off procedure.

Main systems directories are normally initiated via a transaction identifier. Actually, any program or transaction can be triggered in this fashion, but this is a rather sloppy and sometimes impractical way of starting a task. For example, if you need to convey a message via the COMMUNICATIONS AREA, such as a record key, and if that record key is not received by the following program, it might cause an irrevocable error.

Generally speaking, it is easy to develop code for a menu program, since such a program does not require extensive logic, nor does it require the processing of files. There are, of course, some exceptions to the rule. For example, in some systems, you might be controlling security on the menu level, allowing your various users access to an INQUIRY transaction while denying access to other maintenance-related activities. The reason I hesitate to expand on such procedures is because most installations rely on more comprehensive, sophisticated vendor products, such as ACF2 or TOP SECRET, where you can easily develop your own set of rules outside the application.

Case study

As shown in FIG. 2-2, the MCRA billing system relies on a main systems directory to initiate a number of tasks. In most circumstances, you can perform your work via two menu screens, such as the main menu panel and a dependent subdirectory or submenu. In order to delete a customer transaction, enter task 5 on the main systems directory screen, then follow up with task 3 on the invoked subdirectory. (Refer to FIG. 2-4.) In some situations, program specifications might call for a slot to enter the record key directly on the menu screen. This methodology will in no way complicate the menu program, since the reading of the customer master file is performed within the framework of the delete transaction, and all you need to do in the menu program is to save the record key and pass it along in the COMMUNICATIONS AREA.

The purpose of the menu programs or directories presented in this chapter is twofold: to review the infrastructure of a typical menu program, then to explain the relationship between the main menu and a subdirectory, as well as the relationship between the subdirectory and a detailed customer panel.

```
AR1O          MCRA BILLING SYSTEM - MAIN MENU          04/16/91


         1   INVOICING NON-RECURRING CUSTOMERS

         2   INVOICING RECURRING CUSTOMERS

         3   PROJECT FILE MAINTENANCE

         4   INVOICE NUMBER MAINTENANCE

         5   CUSTOMER MASTER MAINTENANCE

         6   HELP MAINTENANCE


             ENTER SELECTION


   CLEAR=RESTART PROCEDURE
```

2-2 Highlights the main systems directory menu for the MCRA billing system

Figure 2-2 represents the main systems directory or program, ARM10C. The second menu program is listed to refine the primary selection, providing a great deal more detail. Once you have issued your second selection on the subsequent subdirectory (ARM90C), you can proceed to maintain the customer database.

FCT and map considerations

Figure 2-3 is a Basic Mapping Support (BMS) representation of the systems directory panel. The output of this, i.e., the actual screen, is shown in FIG. 2-4. The first entry on this map is associated with a DFHMSD statement, ARM10M, which is the name of your mapset. This is immediately followed by a DFHMDI statement highlighting your map. There are three data fields referenced in this program, such as a DATE field, a SELECT field, and an ERMSG or error message field. ERMSG is also available for other systems messages, not necessarily those resulting from an ERROR CONDITION.

SELECT is designed to accommodate user input to a specific selection. ERMSG is the system's or the programmer's response to an error, should a selection be entered erroneously by the user. Figure 2-5 is the BMS portion of the customer subdirectory, and it corresponds to FIG. 2-4, which is the display panel.

The programmer-coded BMS is first converted to a symbolic map through the assembly process. The symbolic map is generated only when your BMS is "clean" of any coding error. This topic will be discussed in detail in the following section. Figure 2-6 shows the FCT, or File Control Table, pointing to the customer master file.

2-3 BMS code for the main systems directory screen

```
          PRINT NOGEN                                                    00010000
ARM10M    DFHMSD  TYPE=&SYSPARM,MODE=INOUT,CTRL=FREEKB,LANG=COBOL,       C00020001
          TIOAPFX=YES                                                    00030000
ARM10M1   DFHMDI   SIZE=(24,80)                                          00040002
          DFHMDF POS=(01,02),LENGTH=04,INITIAL='AR10',                   C00050003
          ATTRB=(BRT,PROT)                                               00060000
          DFHMDF POS=(01,15),LENGTH=32,ATTRB=(ASKIP),                    C00070004
          INITIAL='MCRA  BILLING SYSTEM - MAIN MENU'                     00080000
DATE      DFHMDF POS=(01,60),LENGTH=08,ATTRB=(BRT,PROT),                 00090000
          DFHMDF POS=(06,12),LENGTH=01,INITIAL='1',                      C00100000
          ATTRB=(PROT)                                                   00110000
          DFHMDF POS=(06,16),LENGTH=33,ATTRB=(BRT,PROT),                 C00120000
          INITIAL='INVOICING NON-RECURRING CUSTOMERS'                    00130000
          DFHMDF POS=(08,12),LENGTH=01,INITIAL='2',                      C00140000
          ATTRB=(PROT)                                                   00150000
          DFHMDF POS=(08,16),LENGTH=33,ATTRB=(BRT,PROT),                 C00160000
          INITIAL='INVOICING RECURRING CUSTOMERS'                        00170000
          DFHMDF POS=(10,12),LENGTH=01,INITIAL='3',                      C00180000
          ATTRB=(PROT)                                                   00190000
          DFHMDF POS=(10,16),LENGTH=24,ATTRB=(BRT,PROT),                 C00200000
          INITIAL='PROJECT FILE MAINTENANCE'                             00210000
          DFHMDF POS=(12,12),LENGTH=01,INITIAL='4',                      C00220000
          ATTRB=(PROT)                                                   00230000
          DFHMDF POS=(12,16),LENGTH=26,ATTRB=(BRT,PROT),                 C00240000
          INITIAL='INVOICE NUMBER MAINTENANCE'                           00250000
          DFHMDF POS=(14,12),LENGTH=01,INITIAL='5',                      C00260000
          ATTRB=(PROT)                                                   00270000
          DFHMDF POS=(14,16),LENGTH=39,ATTRB=(BRT,PROT),                 C00280000
          INITIAL='CUSTOMER MASTER MAINTENANCE'                          00290000
          DFHMDF POS=(16,12),LENGTH=01,INITIAL='6',                      C00300000
          ATTRB=(PROT)                                                   00310000
          DFHMDF POS=(16,16),LENGTH=16,ATTRB=(BRT,PROT),                 C00320000
          INITIAL='HELP MAINTENANCE'                                     00330000
SELECT    DFHMDF POS=(19,12),LENGTH=01,ATTRB=(IC,UNPROT,FSET)            00340000
          DFHMDF POS=(19,14),LENGTH=01,ATTRB=ASKIP,INITIAL=' '           00350000
          DFHMDF POS=(19,16),LENGTH=15,INITIAL='ENTER SELECTION',        C00360000
          ATTRB=(BRT,ASKIP)                                              00370000
          DFHMDF POS=(22,02),LENGTH=39,ATTRB=(PROT),                     C00380000
          INITIAL='CLEAR=RESTART PROCEDURE'                              00390000
ERMSG     DFHMDF POS=(24,05),LENGTH=60,ATTRB=(BRT,PROT)                  00400004
          DFHMSD TYPE=FINAL                                              00410000
          END                                                           00420000
```

```
┌──────────────────────────────────────────────────────────────┐
│  AR90       CUSTOMER MAINTENANCE SCREEN                        │
│                                                                │
│                                                                │
│         1   ADD A NEW CUSTOMER TO FILE                         │
│                                                                │
│         2   CHANGES TO AN EXISTING CUSTOMER                    │
│                                                                │
│         3   DELETE A CUSTOMER RECORD                           │
│                                                                │
│         4   BROWSE CUSTOMER DATABASE                           │
│                                                                │
│                                                                │
│             ENTER YOUR SELECTION                               │
│                                                                │
│                                                                │
│                                                                │
│      PF1:  RETURN TO MAIN SYSTEM DIRECTORY                     │
└──────────────────────────────────────────────────────────────┘
```

2-4 Highlights the subdirectory used to maintain the customer master

2-5 Shows the BMS code for the customer master maintenance screen

```
        PRINT  NOGEN
ARM90M  DFHMSD TYPE=&SYSPARM,MODE=INOUT,LANG=COBOL,CTRL=(FREEKB),        C
               TIOAPFX=YES
*
ARM90M7 DFHMDI SIZE=(24,80)
*
TRANSID DFHMDF POS=(1,1),LENGTH=4,ATTRB=(PROT),                          C
               INITIAL='AR90'
        DFHMDF POS=(1,6),LENGTH=6,ATTRB=(ASKIP)
        DFHMDF POS=(1,15),LENGTH=38,ATTRB=(ASKIP,BRT),                   C
               INITIAL='CUSTOMER MAINTENANCE SCREEN           '
DATE    DFHMDF POS=(01,70),LENGTH=08,ATTRB=ASKIP
        DFHMDF POS=(6,14),LENGTH=34,ATTRB=(ASKIP,BRT),                   C
               INITIAL='1  ADD A NEW CUSTOMER TO FILE      '
        DFHMDF POS=(8,14),LENGTH=34,ATTRB=(ASKIP),                       C
               INITIAL='2  CHANGES TO AN EXISTING CUSTOMER'
        DFHMDF POS=(10,14),LENGTH=34,ATTRB=(ASKIP,BRT),                  C
               INITIAL='3  DELETE A CUSTOMER RECORD        '
        DFHMDF POS=(12,14),LENGTH=34,ATTRB=(ASKIP),                      C
               INITIAL='4  BROWSE CUSTOMER DATABASE        '
SELECT  DFHMDF POS=(15,14),LENGTH=1,ATTRB=(UNPROT,IC)
        DFHMDF POS=(15,18),LENGTH=20,ATTRB=(ASKIP,BRT),                  C
               INITIAL='ENTER YOUR SELECTION'
        DFHMDF POS=(23,4),LENGTH=37,ATTRB=(ASKIP,BRT),                   C
               INITIAL='PF1:  RETURN TO MAIN SYSTEM DIRECTORY'
MSSG    DFHMDF POS=(24,4),LENGTH=50,ATTRB=(ASKIP,BRT)
        DFHMSD TYPE=FINAL
        END
```

2-6 Shows the File Control Table (FCT) for the customer database

```
K501    DFHFCT  TYPE=DATASET,ACCMETH=VSAM,LOG=YES,                       C
                DSNAME=K501,                                             C
                SERVREQ=(BROWSE,DELETE,ADD,UPDATE),                      C
                DSNAME=NIRVT.AR.K501,                                    C
                RECFORM=(FIXED,BLOCK),                                   C
                FILSTAT=(ENABLED,CLOSED),                                C
                LSPPOOL=1,DISP=SHR,                                      C
                STRNO=2,BUFNO=3,BUFNI=2
```

Source program listing and narrative

The panel depicting the main systems directory (ARM10C) was presented in FIG. 2-2. The purpose of this program is to utilize the screen for an initial user-selected criterion.

As shown in FIG. 2-7, the WORKING-STORAGE SECTION of ARM10C begins with the layout of a standard error message (statements 8 through 12), which is invoked by the program in case an unavailable task is selected. In developing your menu program, it is practical to say that some options initially displayed on that main systems directory might not be available because of some lag in certain programming activities. When that happens, you need to provide some logic to inform the user that currently no such programming module is available in the system.

Next the DATA DIVISION portion of the COMMUNICATIONS AREA, (lines 14 through 17) defines the use of both ENTER and PF 1. These keys are designed to parallel each other, meaning that whether you press PF 1 or the CLEAR key, you will immediately be logged off the system. Procedures for these function keys are developed in paragraph 0200-PF 1-EXIT, (lines 53 through 62). When completing the sign off process, you need to issue the message SESSION ENDED on the bottom portion of the screen.

Beginning in statements 21 through 24, ARM10C accesses the copy library in order to reference some of the required members during the compilation process. These are, in order:

- The ARM10M map, which is brought into the program so that you can reference each field that appears on the map. (See FIG. 2-3.)
- The CHARATR block lends clarity to some of the attributes that need to be used in a combined fashion, such as an unprotected alpha field that displays in high intensity with its modified data tag turned on. More on this later.
- The DFHBMSCA table is also copied into the program. This table is the original attribute table developed by the vendor (IBM). Although the DFHBMSCA table is quite extensive, it doesn't seem to provide sufficient detail.
- Last, the EIBAID block is requested from the copy library. These entries, as you'll soon see, were copied into your program in case you need to reference them.

At this point you are ready to process your program. So let me start out by giving you some explanation of statement 33. The value "A" means that the message field is to be transformed back to an unprotected alpha field (the actual value stands for low-intensity green) in case such a message was previously intensified. An unprotected status is required so other, less severe messages would be shown in a less "alarming" color.

Next, check the contents of the COMMUNICATIONS AREA in the LINKAGE-SECTION. If, and only if, the DFHCOMMAREA contains a message, you will need to move it directly into your DATA DIVISION. Statement 36, IF EIBTRNID NOT = "AR10," refers to a situation that enables the map to be sent for the first time, including the constants, or title headers. Code for receiving the map is highlighted in lines 47 through 50, invoking 0300-SELECT-OPTION procedures.

The first statement in line 71 now sets up the error message using a protected low-intensity color through the attribute value. In order to provide efficiency in turning out code, most programmers develop a standard menu program that needs to be a bit customized, depending on the specific application. ARM10C or the main directory menu is no exception to the rule, even though some of the tables that were earlier copied into the program were neither fully utilized nor referenced.

If you were to compare the layout of the main systems directory, as shown in FIG. 2-2 and the actual code that generates such a map, you would find a definite correspondence in statements 76 through 99. For example, if you were to select task 1 in line 76 of FIG. 2-7, program logic would have you exit the current transaction through an XCTL statement (lines 76 through 79), sending you to program "ARM2OC," which is the task that handles invoicing for nonrecurring customers. Likewise, by entering option 5 on this menu screen, you would be triggering the transaction AR90, which, as you'll shortly see, is the customer maintenance panel. Finally, 9999-PGM-NOTFND is a statement designed to route erroneous situations, such as when the program or programs used by the system cannot be located in the library.

2-7 ARM10C

```
 1    IDENTIFICATION DIVISION.
 2    PROGRAM-ID.    ARM10C.
 3    DATE-COMPILED. FEBRUARY 23 1990.
 4    ENVIRONMENT DIVISION.
 5    DATA DIVISION.
 6
 7    WORKING-STORAGE SECTION.
 8    01  PGM-MSG.
 9        03   FILLER              PIC X(11) VALUE 'SELECTION  '.
10        03   PGM-SEL             PIC X.
11        03   FILLER              PIC X(15) VALUE '  NOT AVAILABLE'.
12        03   FILLER              PIC X(15) VALUE '  AT THIS TIME.'.
13
14    01  COMM-AREA.
15        03   PF-KEYS        PIC X VALUE '0'.
16             88   PFENTER              VALUE '0'.
17             88   PF1-KEY              VALUE '1'.
18
19    01  END-OF-SESSION-MSG   PIC X(13) VALUE 'SESSION ENDED'.
20
21        COPY ARM10M.
22        COPY CHARATR.
23        COPY DFHBMSCA.
24        COPY DFHAID.
25
26    LINKAGE SECTION.
27    01  DFHCOMMAREA          PIC X.
28
29    PROCEDURE DIVISION.
30
31    0000-MAIN.
32    0100-SET-PFKEYS.
33        MOVE 'A' TO SELECTA ERMSGA.
34        IF EIBCALEN > ZERO
35            MOVE DFHCOMMAREA TO COMM-AREA.
36        IF EIBTRNID NOT = 'AR10'
37            MOVE '0' TO PF-KEYS.
38        EXEC CICS
39            HANDLE AID
40                CLEAR(0200-PF1-EXIT)
41                PF1(0200-PF1-EXIT)
42                ANYKEY(0210-INVALID-SELECT)
43        END-EXEC.
44        IF PFENTER
45            MOVE 'X' TO PF-KEYS
46            GO TO 0500-START-SESSION.
```

```
47        EXEC CICS
48            RECEIVE MAP('ARM10M1')
49                    MAPSET('ARM10M')
50        END-EXEC
51        GO TO 0300-SELECT-OPTION.
52
53    0200-PF1-EXIT.
54        EXEC CICS
55            SEND TEXT FROM(END-OF-SESSION-MSG)
56                    LENGTH(13)
57                    ERASE
58                    FREEKB
59        END-EXEC.
60        EXEC CICS
61            RETURN
62        END-EXEC.
63
64    0210-INVALID-SELECT.
65        MOVE -1 TO SELECTL.
66        MOVE 'I' TO SELECTA ERMSGA.
67        MOVE 'INVALID SELECTION' TO ERMSGO
68        MOVE PROT-BRT TO ERMSGA.
69
70    0300-SELECT-OPTION.
71        MOVE '-' TO ERMSGA.
72            EXEC CICS
73                HANDLE CONDITION
74                    PGMIDERR(9999-PGM-NOTFND)
75            END-EXEC
76        IF SELECTI = '1'
77            EXEC CICS
78                XCTL PROGRAM('ARM20C')
79            END-EXEC
80        ELSE IF SELECTI = '2'
81            EXEC CICS
82                XCTL PROGRAM('ARM40C')
83            END-EXEC
84        ELSE IF SELECTI = '3'
85            EXEC CICS
86                XCTL PROGRAM('ARM60C')
87            END-EXEC
88        ELSE IF SELECTI = '4'
89            EXEC CICS
90                XCTL PROGRAM('ARM70C')
91            END-EXEC
92        ELSE IF SELECTI = '5'
93            EXEC CICS
94                XCTL PROGRAM('ARM90C')
95            END-EXEC
96        ELSE IF SELECTI = '6'
97            EXEC CICS
98                XCTL PROGRAM('ARM80C')
99            END-EXEC
100       ELSE IF SELECTI = LOW-VALUES OR SELECTI = SPACES
101           MOVE 'ENTER SELECTION' TO ERMSGO
102           GO TO 0400-SEND-MAP.
103
104   0400-SEND-MAP.
105   0500-START-SESSION.
106       MOVE -1 TO SELECTL.
107       MOVE CURRENT-DATE TO DATEO.
108       EXEC CICS
109               SEND MAP('ARM10M1')
110                   MAPSET('ARM10M')
111                   ERASE
112                   CURSOR
113       END-EXEC.
114       EXEC CICS
115           RETURN TRANSID('AR10')
116           COMMAREA(COMM-AREA)
117           LENGTH(1)
118       END-EXEC.
119       STOP RUN.
120       GOBACK.
121   9999-PGM-NOTFND.
122       MOVE SELECTI TO PGM-SEL.
123       MOVE PGM-MSG TO ERMSGO.
```

```
124    MOVE 'I' TO ERMSGA.
125    MOVE -1 TO SELECTL.
126    GO TO 0400-SEND-MAP.
127
```

The subdirectory for the customer database

The input map to the subdirectory program was presented in FIG. 2-4. As shown in FIG. 2-8, this program defines the COMMUNICATIONS AREA as a 5-position long data field (statements 8 through 9). The first position is available to differentiate between SEND and RECEIVE operations. The second field is used to store the current customer number field for a change transaction. The dollar signs in the counter simply describe to the subsequent program the destination of the message. The dollar signs also signify that the message comes from a subdirectory program. The purpose of the two copy statements (statements 10 and 11) were explained earlier and I will further expand on them in future sections. The ARM90M in statement 10 is the Basic Mapping required for the current program, while the DFHAID block in line 11 is available for function key assignments. Note that the length of the DFHCOMMAREA (statement 13), initially defined in the LINKAGE SECTION, corresponds to the length of the WORKING-STORAGE definition.

Statements 18 through 23 set up certain conditions that must be provided by the programmer, such as the use of the CLEAR key. It also provides procedures in case PF 1 is pressed (statement 21), which enables you to branch back to the main systems directory. ANYKEY, of course, is sort of a "catch all" routine designed to handle all other undefined keys.

A SEND-REC-FLAG is now tested for an "R," meaning that a branch to a RECEIVE MAP would be triggered on an equal condition. However, since no such code was stored in that indicator, program logic will simply fall through the 030-SEND-RECEIVE-PARAGRAPH, invoking a SEND status. This is highlighted in statements 27 through 36 and continues with the reinvocation of the current task (statements 73 through 78). Note that just as you are setting up the SEND MAP process, you need to replace the current value of the SEND-REC-INDICATOR ("R"), which enables you to invoke a set of RECEIVE procedures the next time around. (This too must then be re-initialized for a subsequent SEND operation.)

As shown in FIG. 2-4, you are allowed four types of selections on this subdirectory:

1. Addition of customers to the file
2. Changes to existing customers

3. Deleting certain customer records
4. Browsing the entire customer database

If the terminal operator enters something other than one of those transactions, an error message will be displayed (statements 44 through 45). In addition to a warning message that will now appear in intensified white (this is done through an attribute value of "Y"), the programmer now "re-colorizes" the erroneous selection in order to display the field in high intensity (unprotected) red. (This is accomplished by moving the character value of "I" into the attribute portion of the SELECT field, SELECTA.)

If your selection is "1," representing an ADD transaction (statements 50 through 54), program logic will exit the current transaction, entering program ARA91C. Selection 2 also enables you to relay a message to a subsequent change program, sending an initialized field (CUST-COMPARE containing four dollar signs) into program ARC92C. Note that while selections 1, 2, and 3 trigger a branch operation out of the current transaction, selection 4 remains unaffected. As I said before, task 4, which is a BROWSE program, has not been completed, and thus only a warning message can be generated at this point. However, once the BROWSE program is completed, you can replace the current procedures assigned to program ARB94C with procedures similar to selections 1, 2, and 3. Actual reinvocation of the program starts in statement 73.

2-8 ARM90C

```
1            IDENTIFICATION DIVISION.
2            PROGRAM-ID. ARM90C.
3            DATE-COMPILED.
4            ENVIRONMENT DIVISION.
5            DATA DIVISION.
6            WORKING-STORAGE SECTION.
7            01  COMM-AREA.
8                05  SEND-REC-FLAG     PIC X.
9                05  CUST-COMPARE      PIC X(4).
10           COPY ARM90M.
11           COPY DFHAID.
12           LINKAGE SECTION.
13           01  DFHCOMMAREA   PIC X(5).
14           PROCEDURE DIVISION.
15           010-CHECK-COMMAREA.
16               IF EIBCALEN > 0
17               MOVE DFHCOMMAREA TO COMM-AREA.
18           020-START-PROCESSING.
19               EXEC CICS HANDLE AID
20                   CLEAR(035-RESEND)
21                   PF1(070-RETURN)
22                   ANYKEY(035-RESEND)
23               END-EXEC.
24           030-SEND-RECEIVE-PARAGRAPH.
25               IF SEND-REC-FLAG = 'R' GO TO
26               040-RECEIVE-MAP.
27           035-RESEND.
28               MOVE 'R' TO SEND-REC-FLAG.
29               MOVE -1 TO SELECTL.
30               EXEC CICS
```

```
31                        SEND MAP('ARM90M7')
32                        MAPSET('ARM90M')
33                        ERASE
34                        CURSOR
35                   END-EXEC.
36                   GO TO 800-REINVOKE-TRANSACTION.
37              040-RECEIVE-MAP.
38                   EXEC CICS RECEIVE MAP('ARM90M7')
39                        MAPSET('ARM90M')
40                   END-EXEC.
41                   MOVE 'S' TO SEND-REC-FLAG.
42                   IF SELECTI = '1', OR, '2', OR '3', OR '4'
43                   NEXT SENTENCE ELSE
44                   MOVE 'INVALID SELECTION CODE, PLEASE RE-ENTER'
45                   TO MSSGO
46                   MOVE 'Y' TO MSSGA
47                   MOVE 'I' TO SELECTA
48                   MOVE -1 TO SELECTL
49                   GO TO 035-RESEND.
50                   IF SELECTI = '1'
51                   EXEC CICS XCTL PROGRAM('ARA91C')
52                        COMMAREA(COMM-AREA)
53                        LENGTH(1)
54                   END-EXEC.
55                   IF SELECTI = '2'
56                   MOVE ' ' TO SEND-REC-FLAG
57                   MOVE '$$$$' TO CUST-COMPARE
58                   EXEC CICS XCTL PROGRAM('ARC92C')
59                        COMMAREA(COMM-AREA)
60                        LENGTH(5)
61                   END-EXEC.
62                   IF SELECTI = '3'
63                   EXEC CICS XCTL PROGRAM('ARD93C')
64                        COMMAREA(COMM-AREA)
65                        LENGTH(1)
66                   END-EXEC.
67                   IF SELECTI = '4'
68                   MOVE 'BROWSE FUNCTION CURRENTLY UNAVAILABLE' TO MSSGO
69                   MOVE '-' TO MSSGA
70                   MOVE -1 TO SELECTL
71                   MOVE 'I' TO SELECTA
72                   GO TO 035-RESEND.
73              800-REINVOKE-TRANSACTION.
74                   EXEC CICS RETURN
75                        TRANSID('AR90')
76                        COMMAREA(COMM-AREA)
77                        LENGTH(7)
78                   END-EXEC.
79              070-RETURN.
80                   EXEC CICS XCTL PROGRAM('ARM10C')
81                   END-EXEC.
82                   STOP RUN.
83                   GOBACK.
84
```

Compiler-generated source code

The first expanded copy statement in the main systems directory (ARM10C), shown in FIG. 2-9, is the symbolic map presented in lines 22 through 46. The map corresponds to the panel shown in FIG. 2-2, and the map is converted from the BMS code through the assembly process. The original BMS version for this map is highlighted in FIG. 2-3. Note that the symbolic map is subdivided into two areas, one that is the input version of the map (ARM10M1I) and a second one (ARM10M1O) representing the output.

Note that each of the three variable fields listed on the map (i.e., a date, a select and an error message field) is defined using four different suffixes. A field ending in an "L" designates the length portion of the field. If DATEL contains zeros, it means that no such field has been entered by the operator during the current transaction cycle, and for programming purposes, DATEL should not be processed. If a field name ends with the character "L," then, an additional "L" will be attached to it via CICS. Thus, the field name TALL would look like TALLL, and a field name L would look like LL.

The second version of the field is created by adding to it the suffix F. F is responsible for initially setting the modified data tags, which can later be overridden in the application program. So our previous TALL field would now look like TALLF.

A third version adds the character "A" to the field, and it stands for an attribute byte. Any time you need to modify the appearance of a particular data field displayed on the screen, you need to manipulate its attribute bit. For example, you might want to display a field in protected and intensified mode. To convey all that to the system, you need to move a particular value into the attribute position of that field. To reset such an entry later on, using, say, an unprotected low-intensity field, you need to overlay its previous value with a blank (hex 40) attribute.

The suffix, "I" merely tells the programmer that the field is an input element, although CICS does not really differentiate between an "I" and an "O," which comes into play with the ARM10M10 output map definition.

Next is the CHARATR table, which summarizes attribute characteristics and makes them available for the user. The advantage of using such a table is that it enables you to use combined attributes and to stay away from using the value portion of the field. It is easier for the programmer to remember the term "UNPROT-ALPHA-BRT-MDT," which refers to an unprotected, intensified (bright) alpha field with its modified data tag turned on, rather than using an absolute (machine value) of "I." In complicated, long programs, as a rule of thumb, it might sometimes be necessary to rely on descriptive field names rather than on machine values. In short, I copied CHARATR into this program simply to show some of the combined selections you can make in your program, and primarily to make you aware of the fact that such tables are feasible to develop. The attribute table is laid out in statements 48 through 73.

A second module that I copied into this program is the DFHBMSCA block, which does very much what the CHARATR table does, except it is a block developed by the vendor (IBM), and I find it rather cumbersome to continually reference it. Let me give you an example. Rather than calling a field UNPRO-ALPHA-BRT-MDT in your program, you can refer to it as DFHUNIMD. To refer to or remember a field such as DFHUNIMD is probably more difficult than remembering the character value "I." This block, by the way, is also laid out (even though it is not referenced in the program) in statements 78 through 141.

An additional block, the DFHAID is shown in lines 144 through 179. The sole purpose of this table is to allow you reference to the keyboard. It is possible, for example, to refer to a function key, such as PF 1, as DFHPF 1 and use it as a procedure division comparison item. For example, the statement: IF EIBAID = DFHCLEAR simply means to do something in your program when the CLEAR key is pressed. All of this is defined and handled in a Handle Aid statement.

The next series of statements running from line 186 all the way down to line 225 merely represents internal storage areas used by CICS, and you, as an application programmer need not reference them in your program. For example, when you issue an exit control statement, such as:

```
IF SELECTI = '4'
EXEC CICS
XCTL PROGRAM('ARM70C')
END-EXEC.
```

the compiler expands your command-level statements to make it look like those presented in lines 362 through 364.

Following the PROCEDURE DIVISION of ARM10C, the Cross Reference Dictionary lists by data names all data fields used in your program. It also shows the original definition of the field, plus occurrences (meaning references) where each of the data fields is being used. This special list continues to show all the Procedure names used in the program.

2-9 ARM10C compiler version

```
00001        IDENTIFICATION DIVISION.
00002        PROGRAM-ID.    ARM10C.
00003        DATE-COMPILED. APR  6,1990.
00004        ENVIRONMENT DIVISION.
00005        DATA DIVISION.
00006
00007        WORKING-STORAGE SECTION.
00008        01  PGM-MSG.
00009            03   FILLER            PIC X(11) VALUE 'SELECTION  '.
00010            03   PGM-SEL           PIC X.
00011            03   FILLER            PIC X(15) VALUE ' NOT AVAILABLE'.
00012            03   FILLER            PIC X(15) VALUE ' AT THIS TIME.'.
00013
00014        01  COMM-AREA.
```

```
00015                03  PF-KEYS              PIC X VALUE '0'.
00016                    88  PFENTER                VALUE '0'.
00017                    88  PF1-KEY                VALUE '1'.
00018
00019            01  END-OF-SESSION-MSG   PIC X(13) VALUE 'SESSION ENDED'.
00020
00021                COPY ARM1OM.
00022 C          01  ARM1OM1I.
00023 C              02  FILLER PIC X(12).
00024 C              02  DATEL     COMP  PIC  S9(4).
00025 C              02  DATEF     PICTURE X.
00026 C              02  FILLER REDEFINES DATEF.
00027 C                  03 DATEA     PICTURE X.
00028 C              02  DATEI PIC X(8).
00029 C              02  SELECTL   COMP  PIC  S9(4).
00030 C              02  SELECTF   PICTURE X.
00031 C              02  FILLER REDEFINES SELECTF.
00032 C                  03 SELECTA   PICTURE X.
00033 C              02  SELECTI  PIC X(1).
00034 C              02  ERMSGL    COMP  PIC  S9(4).
00035 C              02  ERMSGF    PICTURE X.
00036 C              02  FILLER REDEFINES ERMSGF.
00037 C                  03 ERMSGA    PICTURE X.
00038 C              02  ERMSGI PIC X(60).
00039 C          01  ARM1OM1O REDEFINES ARM1OM1I.
00040 C              02  FILLER PIC X(12).
00041 C              02  FILLER PICTURE X(3).
00042 C              02  DATEO PIC X(8).
00043 C              02  FILLER PICTURE X(3).
00044 C              02  SELECTO PIC X(1).
00045 C              02  FILLER PICTURE X(3).
00046 C              02  ERMSGO PIC X(60).
00047                COPY CHARATR.
00048 C      *------------* ATTRIBUTE-BYTES *---------------------------
00049 C          01  CHARATR.
00050 C              05  UNPROT-ALPHA          PIC X   VALUE SPACE.
00051 C              05  UNPROT-ALPHA-MDT      PIC X   VALUE 'A'.
00052 C              05  UNPROT-ALPHA-BRT      PIC X   VALUE 'H'.
00053 C              05  UNPROT-ALPHA-BRT-MDT  PIC X   VALUE 'I'.
00054 C              05  UNPROT-ALPHA-DRK      PIC X   VALUE '<'.
00055 C              05  UNPROT-ALPHA-DRK-MDT  PIC X   VALUE '('.
00056 C              05  UNPROT-NUM            PIC X   VALUE '&'.
00057 C              05  UNPROT-NUM-MDT        PIC X   VALUE 'J'.
00058 C              05  UNPROT-NUM-BRT        PIC X   VALUE 'Q'.
00059 C              05  UNPROT-NUM-BRT-MDT    PIC X   VALUE 'R'.
00060 C              05  UNPROT-NUM-DRK        PIC X   VALUE '*'.
00061 C              05  UNPROT-NUM-DRK-MDT    PIC X   VALUE ')'.
00062 C              05  PROT                  PIC X   VALUE '-'.
00063 C              05  PROT-MDT              PIC X   VALUE '/'.
00064 C              05  PROT-BRT              PIC X   VALUE 'Y'.
00065 C              05  PROT-BRT-MDT          PIC X   VALUE 'Z'.
00066 C              05  PROT-DRK              PIC X   VALUE '%'.
00067 C              05  PROT-DRK-MDT          PIC X   VALUE ' '.
00068 C              05  ASKIP                 PIC X   VALUE '0̄'.
00069 C              05  ASKIP-MDT             PIC X   VALUE '1'.
00070 C              05  ASKIP-BRT             PIC X   VALUE '8'.
00071 C              05  ASKIP-BRT-MDT         PIC X   VALUE '9'.
00072 C              05  ASKIP-DRK             PIC X   VALUE '@'.
00073 C              05  ASKIP-DRK-MDT         PIC X   VALUE QUOTE.
00074 C      *--------------* LENGTH BYTES *----------------------------
00075 C          01  LENGTH-BYTES.
00076 C              05  CSR-REPO              PIC S9(4) COMP VALUE -1.
00077                COPY DFHBMSCA.
00078 C          01  DFHBMSCA.
00079 C              02   DFHBMPEM  PICTURE X   VALUE IS ' '.
00080 C              02   DFHBMPNL  PICTURE X   VALUE IS ' '.
00081 C              02   DFHBMASK  PICTURE X   VALUE IS '0'.
00082 C              02   DFHBMUNP  PICTURE X   VALUE IS ' '.
00083 C              02   DFHBMUNN  PICTURE X   VALUE IS '&'.
00084 C              02   DFHBMPRO  PICTURE X   VALUE IS '-'.
00085 C              02   DFHBMBRY  PICTURE X   VALUE IS 'H'.
00086 C              02   DFHBMDAR  PICTURE X   VALUE IS '<'.
00087 C              02   DFHBMFSE  PICTURE X   VALUE IS 'A'.
00088 C              02   DFHBMPRF  PICTURE X   VALUE IS '/'.
00089 C              02   DFHBMASF  PICTURE X   VALUE IS '1'.
00090 C              02   DFHBMASB  PICTURE X   VALUE IS '8'.
00091 C              02   DFHBMEOF  PICTURE X   VALUE IS ' '.
00092 C              02   DFHBMDET  PICTURE X   VALUE IS ' '.
```

2-9 Continued

```
00093 C       02   DFHBMPSO  PICTURE X   VALUE IS ' '.
00094 C       02   DFHBMPSI  PICTURE X   VALUE IS ' '.
00095 C       02   DFHSA     PICTURE X   VALUE IS ' '.
00096 C       02   DFHCOLOR  PICTURE X   VALUE IS ' '.
00097 C       02   DFHPS     PICTURE X   VALUE IS ' '.
00098 C       02   DFHHLT    PICTURE X   VALUE IS ' '.
00099 C       02   DFH3270   PICTURE X   VALUE IS '{'.
00100 C       02   DFHVAL    PICTURE X   VALUE IS 'A'.
00101 C       02   DFHOUTLN  PICTURE X   VALUE IS 'B'.
00102 C       02   DFHBKTRN  PICTURE X   VALUE IS ' '.
00103 C       02   DFHALL    PICTURE X   VALUE IS ' '.
00104 C       02   DFHERROR  PICTURE X   VALUE IS ' '.
00105 C       02   DFHDFT    PICTURE X   VALUE IS ' '.
00106 C       02   DFHDFCOL  PICTURE X   VALUE IS ' '.
00107 C       02   DFHBLUE   PICTURE X   VALUE IS '1'.
00108 C       02   DFHRED    PICTURE X   VALUE IS '2'.
00109 C       02   DFHPINK   PICTURE X   VALUE IS '3'.
00110 C       02   DFHGREEN  PICTURE X   VALUE IS '4'.
00111 C       02   DFHTURQ   PICTURE X   VALUE IS '5'.
00112 C       02   DFHYELLO  PICTURE X   VALUE IS '6'.
00113 C       02   DFHNEUTR  PICTURE X   VALUE IS '7'.
00114 C       02   DFHBASE   PICTURE X   VALUE IS ' '.
00115 C       02   DFHDFHI   PICTURE X   VALUE IS ' '.
00116 C       02   DFHBLINK  PICTURE X   VALUE IS '1'.
00117 C       02   DFHREVRS  PICTURE X   VALUE IS '2'.
00118 C       02   DFHUNDLN  PICTURE X   VALUE IS '4'.
00119 C       02   DFHMFIL   PICTURE X   VALUE IS ' '.
00120 C       02   DFHMENT   PICTURE X   VALUE IS ' '.
00121 C       02   DFHMFE    PICTURE X   VALUE IS ' '.
00122 C       02   DFHUNNOD  PICTURE X   VALUE IS '('.
00123 C       02   DFHUNIMD  PICTURE X   VALUE IS 'I'.
00124 C       02   DFHUNNUM  PICTURE X   VALUE IS 'J'.
00125 C       02   DFHUNINT  PICTURE X   VALUE IS 'R'.
00126 C       02   DFHUNNON  PICTURE X   VALUE IS ')'.
00127 C       02   DFHPROTI  PICTURE X   VALUE IS 'Y'.
00128 C       02   DFHPROTN  PICTURE X   VALUE IS '%'.
00129 C       02   DFHMT     PICTURE X   VALUE IS ' '.
00130 C       02   DFHMFT    PICTURE X   VALUE IS ' '.
00131 C       02   DFHMET    PICTURE X   VALUE IS ' '.
00132 C       02   DFHMFET   PICTURE X   VALUE IS ' '.
00133 C       02   DFHDFFR   PICTURE X   VALUE IS ' '.
00134 C       02   DFHLEFT   PICTURE X   VALUE IS ' '.
00135 C       02   DFHOVER   PICTURE X   VALUE IS ' '.
00136 C       02   DFHRIGHT  PICTURE X   VALUE IS ' '.
00137 C       02   DFHUNDER  PICTURE X   VALUE IS ' '.
00138 C       02   DFHBOX    PICTURE X   VALUE IS ' '.
00139 C       02   DFHSOSI   PICTURE X   VALUE IS ' '.
00140 C       02   DFHTRANS  PICTURE X   VALUE IS '0'.
00141 C       02   DFHOPAQ   PICTURE X   VALUE IS ' '.
00142              COPY DFHAID.
00143 C  01   DFHAID.
00144 C       02   DFHNULL   PIC X  VALUE IS ' '.
00145 C       02   DFHENTER  PIC X  VALUE IS QUOTE.
00146 C       02   DFHCLEAR  PIC X  VALUE IS ' '.
00147 C       02   DFHCLRP   PIC X  VALUE IS 'T'.
00148 C       02   DFHPEN    PIC X  VALUE IS '='.
00149 C       02   DFHOPID   PIC X  VALUE IS 'W'.
00150 C       02   DFHMSRE   PIC X  VALUE IS 'X'.
00151 C       02   DFHSTRF   PIC X  VALUE IS 'h'.
00152 C       02   DFHTRIG   PIC X  VALUE IS '"'.
00153 C       02   DFHPA1    PIC X  VALUE IS '%'.
00154 C       02   DFHPA2    PIC X  VALUE IS '>'.
00155 C       02   DFHPA3    PIC X  VALUE IS ','.
00156 C       02   DFHPF1    PIC X  VALUE IS '1'.
00157 C       02   DFHPF2    PIC X  VALUE IS '2'.
00158 C       02   DFHPF3    PIC X  VALUE IS '3'.
00159 C       02   DFHPF4    PIC X  VALUE IS '4'.
00160 C       02   DFHPF5    PIC X  VALUE IS '5'.
00161 C       02   DFHPF6    PIC X  VALUE IS '6'.
00162 C       02   DFHPF7    PIC X  VALUE IS '7'.
00163 C       02   DFHPF8    PIC X  VALUE IS '8'.
00164 C       02   DFHPF9    PIC X  VALUE IS '9'.
00165 C       02   DFHPF10   PIC X  VALUE IS ':'.
00166 C       02   DFHPF11   PIC X  VALUE IS '#'.
00167 C       02   DFHPF12   PIC X  VALUE IS '@'.
00168 C       02   DFHPF13   PIC X  VALUE IS 'A'.
```

```
00169 C          02   DFHPF14   PIC   X   VALUE IS 'B'.
00170 C          02   DFHPF15   PIC   X   VALUE IS 'C'.
00171 C          02   DFHPF16   PIC   X   VALUE IS 'D'.
00172 C          02   DFHPF17   PIC   X   VALUE IS 'E'.
00173 C          02   DFHPF18   PIC   X   VALUE IS 'F'.
00174 C          02   DFHPF19   PIC   X   VALUE IS 'G'.
00175 C          02   DFHPF20   PIC   X   VALUE IS 'H'.
00176 C          02   DFHPF21   PIC   X   VALUE IS 'I'.
00177 C          02   DFHPF22   PIC   X   VALUE IS '¢'.
00178 C          02   DFHPF23   PIC   X   VALUE IS '.'.
00179 C          02   DFHPF24   PIC   X   VALUE IS '<'.
00180
00181            01   DFHLDVER PIC X(22) VALUE 'LD TABLE DFHEITAB 210.'.
00182            01   DFHEIDO PICTURE S9(7) COMPUTATIONAL-3 VALUE ZERO.
00183            01   DFHEIBO PICTURE S9(4) COMPUTATIONAL VALUE ZERO.
00184            01   DFHEICB PICTURE X(8) VALUE IS '        '.
00185
00186            01   DFHEIV16  COMP PIC S9(8).
00187            01   DFHB0041  COMP PIC S9(8).
00188            01   DFHB0042  COMP PIC S9(8).
00189            01   DFHB0043  COMP PIC S9(8).
00190            01   DFHB0044  COMP PIC S9(8).
00191            01   DFHB0045  COMP PIC S9(8).
00192            01   DFHB0046  COMP PIC S9(8).
00193            01   DFHB0047  COMP PIC S9(8).
00194            01   DFHB0048  COMP PIC S9(8).
00195            01   DFHEIV11  COMP PIC S9(4).
00196            01   DFHEIV12  COMP PIC S9(4).
00197            01   DFHEIV13  COMP PIC S9(4).
00198            01   DFHEIV14  COMP PIC S9(4).
00199            01   DFHEIV15  COMP PIC S9(4).
00200            01   DFHB0025  COMP PIC S9(4).
00201            01   DFHEIV5   PIC X(4).
00202            01   DFHEIV6   PIC X(4).
00203            01   DFHEIV17  PIC X(4).
00204            01   DFHEIV18  PIC X(4).
00205            01   DFHEIV19  PIC X(4).
00206            01   DFHEIV1   PIC X(8).
00207            01   DFHEIV2   PIC X(8).
00208            01   DFHEIV3   PIC X(8).
00209            01   DFHEIV20  PIC X(8).
00210            01   DFHC0084  PIC X(8).
00211            01   DFHC0085  PIC X(8).
00212            01   DFHC0320  PIC X(32).
00213            01   DFHEIV7   PIC X(2).
00214            01   DFHEIV8   PIC X(2).
00215            01   DFHC0022  PIC X(2).
00216            01   DFHC0023  PIC X(2).
00217            01   DFHEIV10  PIC S9(7) COMP-3.
00218            01   DFHEIV9   PIC X(1).
00219            01   DFHC0011  PIC X(1).
00220            01   DFHEIV4   PIC X(6).
00221            01   DFHC0070  PIC X(7).
00222            01   DFHC0071  PIC X(7).
00223            01   DFHC0440  PIC X(44).
00224            01   DFHDUMMY COMP PIC S9(4).
00225            01   DFHEIVO  PICTURE X(29).
00226       LINKAGE SECTION.
00227            01   DFHEIBLK.
00228            02   EIBTIME  PIC S9(7) COMP-3.
00229            02   EIBDATE  PIC S9(7) COMP-3.
00230            02   EIBTRNID PIC X(4).
00231            02   EIBTASKN PIC S9(7) COMP-3.
00232            02   EIBTRMID PIC X(4).
00233            02   DFHEIGDI COMP PIC S9(4).
00234            02   EIBCPOSN COMP PIC S9(4).
00235            02   EIBCALEN COMP PIC S9(4).
00236            02   EIBAID   PIC X(1).
00237            02   EIBFN    PIC X(2).
00238            02   EIBRCODE PIC X(6).
00239            02   EIBDS    PIC X(8).
00240            02   EIBREQID PIC X(8).
00241            02   EIBRSRCE PIC X(8).
00242            02   EIBSYNC  PIC X(1).
00243            02   EIBFREE  PIC X(1).
00244            02   EIBRECV  PIC X(1).
00245            02   EIBFIL01 PIC X(1).
00246            02   EIBATT   PIC X(1).
```

```
00247          02    EIBEOC   PIC X(1).
00248          02    EIBFMH   PIC X(1).
00249          02    EIBCOMPL PIC X(1).
00250          02    EIBSIG   PIC X(1).
00251          02    EIBCONF  PIC X(1).
00252          02    EIBERR   PIC X(1).
00253          02    EIBERRCD PIC X(4).
00254          02    EIBSYNRB PIC X(1).
00255          02    EIBNODAT PIC X(1).
00256          02    EIBRESP  COMP PIC S9(8).
00257          02    EIBRESP2 COMP PIC S9(8).
00258          02    EIBRLDBK PIC X(1).
00259          01  DFHCOMMAREA          PIC X.
00260
00261          01  DFHBLLSLOT1 PICTURE X(1).
00262          01  DFHBLLSLOT2 PICTURE X(1).
00263          PROCEDURE DIVISION USING DFHEIBLK DFHCOMMAREA.
00264
00265              CALL 'DFHEI1'.
00266              SERVICE RELOAD DFHEIBLK.
00267              SERVICE RELOAD DFHCOMMAREA.
00268          0000-MAIN.
00269          0100-SET-PFKEYS.
00270              MOVE 'A' TO SELECTA ERMSGA.
00271              IF EIBCALEN > ZERO
00272                  MOVE DFHCOMMAREA TO COMM-AREA.
00273              IF EIBTRNID NOT = 'AR10'
00274                  MOVE '0' TO PF-KEYS.
00275          *EXEC CICS
00276          *    HANDLE AID
00277          *        CLEAR(0200-PF1-EXIT)
00278          *        PF1(0200-PF1-EXIT)
00279          *        ANYKEY(0210-INVALID-SELECT)
00280          *END-EXEC.
00281              MOVE ' \                    00038  ' TO DFHEIVO
00282              CALL 'DFHEI1' USING DFHEIVO
00283              GO TO 0200-PF1-EXIT 0200-PF1-EXIT 0210-INVALID-SELECT
00284              DEPENDING ON DFHEIGDI.
00285
00286
00287              IF PFENTER
00288                  MOVE 'X' TO PF-KEYS
00289                  GO TO 0500-START-SESSION.
00290          *EXEC CICS
00291          *    RECEIVE MAP('ARM10M1')
00292          *            MAPSET('ARM10M')
00293          *END-EXEC
00294              MOVE ' }             00047   ' TO DFHEIVO
00295              MOVE 'ARM10M1' TO DFHC0070
00296              MOVE 'ARM10M' TO DFHC0071
00297              CALL 'DFHEI1' USING DFHEIVO  DFHC0070 ARM10M1I DFHDUMMY
00298              DFHC0071
00299              GO TO 0300-SELECT-OPTION.
00300
00301          0200-PF1-EXIT.
00302          *EXEC CICS
00303          *    SEND TEXT FROM(END-OF-SESSION-MSG)
00304          *              LENGTH(13)
00305          *              ERASE
00306          *              FREEKB
00307          *END-EXEC.
00308              MOVE ' -  B         00054   ' TO DFHEIVO
00309              MOVE 13 TO DFHEIV11
00310              CALL 'DFHEI1' USING DFHEIVO  DFHDUMMY END-OF-SESSION-MSG
00311              DFHEIV11.
00312
00313
00314          *EXEC CICS
00315          *    RETURN
00316          *END-EXEC.
00317              MOVE '          00060   ' TO DFHEIVO
00318              CALL 'DFHEI1' USING DFHEIVO.
00319
00320
00321          0210-INVALID-SELECT.
00322              MOVE -1 TO SELECTL.
```

```
00323                    MOVE 'I' TO SELECTA ERMSGA.
00324                    MOVE 'INVALID SELECTION' TO ERMSGO
00325                    MOVE PROT-BRT TO ERMSGA.
00326
00327             0300-SELECT-OPTION.
00328                    MOVE '-' TO ERMSGA.
00329         *EXEC CICS
00330         *     HANDLE CONDITION
00331         *       PGMIDERR(9999-PGM-NOTFND)
00332         *END-EXEC
00333                       MOVE '                    00072     ' TO DFHEIVO
00334                       CALL 'DFHEI1' USING DFHEIVO
00335                       GO TO  9999-PGM-NOTFND DEPENDING ON DFHEIGDI
00336
00337                    IF SELECTI = '1'
00338         *EXEC CICS
00339         *     XCTL PROGRAM('ARM20C')
00340         *END-EXEC
00341                       MOVE '           00077    ' TO DFHEIVO
00342                       MOVE 'ARM20C' TO DFHEIV1
00343                       CALL 'DFHEI1' USING DFHEIVO  DFHEIV1
00344                    ELSE IF SELECTI = '2'
00345         *EXEC CICS
00346         *     XCTL PROGRAM('ARM40C')
00347         *END-EXEC
00348                       MOVE '           00081    ' TO DFHEIVO
00349                       MOVE 'ARM40C' TO DFHEIV1
00350                       CALL 'DFHEI1' USING DFHEIVO  DFHEIV1
00351                    ELSE IF SELECTI = '3'
00352         *EXEC CICS
00353         *     XCTL PROGRAM('ARM60C')
00354         *END-EXEC
00355                       MOVE '           00085    ' TO DFHEIVO
00356                       MOVE 'ARM60C' TO DFHEIV1
00357                       CALL 'DFHEI1' USING DFHEIVO  DFHEIV1
00358                    ELSE IF SELECTI = '4'
00359         *EXEC CICS
00360         *     XCTL PROGRAM('ARM70C')
00361         *END-EXEC
00362                       MOVE '           00089    ' TO DFHEIVO
00363                       MOVE 'ARM70C' TO DFHEIV1
00364                       CALL 'DFHEI1' USING DFHEIVO  DFHEIV1
00365                    ELSE IF SELECTI = '5'
00366         *EXEC CICS
00367         *     XCTL PROGRAM('ARM90C')
00368         *END-EXEC
00369                       MOVE '           00093    ' TO DFHEIVO
00370                       MOVE 'ARM90C' TO DFHEIV1
00371                       CALL 'DFHEI1' USING DFHEIVO  DFHEIV1
00372                    ELSE IF SELECTI = '6'
00373         *EXEC CICS
00374         *     XCTL PROGRAM('ARM80C')
00375         *END-EXEC
00376                       MOVE '           00097    ' TO DFHEIVO
00377                       MOVE 'ARM80C' TO DFHEIV1
00378                       CALL 'DFHEI1' USING DFHEIVO  DFHEIV1
00379                    ELSE IF SELECTI = LOW-VALUES OR SELECTI = SPACES
00380                       MOVE 'ENTER SELECTION' TO ERMSGO
00381                       GO TO 0400-SEND-MAP.
00382
00383             0400-SEND-MAP.
00384             0500-START-SESSION.
00385                    MOVE -1 TO SELECTL.
00386                    MOVE CURRENT-DATE TO DATEO.
00387         *EXEC CICS
00388         *         SEND MAP('ARM10M1')
00389         *              MAPSET('ARM10M')
00390         *              ERASE
00391         *              CURSOR
00392         *END-EXEC.
00393                       MOVE ' J      S    00108    ' TO DFHEIVO
00394                       MOVE 'ARM10M1' TO DFHC0070
00395                       MOVE 'ARM10M' TO DFHC0071
00396                       MOVE -1 TO DFHEIV11
00397                       CALL 'DFHEI1' USING DFHEIVO DFHC0070 ARM10M1O DFHDUMMY
00398                       DFHC0071 DFHDUMMY DFHDUMMY DFHDUMMY DFHEIV11.
00399         *EXEC CICS
00400         *     RETURN TRANSID('AR10')
```

```
00401        *    COMMAREA(COMM-AREA)
00402        *    LENGTH(1)
00403        *END-EXEC.
00404             MOVE ' \    00114 ' TO DFHEIVO
00405             MOVE 'AR10' TO DFHEIV5
00406             MOVE 1 TO DFHEIV11
00407             CALL 'DFHEI1' USING DFHEIVO  DFHEIV5  COMM-AREA DFHEIV11.
00408
00409             STOP RUN.
00410             GOBACK.
00411         9999-PGM-NOTFND.
00412             MOVE SELECTI TO PGM-SEL.
00413             MOVE PGM-MSG TO ERMSGO.
00414             MOVE 'I' TO ERMSGA.
00415             MOVE -1 TO SELECTL.
00416             GO TO 0400-SEND-MAP.
```

```
*STATISTICS*    SOURCE RECORDS =   416    DATA DIVISION STATEMENTS =    242
*OPTIONS IN EFFECT*    SIZE = 524288  BUF =   20480  LINECNT = 57  SPACE1, FL
*OPTIONS IN EFFECT*    NODMAP, NOPMAP, NOCLIST, NOSUPMAP, NOXREF,   SXREF,   L
*OPTIONS IN EFFECT*    NOTERM, NONUM, NOBATCH, NONAME, COMPILE=01, NOSTATE, NO
*OPTIONS IN EFFECT*    NOOPTIMIZE, NOSYMDMP, NOTEST,   VERB,   ZWB, SYST, NOEN
*OPTIONS IN EFFECT*    NOLST , NOFDECK,NOCDECK, LCOL2, L120,   DUMP , NOADV ,
*OPTIONS IN EFFECT*    NOCOUNT, NOVBSUM, NOVBREF, LANGLVL(1)
                                CROSS-REFERENCE DICTIONARY
```

DATA NAMES	DEFN	REFERENCE	
ARM10M1I	000022	000297	
ARM10M10	000039	000397	
ASKIP	000068		DFHC0023
ASKIP-BRT	000070		DFHC0070
ASKIP-BRT-MDT	000071		DFHC0071
ASKIP-DRK	000072		DFHC0084
ASKIP-DRK-MDT	000073		DFHC0085
ASKIP-MDT	000069		DFHC0320
COMM-AREA	000014	000272 000407	DFHC0440
CSR-REPO	000076		DFHDFCOL
DATEA	000027		DFHDFFR
DATEF	000025		DFHDFHI
DATEI	000028		DFHDFT
DATEL	000024		DFHDUMMY
DATEO	000042	000386	DFHEIBLK
DFHAID	000143		DFHEIB0
DFHALL	000103		DFHEICB
DFHBASE	000114		DFHEIDO
DFHBKTRN	000102		DFHEIGDI
DFHBLINK	000116		DFHEIVO
DFHBLLSLOT1	000261		
DFHBLLSLOT2	000262		
DFHBLUE	000107		DFHEIV1
DFHBMASB	000090		
DFHBMASF	000089		DFHEIV10
DFHBMASK	000081		DFHEIV11
DFHBMBRY	000085		DFHEIV12
DFHBMDAR	000086		DFHEIV13
DFHBMDET	000092		DFHEIV14
DFHBMEOF	000091		DFHEIV15
DFHBMFSE	000087		DFHEIV16
DFHBMPEM	000079		DFHEIV17
DFHBMPNL	000080		DFHEIV18
DFHBMPRF	000088		DFHEIV19
DFHBMPRO	000084		DFHEIV2
DFHBMPSI	000094		DFHEIV20
DFHBMPSO	000093		DFHEIV3
DFHBMSCA	000078		DFHEIV4
DFHBMUNN	000083		DFHEIV5
DFHBMUNP	000082		DFHEIV6
DFHBOX	000138		DFHEIV7
DFHB0025	000200		DFHEIV8
DFHB0041	000187		DFHEIV9
DFHB0042	000188		DFHENTER
DFHB0043	000189		DFHERROR
DFHB0044	000190		DFHGREEN

DFHB0045	000191	DFHHLT
DFHB0046	000192	DFHLDVER
DFHB0047	000193	DFHLEFT
DFHB0048	000194	DFHMENT
DFHCLEAR	000146	DFHMET
DFHCLRP	000147	DFHMFE
DFHCOLOR	000096	DFHMFET
DFHCOMMAREA	000259 000272	DFHMFIL
DFHC0011	000219	DFHMFT
DFHC0022	000215	DFHMSRE

```
                      000216
                      000221   000295  000297  000394  000397
                      000222   000296  000297  000395  000397
                      000210
                      000211
                      000212
                      000223
                      000106
                      000133
                      000115
                      000105
                      000224   000297  000310  000397
                      000227
                      000183
                      000184
                      000182
                      000233   000283  000335
                      000225   000281  000282  000294  000297  00030
                               000341  000343  000348  000350  00035
                               000376  000378  000393  000397  00040
                      000206   000342  000343  000349  000350  00035
                               000377  000378
                      000217
                      000195   000309  000310  000396  000397  00040
                      000196
                      000197
                      000198
                      000199
                      000186
                      000203
                      000204
                      000205
                      000207
                      000209
                      000208
                      000220
                      000201   000405  000407
                      000202
                      000213
                      000214
                      000218
                      000145
                      000104
                      000110
                      000098
                      000181
                      000134
                      000120
                      000131
                      000121
                      000132
                      000119
                      000130
                      000150
```

DFHMT	000129
DFHNEUTR	000113
DFHNULL	000144
DFHOPAQ	000141
DFHOPID	000149
DFHOUTLN	000101
DFHOVER	000135
DFHPA1	000153
DFHPA2	000154
DFHPA3	000155
DFHPEN	000148
DFHPF1	000156
DFHPF10	000165
DFHPF11	000166

DFHPF12	000167				
DFHPF13	000168				
DFHPF14	000169				
DFHPF15	000170				
DFHPF16	000171				
DFHPF17	000172				
DFHPF18	000173				
DFHPF19	000174				
DFHPF2	000157				
DFHPF20	000175				
DFHPF21	000176				
DFHPF22	000177				
DFHPF23	000178				
DFHPF24	000179				
DFHPF3	000158				
DFHPF4	000159				
DFHPF5	000160				
DFHPF6	000161				
DFHPF7	000162				
DFHPF8	000163				
DFHPF9	000164				
DFHPINK	000109				
DFHPROTI	000127				
DFHPROTN	000128				
DFHPS	000097				
DFHRED	000108				
DFHREVRS	000117				
DFHRIGHT	000136				
DFHSA	000095				
DFHSOSI	000139				
DFHSTRF	000151				
DFHTRANS	000140				
DFHTRIG	000152				
DFHTURQ	000111				
DFHUNDER	000137				
DFHUNDLN	000118				
DFHUNIMD	000123				
DFHUNINT	000125				
DFHUNNOD	000122				
DFHUNNON	000126				
DFHUNNUM	000124				
DFHVAL	000100				
DFHYELLO	000112				
DFH3270	000099				
EIBAID	000236				
EIBATT	000246				
EIBCALEN	000235	000271			
EIBCOMPL	000249				
EIBCONF	000251				
EIBCPOSN	000234				
EIBDATE	000229				
EIBDS	000239				
EIBEOC	000247				
EIBERR	000252				
EIBERRCD	000253				
EIBFIL01	000245				
EIBFMH	000248				
EIBFN	000237				
EIBFREE	000243				
EIBNODAT	000255				
EIBRCODE	000238				
EIBRECV	000244				
EIBREQID	000240				
EIBRESP	000256				
EIBRESP2	000257				
EIBRLDBK	000258				
EIBRSRCE	000241				
EIBSIG	000250				
EIBSYNC	000242				
EIBSYNRB	000254				
EIBTASKN	000231				
EIBTIME	000228				
EIBTRMID	000232				
EIBTRNID	000230	000273			
END-OF-SESSION-MSG	000019	000310			
ERMSGA	000037	000270	000323	000325	000328	00041

ERMSGF	000035				
ERMSGI	000038				
ERMSGL	000034				
ERMSGO	000046	000324	000380	000413	
LENGTH-BYTES	000075				
PF-KEYS	000015	000274	000288		
PFENTER	000016	000287			
PF1-KEY	000017				
PGM-MSG	000008	000413			
PGM-SEL	000010	000412			
PROT	000062				
PROT-BRT	000064	000325			
PROT-BRT-MDT	000065				
PROT-DRK	000066				
PROT-DRK-MDT	000067				
PROT-MDT	000063				
SELECTA	000032	000270	000323		
SELECTF	000030				
SELECTI	000033	000337	000344	000351	000358	00036
SELECTL	000029	000322	000385	000415	
SELECTO	000044				
UNPROT-ALPHA	000050				
UNPROT-ALPHA-BRT	000052				
UNPROT-ALPHA-BRT-MDT	000053				
UNPROT-ALPHA-DRK	000054				
UNPROT-ALPHA-DRK-MDT	000055				
UNPROT-ALPHA-MDT	000051				
UNPROT-NUM	000056				
UNPROT-NUM-BRT	000058				
UNPROT-NUM-BRT-MDT	000059				
UNPROT-NUM-DRK	000060				
UNPROT-NUM-DRK-MDT	000061				
UNPROT-NUM-MDT	000057				
PROCEDURE NAMES	DEFN	REFERENCE			
0000-MAIN	000268			
0100-SET-PFKEYS	000269			
0200-PF1-EXIT	000301	000283		
0210-INVALID-SELECT	000321	000283		
0300-SELECT-OPTION	000327	000299		
0400-SEND-MAP	000383	000381	000416	
0500-START-SESSION	000384	000289		
9999-PGM-NOTFND	000411	000335		

Subdirectory ARM90C

As shown in FIG. 2-10, the subdirectory program starts out with the expansion of the symbolic map (lines 11 through 42), which is the result of the compilation process. The copy statement is issued in line 10, which triggers the map, ARM90M7I (line 11) and a subsequent layout of your panel. As you can see, much of the copy statements are similar, if not identical, to those in the ARM10C program, including the Cross Reference Dictionary.

2-10 ARM90C compiler version

```
00001        IDENTIFICATION DIVISION.
00002        PROGRAM-ID. ARM90C.
00003        DATE-COMPILED. APR 18,1990.
00004        ENVIRONMENT DIVISION.
00005        DATA DIVISION.
00006        WORKING-STORAGE SECTION.
00007        01  COMM-AREA.
00008            05  SEND-REC-FLAG    PIC X.
00009            05  CUST-COMPARE     PIC X(4).
```

```
00010          COPY ARM90M.
00011 C        01  ARM90M7I.
00012 C            02  FILLER PIC X(12).
00013 C            02  TRANSIDL   COMP PIC  S9(4).
00014 C            02  TRANSIDF   PICTURE X.
00015 C            02  FILLER REDEFINES TRANSIDF.
00016 C                03 TRANSIDA   PICTURE X.
00017 C            02  TRANSIDI PIC X(4).
00018 C            02  DATEL    COMP  PIC  S9(4).
00019 C            02  DATEF    PICTURE X.
00020 C            02  FILLER REDEFINES DATEF.
00021 C                03 DATEA    PICTURE X.
00022 C            02  DATEI PIC X(8).
00023 C            02  SELECTL   COMP  PIC  S9(4).
00024 C            02  SELECTF   PICTURE X.
00025 C            02  FILLER REDEFINES SELECTF.
00026 C                03 SELECTA   PICTURE X.
00027 C            02  SELECTI PIC X(1).
00028 C            02  MSSGL    COMP  PIC  S9(4).
00029 C            02  MSSGF    PICTURE X.
00030 C            02  FILLER REDEFINES MSSGF.
00031 C                03 MSSGA    PICTURE X.
00032 C            02  MSSGI PIC X(50).
00033 C        01  ARM90M7O REDEFINES ARM90M7I.
00034 C            02  FILLER PIC X(12).
00035 C            02  FILLER PICTURE X(3).
00036 C            02  TRANSIDO PIC X(4).
00037 C            02  FILLER PICTURE X(3).
00038 C            02  DATEO PIC X(8).
00039 C            02  FILLER PICTURE X(3).
00040 C            02  SELECTO  PIC X(1).
00041 C            02  FILLER PICTURE X(3).
00042 C            02  MSSGO  PIC X(50).
00043          COPY DFHAID.
00044 C        01   DFHAID.
00045 C            02  DFHNULL   PIC  X  VALUE IS ' '.
00046 C            02  DFHENTER  PIC  X  VALUE IS QUOTE.
00047 C            02  DFHCLEAR  PIC  X  VALUE IS '_'.
00048 C            02  DFHCLRP   PIC  X  VALUE IS '⊤'.
00049 C            02  DFHPEN    PIC  X  VALUE IS '='.
00050 C            02  DFHOPID   PIC  X  VALUE IS 'W'.
00051 C            02  DFHMSRE   PIC  X  VALUE IS 'X'.
00052 C            02  DFHSTRF   PIC  X  VALUE IS 'h'.
00053 C            02  DFHTRIG   PIC  X  VALUE IS '"'.
00054 C            02  DFHPA1    PIC  X  VALUE IS '%'.
00055 C            02  DFHPA2    PIC  X  VALUE IS '>'.
00056 C            02  DFHPA3    PIC  X  VALUE IS ','.
00057 C            02  DFHPF1    PIC  X  VALUE IS '1'.
00058 C            02  DFHPF2    PIC  X  VALUE IS '2'.
00059 C            02  DFHPF3    PIC  X  VALUE IS '3'.
00060 C            02  DFHPF4    PIC  X  VALUE IS '4'.
00061 C            02  DFHPF5    PIC  X  VALUE IS '5'.
00062 C            02  DFHPF6    PIC  X  VALUE IS '6'.
00063 C            02  DFHPF7    PIC  X  VALUE IS '7'.
00064 C            02  DFHPF8    PIC  X  VALUE IS '8'.
00065 C            02  DFHPF9    PIC  X  VALUE IS '9'.
00066 C            02  DFHPF10   PIC  X  VALUE IS ':'.
00067 C            02  DFHPF11   PIC  X  VALUE IS '#'.
00068 C            02  DFHPF12   PIC  X  VALUE IS '@'.
00069 C            02  DFHPF13   PIC  X  VALUE IS 'A'.
00070 C            02  DFHPF14   PIC  X  VALUE IS 'B'.
00071 C            02  DFHPF15   PIC  X  VALUE IS 'C'.
00072 C            02  DFHPF16   PIC  X  VALUE IS 'D'.
00073 C            02  DFHPF17   PIC  X  VALUE IS 'E'.
00074 C            02  DFHPF18   PIC  X  VALUE IS 'F'.
00075 C            02  DFHPF19   PIC  X  VALUE IS 'G'.
00076 C            02  DFHPF20   PIC  X  VALUE IS 'H'.
00077 C            02  DFHPF21   PIC  X  VALUE IS 'I'.
00078 C            02  DFHPF22   PIC  X  VALUE IS ''.
00079 C            02  DFHPF23   PIC  X  VALUE IS '.'.
00080 C            02  DFHPF24   PIC  X  VALUE IS '<'.
00081          01  DFHLDVER PIC X(22) VALUE 'LD TABLE DFHEITAB 210.'.
00082          01  DFHEIDO PICTURE S9(7) COMPUTATIONAL-3 VALUE ZERO.
00083          01  DFHEIBO PICTURE S9(4) COMPUTATIONAL VALUE ZERO.
00084          01  DFHEICB  PICTURE X(8) VALUE IS '        '
00085
```

```
00086          01   DFHEIV16  COMP PIC S9(8).
00087          01   DFHB0041  COMP PIC S9(8).
00088          01   DFHB0042  COMP PIC S9(8).
00089          01   DFHB0043  COMP PIC S9(8).
00090          01   DFHB0044  COMP PIC S9(8).
00091          01   DFHB0045  COMP PIC S9(8).
00092          01   DFHB0046  COMP PIC S9(8).
00093          01   DFHB0047  COMP PIC S9(8).
00094          01   DFHB0048  COMP PIC S9(8).
00095          01   DFHEIV11  COMP PIC S9(4).
00096          01   DFHEIV12  COMP PIC S9(4).
00097          01   DFHEIV13  COMP PIC S9(4).
00098          01   DFHEIV14  COMP PIC S9(4).
00099          01   DFHEIV15  COMP PIC S9(4).
00100          01   DFHB0025  COMP PIC S9(4).
00101          01   DFHEIV5   PIC X(4).
00102          01   DFHEIV6   PIC X(4).
00103          01   DFHEIV17  PIC X(4).
00104          01   DFHEIV18  PIC X(4).
00105          01   DFHEIV19  PIC X(4).
00106          01   DFHEIV1   PIC X(8).
00107          01   DFHEIV2   PIC X(8).
00108          01   DFHEIV3   PIC X(8).
00109          01   DFHEIV20  PIC X(8).
00110          01   DFHC0084  PIC X(8).
00111          01   DFHC0085  PIC X(8).
00112          01   DFHC0320  PIC X(32).
00113          01   DFHEIV7   PIC X(2).
00114          01   DFHEIV8   PIC X(2).
00115          01   DFHC0022  PIC X(2).
00116          01   DFHC0023  PIC X(2).
00117          01   DFHEIV10  PIC S9(7) COMP-3.
00118          01   DFHEIV9   PIC X(1).
00119          01   DFHC0011  PIC X(1).
00120          01   DFHEIV4   PIC X(6).
00121          01   DFHC0070  PIC X(7).
00122          01   DFHC0071  PIC X(7).
00123          01   DFHC0440  PIC X(44).
00124          01   DFHDUMMY COMP PIC S9(4).
00125          01   DFHEIV0  PICTURE X(29).
00126      LINKAGE SECTION.
00127          01  DFHEIBLK.
00128          02    EIBTIME  PIC S9(7) COMP-3.
00129          02    EIBDATE  PIC S9(7) COMP-3.
00130          02    EIBTRNID PIC X(4).
00131          02    EIBTASKN PIC S9(7) COMP-3.
00132          02    EIBTRMID PIC X(4).
00133          02    DFHEIGDI COMP PIC S9(4).
00134          02    EIBCPOSN COMP PIC S9(4).
00135          02    EIBCALEN COMP PIC S9(4).
00136          02    EIBAID   PIC X(1).
00137          02    EIBFN    PIC X(2).
00138          02    EIBRCODE PIC X(6).
00139          02    EIBDS    PIC X(8).
00140          02    EIBREQID PIC X(8).
00141          02    EIBRSRCE PIC X(8).
00142          02    EIBSYNC  PIC X(1).
00143          02    EIBFREE  PIC X(1).
00144          02    EIBRECV  PIC X(1).
00145          02    EIBFIL01 PIC X(1).
00146          02    EIBATT   PIC X(1).
00147          02    EIBEOC   PIC X(1).
00148          02    EIBFMH   PIC X(1).
00149          02    EIBCOMPL PIC X(1).
00150          02    EIBSIG   PIC X(1).
00151          02    EIBCONF  PIC X(1).
00152          02    EIBERR   PIC X(1).
00153          02    EIBERRCD PIC X(4).
00154          02    EIBSYNRB PIC X(1).
00155          02    EIBNODAT PIC X(1).
00156          02    EIBRESP  COMP PIC S9(8).
00157          02    EIBRESP2 COMP PIC S9(8).
00158          02    EIBRLDBK PIC X(1).
00159          01  DFHCOMMAREA    PIC X(5).
00160          01  DFHBLLSLOT1 PICTURE X(1).
00161          01  DFHBLLSLOT2 PICTURE X(1).
00162      PROCEDURE DIVISION USING DFHEIBLK DFHCOMMAREA.
```

```
00163              CALL 'DFHEI1'.
00164              SERVICE RELOAD DFHEIBLK.
00165              SERVICE RELOAD DFHCOMMAREA.
00166          010-CHECK-COMMAREA.
00167              IF EIBCALEN > 0
00168              MOVE DFHCOMMAREA TO COMM-AREA.
00169          020-START-PROCESSING.
00170          *EXEC CICS HANDLE AID
00171          *     CLEAR(035-RESEND)
00172          *     PF1(070-RETURN)
00173          *     ANYKEY(035-RESEND)
00174          *END-EXEC.
00175              MOVE ' \              00019   ' TO DFHEIVO
00176              CALL 'DFHEI1' USING DFHEIVO
00177              GO TO  035-RESEND 070-RETURN 035-RESEND DEPENDING ON
00178              DFHEIGDI.
00179
00180          030-SEND-RECEIVE-PARAGRAPH.
00181              IF SEND-REC-FLAG = 'R' GO TO
00182              040-RECEIVE-MAP.
00183          035-RESEND.
00184              MOVE 'R' TO SEND-REC-FLAG.
00185              MOVE -1 TO SELECTL.
00186          *EXEC CICS
00187          *          SEND MAP('ARM90M7')
00188          *          MAPSET('ARM90M')
00189          *          ERASE
00190          *          CURSOR
00191          *END-EXEC.
00192              MOVE ' J       S   00030   ' TO DFHEIVO
00193              MOVE 'ARM90M7' TO DFHC0070
00194              MOVE 'ARM90M' TO DFHC0071
00195              MOVE -1 TO DFHEIV11
00196              CALL 'DFHEI1' USING DFHEIVO  DFHC0070 ARM90M7O DFHDUMMY
00197              DFHC0071 DFHDUMMY DFHDUMMY DFHEIV11.
00198              GO TO 800-REINVOKE-TRANSACTION.
00199          040-RECEIVE-MAP.
00200          *EXEC CICS RECEIVE MAP('ARM90M7')
00201          *MAPSET('ARM90M')
00202          *END-EXEC.
00203              MOVE ' }              00038   ' TO DFHEIVO
00204              MOVE 'ARM90M7' TO DFHC0070
00205              MOVE 'ARM90M' TO DFHC0071
00206              CALL 'DFHEI1' USING DFHEIVO  DFHC0070 ARM90M7I DFHDUMMY
00207              DFHC0071.
00208              MOVE 'S' TO SEND-REC-FLAG.
00209              IF SELECTI = '1', OR, '2', OR '3', OR '4'
00210              NEXT SENTENCE ELSE
00211              MOVE 'INVALID SELECTION CODE, PLEASE RE-ENTER'
00212              TO MSSGO
00213              MOVE 'Y' TO MSSGA
00214              MOVE 'I' TO SELECTA
00215              MOVE -1 TO SELECTL
00216              GO TO 035-RESEND.
00217              IF SELECTI = '1'
00218          *EXEC CICS XCTL PROGRAM('ARA91C')
00219          *COMMAREA(COMM-AREA)
00220          *LENGTH(1)
00221          *END-EXEC.
00222              MOVE ' \       00051   ' TO DFHEIVO
00223              MOVE 'ARA91C' TO DFHEIV1
00224              MOVE 1 TO DFHEIV11
00225              CALL 'DFHEI1' USING DFHEIVO  DFHEIV1  COMM-AREA DFHEIV11.
00226              IF SELECTI = '2'
00227              MOVE ' ' TO SEND-REC-FLAG
00228              MOVE '$$$$' TO CUST-COMPARE
00229          *EXEC CICS XCTL PROGRAM('ARC92C')
00230          *COMMAREA(COMM-AREA)
00231          *LENGTH(5)
00232          *END-EXEC.
00233              MOVE ' \       00058   ' TO DFHEIVO
00234              MOVE 'ARC92C' TO DFHEIV1
00235              MOVE 5 TO DFHEIV11
00236              CALL 'DFHEI1' USING DFHEIVO  DFHEIV1  COMM-AREA DFHEIV11.

00237              IF SELECTI = '3'
```

```
00238          *EXEC CICS XCTL PROGRAM('ARD93C')
00239          *COMMAREA(COMM-AREA)
00240          *LENGTH(1)
00241          *END-EXEC.
00242              MOVE ' \        00063    ' TO DFHEIV0
00243              MOVE 'ARD93C' TO DFHEIV1
00244              MOVE 1 TO DFHEIV11
00245              CALL 'DFHEI1' USING DFHEIV0 DFHEIV1 COMM-AREA DFHEIV11.

00246              IF SELECTI = '4'
00247              MOVE 'BROWSE FUNCTION CURRENTLY UNAVAILABLE' TO MSSGO
00248              MOVE '-' TO MSSGA
00249              MOVE -1 TO SELECTL
00250              MOVE 'I' TO SELECTA
00251              GO TO 035-RESEND.
00252          800-REINVOKE-TRANSACTION.
00253          *EXEC CICS RETURN
00254          *TRANSID('AR90')
00255          *COMMAREA(COMM-AREA)
00256          *LENGTH(7)
00257          *END-EXEC.
00258              MOVE ' \        00074    ' TO DFHEIV0
00259              MOVE 'AR90' TO DFHEIV5
00260              MOVE 7 TO DFHEIV11
00261              CALL 'DFHEI1' USING DFHEIV0 DFHEIV5 COMM-AREA DFHEIV11.

00262
00263          070-RETURN.
00264          *EXEC CICS XCTL PROGRAM('ARM10C')
00265          *END-EXEC.
00266              MOVE '           00080    ' TO DFHEIV0
00267              MOVE 'ARM10C' TO DFHEIV1
00268              CALL 'DFHEI1' USING DFHEIV0 DFHEIV1.
00269              STOP RUN.
00270              GOBACK.
*STATISTICS*     SOURCE RECORDS =    270     DATA DIVISION STATEMENTS =    151
*OPTIONS IN EFFECT*     SIZE = 524288  BUF =  20480  LINECNT = 57  SPACE1, FL
*OPTIONS IN EFFECT*     NODMAP, NOPMAP, NOCLIST, NOSUPMAP, NOXREF,   SXREF,  L
*OPTIONS IN EFFECT*     NOTERM, NONUM, NOBATCH, NONAME, COMPILE=01, NOSTATE, NO
*OPTIONS IN EFFECT*     NOOPTIMIZE, NOSYMDMP, NOTEST,   VERB,   ZWB, SYST, NOEN
*OPTIONS IN EFFECT*     NOLST , NOFDECK,NOCDECK, LCOL2, L120,   DUMP , NOADV ,
*OPTIONS IN EFFECT*     NOCOUNT, NOVBSUM, NOVBREF, LANGLVL(1)
```

CROSS-REFERENCE DICTIONARY

DATA NAMES	DEFN	REFERENCE			
ARM90M7I	000011	000206			
ARM90M7O	000033	000196			
COMM-AREA	000007	000168	000225	000236	000245	00026
CUST-COMPARE	000009	000228			
DATEA	000021				
DATEF	000019				
DATEI	000022				
DATEL	000018				
DATEO	000038				
DFHAID	000044				
DFHBLLSLOT1	000160				
DFHBLLSLOT2	000161				
DFHB0025	000100				
DFHB0041	000087				
DFHB0042	000088				
DFHB0043	000089				
DFHB0044	000090				
DFHB0045	000091				
DFHB0046	000092				
DFHB0047	000093				
DFHB0048	000094				
DFHCLEAR	000047				
DFHCLRP	000048				
DFHCOMMAREA	000159	000168			
DFHC0011	000119				
DFHC0022	000115				
DFHC0023	000116				
DFHC0070	000121	000193	000196	000204	000206
DFHC0071	000122	000194	000196	000205	000206

DFHC0084	000110				
DFHC0085	000111				
DFHC0320	000112				
DFHC0440	000123				
DFHDUMMY	000124	000196	000206		
DFHEIBLK	000127				
DFHEIB0	000083				
DFHEICB	000084				
DFHEID0	000082				
DFHEIGDI	000133	000177			
DFHEIV0	000125	000175	000176	000192	000196	00020
		000242	000245	000258	000261	00026
DFHEIV1	000106	000223	000225	000234	000236	00024
DFHEIV10	000117				
DFHEIV11	000095	000195	000196	000224	000225	00023
DFHEIV12	000096				
DFHEIV13	000097				
DFHEIV14	000098				
DFHEIV15	000099				
DFHEIV16	000086				
DFHEIV17	000103				
DFHEIV18	000104				
DFHEIV19	000105				
DFHEIV2	000107				
DFHEIV20	000109				
DFHEIV3	000108				
DFHEIV4	000120				
DFHEIV5	000101	000259	000261		
DFHEIV6	000102				
DFHEIV7	000113				
DFHEIV8	000114				
DFHEIV9	000118				
DFHENTER	000046				
DFHLDVER	000081				
DFHMSRE	000051				
DFHNULL	000045				
DFHOPID	000050				
DFHPA1	000054				
DFHPA2	000055				
DFHPA3	000056				
DFHPEN	000049				
DFHPF1	000057				
DFHPF10	000066				
DFHPF11	000067				
DFHPF12	000068				
DFHPF13	000069				
DFHPF14	000070				
DFHPF15	000071				
DFHPF16	000072				
DFHPF17	000073				
DFHPF18	000074				
DFHPF19	000075				
DFHPF2	000058				
DFHPF20	000076				
DFHPF21	000077				
DFHPF22	000078				
DFHPF23	000079				
DFHPF24	000080				
DFHPF3	000059				
DFHPF4	000060				
DFHPF5	000061				
DFHPF6	000062				
DFHPF7	000063				
DFHPF8	000064				
DFHPF9	000065				
DFHSTRF	000052				
DFHTRIG	000053				
EIBAID	000136				
EIBATT	000146				
EIBCALEN	000135	000167			
EIBCOMPL	000149				
EIBCONF	000151				
EIBCPOSN	000134				
EIBDATE	000129				
EIBDS	000139				
EIBEOC	000147				

```
EIBERR                        000152
EIBERRCD                      000153
EIBFIL01                      000145
EIBFMH                        000148
EIBFN                         000137
EIBFREE                       000143
EIBNODAT                      000155
EIBRCODE                      000138
EIBRECV                       000144
EIBREQID                      000140
EIBRESP                       000156
EIBRESP2                      000157
EIBRLDBK                      000158
EIBRSRCE                      000141
EIBSIG                        000150
EIBSYNC                       000142
EIBSYNRB                      000154
EIBTASKN                      000131
EIBTIME                       000128
EIBTRMID                      000132
EIBTRNID                      000130
MSSGA                         000031    000213  000248
MSSGF                         000029
MSSGI                         000032
MSSGL                         000028
MSSGO                         000042    000211  000247
SELECTA                       000026    000214  000250
SELECTF                       000024
SELECTI                       000027    000209  000217  000226  000237  00024
SELECTL                       000023    000185  000215  000249
SELECTO                       000040
SEND-REC-FLAG                 000008    000181  000184  000208  000227
TRANSIDA                      000016
TRANSIDF                      000014
TRANSIDI                      000017
TRANSIDL                      000013
TRANSIDO                      000036
PROCEDURE NAMES               DEFN      REFERENCE
010-CHECK-COMMAREA            000166
020-START-PROCESSING          000169
030-SEND-RECEIVE-PARAGRAPH    000180
035-RESEND                    000183    000177  000216  000251
040-RECEIVE-MAP               000199    000181
070-RETURN                    000263    000177
800-REINVOKE-TRANSACTION      000252    000198
```

3

How to develop an INQUIRY *program*

INQUIRY programs, as a general rule, are simplistic from the programmer's perspective. All you need to do is to read a file based on a user-supplied INQUIRY key, and if such a key happens to be a valid one, that is one representing an existing record on file, you can proceed to display the file on the screen. Display, with the exception of the INQUIRY key, is done where all data fields appear in a protected mode, geared to a low-intensity display. If, on the other hand, no such record can be located on file, a program-generated system message should inform the terminal operator that his or her INQUIRY did not find the proper match.

What might complicate a normally speedy development of an INQUIRY program is the need to read multiple files and/or small VSAM tables to consolidate all requirements into a single display. For example, when you read a file, assuming a successful "hit," you might frequently have to build an additional key to retrieve specific data from another file. This "bouncing" back and forth between master and transaction files, or from file A to file B can require extended code, which is the exception rather than the norm.

INQUIRY programs, as a rule, perform no viable edit functions. If there is an edit problem, your various maintenance transactions ought to address it, unless, of course, file maintenance remains a batch function. In reference to an INQUIRY program, you need to fully describe a record key to attain a match. The record key will not, as you'll soon see, function in a partially defined "generic" format. Compared to BROWSE transactions, INQUIRY programs tend to generate a rather harsh response to a missing or incomplete key, resulting in the rejection of an entire transaction. Thus, the awkward nature of an INQUIRY program might be the lack of generic capabilities (i.e., capabilities to perform a broad search), denying the user even the slightest display capabilities. Because of the comparably restrictive nature of this type of transaction, INQUIRY programs are used infrequently, but they are practical for users with low security clearance restricted to certain display-like transactions.

Case study

This case study entails a relatively simple program. It is designed so that you can invoke it through a subdirectory, through a selection, or by entering the proper transaction identifier (AR49). Once the program is invoked, a panel, identical to the one shown in FIG. 3-1, is displayed on the screen.

```
AR28    INVOICE HEADER SCREEN FOR NON-RECURRING BILLINGS          05/19/90


    PROJECT NO : 00000001
    CREDIT MEMO:            (Y,N)       ORIGINAL INV# : E 00011
    CUSTOMER NO:      0001            CUSTOMER NAME : ALEX VARSEGI
    INVOICE NO :   E 00002           INVOICE AMOUNT: 1244.44
    ACCOUNTING MM/YY : 1288           BILLING DATE  (MMDDYY)
    PERIOD DESCRIPT.:  NO SPECIAL PROCESSING AT THIS TIME

    ------------------ SPECIAL INSTRUCTION -----------------------
    INVESTIGATE PROPER CREDIT MEMO TRANSACTIONS



    ------------------------------------------------------------------

    PF1:RETURN TO MENU
    RECORD DOES NOT EXIST ON FILE
```

3-1 Highlights the INQUIRY panel used in the case study

To inquire about a specific record, you can enter the INQUIRY key, which is made up of two components: an alphabetic prefix followed by a five-position long invoice number. If fewer than five positions are used, the field must be padded with high-order zeros. Thus, the concatenated key of E 00011 is not synonymous with E blank blank blank 11 or E   11. If the record is a valid one, that is, one already in existence, it will be displayed on the screen. If there is no such key in existence, however, the message "RECORD DOES NOT EXIST ON FILE" will appear in line 24. The sole input to the above program is the nonrecurring customer file. Layout for a nonrecurring customer record is highlighted in line 00015 through 00041 in FIG. 3-4.

INQUIRY programs, in fact, bear a great deal of resemblance to DELETE programs in that all data to be displayed on the screen needs to be displayed in protected mode, with the exception of the INQUIRY key. The reason for that is because INQUIRY programs do not possess some of the maintenance apparatus inherent in a CHANGE or ADD transaction that restrict the activities of users with limited access to the system. This highlights the fact that DELETE programs are ideal for creating a logical shell for an INQUIRY program, or vice versa.

Map and FCT considerations

Figure 3-2 shows the Basic Mapping required for a screen definition, which was laid out earlier in FIG. 3-1. Note that every field on this map (except for the prefix and the customer number) is defined in protected mode. Like creating shells for a particular program, this map can easily be converted to a delete map. Compare the BMS in FIG. 3-2 with the symbolic map, which is the assembled version of the program shown in FIG. 3-5. The symbolic map is laid out in lines 43 through 194 of FIG. 3-5. Also note that the File Control Table, or FCT, is shown in FIG. 3-3.

3-2 BMS screen definition for the DELETE screen

```
         PRINT NOGEN
ARB49M   DFHMSD  TYPE=&SYSPARM,MODE=INOUT,CTRL=FREEKB,LANG=COBOL,      C
         TIOAPFX=YES
ARB49M3  DFHMDI  SIZE=(24,80)
TRANS    DFHMDF  POS=(01,02),LENGTH=04,INITIAL='AR49',                 C
         ATTRB=(BRT,ASKIP)
         DFHMDF  POS=(01,10),LENGTH=56,ATTRB=ASKIP,                    C
         INITIAL='INVOICE HEADER SCREEN FOR NON-RECURRING BILLINGC
         S'
DATE     DFHMDF  POS=(01,70),LENGTH=08,ATTRB=(BRT,ASKIP),
MODE     DFHMDF  POS=(03,40),LENGTH=12,ATTRB=(BRT,PROT)
         DFHMDF  POS=(05,03),LENGTH=12,ATTRB=(BRT,PROT),               C
         INITIAL='PROJECT NO :'
PROJECT  DFHMDF  POS=(05,16),LENGTH=06,ATTRB=(BRT,PROT)
         DFHMDF  POS=(05,23),LENGTH=01,INITIAL=' ',ATTRB=ASKIP
         DFHMDF  POS=(06,03),LENGTH=12,ATTRB=ASKIP,                    C
         INITIAL='CREDIT MEMO.'
MEMO     DFHMDF  POS=(06,16),LENGTH=01,ATTRB=(BRT,PROT)
         DFHMDF  POS=(06,18),LENGTH=01,INITIAL=' ',ATTRB=ASKIP
         DFHMDF  POS=(06,20),LENGTH=08,ATTRB=(BRT,PROT),               C
         INITIAL='(Y, N)'
         DFHMDF  POS=(06,31),LENGTH=15,ATTRB=ASKIP,                    C
         INITIAL='ORIGINAL INV# :'
ORGINVF  DFHMDF  POS=(06,47),LENGTH=01,ATTRB=(BRT,ASKIP)
         DFHMDF  POS=(06,49),LENGTH=01,INITIAL=' ',ATTRB=ASKIP
ORGINV   DFHMDF  POS=(06,51),LENGTH=05,ATTRB=(BRT,ASKIP)
         DFHMDF  POS=(06,57),LENGTH=01,INITIAL=' ',ATTRB=ASKIP
         DFHMDF  POS=(07,03),LENGTH=12,ATTRB=ASKIP,                    C
         INITIAL='CUSTOMER NO:'
CUSNUM   DFHMDF  POS=(07,16),LENGTH=14,ATTRB=(BRT,ASKIP,FSET)
         DFHMDF  POS=(07,31),LENGTH=15,ATTRB=ASKIP,                    C
         INITIAL='CUSTOMER NAME :'
CUSNAME  DFHMDF  POS=(07,47),LENGTH=30,ATTRB=(BRT,ASKIP)
         DFHMDF  POS=(07,78),LENGTH=01,INITIAL=' ',ATTRB=ASKIP
         DFHMDF  POS=(08,03),LENGTH=12,ATTRB=(BRT,ASKIP),              C
         INITIAL='INVOICE NO :'
INVPRE   DFHMDF  POS=(08,16),LENGTH=01,ATTRB=(IC,UNPROT,FSET)
INVNO    DFHMDF  POS=(08,18),LENGTH=05,ATTRB=(UNPROT,FSET)
         DFHMDF  POS=(08,24),LENGTH=01,INITIAL=' ',ATTRB=ASKIP
         DFHMDF  POS=(08,31),LENGTH=15,ATTRB=ASKIP,                    C
         INITIAL='INVOICE AMOUNT:'
INVAMNT  DFHMDF  POS=(08,47),LENGTH=11,ATTRB=(PROT,ASKIP)
```

```
            DFHMDF POS=(08,59),LENGTH=01,INITIAL=' ',ATTRB=ASKIP
            DFHMDF POS=(09,03),LENGTH=17,ATTRB=(BRT,ASKIP),            C
                   INITIAL='ACCOUNTING MM/YY:'
ACCPER      DFHMDF POS=(09,21),LENGTH=04,ATTRB=(BRT,ASKIP)
            DFHMDF POS=(09,26),LENGTH=01,INITIAL=' ',ATTRB=ASKIP
            DFHMDF POS=(09,31),LENGTH=21,ATTRB=(BRT,ASKIP),            C
                   INITIAL='BILLING DATE (MMDDYY)'
BILLD       DFHMDF POS=(09,53),LENGTH=08,ATTRB=(BRT,ASKIP)
            DFHMDF POS=(09,62),LENGTH=01,INITIAL=' ',ATTRB=ASKIP
            DFHMDF POS=(10,03),LENGTH=17,ATTRB=ASKIP,                  C
                   INITIAL='PERIOD DESCRIPT.:'
PERDES      DFHMDF POS=(10,21),LENGTH=55,ATTRB=(BRT,ASKIP)
            DFHMDF POS=(10,77),LENGTH=01,INITIAL=' ',ATTRB=ASKIP
            DFHMDF POS=(12,03),LENGTH=23,ATTRB=(BRT,ASKIP),            C
                   INITIAL='                       '
            DFHMDF POS=(12,27),LENGTH=21,ATTRB=ASKIP,                  C
                   INITIAL='SPECIAL INSTRUCTIONS'
            DFHMDF POS=(12,49),LENGTH=23,ATTRB=(BRT,ASKIP),            C
                   INITIAL='                       '
INSTR1      DFHMDF POS=(14,03),LENGTH=70,ATTRB=(ASKIP,FSET)
            DFHMDF POS=(14,74),LENGTH=01,INITIAL=' ',ATTRB=ASKIP
INSTR2      DFHMDF POS=(15,03),LENGTH=70,ATTRB=(ASKIP,FSET)
            DFHMDF POS=(15,74),LENGTH=01,INITIAL=' ',ATTRB=ASKIP
            DFHMDF POS=(17,03),LENGTH=70,ATTRB=(BRT,ASKIP),            C
                   INITIAL='                                         ' C
PFMSG1      DFHMDF POS=(22,05),LENGTH=19,ATTRB=ASKIP,                  C
                   INITIAL='PF1: RETURN TO MENU'
PFMSG2      DFHMDF POS=(22,31),LENGTH=25,ATTRB=(BRT,ASKIP)
PFMSG3      DFHMDF POS=(23,05),LENGTH=19,ATTRB=(BRT,ASKIP),            C
                   INITIAL='                   '
ERMSG       DFHMDF POS=(24,05),LENGTH=60,ATTRB=(BRT,PROT,FSET)
            DFHMSD TYPE=FINAL
            END
```

```
ARA21C  DFHFCT    TYPE DATASET,ACCMETH=VSAM,LOG=YES,        C
                  DATASET=ARA21C,                           C
                  DSNAME=NIRVT.AR,ARA21C,DISP=SHR,          C
                  SERVREQ=(BROWSE,DELETE,ADD,UPDATE),       C
                  RECFORM=(FIXED,BLOCKED),                  C
                  FILSTAT=(ENABLED,CLOSED),                 C
                  LSRPOOL=1,                                C
                  STRNO=2,BUFNO=3,BUFNI=2
```

3-3 File Control Table for the nonrecurring customer master

Source program listing and narrative

As shown in FIG. 3-4, the program starts out with a number of conventionally used fields. Among these are the SEND-RECEIVE-FLAG and STORE-KEY fields. The SEND-RECEIVE-FLAG is used to differentiate between send and receive map cycles, and it is stored and accessed through the COMMAREA in the LINKAGE SECTION. The second field is designed to store the record key for interim purposes. This is shown in lines 11 through 14. As you can see, the DATA DIVISION is just about as simple as it can be, even with a "hard copy" stored in the main body of the program. That is to say that, instead of relying on a copy statement, the invoice record is defined and laid out in the WORKING-STORAGE SECTION of the program, in lines 16 through 42. This is the sole record format used in this transaction.

There are three copy statements requested in this INQUIRY program. The first one is to copy the mapset (and the map) into the IMQUIRY program highlighted in line 44. The purpose of the second copy statement is to establish a reference point to the keyboard in terms of function key usage. This is shown in line 45, but the actual expansion of the above copy statement is highlighted in the next section, in lines 195 through 231. Third, there is an attribute table developed in-house called CHARATR. Using CHARATR is a slick idea when you need to combine a number of different attribute characteristics while giving each function a meaningful name. This statement is shown in line 46 and is expanded in the following section in lines 234 through 260.

The COMMUNICATIONS AREA is defined as a single byte field that directs the traffic between the send and the receive cycle. This is the first piece of data to be checked by the INQUIRY program. The HANDLE AID statement defines two specific keys in the program, followed by a "catch all" ANYKEY option. The CLEAR key (statement 54) is used to reference one of the subroutines in the program, whose logic is highlighted starting in line 64. PF 1 is designed to return (or exit control) from the current procedures and reinvoke a subdirectory just a level higher than the current processing level. If you were to press PF 1, paragraph 170-RETURN-TO-SUBMENU would be executed, as indicated in lines 123 through 128.

Prior to sending a map, two steps need to be considered. The first one is to predefine a condition in case an error should take place during the transmission of a screen. This is referred to via a Handle Condition statement under MAPFAIL (line 59). The second step is designed to check the SEND-RECEIVE-FLAG indicator to decide whether sending a map is the correct procedure to follow, rather than receiving a map. If receive is specified, 004-SEND-MAP paragraph will be omitted, triggering 005-RECEIVE-MAP.

Note that there are two sends in this program. The initial send routine is designed to send not just the data, but the entire map, including the header or constant portion. However, in subsequent send map operations, only the data portion of the map is to be invoked (DATAONLY), to save some valuable time in transmitting data. This would especially be noticed in the system's response time.

In sending the map for the first time, or when rebuilding it after having moved low values into it, you want to start out by redisplaying the screen identifier (same as the transid) in the upper left hand corner of the screen. In sending the ARB49M3 map, (lines 68 through 69), you need to replace the contents of the SEND-RECEIVE-FLAG so that it would receive rather than send the transaction the next time around. This is done by moving the value 'R' into this indicator.

When receiving the above transaction, program logic will branch to the 005-RECEIVE-PARAGRAPH, where the map is received and read. At this point, the programmer needs to set up a HANDLE CONDITION in case a read is issued, but the associated record cannot be located. If this is the case, program logic will be redirected to the 910-RECORD-MISSING paragraph (lines 154 through 163), where a message "RECORD DOES NOT EXIST ON FILE" is displayed.

If, however, the read is a successful one, the above record is displayed using a format specified in FIG. 3-1. Actually, building the panel shown in FIG. 3-1 is done in two separate steps. First, a data field is moved to the output panel from the record. Then, it is enhanced using the PROT attribute byte (low-intensity protected, displayed in blue color). This renders the field unavailable to any modification. These procedures are laid out in lines 92 through 115.

Once the map is built in this fashion, logic is picked up in line 131, where the map is sent using the new data fields. Emphasis must be placed on the term "data fields only" since this time, for reasons of efficiency, only the data portion of the map is transmitted.

Starting in line 117, several subroutine paragraphs need to be highlighted. First and foremost is the RETURN paragraph (lines 117 through 122), designed to reinvoke the current transaction. Paragraph 170-RETURN-TO-SUBMENU was highlighted earlier, which is a procedure used to branch back to the prior subdirectory where the initial task was or could have been initiated. 700-MAPFAIL is designed, on the other hand, to resend the map in case an error occurred during transmission. At this point, the SEND-RECEIVE-FLAG is reset utilizing a previous value (blank), so that sending rather than receiving is performed.

3-4 ARB49C

```
1
2    IDENTIFICATION DIVISION.
3    PROGRAM-ID. ARB49C.
4    DATE-COMPILED.
5    ENVIRONMENT DIVISION.
6    DATA DIVISION.
7    WORKING-STORAGE SECTION.
8    01  COMM-AREA.
9        05  SEND-REC-FLAG      PIC X(01).
10 *
11   01  STORE-KEY.
12       05  STORE-PREFIX      PIC X(01).
13       05  STORE-INVNO       PIC 9(05).
14       05  STORE-FILL        PIC X(24) VALUE '    '.
15 *
16   01  INVOICE-RECORD.
17       05  INVOICE-KEY.
18           10  INVOICE-PREFIX       PIC X.
19           10  INVOICE-NUMBER       PIC 9(5).
20           10  INVOICE-NUMBERX REDEFINES INVOICE-NUMBER
21                                    PIC X(5).
22           10  INVOICE-FILLER       PIC X(24) VALUE '    '.
```

```
23      05  INV-EXPLAIN              PIC X(900).
24      05  INV-EXPLAIN-LINE  REDEFINES INV-EXPLAIN OCCURS 15.
25          10  INV-LINE             PIC X(60).
26      05  INVOICE-AMOUNT           PIC S9(9)V99.
27      05  INVOICE-AMOUNTX REDEFINES INVOICE-AMOUNT
28                                   PIC X(11).
29      05  PERIOD-DESCRIP           PIC X(55).
30      05  ORIGINAL-PREFIX          PIC X.
31      05  ORIGINAL-INV-NUM         PIC X(5).
32      05  ACCOUNTING-PERIOD        PIC X(4).
33      05  FILLER                   PIC X(13).
34      05  PROJECT-NUMBER           PIC X(6).
35      05  INV-SPECIAL-INSTR        PIC X(140).
36      05  OCCUR-INSTR REDEFINES INV-SPECIAL-INSTR.
37          10  INV-INSTR1           PIC X(70).
38          10  INV-INSTR2           PIC X(70).
39      05  CREDIT-MEMO              PIC X.
40      05  FILLER                   PIC X(12).
41      05  INV-CUSTOMER-NO          PIC 9(14).
42      05  FILLER                   PIC X(58).
43
44  COPY  ARB49M.
45  COPY  DFHAID.
46  COPY CHARATR.
47  LINKAGE SECTION.
48  01 DHFCOMMAREA              PIC X(01).
49  PROCEDURE DIVISION.
50  001-START-PROCESSING.
51      IF EIBCALEN > 0,
52      MOVE DFHCOMMAREA TO COMM-AREA.
53          EXEC CICS HANDLE AID
54          CLEAR(004-SEND-MAP)
55          PF1(170-RETURN-TO-SUBMENU)
56          ANYKEY(900-ANYKEY-OPTION)
57      END-EXEC.
58      EXEC CICS HANDLE CONDITION
59      MAPFAIL(700-MAPFAIL)
60      END-EXEC.
61      MOVE SPACES TO ERMSGO.
62      IF SEND-REC-FLAG = 'R' GO TO
63      005-RECEIVE-MAP.
64  004-SEND-MAP.
65      MOVE 'AR49' TO TRANSO.
66      MOVE PROT TO TRANSA.
67      MOVE -1 TO INVPREL.
68      EXEC CICS SEND MAP('ARB49M3')
69      MAPSET('ARB49M')
70      ERASE
71      CURSOR
72      END-EXEC.
73      MOVE 'R' TO SEND-REC-FLAG.
74      MOVE ' ' TO ERMSGO.
75      MOVE UNPROT-ALPHA-MDT TO INVPREA.
76      MOVE UNPROT-NUM-MDT TO INVNOA.
77      GO TO 100-RETURN.
78  005-RECEIVE-MAP.
79      EXEC CICS RECEIVE MAP('ARB49M3')
80      MAPSET('ARB49M')
81      END-EXEC.
82  006-MISSING-RECORD.
83      EXEC CICS HANDLE CONDITION
84      NOTFND(910-RECORD-MISSING)
85      END-EXEC.
86      MOVE INVPREI TO STORE-PREFIX.
87      MOVE INVNOI TO STORE-INVNO.
88      EXEC CICS READ DATASET('ARA21C')
89      INTO(INVOICE-RECORD)
90      RIDFLD(STORE-KEY)
91      END-EXEC.
92  007-MOVE-LINE-TO-MAP.
93      MOVE SPACES TO ERMSGO.
94      MOVE 'A' TO ERMSGA.
95      MOVE PROJECT-NUMBER TO PROJECTO.
96      MOVE PROT TO PROJECTA.
97      MOVE INV-CUSTOMER-NO TO CUSNUMO.
98      MOVE PROT TO CUSNUMA.
99      MOVE INVOICE-PREFIX TO INVPREO.
100     MOVE INVOICE-NUMBERX TO INVNOO.
101     MOVE INVOICE-AMOUNTX TO INVAMNTO.
102     MOVE PROT TO INVAMNTA.
103     MOVE PERIOD-DESCRIP TO PERDESO.
104     MOVE PROT TO PERDESA.
105     MOVE ORIGINAL-PREFIX TO ORGINVFO.
106     MOVE PROT TO ORGINVFA.
107     MOVE ORIGINAL-INV-NUM TO ORGINVO.
108     MOVE PROT TO ORGINVA.
109     MOVE ACCOUNTING-PERIOD TO ACCPERO.
110     MOVE PROT TO ACCPERA.
111     MOVE INV-INSTR1 TO INSTR1O.
112     MOVE PROT TO INSTR1A.
113     MOVE INV-INSTR2 TO INSTR2O.
114     MOVE PROT TO INSTR2A.
115     GO TO 500-RESEND-MAP.
116 ********************************************************
```

```
117   100-RETURN.
118        EXEC CICS RETURN
119            TRANSID('AR49')
120            COMMAREA(COMM-AREA)
121            LENGTH(1)
122        END-EXEC.
123   170-RETURN-TO-SUBMENU.
124        MOVE ' ' TO SEND-REC-FLAG.
125        EXEC CICS XCTL PROGRAM('ARM70C')
126            COMMAREA(COMM-AREA)
127            LENGTH(1)
128        END-EXEC.
129        STOP RUN.
130        GOBACK.
131   500-RESEND-MAP.
132        MOVE UNPROT-ALPHA-MDT TO INVPREA.
133        MOVE UNPROT-NUM-MDT TO INVNOA.
134        MOVE -1 TO INVPREL
135        EXEC CICS SEND MAP('ARB49M3')
136            MAPSET('ARB49M')
137            DATAONLY
138            CURSOR
139        END-EXEC.
140        MOVE 'R' TO SEND-REC-FLAG.
141        MOVE SPACE TO ERMSGO.
142        GO TO 100-RETURN.
143   700-MAPFAIL.
144        MOVE 'ENTER DATA' TO ERMSGO
145        MOVE PROT TO ERMSGA
146        MOVE ' ' TO SEND-REC-FLAG
147        MOVE -1 TO INVPREL
148        GO TO 500-RESEND-MAP.
149   900-ANYKEY-OPTION.
150        MOVE 'INVALID KEY!                         ' TO ERMSGO
151        MOVE PROT TO ERMSGA
152        MOVE -1 TO INVPREL
153        GO TO 500-RESEND-MAP.
154   910-RECORD-MISSING.
155        MOVE -1 TO INVPREL
156        MOVE LOW-VALUES TO ARB49M3O
157        MOVE STORE-PREFIX TO INVPREO
158        MOVE STORE-INVNO TO   INVNOO
159        MOVE UNPROT-ALPHA-BRT TO INVPREA
160        MOVE UNPROT-NUM-BRT-MDT TO INVNOA
161        MOVE 'RECORD DOES NOT EXIST ON FILE' TO ERMSGO
162        MOVE PROT TO ERMSGA
163        GO TO 004-SEND-MAP.
164
```

Compiler-generated source code: excerpts

As shown in FIG. 3-5, the compiler version of the INQUIRY program
ARB49C highlights the symbolic map in its entirety in lines 44
through 150. This portion of the map definition is necessary to
manipulate and analyze each data field, i.e., attribute definition,
length, modified data tag, input/output field definitions, etc. (For
more detail, review FIG. 3-2.)

The next copy statement is that of the DFHAID block (lines 197
through 232), designed to establish reference to the keyboard in
terms of the 24 function keys, PA keys, the enter, as well as the clear
keys. The third copy statement (copy CHARATR) is a programmer-
developed attribute chart or table that allows the programmer
some flexibility (and clarity) in establishing combined attribute
characteristics. Note that most attribute features referenced in the
previous section were from the above ATTRYBYTE table.

```
00001          IDENTIFICATION DIVISION.
00002          PROGRAM-ID. ARB49C.
00003          DATE-COMPILED. MAY 10,1990.
00004          ENVIRONMENT DIVISION.
00005          DATA DIVISION.
00006          WORKING-STORAGE SECTION.
00007          01  COMM-AREA.
00008              05  SEND-REC-FLAG     PIC X(01).
00009          *
00010          01  STORE-KEY.
00011              05  STORE-PREFIX     PIC X(01).
00012              05  STORE-INVNO      PIC 9(05).
00013              05  STORE-FILL       PIC X(24) VALUE ' '.
00014          *
00015          01  INVOICE-RECORD.
00016              05  INVOICE-KEY.
00017              10  INVOICE-PREFIX       PIC X.
00018              10  INVOICE-NUMBER       PIC 9(5).
00019              10  INVOICE-NUMBERX REDEFINES INVOICE-NUMBER
00020                                       PIC X(5).
00021                  10  INVOICE-FILLER     PIC X(24) VALUE ' '.
00022              05  INV-EXPLAIN          PIC X(900).
00023              05  INV-EXPLAIN-LINE  REDEFINES INV-EXPLAIN OCCURS 15.
00024              10  INV-LINE             PIC X(60).
00025              05  INVOICE-AMOUNT       PIC S9(9)V99.
00026              05  INVOICE-AMOUNTX REDEFINES INVOICE-AMOUNT
00027                                       PIC X(11).
00028              05  PERIOD-DESCRIP       PIC X(55).
00029              05  ORIGINAL-PREFIX      PIC X.
00030              05  ORIGINAL-INV-NUM     PIC X(5).
00031              05  ACCOUNTING-PERIOD    PIC X(4).
00032              05  FILLER               PIC X(13).
00033              05  PROJECT-NUMBER       PIC X(6).
00034              05  INV-SPECIAL-INSTR    PIC X(140).
00035              05  OCCUR-INSTR REDEFINES INV-SPECIAL-INSTR.
00036              10  INV-INSTR1           PIC X(70).
00037              10  INV-INSTR2           PIC X(70).
00038              05  CREDIT-MEMO          PIC X.
00039              05  FILLER               PIC X(12).
00040              05  INV-CUSTOMER-NO      PIC 9(14).
00041              05  FILLER               PIC X(58).
00042
00043          COPY  ARB49M.
00044 C        01  ARB49M3I.
00045 C            02  FILLER PIC X(12).
00046 C            02  TRANSL    COMP  PIC  S9(4).
00047 C            02  TRANSF    PICTURE X.
00048 C            02  FILLER REDEFINES TRANSF.
00049 C                03 TRANSA    PICTURE X.
00050 C            02  TRANSI  PIC X(4).
00051 C            02  DATEL    COMP  PIC  S9(4).
00052 C            02  DATEF    PICTURE X.
00053 C            02  FILLER REDEFINES DATEF.
00054 C                03 DATEA    PICTURE X.
00055 C            02  DATEI  PIC X(8).
00056 C            02  MODEL    COMP  PIC  S9(4).
00057 C            02  MODEF    PICTURE X.
00058 C            02  FILLER REDEFINES MODEF.
00059 C                03 MODEA    PICTURE X.
00060 C            02  MODEI  PIC X(12).
00061 C            02  PROJECTL    COMP  PIC  S9(4).
00062 C            02  PROJECTF    PICTURE X.
00063 C            02  FILLER REDEFINES PROJECTF.
00064 C                03 PROJECTA    PICTURE X.
00065 C            02  PROJECTI  PIC X(6).
00066 C            02  MEMOL    COMP  PIC  S9(4).
00067 C            02  MEMOF    PICTURE X.
00068 C            02  FILLER REDEFINES MEMOF.
00069 C                03 MEMOA    PICTURE X.
00070 C            02  MEMOI  PIC X(1).
00071 C            02  ORGINVFL    COMP  PIC  S9(4).
00072 C            02  ORGINVFF    PICTURE X.
00073 C            02  FILLER REDEFINES ORGINVFF.
00074 C                03 ORGINVFA    PICTURE X.
00075 C            02  ORGINVFI  PIC X(1).
00076 C            02  ORGINVL    COMP  PIC  S9(4).
00077 C            02  ORGINVF    PICTURE X.
00078 C            02  FILLER REDEFINES ORGINVF.
00079 C                03 ORGINVA    PICTURE X.
00080 C            02  ORGINVI  PIC X(5).
00081 C            02  CUSNUML    COMP  PIC  S9(4).
00082 C            02  CUSNUMF    PICTURE X.
00083 C            02  FILLER REDEFINES CUSNUMF.
00084 C                03 CUSNUMA    PICTURE X.
00085 C            02  CUSNUMI  PIC X(14).
00086 C            02  CUSNAMEL    COMP  PIC  S9(4).
00087 C            02  CUSNAMEF    PICTURE X.
```

```
00088 C              02  FILLER REDEFINES CUSNAMEF.
00089 C                03  CUSNAMEA    PICTURE X.
00090 C              02  CUSNAMEI  PIC X(30).
00091 C              02  INVPREL    COMP  PIC  S9(4).
00092 C              02  INVPREF    PICTURE X.
00093 C              02  FILLER REDEFINES INVPREF.
00094 C                03  INVPREA    PICTURE X.
00095 C              02  INVPREI  PIC X(1).
00096 C              02  INVNOL    COMP  PIC  S9(4).
00097 C              02  INVNOF    PICTURE X.
00098 C              02  FILLER REDEFINES INVNOF.
00099 C                03  INVNOA    PICTURE X.
00100 C              02  INVNOI  PIC X(5).
00101 C              02  INVAMNTL    COMP  PIC  S9(4).
00102 C              02  INVAMNTF    PICTURE X.
00103 C              02  FILLER REDEFINES INVAMNTF.
00104 C                03  INVAMNTA    PICTURE X.
00105 C              02  INVAMNTI  PIC X(11).
00106 C              02  ACCPERL    COMP  PIC  S9(4).
00107 C              02  ACCPERF    PICTURE X.
00108 C              02  FILLER REDEFINES ACCPERF.
00109 C                03  ACCPERA    PICTURE X.
00110 C              02  ACCPERI  PIC X(4).
00111 C              02  BILLDL    COMP  PIC  S9(4).
00112 C              02  BILLDF    PICTURE X.
00113 C              02  FILLER REDEFINES BILLDF.
00114 C                03  BILLDA    PICTURE X.
00115 C              02  BILLDI  PIC X(8).
00116 C              02  PERDESL    COMP  PIC  S9(4).
00117 C              02  PERDESF    PICTURE X.
00118 C              02  FILLER REDEFINES PERDESF.
00119 C                03  PERDESA    PICTURE X.
00120 C              02  PERDESI  PIC X(55).
00121 C              02  INSTR1L    COMP  PIC  S9(4).
00122 C              02  INSTR1F    PICTURE X.
00123 C              02  FILLER REDEFINES INSTR1F.
00124 C                03  INSTR1A    PICTURE X.
00125 C              02  INSTR1I  PIC X(70).
00126 C              02  INSTR2L    COMP  PIC  S9(4).
00127 C              02  INSTR2F    PICTURE X.
00128 C              02  FILLER REDEFINES INSTR2F.
00129 C                03  INSTR2A    PICTURE X.
00130 C              02  INSTR2I  PIC X(70).
00131 C              02  PFMSG1L    COMP  PIC  S9(4).
00132 C              02  PFMSG1F    PICTURE X.
00133 C              02  FILLER REDEFINES PFMSG1F.
00134 C                03  PFMSG1A    PICTURE X.
00135 C              02  PFMSG1I  PIC X(19).
00136 C              02  PFMSG2L    COMP  PIC  S9(4).
00137 C              02  PFMSG2F    PICTURE X.
00138 C              02  FILLER REDEFINES PFMSG2F.
00139 C                03  PFMSG2A    PICTURE X.
00140 C              02  PFMSG2I  PIC X(25).
00141 C              02  PFMSG3L    COMP  PIC  S9(4).
00142 C              02  PFMSG3F    PICTURE X.
00143 C              02  FILLER REDEFINES PFMSG3F.
00144 C                03  PFMSG3A    PICTURE X.
00145 C              02  PFMSG3I  PIC X(19).
00146 C              02  ERMSGL    COMP  PIC  S9(4).
00147 C              02  ERMSGF    PICTURE X.
00148 C              02  FILLER REDEFINES ERMSGF.
00149 C                03  ERMSGA    PICTURE X.
00150 C              02  ERMSGI  PIC X(60).
00151 C        01  ARB49M3O REDEFINES ARB49M3I.
00152 C              02  FILLER PIC X(12).
00153 C              02  FILLER PICTURE X(3).
00154 C              02  TRANSO  PIC X(4).
00155 C              02  FILLER PICTURE X(3).
00156 C              02  DATEO  PIC X(8).
00157 C              02  FILLER PICTURE X(3).
00158 C              02  MODEO  PIC X(12).
00159 C              02  FILLER PICTURE X(3).
00160 C              02  PROJECTO  PIC X(6).
00161 C              02  FILLER PICTURE X(3).
00162 C              02  MEMOO  PIC X(1).
00163 C              02  FILLER PICTURE X(3).
00164 C              02  ORGINVFO  PIC X(1).
00165 C              02  FILLER PICTURE X(3).
00166 C              02  ORGINVO  PIC X(5).
00167 C              02  FILLER PICTURE X(3).
00168 C              02  CUSNUMO  PIC X(14).
00169 C              02  FILLER PICTURE X(3).
00170 C              02  CUSNAMEO  PIC X(30).
00171 C              02  FILLER PICTURE X(3).
00172 C              02  INVPREO  PIC X(1).
00173 C              02  FILLER PICTURE X(3).
00174 C              02  INVNOO  PIC X(5).
00175 C              02  FILLER PICTURE X(3).
00176 C              02  INVAMNTO  PIC X(11).
00177 C              02  FILLER PICTURE X(3).
00178 C              02  ACCPERO  PIC X(4).
```

```
00179 C          02  FILLER PICTURE X(3).
00180 C          02  BILLDO  PIC X(8).
00181 C          02  FILLER PICTURE X(3).
00182 C          02  PERDESO  PIC X(55).
00183 C          02  FILLER PICTURE X(3).
00184 C          02  INSTR1O  PIC X(70).
00185 C          02  FILLER PICTURE X(3).
00186 C          02  INSTR2O  PIC X(70).
00187 C          02  FILLER PICTURE X(3).
00188 C          02  PFMSG1O  PIC X(19).
00189 C          02  FILLER PICTURE X(3).
00190 C          02  PFMSG2O  PIC X(25).
00191 C          02  FILLER PICTURE X(3).
00192 C          02  PFMSG3O  PIC X(19).
00193 C          02  FILLER PICTURE X(3).
00194 C          02  ERMSGO  PIC X(60).
00195        COPY DFHAID.
00196 C   01   DFHAID.
00197 C          02  DFHNULL    PIC  X   VALUE IS ' '.
00198 C          02  DFHENTER   PIC  X   VALUE IS QUOTE.
00199 C          02  DFHCLEAR   PIC  X   VALUE IS ' '.
00200 C          02  DFHCLRP    PIC  X   VALUE IS '⊤'.
00201 C          02  DFHPEN     PIC  X   VALUE IS '='.
00202 C          02  DFHOPID    PIC  X   VALUE IS 'W'.
00203 C          02  DFHMSRE    PIC  X   VALUE IS 'X'.
00204 C          02  DFHSTRF    PIC  X   VALUE IS 'h'.
00205 C          02  DFHTRIG    PIC  X   VALUE IS '"'.
00206 C          02  DFHPA1     PIC  X   VALUE IS '%'.
00207 C          02  DFHPA2     PIC  X   VALUE IS '>'.
00208 C          02  DFHPA3     PIC  X   VALUE IS ','.
00209 C          02  DFHPF1     PIC  X   VALUE IS '1'.
00210 C          02  DFHPF2     PIC  X   VALUE IS '2'.
00211 C          02  DFHPF3     PIC  X   VALUE IS '3'.
00212 C          02  DFHPF4     PIC  X   VALUE IS '4'.
00213 C          02  DFHPF5     PIC  X   VALUE IS '5'.
00214 C          02  DFHPF6     PIC  X   VALUE IS '6'.
00215 C          02  DFHPF7     PIC  X   VALUE IS '7'.
00216 C          02  DFHPF8     PIC  X   VALUE IS '8'.
00217 C          02  DFHPF9     PIC  X   VALUE IS '9'.
00218 C          02  DFHPF10    PIC  X   VALUE IS ':'.
00219 C          02  DFHPF11    PIC  X   VALUE IS '#'.
00220 C          02  DFHPF12    PIC  X   VALUE IS '@'.
00221 C          02  DFHPF13    PIC  X   VALUE IS 'A'.
00222 C          02  DFHPF14    PIC  X   VALUE IS 'B'.
00223 C          02  DFHPF15    PIC  X   VALUE IS 'C'.
00224 C          02  DFHPF16    PIC  X   VALUE IS 'D'.
00225 C          02  DFHPF17    PIC  X   VALUE IS 'E'.
00226 C          02  DFHPF18    PIC  X   VALUE IS 'F'.
00227 C          02  DFHPF19    PIC  X   VALUE IS 'G'.
00228 C          02  DFHPF20    PIC  X   VALUE IS 'H'.
00229 C          02  DFHPF21    PIC  X   VALUE IS 'I'.
00230 C          02  DFHPF22    PIC  X   VALUE IS '¢'.
00231 C          02  DFHPF23    PIC  X   VALUE IS '.'.
00232 C          02  DFHPF24    PIC  X   VALUE IS '<'.
00233        COPY CHARATR.
00234 C   *------------* ATTRIBUTE-BYTES *---------------------------
00235 C   01   CHARATR.
00236 C          05  UNPROT-ALPHA          PIC X   VALUE SPACE.
00237 C          05  UNPROT-ALPHA-MDT      PIC X   VALUE 'A'.
00238 C          05  UNPROT-ALPHA-BRT      PIC X   VALUE 'H'.
00239 C          05  UNPROT-ALPHA-BRT-MDT  PIC X   VALUE 'I'.
00240 C          05  UNPROT-ALPHA-DRK      PIC X   VALUE '<'.
00241 C          05  UNPROT-ALPHA-DRK-MDT  PIC X   VALUE '('.
00242 C          05  UNPROT-NUM            PIC X   VALUE '&'.
00243 C          05  UNPROT-NUM-MDT        PIC X   VALUE 'J'.
00244 C          05  UNPROT-NUM-BRT        PIC X   VALUE 'Q'.
00245 C          05  UNPROT-NUM-BRT-MDT    PIC X   VALUE 'R'.
00246 C          05  UNPROT-NUM-DRK        PIC X   VALUE '*'.
00247 C          05  UNPROT-NUM-DRK-MDT    PIC X   VALUE ')'.
00248 C          05  PROT                  PIC X   VALUE '-'.
00249 C          05  PROT-MDT              PIC X   VALUE '/'.
00250 C          05  PROT-BRT              PIC X   VALUE 'Y'.
00251 C          05  PROT-BRT-MDT          PIC X   VALUE 'Z'.
00252 C          05  PROT-DRK              PIC X   VALUE '%'.
00253 C          05  PROT-DRK-MDT          PIC X   VALUE ' '.
00254 C          05  ASKIP                 PIC X   VALUE '0̄'.
00255 C          05  ASKIP-MDT             PIC X   VALUE '1'.
00256 C          05  ASKIP-BRT             PIC X   VALUE '8'.
00257 C          05  ASKIP-BRT-MDT         PIC X   VALUE '9'.
00258 C          05  ASKIP-DRK             PIC X   VALUE '@'.
00259 C          05  ASKIP-DRK-MDT         PIC X   VALUE QUOTE.
00260 C   *---------------* LENGTH BYTES -----------------------------
00261 C   01   LENGTH-BYTES.
00262 C          05  CSR-REPO              PIC S9(4) COMP VALUE -1.
00263      01   DFHLDVER PIC X(22) VALUE 'LD TABLE DFHEITAB 210.'.
00264      01   DFHEIDO PICTURE S9(7) COMPUTATIONAL-3 VALUE ZERO.
00265      01   DFHEIBO PICTURE S9(4) COMPUTATIONAL VALUE ZERO.
00266      01   DFHEICB PICTURE X(8) VALUE IS '        '.
00267
00268      01   DFHEIV16  COMP PIC S9(8).
00269      01   DFHB0041  COMP PIC S9(8).
00270      01   DFHB0042  COMP PIC S9(8).
00271      01   DFHB0043  COMP PIC S9(8).
```

```
00272        01    DFHB0044  COMP PIC S9(8).
00273        01    DFHB0045  COMP PIC S9(8).
00274        01    DFHB0046  COMP PIC S9(8).
00275        01    DFHB0047  COMP PIC S9(8).
00276        01    DFHB0048  COMP PIC S9(8).
00277        01    DFHEIV11  COMP PIC S9(4).
00278        01    DFHEIV12  COMP PIC S9(4).
00279        01    DFHEIV13  COMP PIC S9(4).
00280        01    DFHEIV14  COMP PIC S9(4).
00281        01    DFHEIV15  COMP PIC S9(4).
00282        01    DFHB0025  COMP PIC S9(4).
00283        01    DFHEIV5   PIC X(4).
00284        01    DFHEIV6   PIC X(4).
00285        01    DFHEIV17  PIC X(4).
00286        01    DFHEIV18  PIC X(4).
00287        01    DFHEIV19  PIC X(4).
00288        01    DFHEIV1   PIC X(8).
00289        01    DFHEIV2   PIC X(8).
00290        01    DFHEIV3   PIC X(8).
00291        01    DFHEIV20  PIC X(8).
00292        01    DFHC0084  PIC X(8).
00293        01    DFHC0085  PIC X(8).
00294        01    DFHC0320  PIC X(32).
00295        01    DFHEIV7   PIC X(2).
00296        01    DFHEIV8   PIC X(2).
00297        01    DFHC0022  PIC X(2).
00298        01    DFHC0023  PIC X(2).
00299        01    DFHEIV10  PIC S9(7) COMP-3.
00300        01    DFHEIV9   PIC X(1).
00301        01    DFHC0011  PIC X(1).
00302        01    DFHEIV4   PIC X(6).
00303        01    DFHC0070  PIC X(7).
00304        01    DFHC0071  PIC X(7).
00305        01    DFHC0440  PIC X(44).
00306        01    DFHDUMMY  COMP PIC S9(4).
00307        01    DFHEIV0   PICTURE X(29).
00308     LINKAGE SECTION.
00309        01    DFHEIBLK.
00310        02      EIBTIME  PIC S9(7) COMP-3.
00311        02      EIBDATE  PIC S9(7) COMP-3.
00312        02      EIBTRNID PIC X(4).
00313        02      EIBTASKN PIC S9(7) COMP-3.
00314        02      EIBTRMID PIC X(4).
00315        02      DFHEIGDI COMP PIC S9(4).
00316        02      EIBCPOSN COMP PIC S9(4).
00317        02      EIBCALEN COMP PIC S9(4).
00318        02      EIBAID   PIC X(1).
00319        02      EIBFN    PIC X(2).
00320        02      EIBRCODE PIC X(6).
00321        02      EIBDS    PIC X(8).
00322        02      EIBREQID PIC X(8).
00323        02      EIBRSRCE PIC X(8).
00324        02      EIBSYNC  PIC X(1).
00325        02      EIBFREE  PIC X(1).
00326        02      EIBRECV  PIC X(1).
00327        02      EIBFIL01 PIC X(1).
00328        02      EIBATT   PIC X(1).
00329        02      EIBEOC   PIC X(1).
00330        02      EIBFMH   PIC X(1).
00331        02      EIBCOMPL PIC X(1).
00332        02      EIBSIG   PIC X(1).
00333        02      EIBCONF  PIC X(1).
00334        02      EIBERR   PIC X(1).
00335        02      EIBERRCD PIC X(4).
00336        02      EIBSYNRB PIC X(1).
00337        02      EIBNODAT PIC X(1).
00338        02      EIBRESP  COMP PIC S9(8).
00339        02      EIBRESP2 COMP PIC S9(8).
```

4
How to write
a DELETE program

The purpose of this chapter is to illustrate the mechanics of a DELETE operation. When deleting a record, you need to take several procedures into account. First and foremost, you need to retrieve and display a particular record on screen, so that you can visually verify that the correct record is marked for erasure. This process assumes that the record to be deleted already exists on file and contains a valid record key. If this is so, the following conventions should be noted:

1. The SEARCH key is normally entered on a blank screen, or else on a screen used during a previous, but not necessarily related, transaction. Once the ENTER key is pressed, you need to search the file randomly while retrieving and displaying the record.

2. To do a SEARCH, you might have to repeat some of the procedures used during your earlier edit cycle, which initially created and updated the very same record you are about to DELETE. This means that some internal tables need to be in place, such as an employee table that, for example, associates a given employee identifier or social security number with a person's name, his or her department code, job classification, and so forth.

3. Although a DELETE operation is technically considered a maintenance function, you normally retrieve a record as you would in BROWSE or in INQUIRY mode, displaying all data in protected mode. This is done so for several reasons.

First of all, the sole function of a DELETE program is to erase an entire record and not merely to modify parts of it. Deleting one or more data fields is an UPDATE function, not a DELETE function.

4. Another reason for protecting data fields is simply to alert the user that he or she is in a DELETE transaction mode, where a program operates on a record-level rather than on a data field-level. Also, it would make very little sense to modify a field or two only to "throw away" the entire record afterward.

5. Once a proper record is retrieved and displayed on the terminal, you must proceed with extra caution. It is one thing to modify a field where your data can be recovered if a mistake is made. It is much more difficult, however, to restore an entire record once it has been deleted. If the DELETE operation is an erroneous one, a record has to be built from scratch, which might require additional research, especially if the data is not readily available.

To reduce the possibility of an error, it is up to you to caution the user through available programming techniques. A conventional way of doing that would be to display a message on the screen, forcing the operator to press an extra PF key for acknowledgment, or to press the ENTER key for the second time.

Case study

The DELETE program presented in this case study corresponds to the customer database and a set of panels used in Chapter 5 to describe an ADD transaction. The customer master, frequently referred to as a customer database, provides the billing system with a concise demographic profile of MCRA's customers. The term concise refers to a restricted number of data fields necessary for generating invoices before interfacing into an accounts receivable system. The MCRA customer database, also highlighted in Chapter 5, is only partially utilized in this system. Its primary purpose is to supply the necessary data required for printing an invoice.

In this case study, you need to read the customer master based on an inquiry or record key supplied by the user. Once found, delete such a record. What seemingly complicates the process is the way the concatenated key is presented. The concatenated key is thirty-five positions long, but is primarily made up of constants and fillers. (For some additional insight, also review the case study presented in Chapter 5 in reference to an ADD transaction.) Key to the customer master is highlighted in FIG. 4-1.

```
02  FILLER                      PIC  X(01).
02  CUSTOMER-KEY.
    05  CUSTOMER-COMPANY        PIC  X(02)  VALUE  '01'.
    05  CUSTOMER-SEGMENT        PIC  X(01)  VALUE  '2'.
    05  CUSTOMER-NUMBER.
        10  CUSTOMER-PREFIX     PIC  X(10)  VALUE  ZEROS.
        10  CUSTOMER-ID         PIC  X(04).
    05  CUSTOMER-REFERENCE      PIC  X(02)  VALUE  '01'.
    05  FILLER                  PIC  X(16)  VALUE  SPACES.
```

4-1   The concatenated key to the customer database

Note that the only variable area of concern in building the concatenated key is the CUSTOMER-ID, a four-position field entered by the ***terminal operator. This is shown in the shaded area in FIG. 4-1. Note that the high order portion of the key, CUSTOMER-PREFIX, is a 10-position field that is currently not used, but is primarily available for future expansion.

Rather than leaving the contents of the CUSTOMER-PREFIX undefined, I moved high-order zeros into that portion of the key to avoid discrepancies, especially situations where the user would be responsible for entering the entire CUSTOMER-NUMBER field—sometimes as zeros or spaces, and sometimes entering the actual key in high-order positions.

Note that the CUSTOMER-COMPANY is hard-coded in formatting the key. That is because each carrier within the MCRA umbrella is referred to by a company number. In order to simplify procedures, especially data entry, each carrier record is created with a specific company number. Other values required by a subsequent Accounts Receivable system, into which the current billing system interfaces, are a 01 in the customer reference field, spaces or blanks running from column 21 through 35, and a value of 2 in the CUSTOMER-SEGMENT field.

Once the customer master is read, and the particular record to be deleted is found, you can proceed by depressing PF 4. The system will respond by asking you to verify your action. This is done simply by pressing the PF 4 key for the second time. This type of "reassurance" is standard in the industry because of the serious nature of any DELETE operation. In deleting the wrong record, you could spend a substantial amount of time reconstructing that record, and the reconstructed record might not be accurate or timely.

Finally, the submenu panel is shown in FIG. 4-2, and the DELETE panel appears in FIG. 4-3. In selecting task 3 on the Customer Maintenance Screen, the previous (menu) program will exit-control that transaction (AR90) into the current delete activities.

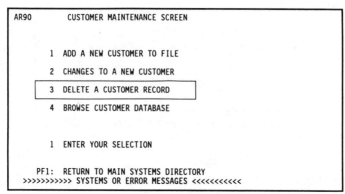

```
AR90         CUSTOMER MAINTENANCE SCREEN


       1   ADD A NEW CUSTOMER TO FILE

       2   CHANGES TO A NEW CUSTOMER

       3   DELETE A CUSTOMER RECORD

       4   BROWSE CUSTOMER DATABASE


       1   ENTER YOUR SELECTION

    PF1:  RETURN TO MAIN SYSTEMS DIRECTORY
    >>>>>>>>>> SYSTEMS OR ERROR MESSAGES <<<<<<<<<<
```

4-2 Second-level customer maintenance menu screen

```
AR91        CUSTOMER DATABASE MAINTENANCE              000000

       CUSTOMER NUMBER    :   1000
       CUSTOMER NAME      :   ALEX VARSEGI
       ADDRESS (1)        :   264 CHANDLER
       ADDRESS (2)        :   WILMINGAM
       ADDRESS (3)        :
       STATE              :   IL
       POSTAL CODE        :   60126-989876
       TELEPHONE          :   456 887 3349
       CONTACT NAME       :   TRXFFG
       ABBREVIATED NAME   :
       ACCOUNT OPENED     :   0189
       DUN * BRADSTREET   :   11234445


       PF1:  RETURN TO MENU    PF4:   DELETE RECORD
```

4-3 The customer DELETE panel prior to user entry

Map considerations

A comprehensive review of the map is presented in FIG. 4-4. Note that every field on this map, with the exception of the inquiry key (CUSTNO), is presented in a protected mode. Although attributes are easy to override in an application program, DELETE, INQUIRY, and BROWSE operations share the same basic concepts in that data cannot be maintained via these transactions individually. Data can only be displayed or deleted. The File Control Table or FCT is presented in FIG. 4-5.

Source program listing and narrative

The DELETE program ARD93C is shown in FIG. 4-6. In this program, there are two initial WORKING-STORAGE fields that are carried via the COMMUNICATIONS AREA. These are a SEND-REC-FLAG, (line 8),

4-4 BMS map for the DELETE operation in ARD93C

```
        PRINT NOGEN                                                      00010001
ARD93M  DFHMSD  TYPE=&SYSPARM,MODE=INOUT,CTRL=FREEKB,LANG=COBOL,         C00020045
        TIOAPFX=YES                                                      00030001
ARD93M7 DFHMDI  SIZE=(24,80)                                             00040045
TRID    DFHMDF POS=(01,02),LENGTH=04,ATTRB=(BRT,ASKIP)                   00050003
        DFHMDF POS=(01,20),LENGTH=31,ATTRB=(PROT,ASKIP),                 C00060022
               INITIAL='CUSTOMER DATABASE MAINTENANCE '                  00070024
TERM    DFHMDF POS=(01,70),LENGTH=08,ATTRB=(BRT,ASKIP)                   00080041
        DFHMDF POS=(05,01),LENGTH=21,ATTRB=(PROT,ASKIP),                 C00090043
               INITIAL='CUSTOMER NUMBER    :'                           00100024
CUSTNO  DFHMDF POS=(05,25),LENGTH=04,ATTRB=(UNPROT,IC)                   00110026
        DFHMDF POS=(06,01),LENGTH=21,ATTRB=(PROT,ASKIP),                 C00120050
               INITIAL='CUSTOMER NAME      :'                           00130024
CUSTNAM DFHMDF POS=(06,25),LENGTH=30,ATTRB=(BRT,ASKIP)                   00140051
        DFHMDF POS=(07,01),LENGTH=21,ATTRB=(PROT,ASKIP),                 C00150048
               INITIAL='ADDRESS (1)        :'                           00160039
ADDR1   DFHMDF POS=(07,25),LENGTH=30,ATTRB=(BRT,ASKIP)                   00170051
        DFHMDF POS=(08,01),LENGTH=21,ATTRB=(PROT,ASKIP),                 C00180043
               INITIAL='ADDRESS (2)        :'                           00190024
ADDR2   DFHMDF POS=(08,25),LENGTH=30,ATTRB=(BRT,ASKIP)                   00200051
        DFHMDF POS=(09,01),LENGTH=21,ATTRB=(PROT,ASKIP),                 C00210047
               INITIAL='ADDRESS (3)        :'                           00220024
ADDR3   DFHMDF POS=(09,25),LENGTH=21,ATTRB=(BRT,ASKIP)                   00230051
        DFHMDF POS=(10,01),LENGTH=21,ATTRB=(PROT,ASKIP),                 C00240049
               INITIAL='STATE              :'                           00250024
STATE   DFHMDF POS=(10,25),LENGTH=02,ATTRB=(PROT,ASKIP)                  00260043
        DFHMDF POS=(11,01),LENGTH=21,ATTRB=(PROT,ASKIP),                 C00270043
               INITIAL='POSTAL CODE        :'                           00280024
POSTCD  DFHMDF POS=(11,25),LENGTH=10,ATTRB=(PROT,ASKIP)                  00290043
        DFHMDF POS=(12,01),LENGTH=21,ATTRB=(PROT,ASKIP),                 C00300043
               INITIAL='TELEPHONE          :'                           00310027
AREA    DFHMDF POS=(12,25),LENGTH=3,ATTRB=(PROT,ASKIP)                   00320043
TEL3    DFHMDF POS=(12,31),LENGTH=3,ATTRB=(PROT,ASKIP)                   00330043
TEL4    DFHMDF POS=(12,37),LENGTH=4,ATTRB=(PROT,ASKIP)                   00340044
        DFHMDF POS=(13,01),LENGTH=21,ATTRB=(PROT,ASKIP),                 C00350032
               INITIAL='CONTACT NAME       :'                           00360024
CONTNAM DFHMDF POS=(13,25),LENGTH=15,ATTRB=(PROT,ASKIP)                  00370043
        DFHMDF POS=(14,01),LENGTH=21,ATTRB=(PROT,ASKIP),                 C00380032
               INITIAL='ABBREVIATED NAME   :'                           00390024
ABBNAME DFHMDF POS=(14,25),LENGTH=15,ATTRB=(PROT,ASKIP)                  00400043
        DFHMDF POS=(15,01),LENGTH=21,ATTRB=(PROT,ASKIP),                 C00410043
               INITIAL='ACCOUNT OPENED     :'                           00420039
MM      DFHMDF POS=(15,25),LENGTH=2,ATTRB=(PROT,ASKIP)                   00430043
YY      DFHMDF POS=(15,30),LENGTH=2,ATTRB=(PROT,ASKIP)                   00440043
        DFHMDF POS=(16,01),LENGTH=21,ATTRB=(PROT,ASKIP),                 C00450033
               INITIAL='DUN * BRADSTREET NO:'                           00460044
DBNO    DFHMDF POS=(16,25),LENGTH=06,ATTRB=(PROT,ASKIP)                  00470043
        DFHMDF POS=(23,01),LENGTH=50,ATTRB=(PROT,ASKIP),                 C00480041
               INITIAL='PF1: RETURN TO MENU    PF4: DELETE RECORD'       00490052
MSSG    DFHMDF POS=(24,01),LENGTH=60,ATTRB=(PROT,ASKIP)                  00500032
        DFHMSD TYPE=FINAL                                                00510001
        END                                                             00520001
```

```
RK501  DFHFCT  TYPE=DATASET,ACCMETH=VSAM,LOG=YES,                  C
               DATASET=RK501,                                     C
               DSNAME=NIRVT.AR.RK501,                             C
               SERVREQ=(BROWSE,DELETE,AD,UPDATE),                 C
               RECFORM=(FIXED,BLOCK),                             C
               FILSTAT=(ENABLED,CLOSED),                         C
               LSRPOOL=1,DISP=SHR,                               C
               STRNO=2,BUFNO=3,BUFNI=2
```

4-5 File Control Table (FCT) for the customer database

```
1           IDENTIFICATION DIVISION.
2           PROGRAM-ID. ARD93C.
3           DATE-COMPILED.
4           ENVIRONMENT DIVISION.
5           DATA DIVISION.
6           WORKING-STORAGE SECTION.
7           01  COMM-AREA.
8               02  SEND-REC-FLAG  PIC X(01).
9               02  DELETE-COUNT   PIC 9(01).
10          01  CUSTOMER-MASTER. COPY RK501.
11          01  STORE-CUSTNO       PIC X(04).
12          01  STORE-TRANSID      PIC X(04).
13          COPY DFHBMSCA.
14          COPY DFHAID.
15          COPY CHARATR.
16          COPY ARD93M.
17          LINKAGE SECTION.
18          01  DFHCOMMAREA        PIC X(02).
19          PROCEDURE DIVISION.
20          001-START-PROCESSING.
21              IF EIBCALEN > 0
22              MOVE DFHCOMMAREA TO COMM-AREA.
23                  EXEC CICS HANDLE AID
24                  CLEAR(004-SEND-MAP)
25                  PF1(170-RETURN-TO-SUBMENU)
26                  PF4
27                  ANYKEY(900-ANYKEY-OPTION)
28              END-EXEC.
29              EXEC CICS HANDLE CONDITION
30              MAPFAIL(700-MAPFAIL)
31              END-EXEC.
32              IF SEND-REC-FLAG = 'R' GO TO
33              005-RECEIVE-MAP.
34          004-SEND-MAP.
35              MOVE 'AR93' TO TRIDO.
36              MOVE EIBTRMID TO TERMO.
37              MOVE PROT TO TRIDA.
38      *
39          004-SEND-MAP-2.
40              MOVE -1 TO CUSTNOL.
41              EXEC CICS SEND MAP('ARD93M7')
42              MAPSET('ARD93M')
43              ERASE
44              CURSOR
45              END-EXEC.
46              MOVE 'R' TO SEND-REC-FLAG.
47              GO TO 100-RETURN.
48          005-RECEIVE-MAP.
49              EXEC CICS RECEIVE MAP('ARD93M7')
50              MAPSET('ARD93M')
51              END-EXEC.
52          006-HANDLE-CONDITION.
53              EXEC CICS HANDLE CONDITION
54              NOTFND(950-CUSTOMER-MISSING)
55              END-EXEC.
56          007-READ-CUSTOMER-MASTER.
57              IF CUSTNOL = ZEROS OR CUSTNOI = SPACES
58              MOVE 'PLEASE ENTER CUSTOMER I.D.' TO MSSGO
59              MOVE PROT TO MSSGA
60              MOVE -1 TO CUSTNOL
61              GO TO 500-RESEND-MAP.
62              MOVE UNPROT-NUM-MDT TO CUSTNOA.
63          ****************************************************************
64          * GET READY TO READ CUSTOMER MASTER                           *
65          ****************************************************************
66              MOVE CUSTNOI TO CUSTOMER-ID
67              EXEC CICS READ DATASET('RK501')
68              INTO(CUSTOMER-MASTER)
69              RIDFLD(CUSTOMER-KEY)
70              END-EXEC.
71          008-DISPLAY-CUSTOMER.
72              MOVE CUSTOMER-NAME TO CUSTNAMI.
73              MOVE PROT-BRT TO CUSTNAMA.
74              MOVE CUSTOMER-ADDRESS1 TO ADDR1I.
75              MOVE PROT-BRT TO ADDR1A.
76              MOVE CUSTOMER-ADDRESS2 TO ADDR2I.
```

```
77            MOVE PROT-BRT TO ADDR2A.
78            MOVE CUSTOMER-ADDRESS3 TO ADDR3I.
79            MOVE PROT-BRT TO ADDR3A.
80            MOVE CUSTOMER-STATE TO STATEI.
81            MOVE PROT TO STATEA.
82            MOVE CUSTOMER-POSTAL-CODE TO POSTCDI.
83            MOVE PROT TO POSTCDA.
84            MOVE CUSTOMER-AREA-CODE TO AREAI.
85            MOVE PROT TO AREAA.
86            MOVE CUSTOMER-TEL1 TO TEL3I.
87            MOVE PROT TO TEL3A.
88            MOVE CUSTOMER-TEL2 TO TEL4I.
89            MOVE PROT TO TEL4A.
90            MOVE CUSTOMER-CONTACT-NAME TO CONTNAMI.
91            MOVE PROT TO CONTNAMA.
92            MOVE CUSTOMER-ABBREVIATED-NAME TO ABBNAMEI.
93            MOVE PROT TO ABBNAMEA.
94            MOVE CUSTOMER-MONTH TO MMI.
95            MOVE PROT TO MMA.
96            MOVE CUSTOMER-YEAR TO YYI.
97            MOVE PROT TO YYA.
98            MOVE CUSTOMER-DB-NUMBER TO DBNOI.
99            MOVE PROT TO DBNOA.
100    ************************************************************
101    * READY TO ADD NEW RECORD TO FILE                         *
102    ************************************************************
103           IF EIBAID = DFHPF4 GO TO 080-DELETE-RECORD ELSE
104           MOVE 'RECORD IS READY TO BE DELETED' TO MSSGO
105           MOVE PROT TO MSSGA
106           MOVE -1 TO CUSTNOL
107           MOVE ZEROS TO DELETE-COUNT
108           GO TO 500-RESEND-MAP.
109    *
110    080-DELETE-RECORD.
111           MOVE CUSTNOI TO STORE-CUSTNO.
112           ADD 1 TO DELETE-COUNT.
113           IF DELETE-COUNT = 1
114           GO TO 960-FIRST-DELETE-COMMENT.
115           MOVE CUSTNOI TO CUSTOMER-ID.
116           EXEC CICS DELETE DATASET('RK501')
117           FROM(CUSTOMER-MASTER)
118           RIDFLD(CUSTOMER-KEY)
119           END-EXEC.
120           MOVE PROT TO MSSGA
121           MOVE -1 TO CUSTNOL
122           MOVE ZEROS TO DELETE-COUNT
123           MOVE LOW-VALUES TO ARD93M70
124           MOVE STORE-CUSTNO TO CUSTNOI
125           MOVE UNPROT-NUM-BRT TO CUSTNOA
126           MOVE 'RECORD IS NOW DELETED' TO MSSGO
127           GO TO 004-SEND-MAP.
128    ************************************************************
129    * SUBROUTINE SECTION                                      *
130    ************************************************************
131    100-RETURN.
132           EXEC CICS RETURN
133               TRANSID('AR93')
134               COMMAREA(COMM-AREA)
135               LENGTH(2)
136           END-EXEC.
137    170-RETURN-TO-SUBMENU.
138           MOVE ' ' TO SEND-REC-FLAG.
139           EXEC CICS XCTL PROGRAM('ARM90C')
140           COMMAREA(COMM-AREA)
141           LENGTH(1)
142           END-EXEC.
143           STOP RUN.
144           GOBACK.
145    500-RESEND-MAP.
146           EXEC CICS SEND MAP('ARD93M7')
147           MAPSET('ARD93M')
148           CURSOR
149           DATAONLY
150           END-EXEC.
151           MOVE 'R' TO SEND-REC-FLAG.
152           GO TO 100-RETURN.
153    700-MAPFAIL.
154           MOVE 'ENTER CUSTOMER NUMBER' TO MSSGO
```

```
155                    MOVE PROT TO MSSGA
156                    MOVE ' ' TO SEND-REC-FLAG
157                    MOVE -1 TO CUSTNOL
158                    GO TO 500-RESEND-MAP.
159            900-ANYKEY-OPTION.
160                    MOVE 'INVALID KEY, PLEASE RESUBMIT' TO MSSGO.
161                    MOVE PROT TO MSSGA
162                    MOVE -1 TO CUSTNOL
163                    GO TO 500-RESEND-MAP.
164            950-CUSTOMER-MISSING.
165                    MOVE CUSTNOI TO STORE-CUSTNO.
166                    MOVE LOW-VALUES TO ARD93M70.
167                    MOVE 'NO SUCH RECORD ON FILE' TO MSSGO.
168                    MOVE PROT TO MSSGA.
169                    MOVE STORE-CUSTNO TO CUSTNOI
170                    MOVE -1 TO CUSTNOL.
171                    MOVE ZEROS TO DELETE-COUNT.
172                    GO TO 004-SEND-MAP.
173            960-FIRST-DELETE-COMMENT.
174                    MOVE 'PLEASE VERIFY DELETE' TO MSSGO.
175                    MOVE PROT TO MSSGA.
176                    MOVE -1 TO CUSTNOL.
177                    GO TO 500-RESEND-MAP.
178
```

and a DELETE-COUNT indicator, (line 9). The first field exists to differentiate between sending and receiving a map in the pseudo-conversational cycle. The second field is defined to allow the program to respond to the terminal operator's request to DELETE a record. Actually, the DELETE-COUNT field is simply a counter that is activated at a time function key 4 (PF 4) is pressed. Thus, when the count is equal to 1, a verification message pops up. When the count is equal to 2, on the other hand, the record marked for deletion is physically erased from the file. More on this during the review of the PROCEDURE DIVISION.

There are, altogether, five copy statements issued in this system. The first one affects the customer master or customer database. Note that a layout of the above file is shown in detail in line 12 through 42 in FIG. 4-7. The customer master is made up of two sections: a record key (lines 12 through 20) and the rest of the data (lines 21 through 42).

Four other copy statements are also brought into ARD93C. These are the DFHBMSCA block, the DFHAID block, a CHARATR table, and the map, or more precisely the map set, ARD93M. These copy statements are executed during the compilation of ARD93C. A comprehensive review of the four other copy statements will be discussed in the next section of this chapter.

The LINKAGE SECTION for the DFHCOMMAREA contains a two-position field. This is to periodically convey messages regarding the SEND-REC-FLAG and the DELETE-COUNT. The PROCEDURE DIVISION, (line 19), starts out with standard "housekeeping" functions. First, the length of the COMMAREA is checked to determine if any message or messages were sent through the previous transaction.

If the answer is yes, the contents of the COMMAREA are moved into WORKING-STORAGE. Next, a HANDLE AID statement is issued to assign procedural labels to certain function keys. For example, simply resend the map when the operator presses clear. PF 1 will take you back to the submenu-related procedures (170-RETURN-TO-SUBMENU), PF 4, which is the actual DELETE key, is initially undefined, but becomes active later on, pointing you in the proper direction.

The ANYKEY option is used to inform the operator that the key pressed was as invalid one, and that it should be reentered once again. The HANDLE CONDITION shown in statements 29 through 33 defines action, if and when the map fails. This is where you need to make your first reference to the SEND-REC-FLAG. If it is equal to the character "R," the program will send you to the 005-RECEIVE-MAP paragraph, where your screen is read and processed (Receive simply means read). If the flag is not an "R," the program is to send the map along with the transaction identifier (AR93), which is to be displayed in the upper left-hand corner of the panel along with a terminal identifier opposite to the transid. This part of the send is only executed after an erase map is issued, and both of the variable data fields need to be rebuilt from scratch. The regularly referenced portion of the SEND MAP instruction is laid out in lines 39 through 47.

Prior to reading the customer master, the program checks to see if the operator has entered a customer number. The program does this by verifying that the above field contains no blanks or low values. If it does, an error message "PLEASE ENTER CUSTOMER I.D." will appear in line 24 of the panel, and the transaction is temporarily suspended until some additional data is supplied by the operator. However, if the above check falls through, then the customer master is read. If the record is missing from the file, the label 950-CUSTOMER-MISSING provides a procedure through a HANDLE CONDITION routine to redirect the logic of the program. If the record is on file, however, an entire paragraph (008-DISPLAY-CUSTOMER), line 71 through 99, is executed to move in protected mode all display fields from the customer master file to the screen.

Once you have successfully displayed the required information, a message, "RECORD IS READY TO BE DELETED" will appear in line 24 of the customer panel. The program constantly checks to verify if PF 4 is pressed in order to erase a record. This is shown in statement: IF EIBAID = DFHPF 4, line 103 of the original source code. If no function key action was initiated by the terminal operator, then the program gets reinvoked, displaying the same record and an associated message.

Once PF 4 is pressed, the next paragraph, 080-DELETE-RECORD is encountered, starting in line 110. Note that the DELETE operation is developed in two phases, centering around the use of a DELETE-COUNT register. When the count is equal to 1, paragraph 960-FIRST-DELETE-COMMENT is triggered, (line 114) which produces a message "PLEASE VERIFY DELETE." This is highlighted in lines 173 through 177. The value contained in the DELETE-COUNT stands at 1. If you were to press PF 1 to invoke a return to the original subdirectory, the contents of the DELETE-COUNT would be erased. Erasure occurs simply by defining the length of the COMM-AREA as 1 at exit control time. Thus, if PF 4 is on during the second cycle, the value placed in the counter would now stand at two, triggering the DELETE. These procedures are highlighted in statements 110 through 119.

What follows the DELETE operation is a number of housekeeping routines, such as deleting or clearing the map for the next set of data, and displaying the message "RECORD IS NOW DELETED." Note that in line 111, I have placed the customer number entered by the terminal operator into storage for subsequent retrieval. The field was later redisplayed right after I had erased the map and displayed it in an unprotected red, line 124. The idea is that after issuing an erase, I want to display such a control number to enable the operator a last-minute visual verification of the record that is now deleted. If I had not saved the above field prior to the erasure of the map, I would not have been able to display it at the proper time.

Four additional subroutines need to be elaborated in this section. The first one is the 100-RETURN paragraph responsible for the timely reinvocation of the DELETE transaction. These procedures are laid out in lines 131 through 136.

Paragraph 170-RETURN-TO-SUBMENU contains the exit routine procedures that will allow you to return to the previous submenu. 500-RESEND-MAP, lines 147 through 152, is developed so that you can send only the data portion of the map, designed to substantially expedite data transfer. Finally, a MAPFAIL, defined in an earlier HANDLE CONDITION, causes the program to reissue the customer panel.

Compiler-generated source code: excerpts

The purpose of this listing is to show you all the file and "block" expansions triggered within the initial source code. Only the DATA DIVISION of the compiled program will be highlighted in this section.

As shown in FIG. 4-7, the first copy expansion brought into ARD93C is that of the customer master format. This was described in the previous section of this book. A second copy statement, copy DFHBMSCA, was brought into this program to provide attribute references for the programmer. This block is shown in lines 45 through 109. The attribute portion of this reference block enables you to refer to certain attribute values. For example, when you use the term DFHBMPRO, (line 52) it will transform an unprotected field into a protected one. With four color terminals, it will also display the field in a low-intensity blue color.

A third copy statement, shown in lines 111 through 147, is that of the DFHAID table. This table is necessary if you need to refer to a particular function key in your program. Look at the statement IF EIBAID = DFHPF 4, (line 103), in the previous section, and how a following set of procedures are executed. This reference could be omitted if you were to assign to a function key a specific label or paragraph via a HANDLE AID statement.

A fourth copy statement, displayed in lines 150 through 174, CHARATR, allows you to combine a number of attribute functions into a unique value while giving the field name a much clearer functional title. For example, the term UNPROT-ALPHA-BRT-MDT (statement 154) informs you that by moving the value "I" into the attribute portion of the field, you will transform the data to an unprotected, alphanumeric field, displayed in high-intensity with the field's modified data tag turned on. This block was copied into the DELETE program, even though a previous copy of the DFHBMSCA block was requested earlier. You can compare the two for efficiency and decide which set you would rather be working with.

Next, the symbolic map is presented, (lines 178 through 308) triggered by the COPY ARD93C statement, which is the map set. Note that this is essentially the result of your BMS assembly shown in FIG. 4-4. The symbolic map enables you to address each data field on the map to determine what portion of such a field needs to be manipulated, i.e., the length, the input/output, the modified data tag setting, or the attribute portion of the data.

Two other blocks are also triggered by the program. These are a set of internally used storage areas, shown in lines 309 through 353, as well as the DFHEIBLK block expanded in lines 355 through 389. The latter is used to receive some useful information from the system, such as systems date, time, terminal and task I.D.'s, and so on. Note that these blocks do not require a copy statement to be invoked; in fact, they are attained automatically through the system.

```
00001         IDENTIFICATION DIVISION.
00002         PROGRAM-ID. ARD93C.
00003         DATE-COMPILED. APR  6,1990.
00004         ENVIRONMENT DIVISION.
00005         DATA DIVISION.
00006         WORKING-STORAGE SECTION.
00007         01  COMM-AREA.
00008             02  SEND-REC-FLAG  PIC X(01).
00009             02  DELETE-COUNT   PIC 9(01).
00010         01  CUSTOMER-MASTER.
00011                          COPY RK501.
00012 C          02  FILLER                     PIC X(01).
00013 C          02  CUSTOMER-KEY.
00014 C              05  CUSTOMER-COMPANY        PIC X(02) VALUE '01'.
00015 C              05  CUSTOMER-SEGMENT        PIC X(01) VALUE '2'.
00016 C              05  CUSTOMER-NUMBER.
00017 C                  10  CUSTOMER-PREFIX     PIC X(10) VALUE ZEROS.
00018 C                  10  CUSTOMER-ID         PIC X(04).
00019 C              05  CUSTOMER-REFERENCE      PIC X(02) VALUE '01'.
00020 C              05  FILLER                  PIC X(16) VALUE SPACES.
00021 C          02  DATA-AREA.
00022 C              05  CUSTOMER-NAME           PIC X(30).
00023 C              05  CUSTOMER-ADDRESS1       PIC X(30).
00024 C              05  CUSTOMER-ADDRESS2       PIC X(30).
00025 C              05  CUSTOMER-ADDRESS3       PIC X(21).
00026 C              05  CUSTOMER-STATE          PIC X(02).
00027 C              05  CUSTOMER-POSTAL-CODE    PIC X(10).
00028 C              05  CUSTOMER-CONTACT-NAME   PIC X(15).
00029 C              05  CUSTOMER-ABBREVIATED-NAME  PIC X(15).
00030 C              05  CUSTOMER-ACCOUNT-OPENED.
00031 C                  10  CUSTOMER-MONTH      PIC X(02).
00032 C                  10  CUSTOMER-YEAR       PIC X(02).
00033 C              05  FILLER                  PIC X(06).
00034 C              05  CUSTOMER-TELEPHONE-NO.
00035 C                  10  FILLER              PIC X(02).
00036 C                  10  CUSTOMER-AREA-CODE  PIC X(03).
00037 C                  10  CUSTOMER-TELEPHONE.
00038 C                      15  CUSTOMER-TEL1   PIC X(03).
00039 C                      15  CUSTOMER-TEL2   PIC X(04).
00040 C              05  FILLER                  PIC X(28).
00041 C              05  CUSTOMER-DB-NUMBER      PIC X(10).
00042 C              05  FILLER                  PIC X(851).
00043         01  STORE-CUSTNO    PIC X(04).
00044         01  STORE-TRANSID   PIC X(04).
00045         COPY DFHBMSCA.
00046 C        01      DFHBMSCA.
00047 C          02      DFHBMPEM  PICTURE X    VALUE IS ' '.
00048 C          02      DFHBMPNL  PICTURE X    VALUE IS ' '.
00049 C          02      DFHBMASK  PICTURE X    VALUE IS '0'.
00050 C          02      DFHBMUNP  PICTURE X    VALUE IS ' '.
00051 C          02      DFHBMUNN  PICTURE X    VALUE IS '&'.
00052 C          02      DFHBMPRO  PICTURE X    VALUE IS '-'.
00053 C          02      DFHBMBRY  PICTURE X    VALUE IS 'H'.
00054 C          02      DFHBMDAR  PICTURE X    VALUE IS '<'.
00055 C          02      DFHBMFSE  PICTURE X    VALUE IS 'A'.
00056 C          02      DFHBMPRF  PICTURE X    VALUE IS '/'.
00057 C          02      DFHBMASF  PICTURE X    VALUE IS '1'.
00058 C          02      DFHBMASB  PICTURE X    VALUE IS '8'.
00059 C          02      DFHBMEOF  PICTURE X    VALUE IS ' '.
00060 C          02      DFHBMDET  PICTURE X    VALUE IS ' '.
00061 C          02      DFHBMPSO  PICTURE X    VALUE IS ' '.
00062 C          02      DFHBMPSI  PICTURE X    VALUE IS ' '.
00063 C          02      DFHSA     PICTURE X    VALUE IS ' '.
00064 C          02      DFHCOLOR  PICTURE X    VALUE IS ' '.
00065 C          02      DFHPS     PICTURE X    VALUE IS ' '.
00066 C          02      DFHHLT    PICTURE X    VALUE IS ' '.
00067 C          02      DFH3270   PICTURE X    VALUE IS '{'.
00068 C          02      DFHVAL    PICTURE X    VALUE IS 'A'.
00069 C          02      DFHOUTLN  PICTURE X    VALUE IS 'B'.
00070 C          02      DFHBKTRN  PICTURE X    VALUE IS ' '.
00071 C          02      DFHALL    PICTURE X    VALUE IS ' '.
00072 C          02      DFHERROR  PICTURE X    VALUE IS ' '.
00073 C          02      DFHDFT    PICTURE X    VALUE IS ' '.
00074 C          02      DFHDFCOL  PICTURE X    VALUE IS ' '.
```

```
00075 C      02   DFHBLUE  PICTURE X   VALUE IS  '1'.
00076 C      02   DFHRED   PICTURE X   VALUE IS  '2'.
00077 C      02   DFHPINK  PICTURE X   VALUE IS  '3'.
00078 C      02   DFHGREEN PICTURE X   VALUE IS  '4'.
00079 C      02   DFHTURQ  PICTURE X   VALUE IS  '5'.
00080 C      02   DFHYELLO PICTURE X   VALUE IS  '6'.
00081 C      02   DFHNEUTR PICTURE X   VALUE IS  '7'.
00082 C      02   DFHBASE  PICTURE X   VALUE IS  ' '.
00083 C      02   DFHDFHI  PICTURE X   VALUE IS  ' '.
00084 C      02   DFHBLINK PICTURE X   VALUE IS  '1'.
00085 C      02   DFHREVRS PICTURE X   VALUE IS  '2'.
00086 C      02   DFHUNDLN PICTURE X   VALUE IS  '4'.
00087 C      02   DFHMFIL  PICTURE X   VALUE IS  ' '.
00088 C      02   DFHMENT  PICTURE X   VALUE IS  ' '.
00089 C      02   DFHMFE   PICTURE X   VALUE IS  ' '.
00090 C      02   DFHUNNOD PICTURE X   VALUE IS  '('.
00091 C      02   DFHUNIMD PICTURE X   VALUE IS  'I'.
00092 C      02   DFHUNNUM PICTURE X   VALUE IS  'J'.
00093 C      02   DFHUNINT PICTURE X   VALUE IS  'R'.
00094 C      02   DFHUNNON PICTURE X   VALUE IS  ')'.
00095 C      02   DFHPROTI PICTURE X   VALUE IS  'Y'.
00096 C      02   DFHPROTN PICTURE X   VALUE IS  '%'.
00097 C      02   DFHMT    PICTURE X   VALUE IS  ' '.
00098 C      02   DFHMFT   PICTURE X   VALUE IS  ' '.
00099 C      02   DFHMET   PICTURE X   VALUE IS  ' '.
00100 C      02   DFHMFET  PICTURE X   VALUE IS  ' '.
00101 C      02   DFHDFFR  PICTURE X   VALUE IS  ' '.
00102 C      02   DFHLEFT  PICTURE X   VALUE IS  ' '.
00103 C      02   DFHOVER  PICTURE X   VALUE IS  ' '.
00104 C      02   DFHRIGHT PICTURE X   VALUE IS  ' '.
00105 C      02   DFHUNDER PICTURE X   VALUE IS  ' '.
00106 C      02   DFHBOX   PICTURE X   VALUE IS  ' '.
00107 C      02   DFHSOSI  PICTURE X   VALUE IS  ' '.
00108 C      02   DFHTRANS PICTURE X   VALUE IS  '0'.
00109 C      02   DFHOPAQ  PICTURE X   VALUE IS  ' '.
00110    COPY DFHAID.
00111 C  01   DFHAID.
00112 C      02   DFHNULL  PIC X VALUE IS ' '.
00113 C      02   DFHENTER PIC X VALUE IS QUOTE.
00114 C      02   DFHCLEAR PIC X VALUE IS ' '.
00115 C      02   DFHCLRP  PIC X VALUE IS 'T'.
00116 C      02   DFHPEN   PIC X VALUE IS '='.
00117 C      02   DFHOPID  PIC X VALUE IS 'W'.
00118 C      02   DFHMSRE  PIC X VALUE IS 'X'.
00119 C      02   DFHSTRF  PIC X VALUE IS 'h'.
00120 C      02   DFHTRIG  PIC X VALUE IS '"'.
00121 C      02   DFHPA1   PIC X VALUE IS '%'.
00122 C      02   DFHPA2   PIC X VALUE IS '>'.
00123 C      02   DFHPA3   PIC X VALUE IS ','.
00124 C      02   DFHPF1   PIC X VALUE IS '1'.
00125 C      02   DFHPF2   PIC X VALUE IS '2'.
00126 C      02   DFHPF3   PIC X VALUE IS '3'.
00127 C      02   DFHPF4   PIC X VALUE IS '4'.
00128 C      02   DFHPF5   PIC X VALUE IS '5'.
00129 C      02   DFHPF6   PIC X VALUE IS '6'.
00130 C      02   DFHPF7   PIC X VALUE IS '7'.
00131 C      02   DFHPF8   PIC X VALUE IS '8'.
00132 C      02   DFHPF9   PIC X VALUE IS '9'.
00133 C      02   DFHPF10  PIC X VALUE IS ':'.
00134 C      02   DFHPF11  PIC X VALUE IS '#'.
00135 C      02   DFHPF12  PIC X VALUE IS '@'.
00136 C      02   DFHPF13  PIC X VALUE IS 'A'.
00137 C      02   DFHPF14  PIC X VALUE IS 'B'.
00138 C      02   DFHPF15  PIC X VALUE IS 'C'.
00139 C      02   DFHPF16  PIC X VALUE IS 'D'.
00140 C      02   DFHPF17  PIC X VALUE IS 'E'.
00141 C      02   DFHPF18  PIC X VALUE IS 'F'.
00142 C      02   DFHPF19  PIC X VALUE IS 'G'.
00143 C      02   DFHPF20  PIC X VALUE IS 'H'.
00144 C      02   DFHPF21  PIC X VALUE IS 'I'.
00145 C      02   DFHPF22  PIC X VALUE IS '¢'.
00146 C      02   DFHPF23  PIC X VALUE IS '.'.
00147 C      02   DFHPF24  PIC X VALUE IS '<'.
00148    COPY CHARATR..
00149 C  *------------* ATTRIBUTE-BYTES *---------------------------
00150 C  01 CHARATR.
00151 C      05  UNPROT-ALPHA       PIC X  VALUE SPACE.
00152 C      05  UNPROT-ALPHA-MDT   PIC X  VALUE 'A'.
```

```
00153 C          05  UNPROT-ALPHA-BRT       PIC X   VALUE 'H'.
00154 C          05  UNPROT-ALPHA-BRT-MDT   PIC X   VALUE 'I'.
00155 C          05  UNPROT-ALPHA-DRK       PIC X   VALUE '<'.
00156 C          05  UNPROT-ALPHA-DRK-MDT   PIC X   VALUE '('.
00157 C          05  UNPROT-NUM             PIC X   VALUE '&'.
00158 C          05  UNPROT-NUM-MDT         PIC X   VALUE 'J'.
00159 C          05  UNPROT-NUM-BRT         PIC X   VALUE 'Q'.
00160 C          05  UNPROT-NUM-BRT-MDT     PIC X   VALUE 'R'.
00161 C          05  UNPROT-NUM-DRK         PIC X   VALUE '*'.
00162 C          05  UNPROT-NUM-DRK-MDT     PIC X   VALUE ')'.
00163 C          05  PROT                   PIC X   VALUE '-'.
00164 C          05  PROT-MDT               PIC X   VALUE '/'.
00165 C          05  PROT-BRT               PIC X   VALUE 'Y'.
00166 C          05  PROT-BRT-MDT           PIC X   VALUE 'Z'.
00167 C          05  PROT-DRK               PIC X   VALUE '%'.
00168 C          05  PROT-DRK-MDT           PIC X   VALUE ' '.
00169 C          05  ASKIP                  PIC X   VALUE '0̄'.
00170 C          05  ASKIP-MDT              PIC X   VALUE '1'.
00171 C          05  ASKIP-BRT              PIC X   VALUE '8'.
00172 C          05  ASKIP-BRT-MDT          PIC X   VALUE '9'.
00173 C          05  ASKIP-DRK              PIC X   VALUE '@'.
00174 C          05  ASKIP-DRK-MDT          PIC X   VALUE QUOTE.
00175 C      *--------------* LENGTH BYTES *-----------------------------
00176 C      01  LENGTH-BYTES.
00177 C          05  CSR-REPO               PIC S9(4) COMP VALUE -1.
00178       COPY ARD93M.
00179 C      01  ARD93M7I.
00180 C          02  FILLER PIC X(12).
00181 C          02  TRIDL    COMP  PIC  S9(4).
00182 C          02  TRIDF    PICTURE X.
00183 C          02  FILLER REDEFINES TRIDF.
00184 C              03  TRIDA    PICTURE X.
00185 C          02  TRIDI PIC X(4).
00186 C          02  TERML    COMP  PIC  S9(4).
00187 C          02  TERMF    PICTURE X.
00188 C          02  FILLER REDEFINES TERMF.
00189 C              03  TERMA    PICTURE X.
00190 C          02  TERMI PIC X(8).
00191 C          02  CUSTNOL   COMP PIC  S9(4).
00192 C          02  CUSTNOF    PICTURE X.
00193 C          02  FILLER REDEFINES CUSTNOF.
00194 C              03  CUSTNOA    PICTURE X.
00195 C          02  CUSTNOI PIC X(4).
00196 C          02  CUSTNAML   COMP  PIC  S9(4).
00197 C          02  CUSTNAMF    PICTURE X.
00198 C          02  FILLER REDEFINES CUSTNAMF.
00199 C              03  CUSTNAMA    PICTURE X.
00200 C          02  CUSTNAMI PIC X(30).
00201 C          02  ADDR1L     COMP  PIC  S9(4).
00202 C          02  ADDR1F     PICTURE X.
00203 C          02  FILLER REDEFINES ADDR1F.
00204 C              03  ADDR1A     PICTURE X.
00205 C          02  ADDR1I PIC X(30).
00206 C          02  ADDR2L     COMP  PIC  S9(4).
00207 C          02  ADDR2F     PICTURE X.
00208 C          02  FILLER REDEFINES ADDR2F.
00209 C              03  ADDR2A     PICTURE X.
00210 C          02  ADDR2I PIC X(30).
00211 C          02  ADDR3L     COMP  PIC  S9(4).
00212 C          02  ADDR3F     PICTURE X.
00213 C          02  FILLER REDEFINES ADDR3F.
00214 C              03  ADDR3A     PICTURE X.
00215 C          02  ADDR3I PIC X(21).
00216 C          02  STATEL     COMP  PIC  S9(4).
00217 C          02  STATEF     PICTURE X.
00218 C          02  FILLER REDEFINES STATEF.
00219 C              03  STATEA     PICTURE X.
00220 C          02  STATEI PIC X(2).
00221 C          02  POSTCDL    COMP  PIC  S9(4).
00222 C          02  POSTCDF     PICTURE X.
00223 C          02  FILLER REDEFINES POSTCDF.
00224 C              03  POSTCDA    PICTURE X.
00225 C          02  POSTCDI PIC X(10).
00226 C          02  AREAL    COMP  PIC  S9(4).
00227 C          02  AREAF    PICTURE X.
00228 C          02  FILLER REDEFINES AREAF.
```

```
00229 C              03 AREAA    PICTURE X.
00230 C           02 AREAI  PIC X(3).
00231 C           02 TEL3L    COMP PIC S9(4).
00232 C           02 TEL3F    PICTURE X.
00233 C           02 FILLER REDEFINES TEL3F.
00234 C              03 TEL3A    PICTURE X.
00235 C           02 TEL3I PIC X(3).
00236 C           02 TEL4L    COMP PIC S9(4).
00237 C           02 TEL4F    PICTURE X.
00238 C           02 FILLER REDEFINES TEL4F.
00239 C              03 TEL4A    PICTURE X.
00240 C           02 TEL4I PIC X(4).
00241 C           02 CONTNAML   COMP PIC S9(4).
00242 C           02 CONTNAMF   PICTURE X.
00243 C           02 FILLER REDEFINES CONTNAMF.
00244 C              03 CONTNAMA    PICTURE X.
00245 C           02 CONTNAMI PIC X(15).
00246 C           02 ABBNAMEL   COMP  PIC S9(4).
00247 C           02 ABBNAMEF   PICTURE X.
00248 C           02 FILLER REDEFINES ABBNAMEF.
00249 C              03 ABBNAMEA    PICTURE X.
00250 C           02 ABBNAMEI PIC X(15).
00251 C           02 MML    COMP PIC S9(4).
00252 C           02 MMF    PICTURE X.
00253 C           02 FILLER REDEFINES MMF.
00254 C              03 MMA    PICTURE X.
00255 C           02 MMI PIC X(2).
00256 C           02 YYL    COMP PIC S9(4).
00257 C           02 YYF    PICTURE X.
00258 C           02 FILLER REDEFINES YYF.
00259 C              03 YYA    PICTURE X.
00260 C           02 YYI PIC X(2).
00261 C           02 DBNOL    COMP PIC S9(4).
00262 C           02 DBNOF    PICTURE X.
00263 C           02 FILLER REDEFINES DBNOF.
00264 C              03 DBNOA    PICTURE X.
00265 C           02 DBNOI PIC X(6).
00266 C           02 MSSGL    COMP PIC S9(4).
00267 C           02 MSSGF    PICTURE X.
00268 C           02 FILLER REDEFINES MSSGF.
00269 C              03 MSSGA    PICTURE X.
00270 C           02 MSSGI PIC X(60).
00271 C        01 ARD93M7O REDEFINES ARD93M7I.
00272 C           02 FILLER PIC X(12).
00273 C           02 FILLER PICTURE X(3).
00274 C           02 TRIDO PIC X(4).
00275 C           02 FILLER PICTURE X(3).
00276 C           02 TERMO PIC X(8).
00277 C           02 FILLER PICTURE X(3).
00278 C           02 CUSTNOO PIC X(4).
00279 C           02 FILLER PICTURE X(3).
00280 C           02 CUSTNAMO PIC X(30).
00281 C           02 FILLER PICTURE X(3).
00282 C           02 ADDR1O PIC X(30).
00283 C           02 FILLER PICTURE X(3).
00284 C           02 ADDR2O PIC X(30).
00285 C           02 FILLER PICTURE X(3).
00286 C           02 ADDR3O PIC X(21).
00287 C           02 FILLER PICTURE X(3).
00288 C           02 STATEO PIC X(2).
00289 C           02 FILLER PICTURE X(3).
00290 C           02 POSTCDO PIC X(10).
00291 C           02 FILLER PICTURE X(3).
00292 C           02 AREAO PIC X(3).
00293 C           02 FILLER PICTURE X(3).
00294 C           02 TEL3O PIC X(3).
00295 C           02 FILLER PICTURE X(3).
00296 C           02 TEL4O PIC X(4).
00297 C           02 FILLER PICTURE X(3).
00298 C           02 CONTNAMO PIC X(15).
00299 C           02 FILLER PICTURE X(3).
00300 C           02 ABBNAMEO PIC X(15).
00301 C           02 FILLER PICTURE X(3).
00302 C           02 MMO  PIC X(2).
00303 C           02 FILLER PICTURE X(3).
00304 C           02 YYO  PIC X(2).
00305 C           02 FILLER PICTURE X(3).
00306 C           02 DBNOO  PIC X(6).
```

Compiler-generated source code: excerpts   **69**

```
00307 C          02  FILLER PICTURE X(3).
00308 C          02  MSSGO  PIC X(60).
00309       01  DFHLDVER PIC X(22) VALUE 'LD TABLE DFHEITAB 210.'.
00310       01  DFHEIDO PICTURE S9(7) COMPUTATIONAL-3 VALUE ZERO.
00311       01  DFHEIBO PICTURE S9(4) COMPUTATIONAL VALUE ZERO.
00312       01  DFHEICB  PICTURE X(8) VALUE IS '        '.
00313
00314       01  DFHEIV16  COMP PIC S9(8).
00315       01  DFHB0041  COMP PIC S9(8).
00316       01  DFHB0042  COMP PIC S9(8).
00317       01  DFHB0043  COMP PIC S9(8).
00318       01  DFHB0044  COMP PIC S9(8).
00319       01  DFHB0045  COMP PIC S9(8).
00320       01  DFHB0046  COMP PIC S9(8).
00321       01  DFHB0047  COMP PIC S9(8).
00322       01  DFHB0048  COMP PIC S9(8).
00323       01  DFHEIV11  COMP PIC S9(4).
00324       01  DFHEIV12  COMP PIC S9(4).
00325       01  DFHEIV13  COMP PIC S9(4).
00326       01  DFHEIV14  COMP PIC S9(4).
00327       01  DFHEIV15  COMP PIC S9(4).
00328       01  DFHB0025  COMP PIC S9(4).
00329       01  DFHEIV5   PIC X(4).
00330       01  DFHEIV6   PIC X(4).
00331       01  DFHEIV17  PIC X(4).
00332       01  DFHEIV18  PIC X(4).
00333       01  DFHEIV19  PIC X(4).
00334       01  DFHEIV1   PIC X(8).
00335       01  DFHEIV2   PIC X(8).
00336       01  DFHEIV3   PIC X(8).
00337       01  DFHEIV20  PIC X(8).
00338       01  DFHC0084  PIC X(8).
00339       01  DFHC0085  PIC X(8).
00340       01  DFHC0320  PIC X(32).
00341       01  DFHEIV7   PIC X(2).
00342       01  DFHEIV8   PIC X(2).
00343       01  DFHC0022  PIC X(2).
00344       01  DFHC0023  PIC X(2).
00345       01  DFHEIV10  PIC S9(7) COMP-3.
00346       01  DFHEIV9   PIC X(1).
00347       01  DFHC0011  PIC X(1).
00348       01  DFHEIV4   PIC X(6).
00349       01  DFHC0070  PIC X(7).
00350       01  DFHC0071  PIC X(7).
00351       01  DFHC0440  PIC X(44).
00352       01  DFHDUMMY COMP PIC S9(4).
00353       01  DFHEIV0   PICTURE X(29).
00354       LINKAGE SECTION.
00355       01  DFHEIBLK.
00356       02  EIBTIME  PIC S9(7) COMP-3.
00357       02   EIBDATE  PIC S9(7) COMP-3.
00358       02   EIBTRNID PIC X(4).
00359       02   EIBTASKN PIC S9(7) COMP-3.
00360       02   EIBTRMID PIC X(4).
00361       02   DFHEIGDI COMP PIC S9(4).
00362       02   EIBCPOSN COMP PIC S9(4).
00363       02   EIBCALEN COMP PIC S9(4).
00364       02   EIBAID   PIC X(1).
00365       02   EIBFN    PIC X(2).
00366       02   EIBRCODE PIC X(6).
00367       02   EIBDS    PIC X(8).
00368       02   EIBREQID PIC X(8).
00369       02   EIBRSRCE PIC X(8).
00370       02   EIBSYNC  PIC X(1).
00371       02   EIBFREE  PIC X(1).
00372       02   EIBRECV  PIC X(1).
00373       02   EIBFIL01 PIC X(1).
00374       02   EIBATT   PIC X(1).
00375       02   EIBEOC   PIC X(1).
00376       02   EIBFMH   PIC X(1).
00377       02   EIBCOMPL PIC X(1).
00378       02   EIBSIG   PIC X(1).
00379       02   EIBCONF  PIC X(1).
00380       02   EIBERR   PIC X(1).
00381       02   EIBERRCD PIC X(4).
00382       02   EIBSYNRB PIC X(1).
```

```
00383          02    EIBNODAT PIC X(1).
00384          02    EIBRESP  COMP PIC S9(8).
00385          02    EIBRESP2 COMP PIC S9(8).
00386          02    EIBRLDBK PIC X(1).
00387       01  DFHCOMMAREA        PIC X(02).
00388       01  DFHBLLSLOT1 PICTURE X(1).
00389       01  DFHBLLSLOT2 PICTURE X(1).
00390       PROCEDURE DIVISION USING DFHEIBLK DFHCOMMAREA.
00391          CALL 'DFHEI1'.
00392          SERVICE RELOAD DFHEIBLK.
00393          SERVICE RELOAD DFHCOMMAREA.
00394       001-START-PROCESSING.
00395          IF EIBCALEN > 0
00396          MOVE DFHCOMMAREA TO COMM-AREA.
00397      *EXEC CICS HANDLE AID
00398      *CLEAR(004-SEND-MAP)
00399      *PF1(170-RETURN-TO-SUBMENU)
00400      *PF4
00401      *ANYKEY(900-ANYKEY-OPTION)                              END
00402      *EXEC.
00403              MOVE ' \            00023  ' TO DFHEIV0
00404              CALL 'DFHEI1' USING DFHEIV0
00405              GO TO  004-SEND-MAP 170-RETURN-TO-SUBMENU
00406          900-ANYKEY-OPTION DEPENDING ON DFHEIGDI.
00407
00408
00409      *EXEC CICS HANDLE CONDITION
00410      *MAPFAIL(700-MAPFAIL)
00411      *END-EXEC.
00412              MOVE '              00029   ' TO DFHEIV0
00413              CALL 'DFHEI1' USING DFHEIV0
00414              GO TO  700-MAPFAIL DEPENDING ON DFHEIGDI.
00415          IF SEND-REC-FLAG = 'R' GO TO
00416          005-RECEIVE-MAP.
00417       004-SEND-MAP.
00418          MOVE 'AR93' TO TRIDO.
00419          MOVE EIBTRMID TO TERMO.
00420          MOVE PROT TO TRIDA.
00421      *
00422       004-SEND-MAP-2.
00423          MOVE -1 TO CUSTNOL.
00424      *EXEC CICS SEND MAP('ARD93M7')
00425      *MAPSET('ARD93M')
00426      *ERASE
00427      *CURSOR
00428      *END-EXEC.
00429              MOVE ' J       S    00041  ' TO DFHEIV0
00430              MOVE 'ARD93M7' TO DFHC0070
00431              MOVE 'ARD93M' TO DFHC0071
00432              MOVE -1 TO DFHEIV11
00433              CALL 'DFHEI1' USING DFHEIV0  DFHC0070 ARD93M7O DFHDUMMY
00434          DFHC0071 DFHDUMMY DFHDUMMY DFHDUMMY DFHEIV11.
00435              MOVE 'R' TO SEND-REC-FLAG.
00436              GO TO 100-RETURN.
00437       005-RECEIVE-MAP.
00438      *EXEC CICS RECEIVE MAP('ARD93M7')
00439      *MAPSET('ARD93M')
00440      *END-EXEC.
00441              MOVE ' }            00049   ' TO DFHEIV0
00442              MOVE 'ARD93M7' TO DFHC0070
00443              MOVE 'ARD93M' TO DFHC0071
00444              CALL 'DFHEI1' USING DFHEIV0  DFHC0070 ARD93M7I DFHDUMMY
00445          DFHC0071.
00446       006-HANDLE-CONDITION.
00447      *EXEC CICS HANDLE CONDITION
00448      *NOTFND(950-CUSTOMER-MISSING)
00449      *END-EXEC.
00450              MOVE '                   00053   ' TO DFHEIV0
00451              CALL 'DFHEI1' USING DFHEIV0
00452              GO TO  950-CUSTOMER-MISSING DEPENDING ON DFHEIGDI.
00453       007-READ-CUSTOMER-MASTER.
00454          IF CUSTNOL = ZEROS OR CUSTNOI = SPACES
00455          MOVE 'PLEASE ENTER CUSTOMER I.D.' TO MSSGO
00456          MOVE PROT TO MSSGA
00457          MOVE -1 TO CUSTNOL
00458          GO TO 500-RESEND-MAP.
00459          MOVE UNPROT-NUM-MDT TO CUSTNOA.
00460      ************************************************************
```

```
00461          * GET READY TO READ CUSTOMER MASTER                        *
00462          ***********************************************************
00463              MOVE CUSTNOI TO CUSTOMER-ID
00464          *EXEC CICS READ DATASET('RK501')
00465          *INTO(CUSTOMER-MASTER)
00466          *RIDFLD(CUSTOMER-KEY)
00467          *END-EXEC.
00468              MOVE ' }       00067   ' TO DFHEIVO
00469              MOVE 'RK501' TO DFHEIV1
00470              CALL 'DFHEI1' USING DFHEIVO DFHEIV1 CUSTOMER-MASTER
00471              DFHDUMMY CUSTOMER-KEY.
00472          008-DISPLAY-CUSTOMER.
00473              MOVE CUSTOMER-NAME TO CUSTNAMI.
00474              MOVE PROT-BRT TO CUSTNAMA.
00475              MOVE CUSTOMER-ADDRESS1 TO ADDR1I.
00476              MOVE PROT-BRT TO ADDR1A.
00477              MOVE CUSTOMER-ADDRESS2 TO ADDR2I.
00478              MOVE PROT-BRT TO ADDR2A.
00479              MOVE CUSTOMER-ADDRESS3 TO ADDR3I.
00480              MOVE PROT-BRT TO ADDR3A.
00481              MOVE CUSTOMER-STATE TO STATEI.
00482              MOVE PROT TO STATEA.
00483              MOVE CUSTOMER-POSTAL-CODE TO POSTCDI.
00484              MOVE PROT TO POSTCDA.
00485              MOVE CUSTOMER-AREA-CODE TO AREAI.
00486              MOVE PROT TO AREAA.
00487              MOVE CUSTOMER-TEL1 TO TEL3I.
00488              MOVE PROT TO TEL3A.
00489              MOVE CUSTOMER-TEL2 TO TEL4I.
00490              MOVE PROT TO TEL4A.
00491              MOVE CUSTOMER-CONTACT-NAME TO CONTNAMI.
00492              MOVE PROT TO CONTNAMA.
00493              MOVE CUSTOMER-ABBREVIATED-NAME TO ABBNAMEI.
00494              MOVE PROT TO ABBNAMEA.
00495              MOVE CUSTOMER-MONTH TO MMI.
00496              MOVE PROT TO MMA.
00497              MOVE CUSTOMER-YEAR TO YYI.
00498              MOVE PROT TO YYA.
00499              MOVE CUSTOMER-DB-NUMBER TO DBNOI.
00500              MOVE PROT TO DBNOA.
00501          ***********************************************************
00502          * READY TO ADD NEW RECORD TO FILE                         *
00503          ***********************************************************
00504              IF EIBAID = DFHPF4 GO TO 080-DELETE-RECORD ELSE
00505              MOVE 'RECORD IS READY TO BE DELETED' TO MSSGO
00506              MOVE PROT TO MSSGA
00507              MOVE -1 TO CUSTNOL
00508              MOVE ZEROS TO DELETE-COUNT
00509              GO TO 500-RESEND-MAP.
00510          *
00511          080-DELETE-RECORD.
00512              MOVE CUSTNOI TO STORE-CUSTNO.
00513              ADD 1 TO DELETE-COUNT.
00514              IF DELETE-COUNT = 1
00515              GO TO 960-FIRST-DELETE-COMMENT.
00516              MOVE CUSTNOI TO CUSTOMER-ID.
00517          *EXEC CICS DELETE DATASET('RK501')
00518          *FROM(CUSTOMER-MASTER)
00519          *RIDFLD(CUSTOMER-KEY)
00520          *END-EXEC.
00521              MOVE '        00116   ' TO DFHEIVO
00522              MOVE 'RK501' TO DFHEIV1
00523              CALL 'DFHEI1' USING DFHEIVO DFHEIV1 DFHDUMMY DFHDUMMY
00524              CUSTOMER-KEY.
00525              MOVE PROT TO MSSGA
00526              MOVE -1 TO CUSTNOL
00527              MOVE ZEROS TO DELETE-COUNT
00528              MOVE LOW-VALUES TO ARD93M70
00529              MOVE STORE-CUSTNO TO CUSTNOI
00530              MOVE UNPROT-NUM-BRT TO CUSTNOA
00531              MOVE 'RECORD IS NOW DELETED' TO MSSGO
00532              GO TO 004-SEND-MAP.
00533          ***********************************************************
00534          * SUBROUTINE SECTION                                      *
00535          ***********************************************************
00536          100-RETURN.
```

```
00537          *EXEC CICS RETURN
00538          *    TRANSID('AR93')
00539          *    COMMAREA(COMM-AREA)
00540          *    LENGTH(2)
00541          *END-EXEC.
00542               MOVE ' \       00132   ' TO DFHEIVO
00543               MOVE 'AR93' TO DFHEIV5
00544               MOVE 2 TO DFHEIV11
00545               CALL 'DFHEI1' USING DFHEIVO  DFHEIV5 COMM-AREA DFHEIV11.
00546
00547           170-RETURN-TO-SUBMENU.
00548               MOVE ' ' TO SEND-REC-FLAG.
00549          *EXEC CICS XCTL PROGRAM('ARM90C')
00550          *COMMAREA(COMM-AREA)
00551          *LENGTH(1)
00552          *END-EXEC.
00553               MOVE ' \       00139   ' TO DFHEIVO
00554               MOVE 'ARM90C' TO DFHEIV1
00555               MOVE 1 TO DFHEIV11
00556               CALL 'DFHEI1' USING DFHEIVO  DFHEIV1 COMM-AREA DFHEIV11.
00557               STOP RUN.
00558               GOBACK.
00559           500-RESEND-MAP.
00560          *EXEC CICS SEND MAP('ARD93M7')
00561          *MAPSET('ARD93M')
00562          *CURSOR
00563          *DATAONLY
00564          *END-EXEC.
00565               MOVE ' J            00146   ' TO DFHEIVO
00566               MOVE 'ARD93M7' TO DFHC0070
00567               MOVE 'ARD93M' TO DFHC0071
00568               MOVE -1 TO DFHEIV11
00569               CALL 'DFHEI1' USING DFHEIVO  DFHC0070 ARD93M7O DFHDUMMY
00570               DFHC0071 DFHDUMMY DFHDUMMY DFHDUMMY DFHEIV11.
00571               MOVE 'R' TO SEND-REC-FLAG.
00572               GO TO 100-RETURN.
00573           700-MAPFAIL.
00574               MOVE 'ENTER CUSTOMER NUMBER' TO MSSGO
00575               MOVE PROT TO MSSGA
00576               MOVE ' ' TO SEND-REC-FLAG
00577               MOVE -1 TO CUSTNOL
00578               GO TO 500-RESEND-MAP.
00579           900-ANYKEY-OPTION.
00580               MOVE 'INVALID KEY, PLEASE RESUBMIT' TO MSSGO.
00581               MOVE PROT TO MSSGA
00582               MOVE -1 TO CUSTNOL
00583               GO TO 500-RESEND-MAP.
00584           950-CUSTOMER-MISSING.
00585               MOVE CUSTNOI TO STORE-CUSTNO.
00586               MOVE LOW-VALUES TO ARD93M7O.
00587               MOVE 'NO SUCH RECORD ON FILE' TO MSSGO.
00588               MOVE PROT TO MSSGA.
00589               MOVE STORE-CUSTNO TO CUSTNOI
00590               MOVE -1 TO CUSTNOL.
00591               MOVE ZEROS TO DELETE-COUNT.
00592               GO TO 004-SEND-MAP.
00593           960-FIRST-DELETE-COMMENT.
00594               MOVE 'PLEASE VERIFY DELETE' TO MSSGO.
00595               MOVE PROT TO MSSGA.
00596               MOVE -1 TO CUSTNOL.
00597               GO TO 500-RESEND-MAP.

*STATISTICS*    SOURCE RECORDS =   597     DATA DIVISION STATEMENTS =   374
*OPTIONS IN EFFECT*     SIZE = 524288  BUF =  20480 LINECNT = 57  SPACE1, FL
*OPTIONS IN EFFECT*     NODMAP, NOPMAP, NOCLIST, NOSUPMAP, NOXREF,   SXREF,  L
*OPTIONS IN EFFECT*     NOTERM, NONUM, NOBATCH, NONAME, COMPILE=01, NOSTATE, NO
*OPTIONS IN EFFECT*     NOOPTIMIZE, NOSYMDMP, NOTEST,   VERB,   ZWB, SYST, NOEN
*OPTIONS IN EFFECT*     NOLST , NOFDECK,NOCDECK, LCOL2, L120,   DUMP , NOADV ,
*OPTIONS IN EFFECT*     NOCOUNT, NOVBSUM, NOVBREF, LANGLVL(1)
                                            CROSS-REFERENCE DICTIONARY


   DATA NAMES                      DEFN    REFERENCE


   ABBNAMEA                        000249  000494
   ABBNAMEF                        000247
   ABBNAMEI                        000250  000493
```

```
ABBNAMEL                        000246
ABBNAMEO                        000300
ADDR1A                          000204    000476
ADDR1F                          000202
ADDR1I                          000205    000475
ADDR1L                          000201
ADDR1O                          000282
ADDR2A                          000209    000478
ADDR2F                          000207
ADDR2I                          000210    000477
ADDR2L                          000206
ADDR2O                          000284
ADDR3A                          000214    000480
ADDR3F                          000212
ADDR3I                          000215    000479
ADDR3L                          000211
ADDR3O                          000286
ARD93M7I                        000179    000444
ARD93M7O                        000271    000433    000528   000569   000586
AREAA                           000229    000486
AREAF                           000227
AREAI                           000230    000485
AREAL                           000226
AREAO                           000292
ASKIP                           000169
ASKIP-BRT                       000171
ASKIP-BRT-MDT                   000172
ASKIP-DRK                       000173
ASKIP-DRK-MDT                   000174
ASKIP-MDT                       000170
ATTRBYTE                        000150
COMM-AREA                       000007    000396    000545   000556
CONTNAMA                        000244    000492
CONTNAMF                        000242
CONTNAMI                        000245    000491
CONTNAML                        000241
CONTNAMO                        000298
CSR-REPO                        000177
CUSTNAMA                        000199    000474
CUSTNAMF                        000197
CUSTNAMI                        000200    000473
CUSTNAML                        000196
CUSTNAMO                        000280
CUSTNOA                         000194    000459    000530
CUSTNOF                         000192
CUSTNOI                         000195    000454    000463   000512   000516   00052
CUSTNOL                         000191    000421    000423   000454   000457   00050
CUSTNOO                         000278
CUSTOMER-ABBREVIATED-NAME       000029    000493
CUSTOMER-ACCOUNT-OPENED         000030
CUSTOMER-ADDRESS1               000023    000475
CUSTOMER-ADDRESS2               000024    000477
CUSTOMER-ADDRESS3               000025    000479
CUSTOMER-AREA-CODE              000036    000485
CUSTOMER-COMPANY                000014
CUSTOMER-CONTACT-NAME           000028    000491
CUSTOMER-DB-NUMBER              000041    000499
CUSTOMER-ID                     000018    000463    000516
CUSTOMER-KEY                    000013    000470    000523
CUSTOMER-MASTER                 000010    000470
CUSTOMER-MONTH                  000031    000495
CUSTOMER-NAME                   000022    000473
CUSTOMER-NUMBER                 000016
CUSTOMER-POSTAL-CODE            000027    000483
CUSTOMER-PREFIX                 000017
CUSTOMER-REFERENCE              000019
CUSTOMER-SEGMENT                000015
CUSTOMER-STATE                  000026    000481
CUSTOMER-TELEPHONE              000037
CUSTOMER-TELEPHONE-NO           000034
CUSTOMER-TEL1                   000038    000487
CUSTOMER-TEL2                   000039    000489
CUSTOMER-YEAR                   000032    000497
DATA-AREA                       000021
DBNOA                           000264    000500
DBNOF                           000262
```

Name						
DBNOI	000265	000499				
DBNOL	000261					
DBNOO	000306					
DELETE-COUNT	000009	000508	000513	000514	000527	00059
DFHAID	000111					
DFHALL	000071					
DFHBASE	000082					
DFHBKTRN	000070					
DFHBLINK	000084					
DFHBLLSLOT1	000388					
DFHBLLSLOT2	000389					
DFHBLUE	000075					
DFHBMASB	000058					
DFHBMASF	000057					
DFHBMASK	000049					
DFHBMBRY	000053					
DFHBMDAR	000054					
DFHBMDET	000060					
DFHBMEOF	000059					
DFHBMFSE	000055					
DFHBMPEM	000047					
DFHBMPNL	000048					
DFHBMPRF	000056					
DFHBMPRO	000052					
DFHBMPSI	000062					
DFHBMPSO	000061					
DFHBMSCA	000046					
DFHBMUNN	000051					
DFHBMUNP	000050					
DFHBOX	000106					
DFHB0025	000328					
DFHB0041	000315					
DFHB0042	000316					
DFHB0043	000317					
DFHB0044	000318					
DFHB0045	000319					
DFHB0046	000320					
DFHB0047	000321					
DFHB0048	000322					
DFHCLEAR	000114					
DFHCLRP	000115					
DFHCOLOR	000064					
DFHCOMMAREA	000387	000396				
DFHC0011	000347					
DFHC0022	000343					
DFHC0023	000344					
DFHC0070	000349	000430	000433	000442	000444	00056
DFHC0071	000350	000431	000433	000443	000444	00056
DFHC0084	000338					
DFHC0085	000339					
DFHC0320	000340					
DFHC0440	000351					
DFHDFCOL	000074					
DFHDFFR	000101					
DFHDFHI	000083					
DFHDFT	000073					
DFHDUMMY	000352	000433	000444	000470	000523	00056
DFHEIBLK	000355					
DFHEIB0	000311					
DFHEICB	000312					
DFHEID0	000310					
DFHEIGDI	000361	000405	000414	000452		
DFHEIV0	000353	000403	000404	000412	000413	00042
		000468	000470	000521	000523	00054
DFHEIV1	000334	000469	000470	000522	000523	00055
DFHEIV10	000345					
DFHEIV11	000323	000432	000433	000544	000545	00055
DFHEIV12	000324					
DFHEIV13	000325					
DFHEIV14	000326					
DFHEIV15	000327					
DFHEIV16	000314					
DFHEIV17	000331					
DFHEIV18	000332					
DFHEIV19	000333					
DFHEIV2	000335					
DFHEIV20	000337					
DFHEIV3	000336					

DFHEIV4	000348		
DFHEIV5	000329	000543	000545
DFHEIV6	000330		
DFHEIV7	000341		
DFHEIV8	000342		
DFHEIV9	000346		
DFHENTER	000113		
DFHERROR	000072		
DFHGREEN	000078		
DFHHLT	000066		
DFHLDVER	000309		
DFHLEFT	000102		
DFHMENT	000088		
DFHMET	000099		
DFHMFE	000089		
DFHMFET	000100		
DFHMFIL	000087		
DFHMFT	000098		
DFHMSRE	000118		
DFHMT	000097		
DFHNEUTR	000081		
DFHNULL	000112		
DFHOPAQ	000109		
DFHOPID	000117		
DFHOUTLN	000069		
DFHOVER	000103		
DFHPA1	000121		
DFHPA2	000122		
DFHPA3	000123		
DFHPEN	000116		
DFHPF1	000124		
DFHPF10	000133		
DFHPF11	000134		
DFHPF12	000135		
DFHPF13	000136		
DFHPF14	000137		
DFHPF15	000138		
DFHPF16	000139		
DFHPF17	000140		
DFHPF18	000141		
DFHPF19	000142		
DFHPF2	000125		
DFHPF20	000143		
DFHPF21	000144		
DFHPF22	000145		
DFHPF23	000146		
DFHPF24	000147		
DFHPF3	000126		
DFHPF4	000127	000504	
DFHPF5	000128		
DFHPF6	000129		
DFHPF7	000130		
DFHPF8	000131		
DFHPF9	000132		
DFHPINK	000077		
DFHPROTI	000095		
DFHPROTN	000096		
DFHPS	000065		
DFHRED	000076		
DFHREVRS	000085		
DFHRIGHT	000104		
DFHSA	000063		
DFHSOSI	000107		
DFHSTRF	000119		
DFHTRANS	000108		
DFHTRIG	000120		
DFHTURQ	000079		
DFHUNDER	000105		
DFHUNDLN	000086		
DFHUNIMD	000091		
DFHUNINT	000093		
DFHUNNOD	000090		
DFHUNNON	000094		
DFHUNNUM	000092		
DFHVAL	000068		
DFHYELLO	000080		

DFH3270	000067					
EIBAID	000364	000504				
EIBATT	000374					
EIBCALEN	000363	000395				
EIBCOMPL	000377					
EIBCONF	000379					
EIBCPOSN	000362					
EIBDATE	000357					
EIBDS	000367					
EIBEOC	000375					
EIBERR	000380					
EIBERRCD	000381					
EIBFIL01	000373					
EIBFMH	000376					
EIBFN	000365					
EIBFREE	000371					
EIBNODAT	000383					
EIBRCODE	000366					
EIBRECV	000372					
EIBREQID	000368					
EIBRESP	000384					
EIBRESP2	000385					
EIBRLDBK	000386					
EIBRSRCE	000369					
EIBSIG	000378					
EIBSYNC	000370					
EIBSYNRB	000382					
EIBTASKN	000359					
EIBTIME	000356					
EIBTRMID	000360	000419				
EIBTRNID	000358					
LENGTH-BYTES	000176					
MMA	000254	000496				
MMF	000252					
MMI	000255	000495				
MML	000251					
MMO	000302					
MSSGA	000269	000456	000506	000525	000575	00058
MSSGF	000267					
MSSGI	000270					
MSSGL	000266					
MSSGO	000308	000455	000505	000531	000574	00058
POSTCDA	000224	000484				
POSTCDF	000222					
POSTCDI	000225	000483				
POSTCDL	000221					
POSTCDO	000290					
PROT	000163	000420	000456	000482	000484	00048
		000498	000500	000506	000525	00057
PROT-BRT	000165	000474	000476	000478	000480	
PROT-BRT-MDT	000166					
PROT-DRK	000167					
PROT-DRK-MDT	000168					
PROT-MDT	000164					
SEND-REC-FLAG	000008	000415	000435	000548	000571	00057
STATEA	000219	000482				
STATEF	000217					
STATEI	000220	000481				
STATEL	000216					
STATEO	000288					
STORE-CUSTNO	000043	000512	000529	000585	000589	
STORE-TRANSID	000044					
TEL3A	000234	000488				
TEL3F	000232					
TEL3I	000235	000487				
TEL3L	000231					
TEL3O	000294					
TEL4A	000239	000490				
TEL4F	000237					
TEL4I	000240	000489				
TEL4L	000236					
TEL4O	000296					
TERMA	000189					
TERMF	000187					
TERMI	000190					
TERML	000186					
TERMO	000276	000419				
TRIDA	000184	000420				

TRIDF	000182	
TRIDI	000185	
TRIDL	000181	
TRIDO	000274	000418
UNPROT-ALPHA	000151	
UNPROT-ALPHA-BRT	000153	
UNPROT-ALPHA-BRT-MDT	000154	
UNPROT-ALPHA-DRK	000155	
UNPROT-ALPHA-DRK-MDT	000156	
UNPROT-ALPHA-MDT	000152	
UNPROT-NUM	000157	
UNPROT-NUM-BRT	000159	000530
UNPROT-NUM-BRT-MDT	000160	
UNPROT-NUM-DRK	000161	
UNPROT-NUM-DRK-MDT	000162	
UNPROT-NUM-MDT	000158	000459
YYA	000259	000498
YYF	000257	
YYI	000260	000497
YYL	000256	
YYO	000304	

PROCEDURE NAMES	DEFN	REFERENCE				
001-START-PROCESSING	000394					
004-SEND-MAP	000417	000405	000532	000592		
004-SEND-MAP-2	000422					
005-RECEIVE-MAP	000437	000415				
006-HANDLE-CONDITION	000446					
007-READ-CUSTOMER-MASTER	000453					
008-DISPLAY-CUSTOMER	000472					
080-DELETE-RECORD	000511	000504				
100-RETURN	000536	000436	000572			
170-RETURN-TO-SUBMENU	000547	000405				
500-RESEND-MAP	000559	000458	000509	000578	000583	00059
700-MAPFAIL	000573	000414				
900-ANYKEY-OPTION	000579	000405				
950-CUSTOMER-MISSING	000584	000452				
960-FIRST-DELETE-COMMENT	000593	000515				

5
How to write
an ADD program

In this chapter, I'm going to illustrate some of the fundamental aspects of developing an ADD program. When designing such a transaction, you need to be especially thorough, since most ADD programs can be easily converted to perform changes on an existing record. Thus, logical flaws or poor habits shown in the ADD program can carry over into the CHANGE program. Writing ADD programs will be further discussed in Chapter 6.

As general error-handling procedures, there are some interesting techniques that will help you highlight errors caused by data omission. Data omission is especially critical during the validation of an ADD, since the initial panel invoked by the terminal operator is displayed without any data, whether the field is optional or mandatory. This, of course, is quite different from standard CHANGE procedures, where all requirements are immediately available at the time the initial map is sent. These requirements will continually remain available unless, in altering the data, you inadvertently blank out or zero out one or more mandatory field components.

To efficiently test for the absence of data under such circumstances, I refer to some of the constant fields on the map as variable data entries. This enables me to make individualized references to certain column headings, while leaving others intact. The reason this can be an important issue is as follows:

- You can diagnose a specific problem, providing the terminal operator with the location of the error on the screen.

- You can present a panel to the terminal operator in a hierarchical fashion, meaning that the system will stop the validation process at a position highlighted on the map until the error is resolved.
- This is especially critical when entering a wrong (search) key in reference to a record that already exists. It is important to be aware of this, since you don't want to waste your time entering a large amount of data that will subsequently be rejected by the system.

In adding a record, the entire premise in handling such a procedure needs to be associated with a NOTFND (not found) routine, part of your HANDLE CONDITION. For example, if a mandatory field is omitted, it goes without saying that it cannot be transformed from a protected low-intensity color to one with high-intensity. Suppose you have a panel containing three data fields. These are:

```
EMPLOYEE I.D.                  :
EMPLOYEE NAME                  :
EMPLOYEE'S MONTHLY SALARY  :
```

Assume that all three of these fields are initially displayed on the panel, each in protected mode. If you were to press ENTER at this point, you would start editing the first (EMPLOYEE I.D.) data field, which, of course, is absent. To call the terminal operator's attention to the fact, you can "recolorize" the title from a low-intensity to a high-intensity, bright color, coupled with a message on the bottom of the screen that would read "EMPLOYEE I.D. IS MISSING, PLEASE ENTER." If a correct EMPLOYEE I.D. field is entered for the second time, and provided you were to press the ENTER key once more, the system will reset the EMPLOYEE I.D. title header to its initial color, while transforming the second title (EMPLOYEE NAME) to a high-intensity, bright field. This is especially critical if you develop programs that show multiple errors in a single cycle. A single message on the bottom of the screen cannot possibly cover an array of problems.

ADD programs, as you will soon see, are ideal for creating a CHANGE shell since:

- All edit procedures, with some minor exceptions, are similar in structure.
- Most file and display requirements are also similar.
- With the exception of a few copy and rewrite statements and a few HANDLE CONDITIONS, all the initial code inherent in an ADD program can be reusable.

For the purpose of coding efficiency, I recommend that the programmer responsible for developing an ADD program also be put in charge of developing a similar transaction to handle changes. Some shops use sophisticated shells to save time in converting (and simplifying) maintenance programs and to perform inquiries in minimum time. The problem with using two or more programmers to develop code for an ADD and a CHANGE transaction within an identical application is that each of them will end up developing the required logic from scratch, thus reinventing the wheel. This is an expensive proposition because it is not only a time-consuming process, but one that could result in different programming styles and techniques. Such features might not be advisable.

Case study

The purpose of this case study is to show you how to invoke an ADD transaction through menu selection. The menu screen is presented in FIG. 5-1. When you select task 1 on this panel, you are in fact exiting the current task, a technique similar to an unconditional branch. (See Chapter 2 for more detail on menu screen structures.)

```
AR90        CUSTOMER MAINTENANCE SCREEN


        1    ADD A NEW CUSTOMER TO FILE

        2    CHANGES TO AN EXISTING CUSTOMER

        3    DELETE A CUSTOMER RECORD

        4    BROWSE CUSTOMER DATABASE


             ENTER YOUR SELECTION




    PF1:  RETURN TO MAIN SYSTEM DIRECTORY
```

5-1 Highlights the subdirectory used to maintain the customer database

The purpose of this program (ARA91C) is to create and edit a customer record on the customer master, frequently referred to as a customer database. Thus, a record is created when all input data is "clean," requiring you to press PF 4 to complete the transaction.

By relying on function keys to complete the process of updating a record, you are verifying that indeed, the process was accurate, and that the record can now be updated. This is a recommended, but not necessarily a mandatory, way of adding a record to the database. You can, for example, provide the user with an automatic process for updating a file, which can result after satisfying all validation rules prescribed by the system. Personally, I do not favor this methodology simply because it takes some of the few visual controls away from the user. Visual verification is over-whelming important at times.

The MCRA Billing System utilizes an 1100-position long record for defining a customer-related demographic database. In addition to some vital information, such as the name, address and telephone number of a particular customer, this database also reflects certain customer paying habits, credit standing, tolerance characteristics, and Dun & Bradstreet related references, etc.

Since the customer database needs to interact with a vendor product, specifically with an accounts receivable system, the customer file must emulate a format used by the MCRA system. Accordingly, the key to the customer master is made up of a 35-position long concatenated key, as depicted in FIG. 5-2. The first two positions of the key designate a company master hand-picked by the user for classification purposes. For our immediate need, I simply used a fixed value of 01. Another constant field in the vendor system to be emulated in the customer file is a record segment having a fixed value of 2, which is also used during the interface process.

```
02  FILLER                    PIC X(01).
02  CUSTOMER-KEY.
    05  CUSTOMER-COMPANY       PIC X(02) VALUE '01'.
    05  CUSTOMER-SEGMENT       PIC X(01) VALUE '2'.
    05  CUSTOMER-NUMBER.
        10  CUSTOMER-PREFIX    PIC X(10) VALUE ZEROS.
        10  CUSTOMER-ID        PIC X(04).
    05  CUSTOMER-REFERENCE     PIC X(02) VALUE '01'.
    05  FILLER                 PIC X(16) VALUE SPACES.
```

5-2 Highlights the concatenated key to the customer master. In order to set up such a key, all you need to do is to move the customer number into the shaded area.

The customer number is used only partially, although it is a 14-position long field designed with future expansion in mind. The first 10 positions are set aside to be referenced later on, probably by accounting. This is the constant portion of the key, containing some 10-position (high-order) zeros. These zeros are automatically formatted by the system and not by you, for reasons of conformity.

If you were to allow the user, for example, to enter this field in "free style," that is, sometimes followed and sometimes preceded by either zeros or blanks, you would have a terrible time matching the record key.

The four positions allotted to the customer number field is the variable portion of the key, to be user-supplied every time a transaction is invoked. Finally, two additional constants are also provided, one with a fixed value of "01" and another one using spaces. Note that in building the concatenated key, you only have to consider the variable portion of the key, since all other components are built for you the minute a copy is requested.

Figure 5-3 represents a logical overview for the ADD transaction. A single file, the Customer database, is accessed in this process. Data on the Customer master can be classified into two general categories: those that are mandatory and those that are optional. Mandatory fields require that you enter them according to priority, that is, the way they are presented on the map. Suppose you have three data fields that are mandatory for creating a record. In this case, and using a specific technology, you would not be able to enter or diagnose field number 2 until field number 1 is corrected, should you enter it erroneously.

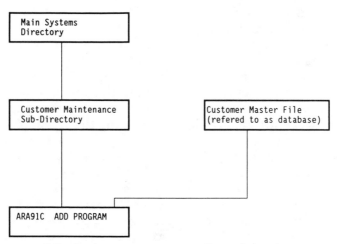

5-3 ARA91C ADD program—path requirements

To put it in more practical terms, when you enter the customer number, which happens to be a key field in processing the customer database, you should immediately press ENTER to see if such a record needs to be added to the file or if it is already in existence. If it is, you certainly do want to waste time entering the rest of the data.

Mandatory data fields in this program are as follows:

- The customer's name. It must not be a blank field.
- Two of the address lines (the third one being optional).
- A state code that must be alphabetic.
- An expanded alphanumeric zip code (also accommodating a hyphen).
- A customer telephone number with a numeric area code.
- An account open field.

All other fields are optional and you can enter them at your discretion.

Map and FCT considerations

Note that the programmer developed BMS map in FIG. 5-4 corresponds to the output panel highlighted in FIG. 5-5. As I mentioned earlier, I have used actual field names for the title headers, since I want to be able to reference them in a given situation. Referencing simply means the use of different colors to highlight a problem when the variable field is omitted. This situation differs slightly when you use extended attributes. Extended attributes allow you to underscore or highlight field omissions.

In processing this or other maps in CICS, you can customize your transaction processing in one of two ways. A more conventional approach to an ADD program, for example, is to diagnose every mandatory field one at a time. Once an error condition is detected by the system, you are to interrupt the edit cycle by sending or retransmitting the map and advising the operator of a pending error condition. This means that you need to reinvoke the transaction from the beginning via the RETURN command.

The above is a conventional way of designing and conceptualizing an ADD program. A second, and certainly less orthodox way, is to diagnose your data in its entirety before sending the map, thus interrupting the edit cycle only after processing the entire record. With this method, you would show a map containing a multiple number of errors, which can be a bit confusing at first.

I am biased toward the first methodology that requires a user notification at the first occurrence of the error. If this procedure is followed, your map will concentrate on a single error, rather than an array of it. (You'll find the coding aspect of the second situation may also be somewhat more complex . . .)

```
         PRINT NOGEN                                                   00010001
ARA91M   DFHMSD  TYPE=&SYSPARM,MODE=INOUT,CTRL=FREEKB,LANG=COBOL,      C00020024
         TIOAPFX=YES                                                   00030001
ARA91M7  DFHMDI   SIZE=(24,80)                                         00040025
TRID     DFHMDF POS=(01,02),LENGTH=04,ATTRB=(BRT,ASKIP)               00050003
         DFHMDF POS=(01,20),LENGTH=31,ATTRB=(PROT,ASKIP),             C00060022
         INITIAL='CUSTOMER DATABASE MAINTENANCE '                     00070024
TERM     DFHMDF POS=(01,70),LENGTH=08,ATTRB=(BRT,ASKIP)               00080041
TCUSTNO  DFHMDF POS=(05,01),LENGTH=21,ATTRB=(PROT,ASKIP),             C00090037
         INITIAL='CUSTOMER NUMBER   :'                                00100024
CUSTNO   DFHMDF POS=(05,25),LENGTH=04,ATTRB=(UNPROT,IC)               00110026
         DFHMDF POS=(05,30),LENGTH=1,ATTRB=ASKIP                      00120034
TCUSTNM  DFHMDF POS=(06,01),LENGTH=21,ATTRB=(PROT,ASKIP),             C00130037
         INITIAL='CUSTOMER NAME     :'                                00140024
CUSTNAM  DFHMDF POS=(06,25),LENGTH=30,ATTRB=UNPROT                    00150035
         DFHMDF POS=(06,56),LENGTH=1,ATTRB=ASKIP                      00160035
TADDR1   DFHMDF POS=(07,01),LENGTH=21,ATTRB=(PROT,ASKIP),             C00170039
         INITIAL='ADDRESS (1)       :'                                00180039
ADDR1    DFHMDF POS=(07,25),LENGTH=30,ATTRB=UNPROT                    00190026
         DFHMDF POS=(07,56),LENGTH=1,ATTRB=ASKIP                      00200034
TADDR2   DFHMDF POS=(08,01),LENGTH=21,ATTRB=(PROT,ASKIP),             C00210023
         INITIAL='ADDRESS (2)       :'                                00220024
ADDR2    DFHMDF POS=(08,25),LENGTH=30,ATTRB=UNPROT                    00230026
         DFHMDF POS=(08,56),LENGTH=1,ATTRB=ASKIP                      00240034
TADDR3   DFHMDF POS=(09,01),LENGTH=21,ATTRB=(PROT,ASKIP),             C00250037
         INITIAL='ADDRESS (3)       :'                                00260024
ADDR3    DFHMDF POS=(09,25),LENGTH=21,ATTRB=UNPROT                    00270040
         DFHMDF POS=(09,56),LENGTH=1,ATTRB=ASKIP                      00280034
TSTATE   DFHMDF POS=(10,01),LENGTH=21,ATTRB=PROT,                     C00290037
         INITIAL='STATE             :'                                00300024
STATE    DFHMDF POS=(10,25),LENGTH=02,ATTRB=UNPROT                    00310026
         DFHMDF POS=(10,28),LENGTH=1,ATTRB=ASKIP                      00320034
TPOSTAL  DFHMDF POS=(11,01),LENGTH=21,ATTRB=(PROT,ASKIP),             C00330037
         INITIAL='POSTAL CODE       :'                                00340024
POSTCD   DFHMDF POS=(11,25),LENGTH=10,ATTRB=UNPROT                    00350040
         DFHMDF POS=(11,41),LENGTH=1,ATTRB=ASKIP                      00360034
TTEL     DFHMDF POS=(12,01),LENGTH=21,ATTRB=(PROT,ASKIP),             C00370037
         INITIAL='TELEPHONE         :'                                00380027
AREA     DFHMDF POS=(12,25),LENGTH=3,ATTRB=UNPROT                     00390028
         DFHMDF POS=(12,29),LENGTH=1,ATTRB=ASKIP                      00400034
TEL3     DFHMDF POS=(12,31),LENGTH=3,ATTRB=UNPROT                     00410036
         DFHMDF POS=(12,35),LENGTH=1,ATTRB=ASKIP                      00420036
TEL4     DFHMDF POS=(12,37),LENGTH=4,ATTRB=UNPROT                     00430036
         DFHMDF POS=(12,42),LENGTH=1,ATTRB=ASKIP                      00440036
         DFHMDF POS=(13,01),LENGTH=21,ATTRB=(PROT,ASKIP),             C00450032
         INITIAL='CONTACT NAME      :'                                00460024
CONTNAM  DFHMDF POS=(13,25),LENGTH=15,ATTRB=UNPROT                    00470026
         DFHMDF POS=(13,41),LENGTH=1,ATTRB=ASKIP                      00480034
         DFHMDF POS=(14,01),LENGTH=21,ATTRB=(PROT,ASKIP),             C00490032
         INITIAL='ABBREVIATED NAME  :'                                00500024
ABBNAME  DFHMDF POS=(14,25),LENGTH=15,ATTRB=UNPROT                    00510040
         DFHMDF POS=(14,41),LENGTH=1,ATTRB=ASKIP                      00520040
MMYY     DFHMDF POS=(15,01),LENGTH=21,ATTRB=(PROT,ASKIP),             C00530039
         INITIAL='ACCOUNT OPENED    :'                                00540039
MM       DFHMDF POS=(15,25),LENGTH=2,ATTRB=UNPROT                     00550026
         DFHMDF POS=(15,28),LENGTH=1,ATTRB=ASKIP                      00560034
YY       DFHMDF POS=(15,30),LENGTH=2,ATTRB=UNPROT                     00570035
         DFHMDF POS=(15,33),LENGTH=1,ATTRB=ASKIP                      00580035
         DFHMDF POS=(16,01),LENGTH=21,ATTRB=(PROT,ASKIP),             C00590033
         INITIAL='DUN & BRADSTREET NO:'                               00600042
DBNO     DFHMDF POS=(16,25),LENGTH=06,ATTRB=UNPROT                    00610040
         DFHMDF POS=(16,32),LENGTH=1,ATTRB=ASKIP                      00620034
         DFHMDF POS=(23,01),LENGTH=50,ATTRB=(PROT,ASKIP),             C00630041
         INITIAL='PF1: RETURN TO MENU    PF4: ADD RECORD'             00640041
MSSG     DFHMDF POS=(24,01),LENGTH=60,ATTRB=(PROT,ASKIP)              00650032
         DFHMDF POS=(24,62),LENGTH=1,ATTRB=ASKIP                      00660034
         DFHMSD TYPE=FINAL                                            00670001
         END                                                          00680001
```

```
AR92          CUSTOMER DATABASE MAINTENANCE                    0001


     CUSTOMER NUMBER     : STANDARD TOOL AND APPLIANCE
     CUSTOMER NAME       : HAMILTON, JOHN J
     ADDRESS (1)         : 12334 W 147TH STREET
     ADDRESS (2)         : CHICAGO
     ADDRESS (3)         :
     STATE               : IL
     POSTAL CODE         : 60607-0998
     TELEPHONE           : 312 765 8876
     CONTACT NAME        : DREW, CAROL
     ABBREVIATED NAME    : STDTA
     ACCOUNT OPENED      : 01 86
     DUN * BRADSTREET NO: 11234456




     PF1: RETURN TO MENU      PF4: ADD RECORD
```

5-5 Maintenance panel to add a customer to the customer database

Source program listing and narrative

As shown in FIG. 5-6, the ARA91C ADD program relies on a single position indicator, SEND-REC-FLAG, to control the initial and subsequent SENDING and RECEIVING cycles. This field is originally defined in line 8, which is a dumping area for the DFHCOMMAREA. Note that when the SEND-REC-FLAG equals the character "R," the system will initiate a receive map, which is how the pseudoconversational cycle is manipulated.

5-6 ARA91C

```
1    IDENTIFICATION DIVISION.
2    PROGRAM-ID. ARA91C.
3    DATE-COMPILED.
4    ENVIRONMENT DIVISION.
5    DATA DIVISION.
6    WORKING-STORAGE SECTION.
7    01   COMM-AREA.
8         02  SEND-REC-FLAG  PIC X(01).
9    01   CUSTOMER-MASTER. COPY RK501.
10   01   STORE-CUSTNO      PIC X(4).
11   COPY DFHBMSCA.
12   COPY DFHAID.
13   COPY CHARATR.
14   COPY ARA91M.
15   LINKAGE SECTION.
16   01   DFHCOMMAREA       PIC X(01).
17   PROCEDURE DIVISION.
18   001-START-PROCESSING.
19        IF EIBCALEN > 0
20        MOVE DFHCOMMAREA TO COMM-AREA.
21           EXEC CICS HANDLE AID
22           CLEAR(004-SEND-MAP)
23           PF1(170-RETURN-TO-SUBMENU)
24           PF4
25           ANYKEY(900-ANYKEY-OPTION)
26        END-EXEC.
27        EXEC CICS HANDLE CONDITION
```

```
28          MAPFAIL(700-MAPFAIL)
29          END-EXEC.
30          IF SEND-REC-FLAG = 'R' GO TO
31          005-RECEIVE-MAP.
32      004-SEND-MAP.
33          MOVE 'AR91' TO TRIDO.
34          MOVE EIBTRMID TO TERMO.
35          MOVE PROT TO TRIDA.
36          MOVE PROT-BRT TO TCUSTNOA.
37          MOVE -1 TO CUSTNOL.
38      004-SEND-MAP-2.
39          EXEC CICS SEND MAP('ARA91M7')
40          MAPSET('ARA91M')
41          ERASE
42          CURSOR
43          END-EXEC.
44          MOVE 'R' TO SEND-REC-FLAG.
45          GO TO 100-RETURN.
46      005-RECEIVE-MAP.
47          EXEC CICS RECEIVE MAP('ARA91M7')
48          MAPSET('ARA91M')
49          END-EXEC.
50      006-HANDLE-CONDITION.
51          EXEC CICS HANDLE CONDITION
52          NOTFND(008-CUSTOMER-MISSING)
53          END-EXEC.
54      007-READ-CUSTOMER-MASTER.
55          IF CUSTNOL = ZEROS OR CUSTNOI = SPACES
56          MOVE 'PLEASE ENTER CUSTOMER I.D.' TO MSSGO
57          MOVE PROT TO MSSGA
58          MOVE -1 TO CUSTNOL
59          MOVE PROT-BRT TO TCUSTNOA
60          GO TO 500-RESEND-MAP.
61          MOVE UNPROT-NUM-MDT TO CUSTNOA.
62          MOVE PROT TO TCUSTNOA.
63      ****************************************************************
64      * GET READY TO READ CUSTOMER MASTER                           *
65      ****************************************************************
66          MOVE CUSTNOI TO CUSTOMER-ID
67          EXEC CICS READ DATASET('RK501')
68          INTO(CUSTOMER-MASTER)
69          RIDFLD(CUSTOMER-KEY)
70          END-EXEC.
71          GO TO 102-RECORD-ALREADY-EXISTS.
72      008-CUSTOMER-MISSING.
73      ****************************************************************
74      * VALIDATE CUSTOMER NAME                                      *
75      ****************************************************************
76          IF CUSTNAML = ZEROS OR
77          CUSTNAMI = SPACES
78          MOVE 'CUSTOMER NAME IS MISSING' TO MSSGO
79          MOVE PROT TO MSSGA
80          MOVE -1 TO CUSTNAML
81          MOVE PROT-BRT TO TCUSTNMA
82          GO TO 500-RESEND-MAP.
83          MOVE UNPROT-NUM-MDT TO CUSTNAMA.
84          MOVE CUSTNAMI TO CUSTOMER-NAME.
85          MOVE PROT TO TCUSTNMA.
86      ****************************************************************
87      * VALIDATE FIRST LINE OF THE CUSTOMER ADDRESS                 *
88      ****************************************************************
89          IF ADDR1L = ZEROS OR ADDR1I = SPACES
90          MOVE 'MISSING STREET ADDRESS' TO MSSGO
91          MOVE -1 TO ADDR1L
92          MOVE PROT-BRT TO TADDR1A
93          MOVE PROT TO MSSGA
94          GO TO 500-RESEND-MAP.
95          MOVE ADDR1I TO CUSTOMER-ADDRESS1.
96          MOVE PROT TO TADDR1A.
97          MOVE UNPROT-ALPHA-MDT TO ADDR1A.
98      ****************************************************************
99      * ADDRESS LINES 2 IS MANDATORY, 3 IS OPTIONAL                 *
100     ****************************************************************
101         IF ADDR2L = 0 OR ADDR2I = SPACES
102         MOVE 'MISSING CITY LOCATION' TO MSSGO
103         MOVE -1 TO ADDR2L
104         MOVE PROT-BRT TO TADDR2A
105         MOVE PROT TO MSSGA
```

```
106        GO TO 500-RESEND-MAP.
107        MOVE PROT TO TADDR2A.
108        MOVE ADDR2I TO CUSTOMER-ADDRESS2.
109        MOVE UNPROT-ALPHA-MDT TO ADDR2A
110  *
111        IF ADDR3L NOT = 0 OR
112        ADDR3I NOT = SPACES
113        MOVE ADDR3I TO CUSTOMER-ADDRESS3.
114        MOVE PROT TO TADDR3A.
115  *****************************************************************
116  * CHECK THE PRESENCE OF THE STATE CODE                         *
117  *****************************************************************
118        IF STATEL = 0 OR STATEI = SPACE
119        MOVE 'MISSING STATE CODE' TO MSSGO
120        MOVE PROT TO MSSGA
121        MOVE -1 TO STATEL
122        MOVE PROT-BRT TO TSTATEA
123        GO TO 500-RESEND-MAP.
124        IF STATEI NUMERIC
125        MOVE 'STATE FIELD CANNOT CONTAIN NUMERICS' TO MSSGO
126        MOVE PROT TO MSSGA
127        MOVE -1 TO STATEL
128        MOVE PROT-BRT TO TSTATEA
129        GO TO 500-RESEND-MAP.
130        MOVE UNPROT-ALPHA-MDT TO STATEA.
131        MOVE STATEI TO CUSTOMER-STATE
132        MOVE PROT TO TSTATEA.
133  *****************************************************************
134  * STORE POSTAL CODE - NOT A MANDATORY FIELD                    *
135  *****************************************************************
136
137        IF POSTCDL = 0 OR POSTCDI = SPACES
138        MOVE 'MISSING ZIP CODE' TO MSSGO
139        MOVE PROT TO MSSGA
140        MOVE -1 TO POSTCDL
141        MOVE PROT-BRT TO TPOSTALA
142        GO TO 500-RESEND-MAP.
143
144        MOVE POSTCDI TO CUSTOMER-POSTAL-CODE.
145        MOVE UNPROT-ALPHA-MDT TO POSTCDA.
146        MOVE PROT TO TPOSTALA.
147
148  *****************************************************************
149  * CHECK THE PRESENCE OF A TELEPHONE NUMBER - MANDATORY FIELD*
150  *****************************************************************
151        IF AREAL = 0 OR AREAI = SPACES
152        MOVE 'YOU MUST ENTER AN AREA CODE' TO  MSSGO
153        MOVE PROT TO MSSGA
154        MOVE -1 TO AREAL
155        MOVE PROT-BRT TO TTELA
156        GO TO 500-RESEND-MAP.
157        MOVE PROT TO TTELA.
158
159        IF AREAI NOT NUMERIC
160        MOVE UNPROT-ALPHA-BRT-MDT TO AREAA
161        MOVE 'AREA CODE CANNOT BE ALPHA' TO MSSGO
162        MOVE PROT TO MSSGA
163        MOVE -1 TO AREAL
164        MOVE PROT-BRT TO TTELA
165        GO TO 500-RESEND-MAP.
166        MOVE UNPROT-ALPHA-MDT TO AREAA.
167        MOVE AREAI TO CUSTOMER-AREA-CODE.
168        MOVE PROT TO TTELA.
169  *
170        IF TEL3L = 0 OR TEL3I = SPACES
171        MOVE 'YOU MUST ENTER A TELEPHONE NUMBER' TO MSSGO
172        MOVE PROT TO MSSGA
173        MOVE -1 TO TEL3L
174        MOVE PROT-BRT TO TTELA
175        GO TO 500-RESEND-MAP.
176        MOVE UNPROT-ALPHA-MDT TO TEL3A.
177        MOVE TEL3I TO CUSTOMER-TEL1.
178        MOVE PROT TO TTELA.
179  *
180        IF TEL4L = 0 OR TEL4I = SPACES
181        MOVE 'YOU MUST ENTER A TELEPHONE NUMBER' TO MSSGO
182        MOVE PROT TO MSSGA
```

```
183        MOVE -1 TO TEL4L
184        MOVE PROT-BRT TO TTELA
185        GO TO 500-RESEND-MAP.
186        MOVE TEL4I TO CUSTOMER-TEL2.
187        MOVE PROT TO TTELA.
188        MOVE UNPROT-ALPHA-MDT TO TEL4A.
189 *
190 ************************************************************
191 * CHECK CONTACT NAME - NOT A MANDATORY FIELD              *
192 ************************************************************
193        IF CONTNAML = 0 OR CONTNAMI = SPACES
194        NEXT SENTENCE, ELSE
195        MOVE CONTNAMI TO CUSTOMER-CONTACT-NAME
196        MOVE UNPROT-ALPHA-MDT TO CONTNAMA.
197 ************************************************************
198 * ABBREVIATED NAME - NOT A MANDATORY FIELD                *
199 ************************************************************
200        IF ABBNAMEL = 0 OR ABBNAMEI = SPACES
201        NEXT SENTENCE, ELSE
202        MOVE ABBNAMEI TO CUSTOMER-ABBREVIATED-NAME
203        MOVE UNPROT-ALPHA-MDT TO ABBNAMEA.
204 ************************************************************
205 * ACCOUNT OPEN FIELDS - MADATORY (NUMERIC) FIELD          *
206 ************************************************************
207        IF MML NOT = 0
208        MOVE UNPROT-NUM-MDT TO MMA.
209        IF MMI = SPACES OR MMI NUMERIC
210        NEXT SENTENCE, ELSE
211        MOVE 'MONTH FIELD IS AN OPTIONAL NUMERIC FIELD'
212        TO MSSGO
213        MOVE PROT TO MSSGA
214        MOVE -1 TO MML
215        MOVE PROT-BRT TO MMYYA
216        GO TO 500-RESEND-MAP.
217        MOVE MMI TO CUSTOMER-MONTH.
218        MOVE UNPROT-NUM-MDT TO MMA.
219        MOVE PROT TO MMYYA.
220
221        IF YYL NOT = 0
222        MOVE UNPROT-NUM-MDT TO YYA.
223        IF YYI = SPACES OR YYI NUMERIC
224        NEXT SENTENCE, ELSE
225        MOVE 'YEAR FIELD IS AN OPTIONAL NUMERIC FIELD'
226        TO MSSGO
227        MOVE PROT TO MSSGA
228        MOVE -1 TO YYL
229        MOVE PROT-BRT TO MMYYA
230        GO TO 500-RESEND-MAP.
231        MOVE YYI TO CUSTOMER-YEAR
232        MOVE UNPROT-NUM-MDT TO YYA.
233        MOVE PROT TO MMYYA.
234
235
236 ************************************************************
237 * ENTER DUNN & BRADSTREET NUMBER                          *
238 ************************************************************
239        IF DBNOL = 0 OR DBNOI = SPACES
240        NEXT SENTENCE, ELSE
241        MOVE DBNOI TO CUSTOMER-DB-NUMBER
242        MOVE UNPROT-ALPHA-MDT TO DBNOA.
243 ************************************************************
244 * READY TO ADD NEW RECORD TO FILE                         *
245 ************************************************************
246        IF EIBAID = DFHPF4 GO TO 080-ADD-RECORD ELSE
247        MOVE 'RECORD IS READY FOR UPDATE' TO MSSGO
248        MOVE PROT TO MSSGA
249        MOVE -1 TO CUSTNOL
250        GO TO 500-RESEND-MAP.
251 *
252 080-ADD-RECORD.
253        MOVE CUSTNOI TO CUSTOMER-ID.
254        EXEC CICS WRITE DATASET('RK501')
255        FROM(CUSTOMER-MASTER)
256        RIDFLD(CUSTOMER-KEY)
257        END-EXEC.
258        MOVE CUSTNOI TO STORE-CUSTNO.
259        MOVE LOW-VALUES TO ARA91M70
260        MOVE -1 TO CUSTNOL
```

```
261        MOVE 'RECORD IS NOW UPDATED' TO MSSGO
262        MOVE STORE-CUSTNO TO CUSTNOI
263        MOVE ZEROS TO STORE-CUSTNO.
264        MOVE UNPROT-NUM-BRT TO CUSTNOA.
265        MOVE PROT TO MSSGA
266        GO TO 004-SEND-MAP.
267  ************************************************************
268  * SUBROUTINE SECTION                                      *
269  ************************************************************
270  100-RETURN.
271        EXEC CICS RETURN
272            TRANSID('AR91')
273            COMMAREA(COMM-AREA)
274            LENGTH(1)
275        END-EXEC.
276  102-RECORD-ALREADY-EXISTS.
277        MOVE 'RECORD ALREADY EXISTS' TO MSSGO
278        MOVE PROT TO MSSGA
279        MOVE -1 TO CUSTNOL
280        GO TO 500-RESEND-MAP.
281  170-RETURN-TO-SUBMENU.
282        MOVE ' ' TO SEND-REC-FLAG.
283        EXEC CICS XCTL PROGRAM('ARM90C')
284        COMMAREA(COMM-AREA)
285        LENGTH(1)
286        END-EXEC.
287        STOP RUN.
288        GOBACK.
289  500-RESEND-MAP.
290        EXEC CICS SEND MAP('ARA91M7')
291        MAPSET('ARA91M')
292        CURSOR
293        DATAONLY
294        END-EXEC.
295        MOVE 'R' TO SEND-REC-FLAG.
296        GO TO 100-RETURN.
297  700-MAPFAIL.
298        MOVE 'ENTER CUSTOMER NUMBER' TO MSSGO
299        MOVE PROT TO MSSGA
300        MOVE ' ' TO SEND-REC-FLAG
301        MOVE -1 TO CUSTNOL
302        GO TO 500-RESEND-MAP.
303  900-ANYKEY-OPTION.
304        MOVE 'INVALID KEY, PLEASE RESUBMIT' TO MSSGO.
305        MOVE PROT TO MSSGA
306        MOVE -1 TO CUSTNOL
307        GO TO 500-RESEND-MAP.
308
```

Line 9 shows a copy statement for the customer master or customer database, which provides a record layout in the copy library under the identifier K501. As shown in FIG. 5-8, this layout is physically loaded into the program. Other copy statements include the DFHBMSCA block (IBM's own attribute table). Some of the handicap associated with this map is that it is neither clear nor descriptive if you use a number of different attributes in a combined fashion.

Another problem with the way the DFHBMSCA is presented is that it is quite extensive, and as a general rule, most programmers do not need such a list. So, to be more practical, I used a table that was developed in-house and is referred to as CHARATR (shown in FIG. 5-8).

If you look at both the DFHBMSCA (shown in FIG. 5-6) and the CHARATR tables comparatively, you'll see how much easier it is to reference the latter, where the field names are more self-explanatory. In referring to attributes, you can also rely on a certain set of values, such as a "J" for an unprotected numeric field with its modified data tag turned on, or an "I" to denote an unprotected, intensified alpha field also using an MDT bit. However, to constantly reference values in this fashion can be confusing and at times difficult to follow for the programmer. It is also difficult to maintain and document such a program.

Other copy statements also include the DFHAID block and the mapset referred to as ARA91M. Although I have previously discussed the BMS (Basic Mapping Support) code required for this map, the actual appearance or output of that panel is shown in FIG. 5-5. The DFHAID is expanded in FIG. 5-8 in statements 109 through 144. The DFHAID block is responsible for describing keyboard usage to the user of the system.

The PROCEDURE DIVISION starts out with standard activities passed on by the previous menu program, such as the processing of a standard message in the communications area (COMMAREA). The reason you need this indicator is to establish a "first-time routine" in your program, which needs to be set apart from the rest. Next, in lines 21 through 26, two keys are defined in detail. These are the CLEAR and PF 1 keys. CLEAR parallels the use of PF 1, which is designed to return you to the previous subdirectory, the customer maintenance screen. PF 4 is initially undefined, but as shown in FIG. 5-6, line 246, PF 4 is used to update a particular record once the validation process is completed. All other keys are summarized under the general default paragraph of 900-ANYKEY-OPTION. This paragraph (lines 303 through 307), merely instructs the system to reissue the map and to display an error message, such as "INVALID KEY, PLEASE RESUBMIT."

The initial HANDLE CONDITION is established for a single purpose—to define to the system an alternate route in case a problem occurs while transmitting the map. This procedure is further expanded in lines 297 through 302, under the paragraph name of 700-MAPFAIL. The test differentiating SEND from RECEIVE MAP activities is performed in statements 30 through 31. Note that once a map is sent, you need to immediately replace the contents of the SEND-REC-FLAG so it will continuously trigger a branch to the right procedure. The fragmentation, or the "chopping up" of the SEND procedures into two different paragraphs (004-SEND-MAP and 004-SEND-MAP-2), is shown in lines 32 through 45.

Normally, you only need to use the latter portion of the send paragraph (004-SEND-MAP-2). However, once a record is completed you will probably issue a clear statement in which you will move low values into the map to blank it out, thus making it ready for the next transaction. In the process, of course, you need to rebuild the display screen from scratch. Once the map is sent, reinvoke the entire transaction, including the screen identifier, which is simply the TRANSID. This is highlighted in statements 270 through 275 of FIG. 5-6.

Once the map is received and processed by CICS, you need to set up an additional HANDLE CONDITION (lines 50 through 53) because of the upcoming READ. In reading a file, you must always instruct the system about an alternate route in case the record you are searching for cannot be located. Always issue a HANDLE-CONDITION prior to a READ operation to make sure that it is not overlaid by an earlier definition. If there is such a record on file, the program will shift to the 008-CUSTOMER-MISSING paragraph, which is further defined in line 72.

Since you are in ADD mode, your primary objective is to activate the ADD procedures only when the record in question cannot be located. An ERROR CONDITION exists only when such a record is already on file. This situation is characterized by the fact that no branching to the 008-CUSTOMER-MISSING paragraph is to take place after you have completed reading the file.

When issuing a READ, make sure you don't include the UPDATE option. If you do, you are going to get an INVREQ (invalid request) error condition, since CICS will not allow you to write a record with that option. Statements associated with the READ instruction are laid out in lines 55 through 71 of FIG. 5-6.

Note that there are two types of SEND statements used in this (as well as in other) programs. The only substantial difference between the two is that initially, you want to relay the entire map, both the data and the constant portions of it, to the terminal. In a subsequent cycle, however, you only need to transmit the data portion of your panel, (DATAONLY), which is entered by the user periodically. DATAONLY procedures are highlighted in statements 289 through 296 (500-RESEND-MAP). Likewise, an initial SEND MAP is shown in lines 38 through 45.

The editing process begins by validating the Customer's name, as well as the name of his or her business entity. Note that I followed a standardized structure in defining the process to the computer. Starting in statement 76, I have checked to see if the customer's name, which is a mandatory field, was entered by the terminal operator. This I know right away, just as soon as I check the length portion of the name (CUSTNAML). If the field contains zeros, I assume that either nothing was entered by the user or simply that whatever was entered must have been blanked out through the erase (EOF) key. In any case, there is nothing to validate in either situation.

The same constraint exists when the customer number is blanked out via the space bar (CUSTNAMI = SPACES). So, if there is an error, you might want to do the following. Generate and display an ERROR message. To display such an ERROR message, say in low-intensity protected blue, you want to move a bit into the field's attribute position, which was initially described in the CHARATR block. More on this later. To complete the error procedures, you must also move a –1 into the length portion of the field. Since the field is missing, you can inform the operator by modifying the original color of the title header. That is the purpose of statement 81, issued just before reissuing the SEND MAP command that contains an error message.

If the customer name is present, you want to:

- Move it into the output file to be written at a later time, when all edit rules have been compiled.

- Transform the associated title header back to its normal color, which is low-intensity blue in this particular situation.

This validation process follows the same logical structure throughout the entire program.

Statements 89 through 97 validate the first (mandatory) line of the customer master. Here again, the procedures just described are followed. If the first address field is present on the screen, it is moved into its specified record equivalent on file. Otherwise, the standard error procedure is to be invoked once again.

Likewise, validation for the second line of the customer address is performed in lines 101 through 114. Unlike the third address field, this entry, which normally contains the customer's city or town, is also a mandatory component. The term "mandatory" refers to the fact that the user needs to enter at least a single character into the field to avoid an edit check.

In viewing and editing the state code, the field must be entered as alphanumeric. The postal code is in its new format, containing 10 positions with an imbedded hyphen. This is described in statements 137 through 146.

In checking the telephone number, the following rules must be observed. The area code, which is a three-position long field, must be numeric and cannot be omitted. The rest of the telephone number (7 positions all together) can be alphanumeric. Blanks are disallowed. Logic for this process is highlighted in statements 151 through 188. Note that the entire telephone number is broken up into three separate fields, so that you can highlight any error caused by data omission.

The contact name and the abbreviated name fields are optional. The account open field, on the other hand, is mandatory to provide the user with some customer history. The term mandatory means that the field must be entered as numeric data. Logic for this procedure is built in lines 207 through 233.

Once the data is entered, the message "RECORD IS READY FOR UPDATE" will be displayed at the terminal. If you keep pressing the ENTER key at this point, for example, you will be reinvoking the edit cycle without physically updating, i.e., writing the record to the customer database. To produce such a record (and provided that the data is "clean," you can press PF 4 to complete the update process. Let me briefly explain to you the logic behind the update process, as shown in lines 252 through 266.

First of all, you need to build the record key, which requires the same process as the one you have already followed in reading the file. Once the record key is built and updated, you'll have to blank out the screen in its entirety to make it ready for the next transaction cycle. When you move low-values into the output map, it will erase all variable information on it, including a display of the transaction identifier used to identify a particular panel. When the screen is re-sent with the message "RECORD IS NOW UPDATED," you'll probably want to retain and display the customer number alone in bright red, to inform the terminal operator that such and such a record has been successfully updated. To accomplish this, I preserved the customer number by moving it into a storage area prior to the erasure (statement 258). Once the map is reinitialized and all subsequent instructions are executed, it will be safe to load the customer reference number back from storage and display it on the screen. A subroutine section is coded starting in statement 270. There are two additional procedures that were not covered in my earlier narrative:

- 102-RECORD-ALREADY-EXISTS
- 170-RETURN-TO-SUBMENU

The 102-RECORD-ALREADY-EXISTS paragraph (lines 276 through 280) is developed in case the operator tries to add an existing record to the customer database. Paragraph 170-RETURN-TO-SUB-MENU (lines 281 through 288) is designed to allow you to exit the current transaction cycle and return to the previous menu screen for another selection.

Compiler-generated source code: entire list

The compiler version of the ARA91C ADD program is shown in FIG. 5-7. Note that you need to rely on the compiled listing because of a number of references you have made earlier through *copy statements*. Copy statements are those denoted by the character "C" in the column immediately following the sequence numbers. As for the use of a particular copy library, you can build your own, or you might be required to use a standard copy library, depending on internal shop standards.

A copy of the customer master file is shown in statements 11 through 41. You have to realize, of course, that the layout presented to you is merely a format for the customer master file. Actual data is kept on a direct access device conforming to the format of the copy library member. Looking at the last data field (FILLER) of this record layout (statement 41), you can tell that this program maintains only a relatively narrow portion of the file. The rest of the file is accessed and utilized by other programs in the system.

Earlier, I recommended creating your own attribute table to make things a bit more clear than the IBM table. The table I suggested, CHARATR, enables you to have a better grasp of what some of the combined attribute bytes stand for, as shown in lines 148 through 175 of FIG. 5-7. Although I briefly reviewed some of the advantages of such a reference table, allow me to present some of my additional thoughts on this topic.

5-7 ARA91C compiler version

```
00001           IDENTIFICATION DIVISION.
00002           PROGRAM-ID. ARA91C.
00003           DATE-COMPILED. APR  6,1990.
00004           ENVIRONMENT DIVISION.
00005           DATA DIVISION.
00006           WORKING-STORAGE SECTION.
00007           01  COMM-AREA.
00008               02  SEND-REC-FLAG  PIC X(01).
00009           01  CUSTOMER-MASTER.
00010                       COPY RK501.
00011 C             02  FILLER                      PIC X(01).
00012 C             02  CUSTOMER-KEY.
00013 C                 05  CUSTOMER-COMPANY        PIC X(02) VALUE '01'.
00014 C                 05  CUSTOMER-SEGMENT        PIC X(01) VALUE '2'.
00015 C                 05  CUSTOMER-NUMBER.
00016 C                     10  CUSTOMER-PREFIX     PIC X(10) VALUE ZEROS.
00017 C                     10  CUSTOMER-ID         PIC X(04).
00018 C                 05  CUSTOMER-REFERENCE      PIC X(02) VALUE '01'.
00019 C                 05  FILLER                  PIC X(16) VALUE SPACES.
00020 C             02  DATA-AREA.
00021 C                 05  CUSTOMER-NAME           PIC X(30).
00022 C                 05  CUSTOMER-ADDRESS1       PIC X(30).
00023 C                 05  CUSTOMER-ADDRESS2       PIC X(30).
00024 C                 05  CUSTOMER-ADDRESS3       PIC X(21).
00025 C                 05  CUSTOMER-STATE          PIC X(02).
00026 C                 05  CUSTOMER-POSTAL-CODE    PIC X(10).
00027 C                 05  CUSTOMER-CONTACT-NAME   PIC X(15).
00028 C                 05  CUSTOMER-ABBREVIATED-NAME  PIC X(15).
00029 C                 05  CUSTOMER-ACCOUNT-OPENED.
```

```
00030 C                    10  CUSTOMER-MONTH           PIC X(02).
00031 C                    10  CUSTOMER-YEAR            PIC X(02).
00032 C              05  FILLER                         PIC X(06).
00033 C              05  CUSTOMER-TELEPHONE-NO.
00034 C                    10  FILLER                   PIC X(02).
00035 C                    10  CUSTOMER-AREA-CODE       PIC X(03).
00036 C                    10  CUSTOMER-TELEPHONE.
00037 C                          15  CUSTOMER-TEL1      PIC X(03).
00038 C                          15  CUSTOMER-TEL2      PIC X(04).
00039 C              05  FILLER                         PIC X(28).
00040 C              05  CUSTOMER-DB-NUMBER             PIC X(10).
00041 C              05  FILLER                         PIC X(851).
00042         01  STORE-CUSTNO       PIC X(4).
00043         COPY DFHBMSCA.
00044 C       01      DFHBMSCA.
00045 C          02    DFHBMPEM   PICTURE X    VALUE IS ' '.
00046 C          02    DFHBMPNL   PICTURE X    VALUE IS ' '.
00047 C          02    DFHBMASK   PICTURE X    VALUE IS '0'.
00048 C          02    DFHBMUNP   PICTURE X    VALUE IS ' '.
00049 C          02    DFHBMUNN   PICTURE X    VALUE IS '&'.
00050 C          02    DFHBMPRO   PICTURE X    VALUE IS '-'.
00051 C          02    DFHBMBRY   PICTURE X    VALUE IS 'H'.
00052 C          02    DFHBMDAR   PICTURE X    VALUE IS '<'.
00053 C          02    DFHBMFSE   PICTURE X    VALUE IS 'A'.
00054 C          02    DFHBMPRF   PICTURE X    VALUE IS '/'.
00055 C          02    DFHBMASF   PICTURE X    VALUE IS '1'.
00056 C          02    DFHBMASB   PICTURE X    VALUE IS '8'.
00057 C          02    DFHBMEOF   PICTURE X    VALUE IS ' '.
00058 C          02    DFHBMDET   PICTURE X    VALUE IS ' '.
00059 C          02    DFHBMPSO   PICTURE X    VALUE IS ' '.
00060 C          02    DFHBMPSI   PICTURE X    VALUE IS ' '.
00061 C          02    DFHSA      PICTURE X    VALUE IS ' '.
00062 C          02    DFHCOLOR   PICTURE X    VALUE IS ' '.
00063 C          02    DFHPS      PICTURE X    VALUE IS ' '.
00064 C          02    DFHHLT     PICTURE X    VALUE IS ' '.
00065 C          02    DFH3270    PICTURE X    VALUE IS '{'.
00066 C          02    DFHVAL     PICTURE X    VALUE IS 'A'.
00067 C          02    DFHOUTLN   PICTURE X    VALUE IS 'B'.
00068 C          02    DFHBKTRN   PICTURE X    VALUE IS ' '.
00069 C          02    DFHALL     PICTURE X    VALUE IS ' '.
00070 C          02    DFHERROR   PICTURE X    VALUE IS ' '.
00071 C          02    DFHDFT     PICTURE X    VALUE IS ' '.
00072 C          02    DFHDFCOL   PICTURE X    VALUE IS ' '.
00073 C          02    DFHBLUE    PICTURE X    VALUE IS '1'.
00074 C          02    DFHRED     PICTURE X    VALUE IS '2'.
00075 C          02    DFHPINK    PICTURE X    VALUE IS '3'.
00076 C          02    DFHGREEN   PICTURE X    VALUE IS '4'.
00077 C          02    DFHTURQ    PICTURE X    VALUE IS '5'.
00078 C          02    DFHYELLO   PICTURE X    VALUE IS '6'.
00079 C          02    DFHNEUTR   PICTURE X    VALUE IS '7'.
00080 C          02    DFHBASE    PICTURE X    VALUE IS ' '.
00081 C          02    DFHDFHI    PICTURE X    VALUE IS ' '.
00082 C          02    DFHBLINK   PICTURE X    VALUE IS '1'.
00083 C          02    DFHREVRS   PICTURE X    VALUE IS '2'.
00084 C          02    DFHUNDLN   PICTURE X    VALUE IS '4'.
00085 C          02    DFHMFIL    PICTURE X    VALUE IS ' '.
00086 C          02    DFHMENT    PICTURE X    VALUE IS ' '.
00087 C          02    DFHMFE     PICTURE X    VALUE IS ' '.
00088 C          02    DFHUNNOD   PICTURE X    VALUE IS '('.
00089 C          02    DFHUNIMD   PICTURE X    VALUE IS 'I'.
00090 C          02    DFHUNNUM   PICTURE X    VALUE IS 'J'.
00091 C          02    DFHUNINT   PICTURE X    VALUE IS 'R'.
00092 C          02    DFHUNNON   PICTURE X    VALUE IS ')'.
00093 C          02    DFHPROTI   PICTURE X    VALUE IS 'Y'.
00094 C          02    DFHPROTN   PICTURE X    VALUE IS '%'.
00095 C          02    DFHMT      PICTURE X    VALUE IS ' '.
00096 C          02    DFHMFT     PICTURE X    VALUE IS ' '.
00097 C          02    DFHMET     PICTURE X    VALUE IS ' '.
00098 C          02    DFHMFET    PICTURE X    VALUE IS ' '.
00099 C          02    DFHDFFR    PICTURE X    VALUE IS ' '.
00100 C          02    DFHLEFT    PICTURE X    VALUE IS ' '.
00101 C          02    DFHOVER    PICTURE X    VALUE IS ' '.
00102 C          02    DFHRIGHT   PICTURE X    VALUE IS ' '.
00103 C          02    DFHUNDER   PICTURE X    VALUE IS ' '.
00104 C          02    DFHBOX     PICTURE X    VALUE IS ' '.
00105 C          02    DFHSOSI    PICTURE X    VALUE IS ' '.
```

```
00106 C         02    DFHTRANS  PICTURE X   VALUE  IS  'O'.
00107 C         02    DFHOPAQ   PICTURE X   VALUE  IS  ' '.
00108           COPY DFHAID.
00109 C    01   DFHAID.
00110 C         02   DFHNULL   PIC  X  VALUE IS ' '.
00111 C         02   DFHENTER  PIC  X  VALUE IS QUOTE.
00112 C         02   DFHCLEAR  PIC  X  VALUE IS ' '.
00113 C         02   DFHCLRP   PIC  X  VALUE IS 'T'.
00114 C         02   DFHPEN    PIC  X  VALUE IS '='.
00115 C         02   DFHOPID   PIC  X  VALUE IS 'W'.
00116 C         02   DFHMSRE   PIC  X  VALUE IS 'X'.
00117 C         02   DFHSTRF   PIC  X  VALUE IS 'h'.
00118 C         02   DFHTRIG   PIC  X  VALUE IS '"'.
00119 C         02   DFHPA1    PIC  X  VALUE IS '%'.
00120 C         02   DFHPA2    PIC  X  VALUE IS '>'.
00121 C         02   DFHPA3    PIC  X  VALUE IS ','.
00122 C         02   DFHPF1    PIC  X  VALUE IS '1'.
00123 C         02   DFHPF2    PIC  X  VALUE IS '2'.
00124 C         02   DFHPF3    PIC  X  VALUE IS '3'.
00125 C         02   DFHPF4    PIC  X  VALUE IS '4'.
00126 C         02   DFHPF5    PIC  X  VALUE IS '5'.
00127 C         02   DFHPF6    PIC  X  VALUE IS '6'.
00128 C         02   DFHPF7    PIC  X  VALUE IS '7'.
00129 C         02   DFHPF8    PIC  X  VALUE IS '8'.
00130 C         02   DFHPF9    PIC  X  VALUE IS '9'.
00131 C         02   DFHPF10   PIC  X  VALUE IS ':'.
00132 C         02   DFHPF11   PIC  X  VALUE IS '#'.
00133 C         02   DFHPF12   PIC  X  VALUE IS '@'.
00134 C         02   DFHPF13   PIC  X  VALUE IS 'A'.
00135 C         02   DFHPF14   PIC  X  VALUE IS 'B'.
00136 C         02   DFHPF15   PIC  X  VALUE IS 'C'.
00137 C         02   DFHPF16   PIC  X  VALUE IS 'D'.
00138 C         02   DFHPF17   PIC  X  VALUE IS 'E'.
00139 C         02   DFHPF18   PIC  X  VALUE IS 'F'.
00140 C         02   DFHPF19   PIC  X  VALUE IS 'G'.
00141 C         02   DFHPF20   PIC  X  VALUE IS 'H'.
00142 C         02   DFHPF21   PIC  X  VALUE IS 'I'.
00143 C         02   DFHPF22   PIC  X  VALUE IS '¢'.
00144 C         02   DFHPF23   PIC  X  VALUE IS '.'.
00145 C         02   DFHPF24   PIC  X  VALUE IS '<'.
00146           COPY CHARATR.
00147 C    *------------*  ATTRIBUTE-BYTES  *----------------------------
00148 C    01   CHARATR.
00149 C         05   UNPROT-ALPHA            PIC X    VALUE SPACE.
00150 C         05   UNPROT-ALPHA-MDT        PIC X    VALUE 'A'.
00151 C         05   UNPROT-ALPHA-BRT        PIC X    VALUE 'H'.
00152 C         05   UNPROT-ALPHA-BRT-MDT    PIC X    VALUE 'I'.
00153 C         05   UNPROT-ALPHA-DRK        PIC X    VALUE '<'.
00154 C         05   UNPROT-ALPHA-DRK-MDT    PIC X    VALUE '('.
00155 C         05   UNPROT-NUM              PIC X    VALUE '&'.
00156 C         05   UNPROT-NUM-MDT          PIC X    VALUE 'J'.
00157 C         05   UNPROT-NUM-BRT          PIC X    VALUE 'Q'.
00158 C         05   UNPROT-NUM-BRT-MDT      PIC X    VALUE 'R'.
00159 C         05   UNPROT-NUM-DRK          PIC X    VALUE '*'.
00160 C         05   UNPROT-NUM-DRK-MDT      PIC X    VALUE ')'.
00161 C         05   PROT                    PIC X    VALUE '-'.
00162 C         05   PROT-MDT                PIC X    VALUE '/'.
00163 C         05   PROT-BRT                PIC X    VALUE 'Y'.
00164 C         05   PROT-BRT-MDT            PIC X    VALUE 'Z'.
00165 C         05   PROT-DRK                PIC X    VALUE '%'.
00166 C         05   PROT-DRK-MDT            PIC X    VALUE ' '.
00167 C         05   ASKIP                   PIC X    VALUE '0'.
00168 C         05   ASKIP-MDT               PIC X    VALUE '1'.
00169 C         05   ASKIP-BRT               PIC X    VALUE '8'.
00170 C         05   ASKIP-BRT-MDT           PIC X    VALUE '9'.
00171 C         05   ASKIP-DRK               PIC X    VALUE '@'.
00172 C         05   ASKIP-DRK-MDT           PIC X    VALUE QUOTE.
00173 C    *--------------*  LENGTH BYTES  *----------------------------
00174 C    01   LENGTH-BYTES.
00175 C         05   CSR-REPO                PIC S9(4) COMP VALUE -1.
00176           COPY ARA91M.
00177 C    01   ARA91M7I.
00178 C         02   FILLER PIC X(12).
00179 C         02   TRIDL    COMP PIC  S9(4).
00180 C         02   TRIDF    PICTURE X.
00181 C         02   FILLER REDEFINES TRIDF.
00182 C           03 TRIDA    PICTURE X.
00183 C         02   TRIDI PIC X(4).
```

```
00184 C        02  TERML    COMP  PIC  S9(4).
00185 C        02  TERMF    PICTURE X.
00186 C        02  FILLER REDEFINES TERMF.
00187 C           03 TERMA    PICTURE X.
00188 C        02  TERMI  PIC X(8).
00189 C        02  TCUSTNOL    COMP  PIC  S9(4).
00190 C        02  TCUSTNOF    PICTURE X.
00191 C        02  FILLER REDEFINES TCUSTNOF.
00192 C           03 TCUSTNOA    PICTURE X.
00193 C        02  TCUSTNOI  PIC X(21).
00194 C        02  CUSTNOL    COMP  PIC  S9(4).
00195 C        02  CUSTNOF    PICTURE X.
00196 C        02  FILLER REDEFINES CUSTNOF.
00197 C           03 CUSTNOA    PICTURE X.
00198 C        02  CUSTNOI  PIC X(4).
00199 C        02  TCUSTNML    COMP  PIC  S9(4).
00200 C        02  TCUSTNMF    PICTURE X.
00201 C        02  FILLER REDEFINES TCUSTNMF.
00202 C           03 TCUSTNMA    PICTURE X.
00203 C        02  TCUSTNMI  PIC X(21).
00204 C        02  CUSTNAML    COMP  PIC  S9(4).
00205 C        02  CUSTNAMF    PICTURE X.
00206 C        02  FILLER REDEFINES CUSTNAMF.
00207 C           03 CUSTNAMA    PICTURE X.
00208 C        02  CUSTNAMI  PIC X(30).
00209 C        02  TADDR1L    COMP  PIC  S9(4).
00210 C        02  TADDR1F    PICTURE X.
00211 C        02  FILLER REDEFINES TADDR1F.
00212 C           03 TADDR1A    PICTURE X.
00213 C        02  TADDR1I  PIC X(21).
00214 C        02  ADDR1L    COMP  PIC  S9(4).
00215 C        02  ADDR1F    PICTURE X.
00216 C        02  FILLER REDEFINES ADDR1F.
00217 C           03 ADDR1A    PICTURE X.
00218 C        02  ADDR1I  PIC X(30).
00219 C        02  TADDR2L    COMP  PIC  S9(4).
00220 C        02  TADDR2F    PICTURE X.
00221 C        02  FILLER REDEFINES TADDR2F.
00222 C           03 TADDR2A    PICTURE X.
00223 C        02  TADDR2I  PIC X(21).
00224 C        02  ADDR2L    COMP  PIC  S9(4).
00225 C        02  ADDR2F    PICTURE X.
00226 C        02  FILLER REDEFINES ADDR2F.
00227 C           03 ADDR2A    PICTURE X.
00228 C        02  ADDR2I  PIC X(30).
00229 C        02  TADDR3L    COMP  PIC  S9(4).
00230 C        02  TADDR3F    PICTURE X.
00231 C        02  FILLER REDEFINES TADDR3F.
00232 C           03 TADDR3A    PICTURE X.
00233 C        02  TADDR3I  PIC X(21).
00234 C        02  ADDR3L    COMP  PIC  S9(4).
00235 C        02  ADDR3F    PICTURE X.
00236 C        02  FILLER REDEFINES ADDR3F.
00237 C           03 ADDR3A    PICTURE X.
00238 C        02  ADDR3I  PIC X(21).
00239 C        02  TSTATEL    COMP  PIC  S9(4).
00240 C        02  TSTATEF    PICTURE X.
00241 C        02  FILLER REDEFINES TSTATEF.
00242 C           03 TSTATEA    PICTURE X.
00243 C        02  TSTATEI  PIC X(21).
00244 C        02  STATEL    COMP  PIC  S9(4).
00245 C        02  STATEF    PICTURE X.
00246 C        02  FILLER REDEFINES STATEF.
00247 C           03 STATEA    PICTURE X.
00248 C        02  STATEI  PIC X(2).
00249 C        02  TPOSTALL    COMP  PIC  S9(4).
00250 C        02  TPOSTALF    PICTURE X.
00251 C        02  FILLER REDEFINES TPOSTALF.
00252 C           03 TPOSTALA    PICTURE X.
00253 C        02  TPOSTALI  PIC X(21).
00254 C        02  POSTCDL    COMP  PIC  S9(4).
00255 C        02  POSTCDF    PICTURE X.
00256 C        02  FILLER REDEFINES POSTCDF.
00257 C           03 POSTCDA    PICTURE X.
00258 C        02  POSTCDI  PIC X(10).
00259 C        02  TTELL    COMP  PIC  S9(4).
```

```
00260 C          02  TTELF    PICTURE X.
00261 C          02  FILLER REDEFINES TTELF.
00262 C             03 TTELA    PICTURE X.
00263 C          02  TTELI  PIC X(21).
00264 C          02  AREAL    COMP  PIC  S9(4).
00265 C          02  AREAF    PICTURE X.
00266 C          02  FILLER REDEFINES AREAF.
00267 C             03 AREAA    PICTURE X.
00268 C          02  AREAI  PIC X(3).
00269 C          02  TEL3L    COMP  PIC  S9(4).
00270 C          02  TEL3F    PICTURE X.
00271 C          02  FILLER REDEFINES TEL3F.
00272 C             03 TEL3A    PICTURE X.
00273 C          02  TEL3I  PIC X(3).
00274 C          02  TEL4L    COMP  PIC  S9(4).
00275 C          02  TEL4F    PICTURE X.
00276 C          02  FILLER REDEFINES TEL4F.
00277 C             03 TEL4A    PICTURE X.
00278 C          02  TEL4I  PIC X(4).
00279 C          02  CONTNAML    COMP PIC  S9(4).
00280 C          02  CONTNAMF    PICTURE X.
00281 C          02  FILLER REDEFINES CONTNAMF.
00282 C             03 CONTNAMA    PICTURE X.
00283 C          02  CONTNAMI PIC X(15).
00284 C          02  ABBNAMEL    COMP PIC  S9(4).
00285 C          02  ABBNAMEF    PICTURE X.
00286 C          02  FILLER REDEFINES ABBNAMEF.
00287 C             03 ABBNAMEA    PICTURE X.
00288 C          02  ABBNAMEI PIC X(15).
00289 C          02  MMYYL    COMP  PIC  S9(4).
00290 C          02  MMYYF    PICTURE X.
00291 C          02  FILLER REDEFINES MMYYF.
00292 C             03 MMYYA    PICTURE X.
00293 C          02  MMYYI  PIC X(21).
00294 C          02  MML    COMP  PIC  S9(4).
00295 C          02  MMF      PICTURE X.
00296 C          02  FILLER REDEFINES MMF.
00297 C             03 MMA    PICTURE X.
00298 C          02  MMI  PIC X(2).
00299 C          02  YYL    COMP  PIC  S9(4).
00300 C          02  YYF      PICTURE X.
00301 C          02  FILLER REDEFINES YYF.
00302 C             03 YYA    PICTURE X.
00303 C          02  YYI  PIC X(2).
00304 C          02  DBNOL    COMP  PIC  S9(4).
00305 C          02  DBNOF    PICTURE X.
00306 C          02  FILLER REDEFINES DBNOF.
00307 C             03 DBNOA    PICTURE X.
00308 C          02  DBNOI  PIC X(6).
00309 C          02  MSSGL    COMP  PIC  S9(4).
00310 C          02  MSSGF    PICTURE X.
00311 C          02  FILLER REDEFINES MSSGF.
00312 C             03 MSSGA    PICTURE X.
00313 C          02  MSSGI  PIC X(60).
00314 C       01  ARA91M7O REDEFINES ARA91M7I.
00315 C          02  FILLER PIC X(12).
00316 C          02  FILLER PICTURE X(3).
00317 C          02  TRIDO  PIC X(4).
00318 C          02  FILLER PICTURE X(3).
00319 C          02  TERMO  PIC X(8).
00320 C          02  FILLER PICTURE X(3).
00321 C          02  TCUSTNOO  PIC X(21).
00322 C          02  FILLER PICTURE X(3).
00323 C          02  CUSTNOO  PIC X(4).
00324 C          02  FILLER PICTURE X(3).
00325 C          02  TCUSTNMO  PIC X(21).
00326 C          02  FILLER PICTURE X(3).
00327 C          02  CUSTNAMO  PIC X(30).
00328 C          02  FILLER PICTURE X(3).
00329 C          02  TADDR1O  PIC X(21).
00330 C          02  FILLER PICTURE X(3).
00331 C          02  ADDR1O  PIC X(30).
00332 C          02  FILLER PICTURE X(3).
00333 C          02  TADDR2O  PIC X(21).
00334 C          02  FILLER PICTURE X(3).
00335 C          02  ADDR2O  PIC X(30).
00336 C          02  FILLER PICTURE X(3).
00337 C          02  TADDR3O  PIC X(21).
```

```
00338 C        02  FILLER PICTURE X(3).
00339 C        02  ADDR3O  PIC X(21).
00340 C        02  FILLER PICTURE X(3).
00341 C        02  TSTATEO  PIC X(21).
00342 C        02  FILLER PICTURE X(3).
00343 C        02  STATEO  PIC X(2).
00344 C        02  FILLER PICTURE X(3).
00345 C        02  TPOSTALO  PIC X(21).
00346 C        02  FILLER PICTURE X(3).
00347 C        02  POSTCDO  PIC X(10).
00348 C        02  FILLER PICTURE X(3).
00349 C        02  TTELO  PIC X(21).
00350 C        02  FILLER PICTURE X(3).
00351 C        02  AREAO  PIC X(3).
00352 C        02  FILLER PICTURE X(3).
00353 C        02  TEL3O  PIC X(3).
00354 C        02  FILLER PICTURE X(3).
00355 C        02  TEL4O  PIC X(4).
00356 C        02  FILLER PICTURE X(3).
00357 C        02  CONTNAMO  PIC X(15).
00358 C        02  FILLER PICTURE X(3).
00359 C        02  ABBNAMEO  PIC X(15).
00360 C        02  FILLER PICTURE X(3).
00361 C        02  MMYYO  PIC X(21).
00362 C        02  FILLER PICTURE X(3).
00363 C        02  MMO  PIC X(2).
00364 C        02  FILLER PICTURE X(3).
00365 C        02  YYO  PIC X(2).
00366 C        02  FILLER PICTURE X(3).
00367 C        02  DBNOO  PIC X(6).
00368 C        02  FILLER PICTURE X(3).
00369 C        02  MSSGO  PIC X(60).
00370      01  DFHLDVER PIC X(22) VALUE 'LD TABLE DFHEITAB 210.'.
00371      01  DFHEIDO PICTURE S9(7) COMPUTATIONAL-3 VALUE ZERO.
00372      01  DFHEIBO PICTURE S9(4) COMPUTATIONAL VALUE ZERO.
00373      01  DFHEICB  PICTURE X(8) VALUE IS '        '.
00374
00375      01  DFHEIV16  COMP PIC S9(8).
00376      01  DFHB0041  COMP PIC S9(8).
00377      01  DFHB0042  COMP PIC S9(8).
00378      01  DFHB0043  COMP PIC S9(8).
00379      01  DFHB0044  COMP PIC S9(8).
00380      01  DFHB0045  COMP PIC S9(8).
00381      01  DFHB0046  COMP PIC S9(8).
00382      01  DFHB0047  COMP PIC S9(8).
00383      01  DFHB0048  COMP PIC S9(8).
00384      01  DFHEIV11  COMP PIC S9(4).
00385      01  DFHEIV12  COMP PIC S9(4).
00386      01  DFHEIV13  COMP PIC S9(4).
00387      01  DFHEIV14  COMP PIC S9(4).
00388      01  DFHEIV15  COMP PIC S9(4).
00389      01  DFHB0025  COMP PIC S9(4).
00390      01  DFHEIV5   PIC X(4).
00391      01  DFHEIV6   PIC X(4).
00392      01  DFHEIV17  PIC X(4).
00393      01  DFHEIV18  PIC X(4).
00394      01  DFHEIV19  PIC X(4).
00395      01  DFHEIV1   PIC X(8).
00396      01  DFHEIV2   PIC X(8).
00397      01  DFHEIV3   PIC X(8).
00398      01  DFHEIV20  PIC X(8).
00399      01  DFHC0084  PIC X(8).
00400      01  DFHC0085  PIC X(8).
00401      01  DFHC0320  PIC X(32).
00402      01  DFHEIV7   PIC X(2).
00403      01  DFHEIV8   PIC X(2).
00404      01  DFHC0022  PIC X(2).
00405      01  DFHC0023  PIC X(2).
00406      01  DFHEIV10  PIC S9(7) COMP-3.
00407      01  DFHEIV9   PIC X(1).
00408      01  DFHC0011  PIC X(1).
00409      01  DFHEIV4   PIC X(6).
00410      01  DFHC0070  PIC X(7).
00411      01  DFHC0071  PIC X(7).
00412      01  DFHC0440  PIC X(44).
00413      01  DFHDUMMY COMP PIC S9(4).
```

```
00414          01   DFHEIVO  PICTURE X(29).
00415          LINKAGE SECTION.
00416          01   DFHEIBLK.
00417          02      EIBTIME  PIC S9(7) COMP-3.
00418          02      EIBDATE  PIC S9(7) COMP-3.
00419          02      EIBTRNID PIC X(4).
00420          02      EIBTASKN PIC S9(7) COMP-3.
00421          02      EIBTRMID PIC X(4).
00422          02      DFHEIGDI COMP PIC S9(4).
00423          02      EIBCPOSN COMP PIC S9(4).
00424          02      EIBCALEN COMP PIC S9(4).
00425          02      EIBAID   PIC X(1).
00426          02      EIBFN    PIC X(2).
00427          02      EIBRCODE PIC X(6).
00428          02      EIBDS    PIC X(8).
00429          02      EIBREQID PIC X(8).
00430          02      EIBRSRCE PIC X(8).
00431          02      EIBSYNC  PIC X(1).
00432          02      EIBFREE  PIC X(1).
00433          02      EIBRECV  PIC X(1).
00434          02      EIBFIL01 PIC X(1).
00435          02      EIBATT   PIC X(1).
00436          02      EIBEOC   PIC X(1).
00437          02      EIBFMH   PIC X(1).
00438          02      EIBCOMPL PIC X(1).
00439          02      EIBSIG   PIC X(1).
00440          02      EIBCONF  PIC X(1).
00441          02      EIBERR   PIC X(1).
00442          02      EIBERRCD PIC X(4).
00443          02      EIBSYNRB PIC X(1).
00444          02      EIBNODAT PIC X(1).
00445          02      EIBRESP  COMP PIC S9(8).
00446          02      EIBRESP2 COMP PIC S9(8).
00447          02      EIBRLDBK PIC X(1).
00448          01   DFHCOMMAREA          PIC X(01).
00449          01   DFHBLLSLOT1 PICTURE X(1).
00450          01   DFHBLLSLOT2 PICTURE X(1).
00451          PROCEDURE DIVISION USING DFHEIBLK DFHCOMMAREA.
00452               CALL 'DFHEI1'.
00453               SERVICE RELOAD DFHEIBLK.
00454               SERVICE RELOAD DFHCOMMAREA.
00455          001-START-PROCESSING.
00456               IF EIBCALEN > 0
00457               MOVE DFHCOMMAREA TO COMM-AREA.
00458          *EXEC CICS HANDLE AID
00459          *CLEAR(004-SEND-MAP)
00460          *PF1(170-RETURN-TO-SUBMENU)
00461          *PF4
00462          *ANYKEY(900-ANYKEY-OPTION)                              END
00463          *EXEC.
00464               MOVE ' \               00021   ' TO DFHEIVO
00465               CALL 'DFHEI1' USING DFHEIVO
00466               GO TO  004-SEND-MAP 170-RETURN-TO-SUBMENU
00467               900-ANYKEY-OPTION DEPENDING ON DFHEIGDI.
00468
00469
00470          *EXEC CICS HANDLE CONDITION
00471          *MAPFAIL(700-MAPFAIL)
00472          *END-EXEC.
00473               MOVE '                00027   ' TO DFHEIVO
00474               CALL 'DFHEI1' USING DFHEIVO
00475               GO TO  700-MAPFAIL DEPENDING ON DFHEIGDI.
00476               IF SEND-REC-FLAG = 'R' GO TO
00477               005-RECEIVE-MAP.
00478          004-SEND-MAP.
00479               MOVE 'AR91' TO TRIDO.
00480               MOVE EIBTRMID TO TERMO.
00481               MOVE PROT TO TRIDA.
00482               MOVE PROT-BRT TO TCUSTNOA.
00483               MOVE -1 TO CUSTNOL.
00484          004-SEND-MAP-2.
00485          *EXEC CICS SEND MAP('ARA91M7')
00486          *MAPSET('ARA91M')
00487          *ERASE
00488          *CURSOR
00489          *END-EXEC.
00490               MOVE ' J      S    00039   ' TO DFHEIVO
00491               MOVE 'ARA91M7' TO DFHC0070
```

```
00492              MOVE 'ARA91M' TO DFHC0071
00493              MOVE -1 TO DFHEIV11
00494              CALL 'DFHEI1' USING DFHEIV0  DFHC0070 ARA91M7O DFHDUMMY
00495              DFHC0071 DFHDUMMY DFHDUMMY DFHDUMMY DFHEIV11.
00496              MOVE 'R' TO SEND-REC-FLAG.
00497              GO TO 100-RETURN.
00498          005-RECEIVE-MAP.
00499      *EXEC CICS RECEIVE MAP('ARA91M7')
00500      *MAPSET('ARA91M')
00501      *END-EXEC.
00502              MOVE ' }              00047   ' TO DFHEIV0
00503              MOVE 'ARA91M7' TO DFHC0070
00504              MOVE 'ARA91M' TO DFHC0071
00505              CALL 'DFHEI1' USING DFHEIV0  DFHC0070 ARA91M7I DFHDUMMY
00506              DFHC0071.
00507          006-HANDLE-CONDITION.
00508      *EXEC CICS HANDLE CONDITION
00509      *NOTFND(008-CUSTOMER-MISSING)
00510      *END-EXEC.
00511              MOVE '                   00051   ' TO DFHEIV0
00512              CALL 'DFHEI1' USING DFHEIV0
00513              GO TO  008-CUSTOMER-MISSING DEPENDING ON DFHEIGDI.
00514          007-READ-CUSTOMER-MASTER.
00515              IF CUSTNOL = ZEROS OR CUSTNOI = SPACES
00516              MOVE 'PLEASE ENTER CUSTOMER I.D.' TO MSSGO
00517              MOVE PROT TO MSSGA
00518              MOVE -1 TO CUSTNOL
00519              MOVE PROT-BRT TO TCUSTNOA
00520              GO TO 500-RESEND-MAP.
00521              MOVE UNPROT-NUM-MDT TO CUSTNOA.
00522              MOVE PROT TO TCUSTNOA.
00523      **************************************************************
00524      * GET READY TO READ CUSTOMER MASTER                         *
00525      **************************************************************
00526              MOVE CUSTNOI TO CUSTOMER-ID
00527      *EXEC CICS READ DATASET('RK501')
00528      *INTO(CUSTOMER-MASTER)
00529      *RIDFLD(CUSTOMER-KEY)
00530      *END-EXEC.
00531              MOVE ' }       00067   ' TO DFHEIV0
00532              MOVE 'RK501' TO DFHEIV1
00533              CALL 'DFHEI1' USING DFHEIV0  DFHEIV1  CUSTOMER-MASTER
00534              DFHDUMMY CUSTOMER-KEY.
00535              GO TO 102-RECORD-ALREADY-EXISTS.
00536          008-CUSTOMER-MISSING.
00537      **************************************************************
00538      * VALIDATE CUSTOMER NAME                                    *
00539      **************************************************************
00540              IF CUSTNAML = ZEROS OR
00541              CUSTNAMI = SPACES
00542              MOVE 'CUSTOMER NAME IS MISSING' TO MSSGO
00543              MOVE PROT TO MSSGA
00544              MOVE -1 TO CUSTNAML
00545              MOVE PROT-BRT TO TCUSTNMA
00546              GO TO 500-RESEND-MAP.
00547              MOVE UNPROT-NUM-MDT TO CUSTNAMA.
00548              MOVE CUSTNAMI TO CUSTOMER-NAME.
00549              MOVE PROT TO TCUSTNMA.
00550      **************************************************************
00551      * VALIDATE FIRST LINE OF THE CUSTOMER ADDRESS               *
00552      **************************************************************
00553              IF ADDR1L = ZEROS OR ADDR1I = SPACES
00554              MOVE 'MISSING STREET ADDRESS' TO MSSGO
00555              MOVE -1 TO ADDR1L
00556              MOVE PROT-BRT TO TADDR1A
00557              MOVE PROT TO MSSGA
00558              GO TO 500-RESEND-MAP.
00559              MOVE ADDR1I TO CUSTOMER-ADDRESS1.
00560              MOVE PROT TO TADDR1A.
00561              MOVE UNPROT-ALPHA-MDT TO ADDR1A.
00562      **************************************************************
00563      * ADDRESS LINES 2 IS MANDATORY, 3 IS OPTIONAL               *
00564      **************************************************************
00565              IF ADDR2L = 0 OR ADDR2I = SPACES
00566              MOVE 'MISSING CITY LOCATION' TO MSSGO
00567              MOVE -1 TO ADDR2L
```

```
00568              MOVE PROT-BRT TO TADDR2A
00569              MOVE PROT TO MSSGA
00570              GO TO 500-RESEND-MAP.
00571              MOVE PROT TO TADDR2A.
00572              MOVE ADDR2I TO CUSTOMER-ADDRESS2.
00573              MOVE UNPROT-ALPHA-MDT TO ADDR2A
00574      *
00575              IF ADDR3L NOT = 0 OR
00576              ADDR3I NOT = SPACES
00577              MOVE ADDR3I TO CUSTOMER-ADDRESS3.
00578              MOVE PROT TO TADDR3A.
00579      ****************************************************************
00580      * CHECK THE PRESENCE OF THE STATE CODE                        *
00581      ****************************************************************
00582              IF STATEL = 0 OR STATEI = SPACE
00583              MOVE 'MISSING STATE CODE' TO MSSGO
00584              MOVE PROT TO MSSGA
00585              MOVE -1 TO STATEL
00586              MOVE PROT-BRT TO TSTATEA
00587              GO TO 500-RESEND-MAP.
00588              IF STATEI NUMERIC
00589              MOVE 'STATE FIELD CANNOT CONTAIN NUMERICS' TO MSSGO
00590              MOVE PROT TO MSSGA
00591              MOVE -1 TO STATEL
00592              MOVE PROT-BRT TO TSTATEA
00593              GO TO 500-RESEND-MAP.
00594              MOVE UNPROT-ALPHA-MDT TO STATEA.
00595              MOVE STATEI TO CUSTOMER-STATE
00596              MOVE PROT TO TSTATEA.
00597      ****************************************************************
00598      * STORE POSTAL CODE - NOT A MANDATORY FIELD                   *
00599      ****************************************************************
00600
00601              IF POSTCDL = 0 OR POSTCDI = SPACES
00602              MOVE 'MISSING ZIP CODE' TO MSSGO
00603              MOVE PROT TO MSSGA
00604              MOVE -1 TO POSTCDL
00605              MOVE PROT-BRT TO TPOSTALA
00606              GO TO 500-RESEND-MAP.
00607
00608              MOVE POSTCDI TO CUSTOMER-POSTAL-CODE.
00609              MOVE UNPROT-ALPHA-MDT TO POSTCDA.
00610              MOVE PROT TO TPOSTALA.
00611
00612      ****************************************************************
00613      * CHECK THE PRESENCE OF A TELEPHONE NUMBER - MANDATORY FIELD*
00614      ****************************************************************
00615              IF AREAL = 0 OR AREAI = SPACES
00616              MOVE 'YOU MUST ENTER AN AREA CODE' TO  MSSGO
00617              MOVE PROT TO MSSGA
00618              MOVE -1 TO AREAL
00619              MOVE PROT-BRT TO TTELA
00620              GO TO 500-RESEND-MAP.
00621              MOVE PROT TO TTELA.
00622
00623              IF AREAI NOT NUMERIC
00624              MOVE UNPROT-ALPHA-BRT-MDT TO AREAA
00625              MOVE 'AREA CODE CANNOT BE ALPHA' TO MSSGO
00626              MOVE PROT TO MSSGA
00627              MOVE -1 TO AREAL
00628              MOVE PROT-BRT TO TTELA
00629              GO TO 500-RESEND-MAP.
00630              MOVE UNPROT-ALPHA-MDT TO AREAA.
00631              MOVE AREAI TO CUSTOMER-AREA-CODE.
00632              MOVE PROT TO TTELA.
00633      *
00634              IF TEL3L = 0 OR TEL3I = SPACES
00635              MOVE 'YOU MUST ENTER A TELEPHONE NUMBER' TO MSSGO
00636              MOVE PROT TO MSSGA
00637              MOVE -1 TO TEL3L
00638              MOVE PROT-BRT TO TTELA
00639              GO TO 500-RESEND-MAP.
00640              MOVE UNPROT-ALPHA-MDT TO TEL3A.
00641              MOVE TEL3I TO CUSTOMER-TEL1.
00642              MOVE PROT TO TTELA.
00643      *
00644              IF TEL4L = 0 OR TEL4I = SPACES
00645              MOVE 'YOU MUST ENTER A TELEPHONE NUMBER' TO MSSGO
```

```
00646                    MOVE PROT TO MSSGA
00647                    MOVE -1 TO TEL4L
00648                    MOVE PROT-BRT TO TTELA
00649                    GO TO 500-RESEND-MAP.
00650                    MOVE TEL4I TO CUSTOMER-TEL2.
00651                    MOVE PROT TO TTELA.
00652                    MOVE UNPROT-ALPHA-MDT TO TEL4A.
00653             *
00654             *****************************************************************
00655             * CHECK CONTACT NAME - NOT A MANDATORY FIELD                    *
00656             *****************************************************************
00657                    IF CONTNAML = 0 OR CONTNAMI = SPACES
00658                    NEXT SENTENCE, ELSE
00659                    MOVE CONTNAMI TO CUSTOMER-CONTACT-NAME
00660                    MOVE UNPROT-ALPHA-MDT TO CONTNAMA.
00661             *****************************************************************
00662             * ABBREVIATED NAME - NOT A MANDATORY FIELD                      *
00663             *****************************************************************
00664                    IF ABBNAMEL = 0 OR ABBNAMEI = SPACES
00665                    NEXT SENTENCE, ELSE
00666                    MOVE ABBNAMEI TO CUSTOMER-ABBREVIATED-NAME
00667                    MOVE UNPROT-ALPHA-MDT TO ABBNAMEA.
00668             *****************************************************************
00669             * ACCOUNT OPEN FIELDS - MANDATORY (NUMERIC) FIELD               *
00670             *****************************************************************
00671                    IF MML NOT = 0
00672                    MOVE UNPROT-NUM-MDT TO MMA.
00673                    IF MMI = SPACES OR MMI NUMERIC
00674                    NEXT SENTENCE, ELSE
00675                    MOVE 'MONTH FIELD IS AN OPTIONAL NUMERIC FIELD'
00676                    TO MSSGO
00677                    MOVE PROT TO MSSGA
00678                    MOVE -1 TO MML
00679                    MOVE PROT-BRT TO MMYYA
00680                    GO TO 500-RESEND-MAP.
00681                    MOVE MMI TO CUSTOMER-MONTH.
00682                    MOVE UNPROT-NUM-MDT TO MMA.
00683                    MOVE PROT TO MMYYA.
00684
00685                    IF YYL NOT = 0
00686                    MOVE UNPROT-NUM-MDT TO YYA.
00687                    IF YYI = SPACES OR YYI NUMERIC
00688                    NEXT SENTENCE, ELSE
00689                    MOVE 'YEAR FIELD IS AN OPTIONAL NUMERIC FIELD'
00690                    TO MSSGO
00691                    MOVE PROT TO MSSGA
00692                    MOVE -1 TO YYL
00693                    MOVE PROT-BRT TO MMYYA
00694                    GO TO 500-RESEND-MAP.
00695                    MOVE YYI TO CUSTOMER-YEAR
00696                    MOVE UNPROT-NUM-MDT TO YYA.
00697                    MOVE PROT TO MMYYA.
00698
00699
00700             *****************************************************************
00701             * ENTER DUNN & BRADSTREET NUMBER                                *
00702             *****************************************************************
00703                    IF DBNOL = 0 OR DBNOI = SPACES
00704                    NEXT SENTENCE, ELSE
00705                    MOVE DBNOI TO CUSTOMER-DB-NUMBER
00706                    MOVE UNPROT-ALPHA-MDT TO DBNOA.
00707             *****************************************************************
00708             * READY TO ADD NEW RECORD TO FILE                               *
00709             *****************************************************************
00710                    IF EIBAID = DFHPF4 GO TO 080-ADD-RECORD ELSE
00711                    MOVE 'RECORD IS READY FOR UPDATE' TO MSSGO
00712                    MOVE PROT TO MSSGA
00713                    MOVE -1 TO CUSTNOL
00714                    GO TO 500-RESEND-MAP.
00715             *
00716              080-ADD-RECORD.
00717                    MOVE CUSTNOI TO CUSTOMER-ID.
00718             *EXEC CICS WRITE DATASET('RK501')
00719             *FROM(CUSTOMER-MASTER)
00720             *RIDFLD(CUSTOMER-KEY)
00721             *END-EXEC.
```

```
00722              MOVE ' }      00254  ' TO DFHEIVO
00723              MOVE 'RK501' TO DFHEIV1
00724              CALL 'DFHEI1' USING DFHEIVO DFHEIV1 CUSTOMER-MASTER
00725          DFHDUMMY CUSTOMER-KEY.
00726              MOVE CUSTNOI TO STORE-CUSTNO.
00727              MOVE LOW-VALUES TO ARA91M70
00728              MOVE -1 TO CUSTNOL
00729              MOVE 'RECORD IS NOW UPDATED' TO MSSGO
00730              MOVE STORE-CUSTNO TO CUSTNOI
00731              MOVE ZEROS TO STORE-CUSTNO.
00732              MOVE UNPROT-NUM-BRT TO CUSTNOA.
00733              MOVE PROT TO MSSGA
00734              GO TO 004-SEND-MAP.
00735      ****************************************************************
00736      * SUBROUTINE SECTION                                          *
00737      ****************************************************************
00738        100-RETURN.
00739      *EXEC CICS RETURN
00740      *    TRANSID('AR91')
00741      *    COMMAREA(COMM-AREA)
00742      *    LENGTH(1)
00743      *END-EXEC.
00744              MOVE ' \      00271  ' TO DFHEIVO
00745              MOVE 'AR91' TO DFHEIV5
00746              MOVE 1 TO DFHEIV11
00747              CALL 'DFHEI1' USING DFHEIVO DFHEIV5 COMM-AREA DFHEIV11.
00748
00749        102-RECORD-ALREADY-EXISTS.
00750              MOVE 'RECORD ALREADY EXISTS' TO MSSGO
00751              MOVE PROT TO MSSGA
00752              MOVE -1 TO CUSTNOL
00753              GO TO 500-RESEND-MAP.
00754        170-RETURN-TO-SUBMENU.
00755              MOVE ' ' TO SEND-REC-FLAG.
00756      *EXEC CICS XCTL PROGRAM('ARM90C')
00757      *COMMAREA(COMM-AREA)
00758      *LENGTH(1)
00759      *END-EXEC.
00760              MOVE ' \      00283  ' TO DFHEIVO
00761              MOVE 'ARM90C' TO DFHEIV1
00762              MOVE 1 TO DFHEIV11
00763              CALL 'DFHEI1' USING DFHEIVO DFHEIV1 COMM-AREA DFHEIV11.
00764              STOP RUN.
00765              GOBACK.
00766        500-RESEND-MAP.
00767      *EXEC CICS SEND MAP('ARA91M7')
00768      *MAPSET('ARA91M')
00769      *CURSOR
00770      *DATAONLY
00771      *END-EXEC.
00772              MOVE ' J           00290  ' TO DFHEIVO
00773              MOVE 'ARA91M7' TO DFHC0070
00774              MOVE 'ARA91M' TO DFHC0071
00775              MOVE -1 TO DFHEIV11
00776              CALL 'DFHEI1' USING DFHEIVO DFHC0070 ARA91M70 DFHDUMMY
00777          DFHC0071 DFHDUMMY DFHDUMMY DFHDUMMY DFHEIV11.
00778              MOVE 'R' TO SEND-REC-FLAG.
00779              GO TO 100-RETURN.
00780        700-MAPFAIL.
00781              MOVE 'ENTER CUSTOMER NUMBER' TO MSSGO
00782              MOVE PROT TO MSSGA
00783              MOVE ' ' TO SEND-REC-FLAG
00784              MOVE -1 TO CUSTNOL
00785              GO TO 500-RESEND-MAP.
00786        900-ANYKEY-OPTION.
00787              MOVE 'INVALID KEY, PLEASE RESUBMIT' TO MSSGO.
00788              MOVE PROT TO MSSGA
00789              MOVE -1 TO CUSTNOL
00790              GO TO 500-RESEND-MAP.

*STATISTICS*    SOURCE RECORDS =   790    DATA DIVISION STATEMENTS =   435
*OPTIONS IN EFFECT*    SIZE = 524288  BUF =  20480 LINECNT = 57   SPACE1, FL
*OPTIONS IN EFFECT*    NODMAP, NOPMAP, NOCLIST, NOSUPMAP, NOXREF,   SXREF,  L
*OPTIONS IN EFFECT*    NOTERM, NONUM, NOBATCH, NONAME, COMPILE=01, NOSTATE, NO
*OPTIONS IN EFFECT*    NOOPTIMIZE, NOSYMDMP, NOTEST,   VERB,   ZWB, SYST, NOEN
*OPTIONS IN EFFECT*    NOLST , NOFDECK,NOCDECK, LCOL2,  L120,   DUMP , NOADV ,
*OPTIONS IN EFFECT*    NOCOUNT, NOVBSUM, NOVBREF, LANGLVL(1)
                                        CROSS-REFERENCE DICTIONARY
```

DATA NAMES	DEFN	REFERENCE			
ABBNAMEA	000287	000667			
ABBNAMEF	000285				
ABBNAMEI	000288	000664	000666		
ABBNAMEL	000284	000664			
ABBNAMEO	000359				
ADDR1A	000217	000561			
ADDR1F	000215				
ADDR1I	000218	000553	000559		
ADDR1L	000214	000553	000555		
ADDR1O	000331				
ADDR2A	000227	000573			
ADDR2F	000225				
ADDR2I	000228	000565	000572		
ADDR2L	000224	000565	000567		
ADDR2O	000335				
ADDR3A	000237				
ADDR3F	000235				
ADDR3I	000238	000575	000577		
ADDR3L	000234	000575			
ADDR3O	000339				
ARA91M7I	000177	000505			
ARA91M7O	000314	000494	000727	000776	
AREAA	000267	000624	000630		
AREAF	000265				
AREAI	000268	000615	000623	000631	
AREAL	000264	000615	000618	000627	
AREAO	000351				
ASKIP	000167				
ASKIP-BRT	000169				
ASKIP-BRT-MDT	000170				
ASKIP-DRK	000171				
ASKIP-DRK-MDT	000172				
ASKIP-MDT	000168				
ATTRBYTE	000148				
COMM-AREA	000007	000457	000747	000763	
CONTNAMA	000282	000660			
CONTNAMF	000280				
CONTNAMI	000283	000657	000659		
CONTNAML	000279	000657			
CONTNAMO	000357				
CSR-REPO	000175				
CUSTNAMA	000207	000547			
CUSTNAMF	000205				
CUSTNAMI	000208	000540	000548		
CUSTNAML	000204	000540	000544		
CUSTNAMO	000327				
CUSTNOA	000197	000521	000732		
CUSTNOF	000195				
CUSTNOI	000198	000515	000526	000717	000726	00073
CUSTNOL	000194	000483	000515	000518	000713	00072
CUSTNOO	000323				
CUSTOMER-ABBREVIATED-NAME	000028	000666			
CUSTOMER-ACCOUNT-OPENED	000029				
CUSTOMER-ADDRESS1	000022	000559			
CUSTOMER-ADDRESS2	000023	000572			
CUSTOMER-ADDRESS3	000024	000577			
CUSTOMER-AREA-CODE	000035	000631			
CUSTOMER-COMPANY	000013				
CUSTOMER-CONTACT-NAME	000027	000659			
CUSTOMER-DB-NUMBER	000040	000705			
CUSTOMER-ID	000017	000526	000717		
CUSTOMER-KEY	000012	000533	000724		
CUSTOMER-MASTER	000009	000533	000724		
CUSTOMER-MONTH	000030	000681			
CUSTOMER-NAME	000021	000548			
CUSTOMER-NUMBER	000015				
CUSTOMER-POSTAL-CODE	000026	000608			
CUSTOMER-PREFIX	000016				
CUSTOMER-REFERENCE	000018				
CUSTOMER-SEGMENT	000014				
CUSTOMER-STATE	000025	000595			
CUSTOMER-TELEPHONE	000036				
CUSTOMER-TELEPHONE-NO	000033				

CUSTOMER-TEL1	000037	000641			
CUSTOMER-TEL2	000038	000650			
CUSTOMER-YEAR	000031	000695			
DATA-AREA	000020				
DBNOA	000307	000706			
DBNOF	000305				
DBNOI	000308	000703	000705		
DBNOL	000304	000703			
DBNOO	000367				
DFHAID	000109				
DFHALL	000069				
DFHBASE	000080				
DFHBKTRN	000068				
DFHBLINK	000082				
DFHBLLSLOT1	000449				
DFHBLLSLOT2	000450				
DFHBLUE	000073				
DFHBMASB	000056				
DFHBMASF	000055				
DFHBMASK	000047				
DFHBMBRY	000051				
DFHBMDAR	000052				
DFHBMDET	000058				
DFHBMEOF	000057				
DFHBMFSE	000053				
DFHBMPEM	000045				
DFHBMPNL	000046				
DFHBMPRF	000054				
DFHBMPRO	000050				
DFHBMPSI	000060				
DFHBMPSO	000059				
DFHBMSCA	000044				
DFHBMUNN	000049				
DFHBMUNP	000048				
DFHBOX	000104				
DFHB0025	000389				
DFHB0041	000376				
DFHB0042	000377				
DFHB0043	000378				
DFHB0044	000379				
DFHB0045	000380				
DFHB0046	000381				
DFHB0047	000382				
DFHB0048	000383				
DFHCLEAR	000112				
DFHCLRP	000113				
DFHCOLOR	000062				
DFHCOMMAREA	000448	000457			
DFHC0011	000408				
DFHC0022	000404				
DFHC0023	000405				
DFHC0070	000410	000491	000494	000503	000505	00077
DFHC0071	000411	000492	000494	000504	000505	00077
DFHC0084	000399				
DFHC0085	000400				
DFHC0320	000401				
DFHC0440	000412				
DFHDFCOL	000072				
DFHDFFR	000099				
DFHDFHI	000081				
DFHDFT	000071				
DFHDUMMY	000413	000494	000505	000533	000724	00077
DFHEIBLK	000416				
DFHEIB0	000372				
DFHEICB	000373				
DFHEID0	000371				
DFHEIGDI	000422	000466	000475	000513		
DFHEIV0	000414	000464	000465	000473	000474	00049
		000531	000533	000722	000724	00074
DFHEIV1	000395	000532	000533	000723	000724	00076
DFHEIV10	000406				
DFHEIV11	000384	000493	000494	000746	000747	00076
DFHEIV12	000385				
DFHEIV13	000386				
DFHEIV14	000387				
DFHEIV15	000388				
DFHEIV16	000375				
DFHEIV17	000392				

5-7 Continued

DFHEIV18	000393		
DFHEIV19	000394		
DFHEIV2	000396		
DFHEIV20	000398		
DFHEIV3	000397		
DFHEIV4	000409		
DFHEIV5	000390	000745	000747
DFHEIV6	000391		
DFHEIV7	000402		
DFHEIV8	000403		
DFHEIV9	000407		
DFHENTER	000111		
DFHERROR	000070		
DFHGREEN	000076		
DFHHLT	000064		
DFHLDVER	000370		
DFHLEFT	000100		
DFHMENT	000086		
DFHMET	000097		
DFHMFE	000087		
DFHMFET	000098		
DFHMFIL	000085		
DFHMFT	000096		
DFHMSRE	000116		
DFHMT	000095		
DFHNEUTR	000079		
DFHNULL	000110		
DFHOPAQ	000107		
DFHOPID	000115		
DFHOUTLN	000067		
DFHOVER	000101		
DFHPA1	000119		
DFHPA2	000120		
DFHPA3	000121		
DFHPEN	000114		
DFHPF1	000122		
DFHPF10	000131		
DFHPF11	000132		
DFHPF12	000133		
DFHPF13	000134		
DFHPF14	000135		
DFHPF15	000136		
DFHPF16	000137		
DFHPF17	000138		
DFHPF18	000139		
DFHPF19	000140		
DFHPF2	000123		
DFHPF20	000141		
DFHPF21	000142		
DFHPF22	000143		
DFHPF23	000144		
DFHPF24	000145		
DFHPF3	000124		
DFHPF4	000125	000710	
DFHPF5	000126		
DFHPF6	000127		
DFHPF7	000128		
DFHPF8	000129		
DFHPF9	000130		
DFHPINK	000075		
DFHPROTI	000093		
DFHPROTN	000094		
DFHPS	000063		
DFHRED	000074		
DFHREVRS	000083		
DFHRIGHT	000102		
DFHSA	000061		
DFHSOSI	000105		
DFHSTRF	000117		
DFHTRANS	000106		
DFHTRIG	000118		
DFHTURQ	000077		
DFHUNDER	000103		
DFHUNDLN	000084		
DFHUNIMD	000089		
DFHUNINT	000091		

DFHUNNOD	000088				
DFHUNNON	000092				
DFHUNNUM	000090				
DFHVAL	000066				
DFHYELLO	000078				
DFH3270	000065				
EIBAID	000425	000710			
EIBATT	000435				
EIBCALEN	000424	000456			
EIBCOMPL	000438				
EIBCONF	000440				
EIBCPOSN	000423				
EIBDATE	000418				
EIBDS	000428				
EIBEOC	000436				
EIBERR	000441				
EIBERRCD	000442				
EIBFIL01	000434				
EIBFMH	000437				
EIBFN	000426				
EIBFREE	000432				
EIBNODAT	000444				
EIBRCODE	000427				
EIBRECV	000433				
EIBREQID	000429				
EIBRESP	000445				
EIBRESP2	000446				
EIBRLDBK	000447				
EIBRSRCE	000430				
EIBSIG	000439				
EIBSYNC	000431				
EIBSYNRB	000443				
EIBTASKN	000420				
EIBTIME	000417				
EIBTRMID	000421	000480			
EIBTRNID	000419				
LENGTH-BYTES	000174				
MMA	000297	000672	000682		
MMF	000295				
MMI	000298	000673	000681		
MML	000294	000671	000678		
MMO	000363				
MMYYA	000292	000679	000683	000693	000697
MMYYF	000290				
MMYYI	000293				
MMYYL	000289				
MMYYO	000361				
MSSGA	000312	000517	000543	000557	000569	00058
		000646	000677	000691	000712	00073
MSSGF	000310				
MSSGI	000313				
MSSGL	000309				
MSSGO	000369	000516	000542	000554	000566	00058
		000645	000675	000689	000711	00072
POSTCDA	000257	000609			
POSTCDF	000255				
POSTCDI	000258	000601	000608		
POSTCDL	000254	000601	000604		
POSTCDO	000347				
PROT	000161	000481	000517	000522	000543	00054
		000584	000590	000596	000603	00061
		000642	000646	000651	000677	00068
		000782	000788			
PROT-BRT	000163	000482	000519	000545	000556	00056
		000638	000648	000679	000693	
PROT-BRT-MDT	000164				
PROT-DRK	000165				
PROT-DRK-MDT	000166				
PROT-MDT	000162				
SEND-REC-FLAG	000008	000476	000496	000755	000778	00078
STATEA	000247	000594			
STATEF	000245				
STATEI	000248	000582	000588	000595	
STATEL	000244	000582	000585	000591	
STATEO	000343				
STORE-CUSTNO	000042	000726	000730	000731	
TADDR1A	000212	000556	000560		
TADDR1F	000210				

TADDR1I	000213				
TADDR1L	000209				
TADDR1O	000329				
TADDR2A	000222	000568	000571		
TADDR2F	000220				
TADDR2I	000223				
TADDR2L	000219				
TADDR2O	000333				
TADDR3A	000232	000578			
TADDR3F	000230				
TADDR3I	000233				
TADDR3L	000229				
TADDR3O	000337				
TCUSTNMA	000202	000545	000549		
TCUSTNMF	000200				
TCUSTNMI	000203				
TCUSTNML	000199				
TCUSTNMO	000325				
TCUSTNOA	000192	000482	000519	000522	
TCUSTNOF	000190				
TCUSTNOI	000193				
TCUSTNOL	000189				
TCUSTNOO	000321				
TEL3A	000272	000640			
TEL3F	000270				
TEL3I	000273	000634	000641		
TEL3L	000269	000634	000637		
TEL3O	000353				
TEL4A	000277	000652			
TEL4F	000275				
TEL4I	000278	000644	000650		
TEL4L	000274	000644	000647		
TEL4O	000355				
TERMA	000187				
TERMF	000185				
TERMI	000188				
TERML	000184				
TERMO	000319	000480			
TPOSTALA	000252	000605	000610		
TPOSTALF	000250				
TPOSTALI	000253				
TPOSTALL	000249				
TPOSTALO	000345				
TRIDA	000182	000481			
TRIDF	000180				
TRIDI	000183				
TRIDL	000179				
TRIDO	000317	000479			
TSTATEA	000242	000586	000592	000596	
TSTATEF	000240				
TSTATEI	000243				
TSTATEL	000239				
TSTATEO	000341				
TTELA	000262	000619	000621	000628	000632	00063
TTELF	000260				
TTELI	000263				
TTELL	000259				
TTELO	000349				
UNPROT-ALPHA	000149				
UNPROT-ALPHA-BRT	000151				
UNPROT-ALPHA-BRT-MDT	000152	000624			
UNPROT-ALPHA-DRK	000153				
UNPROT-ALPHA-DRK-MDT	000154				
UNPROT-ALPHA-MDT	000150	000561	000573	000594	000609	00063
UNPROT-NUM	000155				
UNPROT-NUM-BRT	000157	000732			
UNPROT-NUM-BRT-MDT	000158				
UNPROT-NUM-DRK	000159				
UNPROT-NUM-DRK-MDT	000160				
UNPROT-NUM-MDT	000156	000521	000547	000672	000682	00068
YYA	000302	000686	000696		
YYF	000300				
YYI	000303	000687	000695		
YYL	000299	000685	000692		
YYO	000365				

```
PROCEDURE NAMES                    DEFN     REFERENCE


001-START-PROCESSING              000455
004-SEND-MAP                      000478    000466   000734
004-SEND-MAP-2                    000484
005-RECEIVE-MAP                   000498    000476
006-HANDLE-CONDITION              000507
007-READ-CUSTOMER-MASTER          000514
008-CUSTOMER-MISSING              000536    000513
080-ADD-RECORD                    000716    000710
100-RETURN                        000738    000497   000779
102-RECORD-ALREADY-EXISTS         000749    000535
170-RETURN-TO-SUBMENU             000754    000466
500-RESEND-MAP                    000766    000520   000546   000558   000570   00058
                                            000649   000680   000694   000714   00075

700-MAPFAIL                       000780    000475
900-ANYKEY-OPTION                 000786    000466
```

As you can see, in FIG. 5-8, I expanded the attribute chart by recording some basic color schemes currently available on most IBM3270 (and compatible) type terminals. For example, in referring to the field name UNPROT-ALPHA-BRT-MDT, CICS will create for you a high-intensity data field that is red. You can also use a certain value assigned to such a field, such as the value "I." Clearly, it is easier to reference values through color than through nomenclature. In producing an intensified white display, for example, you can define a field as a protected bright field (a value of "Y"), or as a protected bright white data field, with its modified data tag turned on ("Z").

The next copy statement brought into this ADD program is the symbolic map. The complete listing of this expanded map is shown in lines 177 through 369 in FIG. 5-7. As you will see later in this book, you can actually modify the symbolic map itself by placing it into your copy library and recalling it from there for maintenance.

Following the symbolic map is a comprehensive list of fields required by the execute interface program. This module is compiler-generated, so you are going to get it whether you need it or not. A layout of the EIB block is shown in lines 370 through 414.

The DFHEIBLK block is also compiler-generated for your convenience. EIB, or Execute Interface Block, contains a number of fields that you will probably want to use in your application program. For example the EIBTIME, statement 417, or the EIBDATE, statement 418, are necessary if you want to display those fields on the screen. EIBTRMID, or terminal identifier, displays a particular terminal I.D. as needed.

EIBCALEN (line 424) is used to check if any message was sent through the current transaction from the prior transaction via the COMMUNICATIONS AREA. EIBAID enables you to maintain reference to the keyboard and what has or hasn't been activated during the current pseudoconversational cycle. For example, consider the statement:

IF EIBAID = DFHPF 4 GO TO 080-ADD-RECORD

That statement means that an action is to be triggered, directing the path of your program to the paragraph 080-ADD-RECORD whenever function key 4 is pressed. Note that this block is laid out in its entirety in statements 416 through 450.

Following the last statement shown in line 790, CICS provides a list of some of the options used during your transaction cycle. This is followed by a directory in which every data field name used in the system is arranged alphabetically. Actually, the list provides you with the following information. The first one gives you the name, such as ABBNAMEA. The second column shows where such a field was originally defined, as well as where it was used. Look at the term "PROT," which was referenced through the ATTRBYTE copy statement. This attribute field was utilized every time a field was placed into a low-intensity protected field. Altogether, this was referenced in the ADD program (ARA91C) some 18 times, giving the location of each. Note that PROCEDURE names are also referenced in this directory, very much like their data field equivalent.

5-8 CHARATR

```
01   CHARATR.

        05   UNPROT-ALPHA          PIC X    VALUE SPACE.

        05   UNPROT-ALPHA-MDT      PIC X    VALUE 'A'.

*  A=GREEN

        05   UNPROT-ALPHA-BRT      PIC X    VALUE 'H'.

*  H=RED

        05   UNPROT-ALPHA-BRT-MDT  PIC X    VALUE 'I'.

*  I=RED

        05   UNPROT-ALPHA-DRK      PIC X    VALUE '<'.

        05   UNPROT-ALPHA-DRK-MDT  PIC X    VALUE '('.

        05   UNPROT-NUM            PIC X    VALUE '&'.

        05   UNPROT-NUM-MDT        PIC X    VALUE 'J'.
```

```
* J=GREEN

      05   UNPROT-NUM-BRT          PIC X    VALUE 'Q'.

* Q=RED

      05   UNPROT-NUM-BRT-MDT      PIC X    VALUE 'R'.

      05   UNPROT-NUM-DRK          PIC X    VALUE '*'.

      05   UNPROT-NUM-DRK-MDT      PIC X    VALUE ')'.

      05   PROT                    PIC X    VALUE '-'.

* -=BLUE

      05   PROT-MDT                PIC X    VALUE '/'.

* /=BLUE

      05   PROT-BRT                PIC X    VALUE 'Y'.

* Y=WHITE

      05   PROT-BRT-MDT            PIC X    VALUE 'Z'.

* Z=WHITE

      05   PROT-DRK                PIC X    VALUE '%'.

      05   PROT-DRK-MDT            PIC X    VALUE '_'.

      05   ASKIP                   PIC X    VALUE '0'.

      05   ASKIP-MDT               PIC X    VALUE '1'.

      05   ASKIP-BRT               PIC X    VALUE '8'.

      05   ASKIP-BRT-MDT           PIC X    VALUE '9'.

      05   ASKIP-DRK               PIC X    VALUE '@'.

      05   ASKIP-DRK-MDT           PIC X    VALUE QUOTE.
```

6

How to develop a CHANGE program

The purpose of this chapter is to show you some of the techniques required to develop a CHANGE program. CHANGE programs represent probably the most complicated type of transaction, due to excessive edit requirements and procedures that are frequently not associated with any other CICS task.

In discussing some of the inherent features of a CHANGE program, the following situations can substantially complicate an already complex transaction. These are:

1. When you combine a CHANGE and a BROWSE transaction into a single program that will provide you with a great deal of flexibility.
2. When you develop an exit routine to an external module or subroutine, such as a tutorial program or some specialized search technique.

Combining a CHANGE with a BROWSE transaction might be preferable if you need to perform a considerable volume of sequential updates interactively. This technique will save you time in entering a new key, especially when you perform a sequential search on that file. Please note that no such combined option is available when coding an ADD program.

The most complicated situation comes into play when combining a CHANGE, a BROWSE, and a DELETE transaction into a single program. A valid reason for such a program lies in the user's need to perform maintenance procedures randomly, where branching back and forth between a subdirectory and a detailed maintenance screen is just not feasible.

In developing an exit point for a tutorial subsystem, at least one aspect of advanced programming needs to be taken into consideration. When requesting help, it will be necessary for you to retain the position that the cursor held prior to branching. This is the case because you want to be able to highlight the same data field upon return, in order to continue the edit process uninterrupted. A more involved technique, referred to as a cursor sensitive technique, is one that enables the user to provide specific information on a data field by pointing the cursor at such a data field and pressing the ENTER key or a predefined function key. (More on this in Chapter 9.)

CHANGE programs need to be extensively diagnostics-oriented for clarity. This means that the programmer has to communicate or "report" to the user an array of data errors on several levels. On a primary level, of course, a field that is in error can be highlighted using an attribute scheme that is different from the one designating a normal situation. A numeric field that is keyed in as an alpha field can be presented to the user in reverse video, blinking, or using an altogether different set of colors. On a secondary level, any error can be coupled with a specific error message to inform the user of the nature of the problem. Finally, and in more sophisticated environments, a tutorial screen can be invoked from the location of a specific data element.

Diagnostics for a CHANGE program can be as comprehensive, if not more so, than diagnostics for an ADD transaction. Thus, you can diagnose a specific problem on a field-by-field level until resolving it. You can also diagnose the entire panel all at once, showing more than a single occurrence of error. One of the many problems with multiple error tracking using a single display is a somewhat confusing screen, where numerous problems might be highlighted for your immediate attention. A second problem, equally compelling in developing such a program, is that multiple error tracking requires a great deal more complexity than a conventional approach, i.e., displaying only a single error per cycle.

Creating shells

Once you have developed an ADD program, it will be fairly easy to modify it into a CHANGE transaction. This will save you substantial development time in some of the edit procedures that are common to both programs. The purpose of this section is to highlight some of the differences (and similarities) that exist between two types of transactions necessary to create a program shell.

In creating program shells, you need to narrow down certain transaction types into functional areas. This process requires you to "pair" similar transaction types within an identical application program, such as a CHANGE and an ADD program or an INQUIRY and a DELETE program, where the procedures and the internal logic of these programs calls for similar or identical routines. The process of creating a shell in this fashion is referred to as an internally developed process since, as I said before, you are modifying one of your existing transaction types by creating a replica.

But, suppose you need to develop a shell for a BROWSE program that displays fourteen concurrent lines, and by pressing a PF key, fourteen more lines are to be invoked. It is unlikely that it would be feasible to clone a change or a delete transaction to perform such a task. BROWSE programs, as a general rule, do not possess a great deal of editing facilities; logically, a BROWSE program ranks with an INQUIRY program, yet the technology to develop a BROWSE program is completely different.

The first set of modifications in transforming an ADD to a CHANGE program is to redefine the HANDLE CONDITION. This is necessary since you are no longer dependent on a NOTFND condition to drive your present transaction, as was called for during an ADD type. Rather, it now becomes an exception, meaning that if the record is not found, you are logically dealing with an error condition.

There is a second major difference in developing a shell. When creating (i.e., adding) a new record to a file, you only have to verify that the record currently does not exist. This normally requires editing such a record only once, even if you were to change the key before physically writing it. In CHANGE mode, however, this methodology simply won't do. First, you must check for an existing record, but once this criterion is fulfilled, you still need to check to see if the record key was somehow altered by the terminal operator prior to an update. If this is the case, you need to read and redisplay the entire record in question, provided that there is such a record in existence. When displaying a record, the message "READY TO UPDATE" should not be highlighted at first. Rather, a message requesting the user to start entering the required changes needs to be displayed. This amounts to creating an additional (pseudo-conversational) cycle between sends and receives.

If you are using a predefined function key to update a record (rather than letting the program automatically do it for you), you need to store the original record key and pass it along in the COMMAREA. This is a necessary precaution in case the user decides to press the enter key a couple of times before finally using the required function key.

Paragraph names in the program need to be overhauled, especially with regard to messages. For example, the message "RECORD ALREADY EXISTS ON FILE" is no longer viable, since such a condition is now the norm and not the exception. Thus, you'd want to replace such a message to read "REQUESTED RECORD DOES NOT EXIST, PLEASE RESUBMIT." Likewise, and mainly for clarity in maintaining your application program, you must replace some of the paragraph names to reflect functional changes. For example, a function key used to update a particular record should not be referenced in a paragraph titled "1000-MISSING-PAYRECORD," even if the procedure is logically sound. Rather, you probably want to say something like "1000-RECORD-FOUND" or "1000-RECORD-READY-FOR-UPDATE" to provide the maintenance programmer some future clue as to the structure of the program.

In creating a shell for a CHANGE transaction, an ADD program is not the only source that can be modified in this fashion. A basic map layout or BMS, for example, can also be reused, frequently without any change. This, of course, depends very much on how standardized a particular shop happens to be in formatting a screen. In the case of a subdirectory, for example, the number of available selections on the subdirectory determines if the subdirectory can be reused. Cloning a subdirectory can be done in the matter of minutes, provided all the necessary table entries are all set and you only need to modify certain constant titles in your program. For example, in place of a "PERSONNEL PROFILE" screen, you want to say "INVENTORY" or "ACCOUNTS PAYABLE" screen and keep most, if not all of the logic imbedded into the menu program. Figure 6-1 highlights such a technique.

Figure 6-1 starts out with a Personnel Profile panel, initially showing four major tasks to select from. This is a relatively simple panel drawn to convey the idea of preparing a shell. It is to be transformed into an Accounts Payable subdirectory appearing in the upper left-hand corner of FIG. 6-1. In order to convert a menu program to reflect these changes, which are minimal, I simply highlighted the changes in shaded areas. Thus, the rest of the code (conservatively, over 90%) remains unchanged.

When modifying an existing program into a generic shell, the following topics should be taken into consideration:

- Can you transplant all the applicable edit rules into this shell without disrupting the logical flow of the new program?
- Can you identify some of the frequent changes that are characteristic when modifying, for example, an add into a

change program, so that you can implement these changes efficiently?

Figure 6-2 highlights a chart to evaluate the extent of modification necessary to create a CHANGE program from an ADD program. If you have a text editor, such as ISPF, you can issue a "CHANGE ALL" command, replacing all map and mapset commands with a new name. In reading a file, you need to modify the dataset name (or names), depending on the complexity of a particular transaction (you should only read in a single place in your program). In recording a transaction, delete the command WRITE, which normally refers to an ADD transaction, and promptly replace WRITE with a REWRITE statement.

```
    PERSONNEL PROFILE                    ACCOUNTS PAYABLE

1   EMPLOYEE SKILLS              1   VENDOR MAINTENANCE
2   EMPLOYEE EDUCATIONAL         2   A/R INQUIRIES
3   EMPLOYEE WORK HISTORY        3   G/L INQUIRIES
4   SALARIES & INCENTIVES        4   ON-LINE REPORTS


_   ENTER SELECTION             _   ENTER SELECTION
                                                 •


PF1: REURN TO SUB-MENU          PF1: RETURN TO SUB-MENU
....SYSTEMS MESAGES....          ....SYSTEMS MESSAGES
```

```
EXEC CICS RECEIVE MAP('PAY002')   EXEC CICS RECEIVE MAP('AP7009')
MAPSET('PAY002M')                 MAPSET('AP7009M')
                MOVE 'S' TO SEND-REC-FLAG.
                IF SELECTI = '1' OR '2' OR '3' OR '4'
                NEXT SENTENCE ELSE
                MOVE 'INVALID SELECTION CODE, PLEASE RE-ENTER'
                TO MSSGO
                MOVE 'Y' TO MSSGA
                MOVE 'I' TO SELECTA
                MOVE -1 TO SELECTL
                GO TO 035-RESEND.
                IF SELECTI = '1'
                EXEC CICS XCTL PROGRAM('ARA91C')
                COMMAREA(COMM-AREA)
                LENGTH(1), END-EXEC.
                IF SELECTI = '2'
                MOVE ' ' TO SEND-REC-FLAG
                EXEC CICS XCTL PROGRAM('ARC92C')
                COMMAREA(COMM-AREA)
                LENGTH(1) END-EXEC.
                IF SELECTI = '3'
                MOVE ' ' TO SEND-REC-FLAG
                EXEC CICS XCTL PROGRAM('ARD93C')
                COMMAREA(COMM-AREA)
                LENGTH(1) END-EXEC.
                IF SELECTI = '4'
                MOVE ' ' TO SEND-REC-FLAG
                EXEC CICS XCTL PROGRAM('ARB94C')
                COMMAREA(COMM-AREA)
                LENGTH(1) END-EXEC.
```

6-1 Highlights the reusability of generic code

	Current ADD Pgm	Shell	New Change Pgm
Map	MAPADD1		MAPCHG1
Mapset	MSETAD1		MSETCHG1
READ (file name)	ARA21M		ARA21M
			INVPREF
WRITE	YES		NO
REWRITE	NO		YES
COPY STATEMENTS	NREINV		NREINV
NOTFND(normal path)			
. ERROR	NO		YES
. EDIT	YES		NO
CHANGES IN PF KEY ASSGNMENT			
HELP SCREEN	NO		YES
(all others are identical)			
XCTL Path			GL07100A
Commarea			Spec Ind.
RETURN Command			
. Single Edit			
. Multiple Edit			
Use of Attributes i.e. color, highlights, etc.			

6-2 An overview of modifications

Copy statements, like files, can also differ in their overall applicability when it comes to a CHANGE rather than an ADD transaction. In a CHANGE transaction, you are not primarily concerned with a standard copy routine, such as the one required to copy a DFHAID or DFHBMSCA block. Rather, you are concerned with identifying a map or a dataset that is particularly referenced in a given transaction.

The NOTFND statement is defined through a HANDLE CONDITION statement. The NOTFND statement is an important one, since it determines whether such a condition represents an error, as opposed to a normal processing path. There needs to be some structural reorganization in transforming an ADD to a CHANGE program, requiring that you also perform, most, if not all the validation criteria following a READ command. You might also need to redefine your initial function key assignments, mainly to highlight some of the new requirements, i.e., special data routines or perhaps a user defined HELP screen that might have been unavailable in ADD mode, but is a necessity in using a CHANGE program.

When exit controlling out of a current transaction, you might need to spend some time reviewing the associated programs in reference. For example, as you can see in FIG. 6-1, in converting a Payroll Profile subdirectory into an Inventory menu screen, every XCTL statement has to be replaced with a new program. The new CHANGE program in the example requires access to a different program, such as the GL07100A module developed to interface with the General Ledger Chart of Account file online.

You might also need to consider some important changes in the layout of the communications area. In CHANGE mode, for example, you might want to carry an extra field, such as a special indicator designed to tell the programmer if he or she is still dealing with the same record key, and after reading a record, whether to rewrite it or display it from the initial cycle. Suppose you are in the process of making changes to an existing record. You have just completed the editing process and are about to display the message "RECORD IS NOW READY TO BE UPDATED—PRESS PF 5." Just at that point the operator decides to change the record key instead of issuing the update. Obviously, that record now cannot be updated as is without reading the file for the second time via the new record key and displaying all that information from scratch, thus nullifying all the previously entered changes.

Next, change the transaction identifier imbedded in the RETURN command to reinvoke the current transaction. This hopefully occurs only in a single place in the program. Finally, you might want to reconsider your earlier attribute scheme. For example, during the edit of an ADD program, you might want to use extended attributes to underscore mandatory data elements that must be filled in by the terminal operator in this initial stage. In a CHANGE program, however, underscoring is not too terribly important, since it is unlikely that you will encounter a missing field that was initially defined as a mandatory one, unless you have, for some reason, deleted or truncated a field.

Case study

The purpose of this exercise is twofold. First, to show you just how to develop a CHANGE program. Second, to explain how a particular module, such as a HELP screen can be accessed and brought into your program temporarily, although the actual tutorial mechanism is laid out in detail in Chapter 9. The panel containing the nonrecurring customer billing, which is the sole vehicle for entering the required changes, is shown in FIG. 6-3. Note that this panel was presented in Chapter 3 in conjunction with an inquiry program, where every field, with the exception of the inquiry key, was highlighted in protected mode. An overview of the CHANGE program is shown in FIG. 6-4.

Two of the main components of this mechanism is the nonrecurring billing and the customer master files, each presented in detail in FIG. 6-14 in lines 33 through 60 and in lines 64 through 94, respectively. The customer master is accessed to be utilized only in

INQUIRY mode for customer description. The nonrecurring master is maintained through the ARC24C CHANGE program utilizing a change panel.

The invoice number for each nonrecurring customer, which is the key to the customer master file, is created in the prior ADD transaction, but you can also maintain it in this program. Two other fields also appear in protected mode on the Invoice Header. These are the customer number and name. Note that both data components are denoted by a string of D's meaning "display" items.

```
┌──────────────────────────────────────────────────────────────────────┐
│ AR24    INVOICE HEADER SCREEN FOR NON-RECURING BILLINGS   __/__/__     │
│                                                                        │
│    PROJECT NO:        _____                                         │
│    CREDIT MEMO.   _           ORIGIAL INV# :  _____                   │
│    CUSTOMER NO:       DDDD     CUSTOMER NAME : DDDDDDDDDDDDDDDDDDDDDDDDDDDD│
│    INVOICE NO :   _____       INVOICE AMOUNT: _____                  │
│    ACCOUNTING MM/YY: ____      BILLING DATE (MMDDYY)  _____            │
│    PERIOD DESCRIPT.: _____                  │
│                                                                        │
│    _____ SPECIAL INSTRUCTION _____       │
│                                                                        │
│                                                                        │
│                                                                        │
│    PF1: RETURN TO MENU       PF2: INVOICE DESCRIPTION PANEL            │
│    PF3: HELP                                                            │
│    >>>>>>>>>>>>>>>>>>> SYSTEMS OR ERROR MESSAGES <<<<<<<<<<<<<<<<<<<<<<  │
└──────────────────────────────────────────────────────────────────────┘
```

6-3 Maintenance header to implement changes

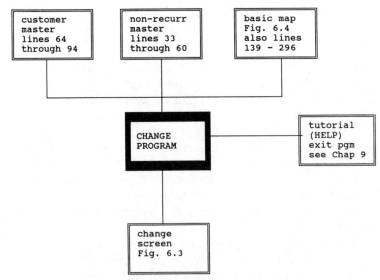

6-4 Overview of the change apparatus

Adding or changing a record on the nonrecurring customer master requires some explanation. The nonrecurring mechanism follows a path that is made up of three panels. These are, as I indicated earlier, the Invoice Header (see FIG. 6-3), as well as a Description and a Distribution panel designed to access the General Ledger. Thus, to update a nonrecurring customer record requires three basic steps, and until such steps are completed, the information entered is stored and passed on to the next step for verification, and only written out to a file afterwards.

When invoking the help module through PF 3 (see FIG. 6-4 for an initial overview), the CHANGE program branches to an external program module responsible for performing the forward and backward BROWSE operation, while displaying the tutorial text, as needed. When the branch occurs, the program retains the relative position of each field at cursor location. This enables the programmer to point to the exact data field that the user was pointing when an exit was requested. Please note that the entire tutorial apparatus will be described in detail in Chapter 9.

Map and FCT considerations

The Basic Mapping code for nonrecurring customers is shown in FIG. 6-5. This corresponds to the screen design highlighted in FIG. 6-3 and expanded in detail in a machine-generated symbolic map in lines 139 through 296 of FIG. 6-14. This symbolic map is rather straightforward, and if you were to place it next to FIG. 6-3, you would see a one-to-one relationship between the two. Actually, this map shows very little variation from that of its ADD counterpart, other than some of the attribute changes that were made to reflect a more customized CHANGE operation.

All data fields to be used during the cycle are defined with the FSET option, meaning that they are used initially with their modified data tag turned on. These definitions are later replaced in the program, pending the result of edit and verification criteria. Figure 6-6 shows the FCT (File Control Table) for the nonrecurring customers file.

Source program listing and narrative

As you can see in FIG. 6-13, the COMMAREA is a lengthy, 79-byte, highly customized format designed to serve a number of purposes. In the first position, it contains an indicator with a specific value, which is either a zero ("0") or the character "T". A zero conventionally denotes a first-time routine. It is also there to detect possible operator "tampering" with the record key prior to updating a

6-5 BMS for the nonrecurring customer CHANGE panel

```
           PRINT NOGEN
ARC24M     DFHMSD  TYPE=&SYSPARM,MODE=INOUT,CTRL=FREEKB,LANG=COBOL,      C
               TIOAPFX=YES
ARC24M2    DFHMDI   SIZE=(24,80)
TRANS      DFHMDF POS=(01,02),LENGTH=04,INITIAL='AR28',                  C
               ATTRB=(BRT,ASKIP)
           DFHMDF POS=(01,10),LENGTH=56,ATTRB=ASKIP,                     C
               INITIAL='INVOICE HEADER SCREEN FOR NON-RECURRING BILLINGC
               S'
DATE       DFHMDF POS=(01,70),LENGTH=08,ATTRB=(BRT,ASKIP),
MODE       DFHMDF POS=(03,28),LENGTH=12,ATTRB=(BRT,PROT)
           DFHMDF POS=(05,03),LENGTH=12,ATTRB=(BRT,PROT),               C
               INITIAL='PROJECT NO :'
PROJECT    DFHMDF POS=(05,16),LENGTH=06,ATTRB=(ASKIP,FSET)
           DFHMDF POS=(05,23),LENGTH=01,INITIAL=' ',ATTRB=ASKIP
           DFHMDF POS=(06,03),LENGTH=12,ATTRB=ASKIP,                     C
               INITIAL='CREDIT MEMO.'
MEMO       DFHMDF POS=(06,16),LENGTH=01,ATTRB=(UNPROT,FSET)
           DFHMDF POS=(06,18),LENGTH=01,INITIAL=' ',ATTRB=ASKIP
           DFHMDF POS=(06,20),LENGTH=08,ATTRB=(BRT,PROT),               C
               INITIAL='(Y, N)'
           DFHMDF POS=(06,31),LENGTH=15,ATTRB=ASKIP,                     C
               INITIAL='ORIGINAL INV# :'
ORGINVF    DFHMDF POS=(06,47),LENGTH=01,ATTRB=(UNPROT,FSET)
           DFHMDF POS=(06,49),LENGTH=01,INITIAL=' ',ATTRB=ASKIP
ORGINV     DFHMDF POS=(06,51),LENGTH=05,ATTRB=(UNPROT,FSET)
           DFHMDF POS=(06,57),LENGTH=01,INITIAL=' ',ATTRB=ASKIP
           DFHMDF POS=(07,03),LENGTH=12,ATTRB=ASKIP,                     C
               INITIAL='CUSTOMER NO:'
CUSNUM     DFHMDF POS=(07,16),LENGTH=14,ATTRB=(BRT,ASKIP,FSET)
           DFHMDF POS=(07,31),LENGTH=15,ATTRB=ASKIP,                     C
               INITIAL='CUSTOMER NAME :'
CUSNAME    DFHMDF POS=(07,47),LENGTH=30,ATTRB=(BRT,ASKIP)
           DFHMDF POS=(07,78),LENGTH=01,INITIAL=' ',ATTRB=ASKIP
           DFHMDF POS=(08,03),LENGTH=12,ATTRB=(BRT,ASKIP),              C
               INITIAL='INVOICE NO :'
INVPRE     DFHMDF POS=(08,16),LENGTH=01,ATTRB=(UNPROT,FSET)
INVNO      DFHMDF POS=(08,18),LENGTH=05,ATTRB=(UNPROT,FSET)
           DFHMDF POS=(08,24),LENGTH=01,INITIAL=' ',ATTRB=ASKIP
           DFHMDF POS=(08,31),LENGTH=15,ATTRB=ASKIP,                     C
               INITIAL='INVOICE AMOUNT:'
INVAMNT    DFHMDF POS=(08,47),LENGTH=11,ATTRB=(UNPROT,FSET)
           DFHMDF POS=(08,59),LENGTH=01,INITIAL=' ',ATTRB=ASKIP
           DFHMDF POS=(09,03),LENGTH=17,ATTRB=(BRT,ASKIP),              C
               INITIAL='ACCOUNTING MM/YY:'
ACCPER     DFHMDF POS=(09,21),LENGTH=04,ATTRB=(UNPROT,FSET)
           DFHMDF POS=(09,26),LENGTH=01,INITIAL=' ',ATTRB=ASKIP
           DFHMDF POS=(09,31),LENGTH=21,ATTRB=(BRT,ASKIP),              C
               INITIAL='BILLING DATE (MMDDYY)'
BILLD      DFHMDF POS=(09,53),LENGTH=06,ATTRB=(UNPROT,FSET)
           DFHMDF POS=(09,60),LENGTH=01,INITIAL=' ',ATTRB=ASKIP
           DFHMDF POS=(10,03),LENGTH=17,ATTRB=ASKIP,                     C
               INITIAL='PERIOD DESCRIPT.:'
PERDES     DFHMDF POS=(10,21),LENGTH=55,ATTRB=(UNPROT,FSET)
           DFHMDF POS=(10,77),LENGTH=01,INITIAL=' ',ATTRB=ASKIP
           DFHMDF POS=(12,03),LENGTH=23,ATTRB=(BRT,ASKIP),              C
               INITIAL='                      '
           DFHMDF POS=(12,27),LENGTH=21,ATTRB=ASKIP,                     C
               INITIAL='SPECIAL INSTRUCTIONS'
           DFHMDF POS=(12,49),LENGTH=23,ATTRB=(BRT,ASKIP),              C
               INITIAL='                      '
INSTR1     DFHMDF POS=(14,03),LENGTH=70,ATTRB=(UNPROT,FSET)
           DFHMDF POS=(14,74),LENGTH=01,INITIAL=' ',ATTRB=ASKIP
INSTR2     DFHMDF POS=(15,03),LENGTH=70,ATTRB=(UNPROT,FSET)
           DFHMDF POS=(15,74),LENGTH=01,INITIAL=' ',ATTRB=ASKIP
           DFHMDF POS=(17,03),LENGTH=70,ATTRB=(BRT,ASKIP),              C
               INITIAL='                                              C
                                                                        '
PFMSG1     DFHMDF POS=(22,05),LENGTH=19,ATTRB=ASKIP,                     C
               INITIAL='PF1: RETURN TO MENU'
PFMSG2     DFHMDF POS=(22,31),LENGTH=35,ATTRB=(BRT,ASKIP),              C
               INITIAL='PF2: INVOICE DESCRIPTION PANEL'
PFMSG3     DFHMDF POS=(23,05),LENGTH=19,ATTRB=(BRT,ASKIP),              C
               INITIAL='PF3: HELP'
```

```
PFMSG4    DFHMDF  POS=(23,31),LENGTH=25,ATTRB=(BRT,ASKIP)
ERMSG     DFHMDF  POS=(24,05),LENGTH=60,ATTRB=(BRT,PROT,FSET)
          DFHMSD  TYPE=FINAL
          END
```

```
ARA21C  DFHFCT  TYPE=DATASET,ACCMETH=VSAM,LOG=YES,          C
                DATASE=ARA21C,                              C
                DSNAME=NIRVT.AR.ARA21C,DISP=SHR,            C
                SEVREQ=(BROWSE,DELETE,ADD,UPDATE),          C
                RCFORM=(FIXED,BLOCK),                       C
                FILSTAT=(ENABLED,CLOSED),                   C
                LSRPOOL=1,                                  C
                STRNO=2,BUFND=3,BUFNI=2
```

6-6   FCT (File Control Table) for the nonrecurring customer master billing file

particular dataset. Thus, you need to verify that there has been no tampering with the record key.

The next 30 positions reflect the full key of the nonrecurring billing master: one position allocated to an invoice prefix, five numeric positions allocated to an invoice number, while the rest of the 24 positions are filled with blanks. From position 32 on, (statement 15) down to the location of the cursor (statement 29), this COMMAREA contains multiple switches and indicators that I am going to describe in detail momentarily.

There are four copy statements issued in this program. These are: a nonrecurring customer billing master (statement 31), a customer master containing some essential demographic data required for producing an invoice statement (line 33), a DFHAID block to develop a standard reference to the keyboard (statement 39), and an associated map (statement 40).

Paragraph 0000-MAIN checks the length of the message in the communications area by examining the EIBCALEN byte. If any recent messages have been transmitted in the COMMAREA, they will promptly be moved into a formatted DATA DIVISION storage area for subsequent reference. In lines 48 through 50, the program checks the contents of the tutorial return field to see if a HELP screen was issued during the previous cycle. This situation is designated by an indicator value of "T," and it will initiate the following procedures:

- Clear the above indicator, replacing the character "T" with the value "X." The reason for that is so that it would bypass the tutorial session the next time around.
- It will invoke a paragraph, 0400-TUTORIAL-RETURN (lines 241 through 272), which I will discuss shortly. If the tutorial session is not applicable under the circumstances, a final "IF" statement is to be performed. This is essentially triggered by comparing EIBTRNID to the current transaction identifier,

which is AR24. A first-time routine is then promptly followed, provided that the current transid is other than AR24, simply meaning that it is the beginning of the program and no RETURN statement had been issued up to this point. This will direct you to the 0800-START-SESSION paragraph.

If the program is being invoked for the first time, program logic will follow a number of PF key assignments through a HANDLE AID command (lines 53 through 60). Accordingly, PF 1 will return you to a prior subdirectory (or menu) screen. PF 2 triggers an edit function that deserves some additional explanation. As I briefly explained in the case study, physical update requires sequential interaction through three panels. That means that the amount of data required to update the nonrecurring customer billing file is contained on several panels. Of these panels, only the current procedures use an invoice header screen (see FIG. 6-3), which happens to be the first panel in the series. Thus, by pressing PF 2 (provided all edit requirements have been previously fulfilled), you are only updating a "dummy" record. This is like placing part of the information needed to update a file into a storage area for subsequent retrieval, provided all three screens successfully pass the required validation. PF 3 is designed to invoke a HELP screen, which is invoked through a tutorial program. The source listing of this independent piece of program, including a comprehensive narrative, will be presented in Chapter 9.

Let me proceed by describing all the attribute values in this program, which is very much standard in CICS.

A   This value is used to describe an unprotected alpha field with its modified data tag turned on. This is a low-intensity field.

H   This value stands for an unprotected alpha field displayed in high-intensity.

I   The attribute "I" denotes an unprotected, high-intensity alpha field with its modified data tag turned on.

Y   Stands for a protected, high-intensity field.

Z   This field, just like the above Y field, stands for a protected, high-intensity field with its modified data tag turned on.

–   This sign means a protected, low-intensity field.

Using a basic attribute scheme, each of these values are assigned a particular color. These are: green, encompassing the value "A"; blue, associated with a " – "; red, associated with the character values of "H" and "I"; and white, denoting the values for "Y" and "Z."

Prior to sending the map, a few lines of maintenance procedures are performed as part of paragraph 0100-START-PROCESS, such as turning on the modified data tag for a number of fields and resetting the error message to a low-intensity, protected field (line 65), in case such a field has other characteristics from a previous instruction (i.e., a high-intensity display message, etc.). Next, the program checks the invoice number field which, is made up of a prefix (one-position, alphanumeric) and an invoice number field. Thus, in order to display a particular record on the screen, you need to check the validity of the key to verify what the user initially entered. These procedures and follow up error messages are presented in lines 70 through 85 of FIG. 6-13. In case of an error condition, paragraph 0910-SEND-MAP-DATAONLY is invoked, which will physically carry and transmit one of the error messages.

Paragraph 0210-ENTER-EDIT (lines 117 through 159) is executed when the value of the EDIT-RECORD field (originally shown in line 23) is equal to a "Y." Paragraph 0210-ENTER-EDIT is invoked after the program successfully performs paragraph 0500-READ-INVOICE-RECORD (shown in line 275 through 289), where the switch is set to equal the character "Y." Here are the logical sequences I refer to as "events."

The first event takes place when you select the "UPDATE AN INVOICE RECORD" from the associated subdirectory. This is shown in FIG. 6-7. Once you have selected task 2, program logic will branch to the Invoice Header Screen for Nonrecurring Billings. Thus, the screen appears to display only the constant or header portion of the screen. This screen is highlighted in FIG. 6-8, coupled with a message (ENTER PREFIX AND HIT ENTER). At this point, the program expects you to key in the concatenated key (prefix + invoice number) that looks like this: E 00001.

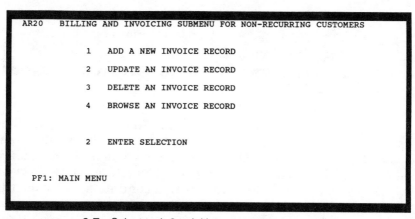

```
AR20    BILLING AND INVOICING SUBMENU FOR NON-RECURRING CUSTOMERS

          1    ADD A NEW INVOICE RECORD

          2    UPDATE AN INVOICE RECORD

          3    DELETE AN INVOICE RECORD

          4    BROWSE AN INVOICE RECORD


          2    ENTER SELECTION


   PF1: MAIN MENU
```

6-7 Select task 2 to initiate a CHANGE transaction

```
AR24    INVOICE HEADER SCREEN FOR NON RECURRING BILLINGS    05/31/90
                        UPDATE MODE

    PROJECT NO :
    CREDIT MEMO.        (Y, N)      ORIGINAL INV# :
    CUSTOMER NO:                    CUSTOMER NAME :
    INVOICE NO :                    INVOICE AMOUNT:
    ACCOUNTING MM/YY:               BILLING DATE   (MMDDYY)
    PERIOD DESCRIPT.:

    -------------------- SPECIAL INSTRUCTION ------------------------



    ----------------------------------------------------------------

    PF1: RETURN TO MENU       PF2: INVOICE DESCRIPTION PANEL
    PF3: HELP
    ENTER PREFIX AND HIT ENTER
```

6-8 Displays a blank screen for entering an INQUIRY key

In the second event, I entered E 0001 (FIG. 6-9) and pressed the ENTER key. This resulted in the display of the requested record (provided that such a key is pointing to an existing record on file). The display panel representing this situation is highlighted in FIG. 6-10. Note that line 24 now contains a systems message that reads: "TYPE IN THE CHANGES, HIT PF 2 WHEN RECORD COMPLETE."

```
AR24    INVOICE HEADER SCREEN FOR NON RECURRING BILLINGS    05/31/90
                        UPDATE MODE

    PROJECT NO :
    CREDIT MEMO.        (Y, N)      ORIGINAL INV# :
    CUSTOMER NO:                    CUSTOMER NAME :
    INVOICE NO : E 00001            INVOICE AMOUNT:
    ACCOUNTING MM/YY:               BILLING DATE   (MMDDYY)
    PERIOD DESCRIPT.:

    -------------------- SPECIAL INSTRUCTION ------------------------



    ----------------------------------------------------------------

    PF1: RETURN TO MENU       PF2: INVOICE DESCRIPTION PANEL
    PF3: HELP
    ENTER PREFIX AND HIT ENTER
```

6-9 Entering the INQUIRY key on a blank screen

A third event is now initiated, which is the edit cycle. Whether you leave the displayed items intact or substantially modify them, this is the place to do so. Once the ENTER key is pressed, you are signalling to the program the end of your modifications. This cycle is highlighted in 0210-ENTER-EDIT, which continuously reedits the screen on a field by field basis. Thus, the program checks and validates the invoice amount (i.e., to make sure that the invoice

```
AR24    INVOICE HEADER SCREEN FOR NON RECURRING BILLINGS    05/31/90
                       UPDATE MODE

    PROJECT NO : 000001
    CREDIT MEMO. 0101 (Y, N)    ORIGINAL INV# :
    CUSTOMER NO:               CUSTOMER NAME : CONSOLIDATED METAL
    INVOICE NO : E 00001       INVOICE AMOUNT: 009000000
    ACCOUNTING MM/YY: 0991     BILLING DATE  (MMDDYY)  090991
    PERIOD DESCRIPT.: THIS INVOICE IS FOR THE PERIOD ENDING 0909

    -------------------- SPECIAL INSTRUCTION ------------------------
    REVIEW ALL E SERIES INVOICES


    ----------------------------------------------------------------

    PF1: RETURN TO MENU       PF2: INVOICE DESCRIPTION PANEL
    PF3: HELP
    TYPE IN THE CHANGES, HIT PF2 WHEN RECORD COMPLETE
```

6-10 Displaying the nonrecurring record based on the E00001 key

amount field was not omitted and that it is numeric). It also verifies the presence of a credit memo field (line 129). If the indicator contains a "Y" ("Y" meaning YES), the program also checks the contents of the original invoice number for validity. Afterward, the prefix (ORGINVFO) and the original invoice number (ORIGINVO) are checked, along with all other required fields. If no edit problems are encountered in this cycle, a message: "IF SATISFIED HIT PF 2" appears in line 24, which initiates a subsequent event. Note that if you were to constantly press the ENTER key at this point, you would keep reediting your data, leaving the panel displayed in FIG. 6-11 unchanged.

```
AR24    INVOICE HEADER SCREEN FOR NON RECURRING BILLINGS    05/31/90
                       UPDATE MODE

    PROJECT NO : 000001
    CREDIT MEMO. 0101 (Y, N)    ORIGINAL INV# :
    CUSTOMER NO:               CUSTOMER NAME : CONSOLIDATED METAL
    INVOICE NO : E 00001       INVOICE AMOUNT: 009000000
    ACCOUNTING MM/YY: 0991     BILLING DATE  (MMDDYY)  090991
    PERIOD DESCRIPT.: THIS INVOICE IS FOR THE PERIOD ENDING 0909

    -------------------- SPECIAL INSTRUCTION ------------------------
    REVIEW ALL E SERIES INVOICES


    ----------------------------------------------------------------

    PF1: RETURN TO MENU       PF2: INVOICE DESCRIPTION PANEL
    PF3: HELP
    IF SATISFIED HIT PF2
```

6-11 After-edit-cycle display expecting PF key action

The fourth event is triggered when you press PF 2. This logic is laid out for you in detail in paragraph 0220-PF 2-EDIT. Editing is done once again in case this paragraph was invoked via the initial HAN-

DLE-AID command, which needs to duplicate all prior edits before updating the file. Once editing is performed, paragraph 0600-REWRITE-INVOICE is to be executed (line 333), which stores all prior information while branching via an exit procedure to an Invoice Description Screen (see FIG. 6-12). Note that the entire life cycle of this change mechanism is described in FIGS. 6-7 through 6-11. Also, the entire ARC24C source code is shown in FIG. 6-13.

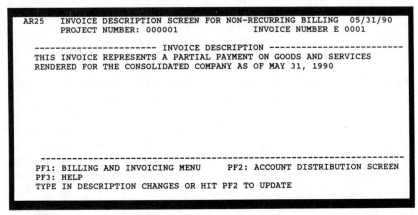

```
AR25   INVOICE DESCRIPTION SCREEN FOR NON-RECURRING BILLING  05/31/90
       PROJECT NUMBER: 000001                   INVOICE NUMBER E 0001

       ----------------------- INVOICE DESCRIPTION -----------------------
       THIS INVOICE REPRESENTS A PARTIAL PAYMENT ON GOODS AND SERVICES
       RENDERED FOR THE CONSOLIDATED COMPANY AS OF MAY 31, 1990




       --------------------------------------------------------------------
       PF1: BILLING AND INVOICING MENU      PF2: ACCOUNT DISTRIBUTION SCREEN
       PF3: HELP
       TYPE IN DESCRIPTION CHANGES OR HIT PF2 TO UPDATE
```

6-12   A panel reached by the CHANGE program through exit control

6-13   ARC24C

```
1    IDENTIFICATION DIVISION.
2    PROGRAM-ID. ARC24C.
3    DATE-COMPILED. MAY 22 1990.
4    ENVIRONMENT DIVISION.
5    DATA DIVISION.
6    WORKING-STORAGE SECTION.
7    01  COMM-AREA.
8        03  ENTRY-SW           PIC X   VALUE '0'.
9            88  TUTORIAL-RETURN         VALUE 'T'.
10       03  SEARCH-KEYS.
11           05  INV-KEY.
12               10  I-KEY      PIC X.
13               10  I-NUM      PIC X(5).
14               10  I-FILLER   PIC X(24) VALUE SPACES.
15           05  PRJ-KEY        PIC X(6).
16       03  RECORD-READ-SW     PIC X   VALUE 'N'.
17           88  RECORD-READ            VALUE 'Y'.
18       03  UPDATE-RECORD-SW   PIC X   VALUE 'N'.
19           88  UPDATE-RECORD          VALUE 'Y'.
20       03  RECORD-UPDATED-SW  PIC X   VALUE 'N'.
21           88  RECORD-UPDATED         VALUE 'Y'.
22       03  EDIT-RECORD-SW     PIC X   VALUE 'N'.
23           88  EDIT-RECORD            VALUE 'Y'.
24       03  COM-ACC-PER        PIC X(4).
25       03  DUMMY-KEY.
26           05  D-KEY          PIC X .
27           05  D-NUM          PIC X(5).
28           05  D-FILLER       PIC X(24).
29       03  CURSOR-POSITION    PIC 9(4) VALUE ZERO.
30
31   01  INVOICE-RECORD.        COPY NREINV.
32
33   01  CUSTOMER-RECORD.       COPY RK501.
34
35   01  HOLD-DATE.
```

```
36        05  HOLD-MONTH              PIC XX.
37        05  HOLD-YEAR               PIC XX.
38
39    COPY DFHAID.
40    COPY ARC24M.
41    LINKAGE SECTION.
42    01  DFHCOMMAREA                 PIC X(79).
43
44    PROCEDURE DIVISION.
45    0000-MAIN.
46        IF EIBCALEN > ZERO
47            MOVE DFHCOMMAREA TO COMM-AREA.
48        IF TUTORIAL-RETURN
49            MOVE 'X' TO ENTRY-SW
50            GO TO 0400-TUTORIAL-RETURN.
51        IF EIBTRNID NOT = 'AR24'
52            GO TO 0800-START-SESSION.
53        EXEC CICS
54            HANDLE AID
55                    CLEAR(0200-PF1-MAIN-MENU)
56                    PF1(0200-PF1-MAIN-MENU)
57                    PF2(0220-PF2-EDIT)
58                    PF3(0230-PF3-HELP)
59                    ANYKEY(0230-INVALID-KEY)
60        END-EXEC.
61
62    0100-START-PROCESS.
63        MOVE 'A' TO INVAMNTA ERMSGA ACCPERA ORGINVFA
64            ORGINVA BILLDA.
65        MOVE '-' TO ERMSGA.
66        EXEC CICS
67            RECEIVE MAP('ARC24M2')
68                    MAPSET('ARC24M')
69        END-EXEC.
70        IF INVPREO = SPACE
71            OR INVPREL = ZERO
72            MOVE 'ENTER PREFIX & HIT ENTER' TO ERMSGO
73            MOVE -1 TO INVPREL
74            GO TO 0910-SEND-MAP-DATAONLY.
75        IF INVNOO = SPACE
76            OR INVNOL = ZERO
77            MOVE 'ENTER PREFIX NUMBER & HIT ENTER' TO ERMSGO
78            MOVE -1 TO INVNOL
79            GO TO 0910-SEND-MAP-DATAONLY.
80        IF INVNOO NOT NUMERIC
81            MOVE 'INVPRE NUMBER NOT NUMERIC PLEASE REENTER'
82                TO ERMSGO
83            MOVE -1 TO INVNOL
84            MOVE 'I' TO INVNOA
85            GO TO 0910-SEND-MAP-DATAONLY.
86        IF EDIT-RECORD
87            GO TO 0210-ENTER-EDIT.
88        IF RECORD-READ
89            GO TO 0300-CONTINUE-PROCESS.
90        MOVE INVNOO TO INVOICE-NUMBERX.
91        MOVE INVPREO TO INVOICE-PREFIX-KEY.
92        MOVE SPACES TO INVOICE-FILLER.
93        MOVE INVOICE-KEY TO INV-KEY.
94        MOVE INV-KEY TO DUMMY-KEY.
95        MOVE 'DUMMY' TO D-NUM.
96        GO TO 0500-READ-INVOICE-RECORD.
97
98    0200-PF1-MAIN-MENU.
99        EXEC CICS
100           HANDLE CONDITION
101                   NOTFND(0200-PF1-CONT-MENU)
102       END-EXEC.
103       EXEC CICS
104           READ DATASET('ARA21C')
105                   INTO(INVOICE-RECORD)
106                   RIDFLD(DUMMY-KEY)
107       END-EXEC.
108       EXEC CICS
109           DELETE DATASET('ARA21C')
110                   RIDFLD(DUMMY-KEY)
111       END-EXEC.
112   0200-PF1-CONT-MENU.
113       EXEC CICS
```

```
114                    XCTL PROGRAM('ARM20C')
115            END-EXEC.
116
117    0210-ENTER-EDIT.
118            MOVE 'A' TO PROJECTA INVAMNTA ERMSGA ACCPERA ORGINVFA
119                ORGINVA.
120            MOVE '-' TO ERMSGA.
121            MOVE ' ' TO ERMSGO.
122            MOVE 'Z' TO CUSNUMA.
123            MOVE 'X' TO ENTRY-SW.
124            IF INVAMNTO NOT NUMERIC
125                MOVE 'AMOUNT NOT NUMERIC PLEASE RENTER' TO ERMSGO
126                MOVE 'I' TO INVAMNTA ERMSGA
127                MOVE -1 TO INVAMNTL
128                GO TO 0910-SEND-MAP-DATAONLY.
129            IF (MEMOO = 'Y') AND
130                (ORGINVFO = SPACES OR LOW-VALUES)
131                    MOVE 'ORIGINAL INVOICE MUST BE ENTERED' TO
132                    ERMSGO
133                    MOVE 'I' TO ORGINVFA ERMSGA
134                    MOVE -1 TO ORGINVFL
135                    GO TO 0910-SEND-MAP-DATAONLY.
136            IF (MEMOO = 'Y') AND
137                (ORGINVO = SPACES OR LOW-VALUES)
138                    MOVE 'ORIGINAL INVOICE MUST BE ENTERED' TO
139                    ERMSGO
140                    MOVE 'I' TO ORGINVFA ERMSGA
141                    MOVE -1 TO ORGINVFL
142                    GO TO 0910-SEND-MAP-DATAONLY.
143            MOVE ACCPERO TO HOLD-DATE.
144            IF ACCPERO NOT NUMERIC
145                MOVE 'ACCOUNTING PERIOD NUMT NUMERIC PLEASE
146                RE-ENTER'
147                    TO ERMSGO
148                MOVE 'I' TO ACCPERA ERMSGA
149                MOVE -1 TO ACCPERL
150                GO TO 0910-SEND-MAP-DATAONLY.
151            IF HOLD-MONTH > 12
152                MOVE 'MONTH IS INVALID PLEASE REENTER' TO ERMSGO
153                MOVE 'I' TO ACCPERA ERMSGA
154                MOVE -1 TO ACCPERL
155                GO TO 0910-SEND-MAP-DATAONLY.
156            MOVE 'Y' TO UPDATE-RECORD-SW.
157            MOVE -1 TO INVPREL.
158            MOVE 'IF SATISFIED HIT PF2 ' TO ERMSGO.
159            GO TO 0910-SEND-MAP-DATAONLY.
160
161    0220-PF2-EDIT.
162            MOVE 'A' TO PROJECTA INVAMNTA ERMSGA ACCPERA ORGINVFA
163                ORGINVA.
164            MOVE ' ' TO ERMSGO.
165            MOVE 'Z' TO CUSNUMA.
166            MOVE 'X' TO ENTRY-SW.
167            IF INVAMNTO NOT NUMERIC
168                MOVE 'AMOUNT NOT NUMERIC PLEASE RENTER' TO ERMSGO
169                MOVE 'I' TO INVAMNTA ERMSGA
170                MOVE -1 TO INVAMNTL
171                GO TO 0910-SEND-MAP-DATAONLY.
172            IF (MEMOO = 'Y') AND
173                (ORGINVFO = SPACES OR LOW-VALUES)
174                    MOVE 'ORIGINAL INVOICE MUST BE ENTERED' TO
175                    ERMSGO
176                    MOVE 'I' TO ORGINVFA ERMSGA
177                    MOVE -1 TO ORGINVFL
178                    GO TO 0910-SEND-MAP-DATAONLY.
179            IF (MEMOO = 'Y') AND
180                (ORGINVO = SPACES OR LOW-VALUES)
181                    MOVE 'ORIGINAL INVOICE MUST BE ENTERED' TO
182                    ERMSGO
183                    MOVE 'I' TO ORGINVFA ERMSGA
184                    MOVE -1 TO ORGINVFL
185                    GO TO 0910-SEND-MAP-DATAONLY.
186            MOVE ACCPERO TO HOLD-DATE.
187            IF ACCPERO NOT NUMERIC
188                MOVE 'ACCOUNTING PERIOD NUMT NUMERIC PLEASE
189                RE-ENTER'
```

```
190                         TO ERMSGO
191                     MOVE 'I' TO ACCPERA ERMSGA
192                     MOVE -1 TO ACCPERL
193                     GO TO 0910-SEND-MAP-DATAONLY.
194             IF HOLD-MONTH > 12
195                 MOVE 'MONTH IS INVALID PLEASE REENTER' TO ERMSGO
196                 MOVE 'I' TO ACCPERA ERMSGA
197                 MOVE -1 TO ACCPERL
198                 GO TO 0910-SEND-MAP-DATAONLY.
199             IF UPDATE-RECORD
200                 PERFORM 0600-REWRITE-INVOICE.
201             MOVE 'Y' TO UPDATE-RECORD-SW.
202             MOVE -1 TO INVPREL.
203             MOVE 'IF SATISFIED HIT PF2 ' TO ERMSGO.
204             GO TO 0910-SEND-MAP-DATAONLY.
205
206         0230-PF3-HELP.
207             EXEC CICS
208                     READ DATASET('ARA21C')
209                             INTO(INVOICE-RECORD)
210                             RIDFLD(INV-KEY)
211             END-EXEC.
212             PERFORM 0610-REWRITE-LINE.
213             EXEC CICS
214                     WRITE DATASET('ARA21C')
215                             FROM(INVOICE-RECORD)
216                             RIDFLD(DUMMY-KEY)
217             END-EXEC.
218             MOVE EIBCPOSN TO CURSOR-POSITION.
219                 EXEC CICS
220                     XCTL PROGRAM('ARB83C')
221                             COMMAREA(COMM-AREA)
222                             LENGTH(79)
223                 END-EXEC.
224
225
226         0230-INVALID-KEY.
227             MOVE 'INVALID KEY USED' TO ERMSGO.
228             GO TO 0910-SEND-MAP-DATAONLY.
229
230         0300-CONTINUE-PROCESS.
231             MOVE 'A' TO INVPREA INVNOA PROJECTA.
232             MOVE 'N' TO RECORD-READ-SW.
233             MOVE 'Y' TO EDIT-RECORD-SW.
234             MOVE 'Z' TO CUSNUMA.
235             MOVE 'TYPE IN THE CHANGES, HIT PF2 WHEN RECORD
236         COMPLETE'
237                 TO ERMSGO.
238             MOVE -1 TO INVAMNTL.
239             GO TO 0910-SEND-MAP-DATAONLY.
240
241         0400-TUTORIAL-RETURN.
242             EXEC CICS
243                 HANDLE CONDITION
244                     NOTFND(0530-INVALID-INVOICE)
245             END-EXEC.
246             MOVE 'A' TO INVPREA INVNOA.
247             EXEC CICS
248                     READ DATASET('ARA21C')
249                             INTO(INVOICE-RECORD)
250                             RIDFLD(DUMMY-KEY)
251             END-EXEC.
252             MOVE 'X' TO ENTRY-SW.
253             PERFORM 0510-MOVE-LINE.
254             MOVE I-NUM TO INVNOO.
255             PERFORM 0520-READ-CUSTOMER-MSTR.
256             PERFORM 0810-FIND-CURSOR.
257             MOVE 'A' TO INVPREA INVNOA PROJECTA.
258             MOVE 'N' TO RECORD-READ-SW.
259             MOVE 'Y' TO EDIT-RECORD-SW.
260             MOVE 'Z' TO CUSNUMA.
261             MOVE 'TYPE IN THE CHANGES, HIT PF2 WHEN RECORD
262         COMPLETE'
263                 TO ERMSGO.
264     *       MOVE -1 TO INVAMNTL.
265             EXEC CICS
266                     DELETE DATASET('ARA21C')
267                             RIDFLD(DUMMY-KEY)
```

```
268          END-EXEC.
269          EXEC CICS
270              UNLOCK DATASET('ARA21C')
271          END-EXEC.
272          GO TO 0900-SEND-MAP.
273
274
275      0500-READ-INVOICE-RECORD.
276          EXEC CICS
277              HANDLE CONDITION
278                  NOTFND(0530-INVALID-INVOICE)
279          END-EXEC.
280          MOVE 'A' TO INVPREA INVNOA.
281          EXEC CICS
282              READ DATASET('ARA21C')
283                      INTO(INVOICE-RECORD)
284                      RIDFLD(INV-KEY)
285          END-EXEC.
286          MOVE 'Y' TO RECORD-READ-SW.
287          PERFORM 0510-MOVE-LINE.
288          PERFORM 0520-READ-CUSTOMER-MSTR.
289          GO TO 0300-CONTINUE-PROCESS.
290
291      0510-MOVE-LINE.
292          MOVE INVOICE-PREFIX-KEY TO INVPREO.
293          MOVE INVOICE-NUMBERX TO INVNOO.
294          MOVE INVOICE-AMOUNTX TO INVAMNTO.
295          MOVE PERIOD-DESCRIP TO PERDESO
296          MOVE PROJECT-NUMBER TO PROJECTO
297          MOVE CREDIT-MEMO TO MEMOO.
298          MOVE ORIGINAL-PREFIX TO ORGINVFO.
299          MOVE ORIGINAL-INV-NUM TO ORGINVO.
300          MOVE INV-CUSTOMER-NO TO CUSNUMO CUSTOMER-NUMBER.
301          MOVE ACCOUNTING-PERIOD TO ACCPERO.
302          MOVE INV-INSTR1 TO INSTR1O.
303          MOVE INV-INSTR2 TO INSTR2O.
304          MOVE BILLING-DATE TO BILLDO.
305
306      0520-READ-CUSTOMER-MSTR.
307          MOVE 'Z' TO CUSNUMA.
308          MOVE CUSNUMO TO CUSTOMER-NUMBER.
309          EXEC CICS
310              HANDLE CONDITION
311                  NOTFND(0540-INVALID-CUST)
312          END-EXEC.
313          EXEC CICS
314              READ DATASET('RK501')
315                      INTO(CUSTOMER-RECORD)
316                      RIDFLD(CUSTOMER-KEY)
317          END-EXEC.
318          MOVE 'Y' TO CUSNAMEA.
319          MOVE CUSTOMER-NAME TO CUSNAMEO.
320
321      0530-INVALID-INVOICE.
322          MOVE -1 TO INVNOL.
323          MOVE 'I' TO INVNOA.
324          MOVE 'INVOICE NUMBER DOES NOT EXISTS ' TO ERMSGO.
325          GO TO 0910-SEND-MAP-DATAONLY.
326
327      0540-INVALID-CUST.
328          MOVE -1 TO CUSNUML.
329          MOVE 'I' TO CUSNUMA.
330          MOVE 'CUSTOMER NUMBER DOES NOT EXISTS' TO ERMSGO.
331          GO TO 0910-SEND-MAP-DATAONLY.
332
333      0600-REWRITE-INVOICE.
334          EXEC CICS
335              READ DATASET('ARA21C')
336                      INTO(INVOICE-RECORD)
337                      RIDFLD(INV-KEY)
338          END-EXEC.
339          PERFORM 0610-REWRITE-LINE.
340          EXEC CICS
341              WRITE DATASET('ARA21C')
342                      FROM(INVOICE-RECORD)
343                      RIDFLD(DUMMY-KEY)
```

```
344          END-EXEC.
345          MOVE 'N' TO RECORD-READ-SW UPDATE-RECORD-SW
346          EDIT-RECORD-SW.
347              EXEC CICS
348                  XCTL PROGRAM('ARC25C')
349                          COMMAREA(COMM-AREA)
350                          LENGTH(79)
351              END-EXEC
352
353      0610-REWRITE-LINE.
354          MOVE DUMMY-KEY TO INVOICE-KEY.
355          IF  INVAMNTO NUMERIC
356              MOVE INVAMNTO TO INVOICE-AMOUNTX
357          ELSE
358              MOVE SPACES TO INVOICE-AMOUNTX.
359          IF  PERDESO NOT = SPACES OR LOW-VALUES
360              MOVE PERDESO TO PERIOD-DESCRIP
361          ELSE
362              MOVE SPACES TO PERIOD-DESCRIP.
363          IF  PROJECTO NOT = SPACES OR LOW-VALUES
364              MOVE PROJECTO TO PROJECT-NUMBER PRJ-KEY
365          ELSE
366              MOVE SPACES TO PROJECT-NUMBER.
367          IF  MEMOO NOT = SPACES OR LOW-VALUES
368              MOVE MEMOO TO CREDIT-MEMO
369          ELSE
370              MOVE SPACES TO CREDIT-MEMO.
371          IF  ORGINVFO NOT = SPACES OR LOW-VALUES
372              MOVE ORGINVFO TO ORIGINAL-PREFIX
373          ELSE
374              MOVE SPACES TO ORIGINAL-PREFIX.
375          IF  ORGINVO NUMERIC
376              MOVE ORGINVO TO ORIGINAL-INV-NUM
377          ELSE
378              MOVE SPACES TO ORIGINAL-INV-NUM.
379          IF  CUSNUMO NUMERIC
380              MOVE CUSNUMO TO INV-CUSTOMER-NOX
381          ELSE
382              MOVE SPACES TO INV-CUSTOMER-NOX.
383          MOVE ACCPERO TO ACCOUNTING-PERIOD COM-ACC-PER.
384          IF  INSTR1O NOT = SPACES OR LOW-VALUES
385              MOVE INSTR1O TO INV-INSTR1
386          ELSE
387              MOVE SPACES TO INV-INSTR1.
388          IF  INSTR2O NOT = SPACES OR LOW-VALUES
389              MOVE INSTR2O TO INV-INSTR2
390          ELSE
391              MOVE SPACES TO INV-INSTR2.
392          MOVE BILLDO TO BILLING-DATE.
393
394      0800-START-SESSION.
395          MOVE LOW-VALUE TO ARC24M2O.
396          MOVE CURRENT-DATE TO DATEO.
397          MOVE 'UPDATE MODE ' TO MODEO.
398          MOVE 'ENTER PREFIX AND PREFIX NUMBER'
399              TO ERMSGO.
400          MOVE -1 TO INVPREL.
401          EXEC CICS
402              HANDLE CONDITION
403                      NOTFND(0900-SEND-MAP)
404          END-EXEC.
405          EXEC CICS
406              READ DATASET('ARA21C')
407                          INTO(INVOICE-RECORD)
408                          RIDFLD(DUMMY-KEY)
409          END-EXEC.
410          EXEC CICS
411              DELETE DATASET('ARA21C')
412                          RIDFLD(DUMMY-KEY)
413          END-EXEC.
414          GO TO 0900-SEND-MAP.
415
416      0810-FIND-CURSOR.
417          IF CURSOR-POSITION > 0 AND CURSOR-POSITION < 416
418              MOVE -1 TO PROJECTL
419          ELSE IF CURSOR-POSITION = 416
420              MOVE -1 TO MEMOL
421          ELSE IF CURSOR-POSITION = 447
```

```
422             MOVE -1 TO ORGINVFL
423         ELSE IF CURSOR-POSITION = 451
424             MOVE -1 TO ORGINVL
425         ELSE IF CURSOR-POSITION = 451
426             MOVE -1 TO ORGINVL
427         ELSE IF CURSOR-POSITION > 451 AND CURSOR-POSITION <
428                                                         527
429             MOVE -1 TO CUSNUML
430         ELSE IF CURSOR-POSITION > 526 AND CURSOR-POSITION <
431                                                         576
432             MOVE -1 TO CUSNAMEL
433         ELSE IF CURSOR-POSITION = 576
434             MOVE -1 TO INVPREL
435         ELSE IF CURSOR-POSITION > 576 AND CURSOR-POSITION <
436                                                         607
437             MOVE -1 TO INVNOL
438         ELSE IF CURSOR-POSITION > 606 AND CURSOR-POSITION <
439                                                         660
440             MOVE -1 TO INVAMNTL
441         ELSE IF CURSOR-POSITION > 660 AND CURSOR-POSITION <
442                                                         692
443             MOVE -1 TO ACCPERL
444         ELSE IF CURSOR-POSITION > 692 AND CURSOR-POSITION <
445                                                         740
446             MOVE -1 TO BILLDL
447         ELSE IF CURSOR-POSITION > 740 AND CURSOR-POSITION <
448                                                         1042
449             MOVE -1 TO PERDESL
450         ELSE IF CURSOR-POSITION > 1042 AND CURSOR-POSITION <
451                                                         1103
452             MOVE -1 TO INSTR1L
453         ELSE IF CURSOR-POSITION > 1123 AND CURSOR-POSITION <
454                                                         1193
455             MOVE -1 TO INSTR2L
456         ELSE
457             MOVE -1 TO INVPREL.
458
459     0900-SEND-MAP.
460         MOVE CURRENT-DATE TO DATEO.
461         MOVE 'AR24' TO TRANSO.
462         MOVE 'PF2: INVOICE DESCRIPTION PANEL' TO PFMSG2O.
463         MOVE 'PF3: HELP'  TO PFMSG3O.
464         EXEC CICS
465             SEND MAP('ARC24M2')
466                  MAPSET('ARC24M')
467                  ERASE
468                  CURSOR
469         END-EXEC.
470         EXEC CICS
471             RETURN TRANSID('AR24')
472                    COMMAREA(COMM-AREA)
473                    LENGTH(79)
474         END-EXEC.
475
476     0910-SEND-MAP-DATAONLY.
477         MOVE CURRENT-DATE TO DATEO.
478         EXEC CICS
479             SEND MAP('ARC24M2')
480                  MAPSET('ARC24M')
481                  DATAONLY
482                  CURSOR
483         END-EXEC.
484         EXEC CICS
485             RETURN TRANSID('AR24')
486                    COMMAREA(COMM-AREA)
487                    LENGTH(79)
488         END-EXEC.
489         STOP RUN.
490         GOBACK.
491
492
```

In using the tutorial module in this change program, it is essential that the reader understand the two-stage mechanism involved in the process. The first, which I briefly touched on before, consists of the user pressing PF 3, causing an exit out of the current transaction into the HELP module. This is done so that the position of the cursor is retained in storage. A second stage takes place when the user returns from the above HELP module. This logic is incorporated into paragraph 0400-TUTORIAL-RETURN, lines 241 through 272.

The 0400-TUTORIAL-RETURN paragraph contains a couple of standard procedures, such as a HANDLE CONDITION for a follow up READ operation, and an ENTRY SWITCH (line 252) with the value of "X." Next, the 0810-FIND-CURSOR paragraph is promptly executed (line 256), which now locates the cursor based on its current position on the screen. Logic for these procedures is coded in lines 416 through 452.

Paragraph 0400-TUTORIAL-RETURN highlights two separate operations against the ARA21C dataset (lines 247 through 251 and lines 265 through 268, respectively), which is the nonrecurring customer billing file. This corresponds to the READ and WRITE operation part of the 0230-PF 3-HELP paragraph.

When you issue the first READ instruction (line 208), you are in fact reading the actual nonrecurring customer billing dataset, but in writing it out you need to create a dummy record the way I did lines 213 through 217. This is necessary in order to save your data while exiting out of the current transaction into the tutorial subsystem. In paragraph 0400-TUTORIAL-RETURN prior to returning to the current change transaction you need to read back the same dummy record you have just written into memory, then promptly delete the dummy record. This logic is highlighted for you in detail in lines 256 through 269. Note that this mechanism is also part of the 0200-PF 1-MAIN-MENU paragraph, lines 98 through 115, with a brief scenario incorporated into the 0601-REWRITE-LINE paragraph (356 through 392), as well as the 0800-START-SESSION paragraph shown in statements 395 through 414.

Two send map procedures are also highlighted in lines 459 through 490. The first one, 0900-SEND-MAP is designed to transmit a map in its entirety. A second set of procedures, 0910-SEND-MAP-DATAONLY, is only geared to transmit the data portion of the map, for reasons of efficiency.

Compiler-generated source code: excerpts

As shown in FIG. 6-14, the first copy statement, which is a record layout for the nonrecurring customer billing, is expanded in lines

33 through 60. This record is essentially the driver in updating and eventually printing all the associated invoices, once the files are closed to the online processing. A second copy statement is the customer master, which I have referred to earlier in both Chapters 3 and 5, in conjunction with a DELETE and an ADD transaction. The customer master is laid out in lines 64 through 94.

The third copy statement brings the DFHAID block into the change program, which is required to have reference to the keyboard. This copy statement enables you to use up to 24 keys in your HANDLE AID statement. In addition, the DFHAID block also contains 3 PA keys (lines 111 through 113), an ENTER and a CLEAR key, a light pen, etc. This definition is shown in lines 101 through 137.

A fourth copy statement is that of the symbolic map. As shown in FIG. 6-5, the current change program takes your initial BMS (Basic Mapping Support) definition and, once assembled, places it into a predefined copy library. The symbolic map is shown in lines 139 through 296. As I mentioned earlier, the symbolic map use five different character values in its suffix position for the following reasons:

- The suffix "L" enables you to check the length of a particular data field. This will allow you to check for any data entry (or data omission) on the screen in the current pseudoconversational cycle.
- The suffix "F" means that the particular data field has its modified data tag turned on. Modification means that any field with an "F" suffix can be redefined through the map (or through the program) from a 0 value (meaning no data has been entered in the current cycle), to +1, meaning the opposite.
- The prefix "I" denotes an input field, while an "O" refers to an output field.
- Finally, the character "A" stands for an attribute position required in order to display information on the screen. Attributes actually determine how a particular data field will appear on the screen, whether it is to be protected, highlighted, underscored, shown in reverse video, and so on.

Two other blocks are also part of the "expansion" process by the COBOL compiler, both of them printed without a corresponding copy statement. The first one is a block (DFHEIV) that is used internally by CICS for referencing. A second block, part of the LINKAGE SECTION, is the DFHEIBLK. This block contains valuable information for the program, such as a date and a time field, a terminal

address, a cursor location, the specific contents of the COMMUNICA-
TIONS AREA, etc. This block is laid out in the program in lines 343
through 374.

6-14 ARC24C compiler version

```
00001          IDENTIFICATION DIVISION.
00002          PROGRAM-ID. ARC24C.
00003          DATE-COMPILED. MAY 23,1990.
00004          ENVIRONMENT DIVISION.
00005          DATA DIVISION.
00006          WORKING-STORAGE SECTION.
00007       01  COMM-AREA.
00008           03  ENTRY-SW              PIC X   VALUE '0'.
00009               88  TUTORIAL-RETURN           VALUE 'T'.
00010           03  SEARCH-KEYS.
00011               05  INV-KEY.
00012                   10  I-KEY         PIC X.
00013                   10  I-NUM         PIC X(5).
00014                   10  I-FILLER      PIC X(24) VALUE
                                                   SPACES.
00015               05  PRJ-KEY           PIC X(6).
00016           03  RECORD-READ-SW        PIC X   VALUE 'N'.
00017               88  RECORD-READ               VALUE 'Y'.
00018           03  UPDATE-RECORD-SW      PIC X   VALUE 'N'.
00019               88  UPDATE-RECORD             VALUE 'Y'.
00020           03  RECORD-UPDATED-SW     PIC X   VALUE 'N'.
00021               88  RECORD-UPDATED            VALUE 'Y'.
00022           03  EDIT-RECORD-SW        PIC X   VALUE 'N'.
00023               88  EDIT-RECORD               VALUE 'Y'.
00024           03  COM-ACC-PER           PIC X(4).
00025           03  DUMMY-KEY.
00026               05  D-KEY             PIC X .
00027               05  D-NUM             PIC X(5).
00028               05  D-FILLER          PIC X(24).
00029           03  CURSOR-POSITION       PIC 9(4) VALUE ZERO.
00030
00031       01  INVOICE-RECORD.
00032                                     COPY NREINV.
00033 C         05  INVOICE-KEY.
00034 C             10  INVOICE-PREFIX-KEY    PIC X.
00035 C             10  INVOICE-NUMBER        PIC 9(5).
00036 C             10  INVOICE-NUMBERX REDEFINES INVOICE-NUMBER
00037 C                                       PIC X(5).
00038 C             10  INVOICE-FILLER        PIC X(24).
00039 C         05  INV-EXPLAIN           PIC X(900).
00040 C         05  INV-EXPLAIN-LINE  REDEFINES INV-EXPLAIN OCCURS 15.
00041 C             10  INV-LINE          PIC X(60).
00042 C         05  INVOICE-AMOUNT        PIC S9(9)V99.
00043 C         05  INVOICE-AMOUNTX REDEFINES INVOICE-AMOUNT
00044 C                                       PIC X(11).
00045 C         05  PERIOD-DESCRIP        PIC X(55).
00046 C         05  ORIGINAL-PREFIX       PIC X.
00047 C         05  ORIGINAL-INV-NUM      PIC X(5).
00048 C         05  ACCOUNTING-PERIOD     PIC X(4).
00049 C         05  FILLER                PIC X(13).
00050 C         05  PROJECT-NUMBER        PIC X(6).
00051 C         05  INV-SPECIAL-INSTR     PIC X(140).
00052 C         05  OCCUR-INSTR REDEFINES INV-SPECIAL-INSTR.
00053 C             10  INV-INSTR1        PIC X(70).
00054 C             10  INV-INSTR2        PIC X(70).
00055 C         05  CREDIT-MEMO           PIC X.
00056 C         05  FILLER                PIC X(12).
00057 C         05  INV-CUSTOMER-NO       PIC 9(14).
00058 C         05  INV-CUSTOMER-NOX REDEFINES INV-CUSTOMER-NO PIC X(14).
00059 C         05  BILLING-DATE          PIC X(6).
00060 C         05  FILLER                PIC X(52).
00061
00062       01  CUSTOMER-RECORD.
00063                                     COPY RK501.
00064 C         02  FILLER                        PIC X(01).
00065 C         02  CUSTOMER-KEY.
00066 C             05  CUSTOMER-COMPANY          PIC X(02) VALUE '01'.
```

```
00067 C                   05   CUSTOMER-SEGMENT                 PIC X(01) VALUE '2'.
00068 C                   05   CUSTOMER-NUMBER.
00069 C                        10   CUSTOMER-PREFIX             PIC X(10) VALUE ZEROS.
00070 C                        10   CUSTOMER-ID                 PIC X(04).
00071 C                   05   CUSTOMER-REFERENCE               PIC X(02) VALUE '01'.
00072 C                   05   FILLER                           PIC X(16) VALUE
                                                                          SPACES.
00073 C              02   DATA-AREA.
00074 C                   05   CUSTOMER-NAME                    PIC X(30).
00075 C                   05   CUSTOMER-ADDRESS1                PIC X(30).
00076 C                   05   CUSTOMER-ADDRESS2                PIC X(30).
00077 C                   05   CUSTOMER-ADDRESS3                PIC X(21).
00078 C                   05   CUSTOMER-STATE                   PIC X(02).
00079 C                   05   CUSTOMER-POSTAL-CODE             PIC X(10).
00080 C                   05   CUSTOMER-CONTACT-NAME            PIC X(15).
00081 C                   05   CUSTOMER-ABBREVIATED-NAME        PIC X(15).
00082 C                   05   CUSTOMER-ACCOUNT-OPENED.
00083 C                        10   CUSTOMER-MONTH              PIC X(02).
00084 C                        10   CUSTOMER-YEAR               PIC X(02).
00085 C                   05   FILLER                           PIC X(06).
00086 C                   05   CUSTOMER-TELEPHONE-NO.
00087 C                        10   FILLER                      PIC X(02).
00088 C                        10   CUSTOMER-AREA-CODE          PIC X(03).
00089 C                        10   CUSTOMER-TELEPHONE.
00090 C                             15   CUSTOMER-TEL1          PIC X(03).
00091 C                             15   CUSTOMER-TEL2          PIC X(04).
00092 C                   05   FILLER                           PIC X(28).
00093 C                   05   CUSTOMER-DB-NUMBER               PIC X(10).
00094 C                   05   FILLER                           PIC X(851).
00095
00096              01   HOLD-DATE.
00097                   05   HOLD-MONTH              PIC XX.
00098                   05   HOLD-YEAR               PIC XX.
00099
00100              COPY DFHAID.
00101 C            01    DFHAID.
00102 C                  02   DFHNULL   PIC X   VALUE IS ' '.
00103 C                  02   DFHENTER  PIC X   VALUE IS QUOTE.
00104 C                  02   DFHCLEAR  PIC X   VALUE IS ' '.
00105 C                  02   DFHCLRP   PIC X   VALUE IS 'T'.
00106 C                  02   DFHPEN    PIC X   VALUE IS '='.
00107 C                  02   DFHOPID   PIC X   VALUE IS 'W'.
00108 C                  02   DFHMSRE   PIC X   VALUE IS 'X'.
00109 C                  02   DFHSTRF   PIC X   VALUE IS 'h'.
00110 C                  02   DFHTRIG   PIC X   VALUE IS '"'.
00111 C                  02   DFHPA1    PIC X   VALUE IS '%'.
00112 C                  02   DFHPA2    PIC X   VALUE IS '>'.
00113 C                  02   DFHPA3    PIC X   VALUE IS ','.
00114 C                  02   DFHPF1    PIC X   VALUE IS '1'.
00115 C                  02   DFHPF2    PIC X   VALUE IS '2'.
00116 C                  02   DFHPF3    PIC X   VALUE IS '3'.
00117 C                  02   DFHPF4    PIC X   VALUE IS '4'.
00118 C                  02   DFHPF5    PIC X   VALUE IS '5'.
00119 C                  02   DFHPF6    PIC X   VALUE IS '6'.
00120 C                  02   DFHPF7    PIC X   VALUE IS '7'.
00121 C                  02   DFHPF8    PIC X   VALUE IS '8'.
00122 C                  02   DFHPF9    PIC X   VALUE IS '9'.
00123 C                  02   DFHPF10   PIC X   VALUE IS ':'.
00124 C                  02   DFHPF11   PIC X   VALUE IS '#'.
00125 C                  02   DFHPF12   PIC X   VALUE IS '@'.
00126 C                  02   DFHPF13   PIC X   VALUE IS 'A'.
00127 C                  02   DFHPF14   PIC X   VALUE IS 'B'.
00128 C                  02   DFHPF15   PIC X   VALUE IS 'C'.
00129 C                  02   DFHPF16   PIC X   VALUE IS 'D'.
00130 C                  02   DFHPF17   PIC X   VALUE IS 'E'.
00131 C                  02   DFHPF18   PIC X   VALUE IS 'F'.
00132 C                  02   DFHPF19   PIC X   VALUE IS 'G'.
00133 C                  02   DFHPF20   PIC X   VALUE IS 'H'.
00134 C                  02   DFHPF21   PIC X   VALUE IS 'I'.
00135 C                  02   DFHPF22   PIC X   VALUE IS '¢'.
00136 C                  02   DFHPF23   PIC X   VALUE IS '.'.
00137 C                  02   DFHPF24   PIC X   VALUE IS '<'.
00138              COPY ARC24M.
00139 C            01   ARC24M2I.
00140 C                 02   FILLER PIC X(12).
```

```
00141 C          02  TRANSL    COMP  PIC  S9(4).
00142 C          02  TRANSF    PICTURE  X.
00143 C          02  FILLER REDEFINES TRANSF.
00144 C              03 TRANSA    PICTURE  X.
00145 C          02  TRANSI  PIC X(4).
00146 C          02  DATEL     COMP  PIC  S9(4).
00147 C          02  DATEF     PICTURE  X.
00148 C          02  FILLER REDEFINES DATEF.
00149 C              03 DATEA     PICTURE  X.
00150 C          02  DATEI  PIC X(8).
00151 C          02  MODEL     COMP  PIC  S9(4).
00152 C          02  MODEF     PICTURE  X.
00153 C          02  FILLER REDEFINES MODEF.
00154 C              03 MODEA     PICTURE  X.
00155 C          02  MODEI  PIC X(12).
00156 C          02  PROJECTL    COMP  PIC  S9(4).
00157 C          02  PROJECTF    PICTURE  X.
00158 C          02  FILLER REDEFINES PROJECTF.
00159 C              03 PROJECTA    PICTURE  X.
00160 C          02  PROJECTI  PIC X(6).
00161 C          02  MEMOL     COMP  PIC  S9(4).
00162 C          02  MEMOF     PICTURE  X.
00163 C          02  FILLER REDEFINES MEMOF.
00164 C              03 MEMOA     PICTURE  X.
00165 C          02  MEMOI  PIC X(1).
00166 C          02  ORGINVFL    COMP  PIC  S9(4).
00167 C          02  ORGINVFF    PICTURE  X.
00168 C          02  FILLER REDEFINES ORGINVFF.
00169 C              03 ORGINVFA    PICTURE  X.
00170 C          02  ORGINVFI  PIC X(1).
00171 C          02  ORGINVL    COMP  PIC  S9(4).
00172 C          02  ORGINVF    PICTURE  X.
00173 C          02  FILLER REDEFINES ORGINVF.
00174 C              03 ORGINVA    PICTURE  X.
00175 C          02  ORGINVI  PIC X(5).
00176 C          02  CUSNUML    COMP  PIC  S9(4).
00177 C          02  CUSNUMF    PICTURE  X.
00178 C          02  FILLER REDEFINES CUSNUMF.
00179 C              03 CUSNUMA    PICTURE  X.
00180 C          02  CUSNUMI  PIC X(14).
00181 C          02  CUSNAMEL    COMP  PIC  S9(4).
00182 C          02  CUSNAMEF    PICTURE  X.
00183 C          02  FILLER REDEFINES CUSNAMEF.
00184 C              03 CUSNAMEA    PICTURE  X.
00185 C          02  CUSNAMEI  PIC X(30).
00186 C          02  INVPREL    COMP  PIC  S9(4).
00187 C          02  INVPREF    PICTURE  X.
00188 C          02  FILLER REDEFINES INVPREF.
00189 C              03 INVPREA    PICTURE  X.
00190 C          02  INVPREI  PIC X(1).
00191 C          02  INVNOL    COMP  PIC  S9(4).
00192 C          02  INVNOF    PICTURE  X.
00193 C          02  FILLER REDEFINES INVNOF.
00194 C              03 INVNOA    PICTURE  X.
00195 C          02  INVNOI  PIC X(5).
00196 C          02  INVAMNTL    COMP  PIC  S9(4).
00197 C          02  INVAMNTF    PICTURE  X.
00198 C          02  FILLER REDEFINES INVAMNTF.
00199 C              03 INVAMNTA    PICTURE  X.
00200 C          02  INVAMNTI  PIC X(11).
00201 C          02  ACCPERL    COMP  PIC  S9(4).
00202 C          02  ACCPERF    PICTURE  X.
00203 C          02  FILLER REDEFINES ACCPERF.
00204 C              03 ACCPERA    PICTURE  X.
00205 C          02  ACCPERI  PIC X(4).
00206 C          02  BILLDL    COMP  PIC  S9(4).
00207 C          02  BILLDF    PICTURE  X.
00208 C          02  FILLER REDEFINES BILLDF.
00209 C              03 BILLDA    PICTURE  X.
00210 C          02  BILLDI  PIC X(6).
00211 C          02  PERDESL    COMP  PIC  S9(4).
00212 C          02  PERDESF    PICTURE  X.
00213 C          02  FILLER REDEFINES PERDESF.
00214 C              03 PERDESA    PICTURE  X.
00215 C          02  PERDESI  PIC X(55).
00216 C          02  INSTR1L    COMP  PIC  S9(4).
```

```
00217 C          02  INSTR1F    PICTURE X.
00218 C          02  FILLER REDEFINES INSTR1F.
00219 C            03 INSTR1A    PICTURE X.
00220 C          02  INSTR1I  PIC X(70).
00221 C          02  INSTR2L    COMP  PIC  S9(4).
00222 C          02  INSTR2F    PICTURE X.
00223 C          02  FILLER REDEFINES INSTR2F.
00224 C            03 INSTR2A    PICTURE X.
00225 C          02  INSTR2I  PIC X(70).
00226 C          02  PFMSG1L    COMP  PIC  S9(4).
00227 C          02  PFMSG1F    PICTURE X.
00228 C          02  FILLER REDEFINES PFMSG1F.
00229 C            03 PFMSG1A    PICTURE X.
00230 C          02  PFMSG1I  PIC X(19).
00231 C          02  PFMSG2L    COMP  PIC  S9(4).
00232 C          02  PFMSG2F    PICTURE X.
00233 C          02  FILLER REDEFINES PFMSG2F.
00234 C            03 PFMSG2A    PICTURE X.
00235 C          02  PFMSG2I  PIC X(35).
00236 C          02  PFMSG3L    COMP  PIC  S9(4).
00237 C          02  PFMSG3F    PICTURE X.
00238 C          02  FILLER REDEFINES PFMSG3F.
00239 C            03 PFMSG3A    PICTURE X.
00240 C          02  PFMSG3I  PIC X(19).
00241 C          02  PFMSG4L    COMP  PIC  S9(4).
00242 C          02  PFMSG4F    PICTURE X.
00243 C          02  FILLER REDEFINES PFMSG4F.
00244 C            03 PFMSG4A    PICTURE X.
00245 C          02  PFMSG4I  PIC X(25).
00246 C          02  ERMSGL     COMP  PIC  S9(4).
00247 C          02  ERMSGF     PICTURE X.
00248 C          02  FILLER REDEFINES ERMSGF.
00249 C            03 ERMSGA     PICTURE X.
00250 C          02  ERMSGI  PIC X(60).
00251 C      01  ARC24M2O REDEFINES ARC24M2I.
00252 C          02  FILLER PIC X(12).
00253 C          02  FILLER PICTURE X(3).
00254 C          02  TRANSO   PIC X(4).
00255 C          02  FILLER PICTURE X(3).
00256 C          02  DATEO  PIC X(8).
00257 C          02  FILLER PICTURE X(3).
00258 C          02  MODEO  PIC X(12).
00259 C          02  FILLER PICTURE X(3).
00260 C          02  PROJECTO  PIC X(6).
00261 C          02  FILLER PICTURE X(3).
00262 C          02  MEMOO  PIC X(1).
00263 C          02  FILLER PICTURE X(3).
00264 C          02  ORGINVFO  PIC X(1).
00265 C          02  FILLER PICTURE X(3).
00266 C          02  ORGINVO  PIC X(5).
00267 C          02  FILLER PICTURE X(3).
00268 C          02  CUSNUMO  PIC X(14).
00269 C          02  FILLER PICTURE X(3).
00270 C          02  CUSNAMEO  PIC X(30).
00271 C          02  FILLER PICTURE X(3).
00272 C          02  INVPREO  PIC X(1).
00273 C          02  FILLER PICTURE X(3).
00274 C          02  INVNOO  PIC X(5).
00275 C          02  FILLER PICTURE X(3).
00276 C          02  INVAMNTO  PIC X(11).
00277 C          02  FILLER PICTURE X(3).
00278 C          02  ACCPERO  PIC X(4).
00279 C          02  FILLER PICTURE X(3).
00280 C          02  BILLDO  PIC X(6).
00281 C          02  FILLER PICTURE X(3).
00282 C          02  PERDESO  PIC X(55).
00283 C          02  FILLER PICTURE X(3).
00284 C          02  INSTR1O  PIC X(70).
00285 C          02  FILLER PICTURE X(3).
00286 C          02  INSTR2O  PIC X(70).
00287 C          02  FILLER PICTURE X(3).
00288 C          02  PFMSG1O  PIC X(19).
00289 C          02  FILLER PICTURE X(3).
00290 C          02  PFMSG2O  PIC X(35).
00291 C          02  FILLER PICTURE X(3).
```

```
00292 C          02  PFMSG3O  PIC X(19).
00293 C          02  FILLER PICTURE X(3).
00294 C          02  PFMSG4O  PIC X(25).
00295 C          02  FILLER PICTURE X(3).
00296 C          02  ERMSGO  PIC X(60).
00297      01  DFHLDVER PIC X(22) VALUE 'LD TABLE DFHEITAB 210.'.
00298      01  DFHEID0 PICTURE S9(7) COMPUTATIONAL-3 VALUE ZERO.
00299      01  DFHEIB0 PICTURE S9(4) COMPUTATIONAL VALUE ZERO.
00300      01  DFHEICB  PICTURE X(8) VALUE IS '        '.
00301
00302      01  DFHEIV16  COMP PIC S9(8).
00303      01  DFHB0041  COMP PIC S9(8).
00304      01  DFHB0042  COMP PIC S9(8).
00305      01  DFHB0043  COMP PIC S9(8).
00306      01  DFHB0044  COMP PIC S9(8).
00307      01  DFHB0045  COMP PIC S9(8).
00308      01  DFHB0046  COMP PIC S9(8).
00309      01  DFHB0047  COMP PIC S9(8).
00310      01  DFHB0048  COMP PIC S9(8).
00311      01  DFHEIV11  COMP PIC S9(4).
00312      01  DFHEIV12  COMP PIC S9(4).
00313      01  DFHEIV13  COMP PIC S9(4).
00314      01  DFHEIV14  COMP PIC S9(4).
00315      01  DFHEIV15  COMP PIC S9(4).
00316      01  DFHB0025  COMP PIC S9(4).
00317      01  DFHEIV5   PIC X(4).
00318      01  DFHEIV6   PIC X(4).
00319      01  DFHEIV17  PIC X(4).
00320      01  DFHEIV18  PIC X(4).
00321      01  DFHEIV19  PIC X(4).
00322      01  DFHEIV1   PIC X(8).
00323      01  DFHEIV2   PIC X(8).
00324      01  DFHEIV3   PIC X(8).
00325      01  DFHEIV20  PIC X(8).
00326      01  DFHC0084  PIC X(8).
00327      01  DFHC0085  PIC X(8).
00328      01  DFHC0320  PIC X(32).
00329      01  DFHEIV7   PIC X(2).
00330      01  DFHEIV8   PIC X(2).
00331      01  DFHC0022  PIC X(2).
00332      01  DFHC0023  PIC X(2).
00333      01  DFHEIV10  PIC S9(7) COMP-3.
00334      01  DFHEIV9   PIC X(1).
00335      01  DFHC0011  PIC X(1).
00336      01  DFHEIV4   PIC X(6).
00337      01  DFHC0070  PIC X(7).
00338      01  DFHC0071  PIC X(7).
00339      01  DFHC0440  PIC X(44).
00340      01  DFHDUMMY COMP PIC S9(4).
00341      01  DFHEIV0  PICTURE X(29).
00342  LINKAGE SECTION.
00343      01  DFHEIBLK.
00344          02  EIBTIME  PIC S9(7) COMP-3.
00345          02  EIBDATE  PIC S9(7) COMP-3.
00346          02  EIBTRNID PIC X(4).
00347          02  EIBTASKN PIC S9(7) COMP-3.
00348          02  EIBTRMID PIC X(4).
00349          02  DFHEIGDI COMP PIC S9(4).
00350          02  EIBCPOSN COMP PIC S9(4).
00351          02  EIBCALEN COMP PIC S9(4).
00352          02  EIBAID   PIC X(1).
00353          02  EIBFN    PIC X(2).
00354          02  EIBRCODE PIC X(6).
00355          02  EIBDS    PIC X(8).
00356          02  EIBREQID PIC X(8).
00357          02  EIBRSRCE PIC X(8).
00358          02  EIBSYNC  PIC X(1).
00359          02  EIBFREE  PIC X(1).
00360          02  EIBRECV  PIC X(1).
00361          02  EIBFIL01 PIC X(1).
00362          02  EIBATT   PIC X(1).
00363          02  EIBEOC   PIC X(1).
00364          02  EIBFMH   PIC X(1).
00365          02  EIBCOMPL PIC X(1).
00366          02  EIBSIG   PIC X(1).
00367          02  EIBCONF  PIC X(1).
00368          02  EIBERR   PIC X(1).
```

6-14 Continued.

```
00369        02     EIBERRCD PIC X(4).
00370        02     EIBSYNRB PIC X(1).
00371        02     EIBNODAT PIC X(1).
00372        02     EIBRESP  COMP PIC S9(8).
00373        02     EIBRESP2 COMP PIC S9(8).
00374        02     EIBRLDBK PIC X(1).
00375        01  DFHCOMMAREA              PIC X(79).
00376
00377        01  DFHBLLSLOT1 PICTURE X(1).
00378        01  DFHBLLSLOT2 PICTURE X(1).
```

7

BROWSE *mechanisms*

Multiple-line BROWSE procedures refer to mechanisms that enable you to display a number of records on the screen using an abridged format. Since you are only dedicating one or two lines of displayable data to a single record, it is practical to show such data on a priority basis. For example, if you are only interested in those employees whose annual gross earnings are in excess of $60,000, and who will be permanently retiring at the age of 60 within the next five years, you might want to consider the panel shown in FIG. 7-1. In this situation, you can easily display 16 to 20 employees on a given page, allowing for some format requirements such as the title heading and corresponding systems messages. To display multiple lines on a single panel referred to as a "page," you need to build each page either in temporary storage queues, or in the COMMUNICATIONS AREA. (More on this shortly.)

The source program listed in FIG. 7-13 relies on temporary storage facilities. To initiate a BROWSE operation, code a STARTBR or START BROWSE command to indicate to CICS that a sequential retrieval is about to begin. This process then continues with a READNEXT instruction, which simply takes the next sequential record on file and displays it. A READPREV instruction retrieves a record in reverse order. So, If Sullivan, Mary is shown as the first record on the top of the page, then, assuming that the records are keyed in the employee's full name, the following would be a valid retrieval order (see FIG. 7-1):

Sullivan, Segraves, Newton, Middleton, Henderson.

```
EMPLOYEE NAME            EMP. I.D.     GROSS        SCHEDULED
                                       EARNING      RETIREMENT

HENDERSON, JOHN          128908872     62,560       01/10/92
MIDDLEBROOKS, LARRY      773645409     72,450       04/25/92
NEWTON, KIM, A          802345672     60,700       04/31/93
SEGRAVES, JULIE, A       340987713     67,543       02/20/92
SULLIVAN, MARY           311096741     76,900       01/12/91
>>>>>>END OF FILE<<<<<<
```

7-1   Display illustrating forward and backward retrieval

The ENDBR and the RESETBR commands can be used interchangeably. ENDBR simply terminates a BROWSE operation. If, however, you perform a number of BROWSE operations in your program, you can issue a RESETBR command to indicate to CICS that your current BROWSE has expired. This will also trigger a STARTBR operation for you, redirecting your position in the file.

In a multiple line BROWSE program, you need to perform a series of READNEXT (or READPREV) instructions and store the result each time until those records are ready for a simultaneous display. In this process, you will keep track of each page placed into a temporary storage queue, including the first and the last record on that page. Consider the example shown in FIG. 7-2. Each employee, Ardmore, Ballantine, Brahms, etc., represents a complete record

```
Ardmore, Ballantine, Brahms, Darwin, Henderson, Johnson,
Middleton, Newton, Segraves, Sullivan, Varsegi, Warfield,
Watts............................................................
```

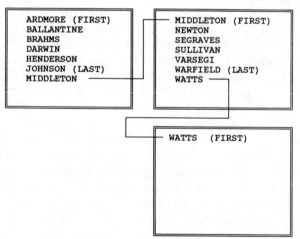

7-2   Logical multi-browse structure for a forward mechanism

written to the queue. Assume that a single page is to be built containing 6 records, starting with Ardmore. Once you have completed writing the first page in temporary storage, you can proceed to build the second page in memory, starting with Middleton, which happens to be the seventh physical record on file.

Developing multiline, multipage programs

Page building involving temporary storage facilities is probably the most common technique in the industry. Temporary storage is called so because it is an area provided by CICS where you can store and maintain data on a temporary basis. You can actually accomplish the same results by creating a VSAM file. This method, however, requires you to build a VSAM cluster, to define your file in the FCT (File Control Table), and to develop an array of maintenance procedures.

All this is not required with temporary storage, which in essence is an internally managed set of VSAM clusters. The problem that comes into play is that since queues can be created without the use of tables, you need to have in place a mechanism to keep them consistently unique. One of these methods uses the terminal identifier through the EIB (Execute Interface Block).

In the EIB, the field IEBTRIMID contains a value representing your terminal identifier, which is unique. To be specific:

```
MOVE IEBTRMID TO YOUR-TERMINAL-ID
```

The queue can be set up in the DATA DIVISION as follows:

```
01   TEMP-STORAGE-QUEUE
     05 YOUR-TERMINAL-ID    PIC X(4).
     05 FILLER              PIC X(4) VALUE 'ACCT'.
```

So in the PROCEDURE DIVISION, you simply say:

```
EXEC CICS
WRITEQ TS QUEUE(TEMP-STORAGE-QUEUE) tells you just where the
   record will be written
FROM        (... an area this information is written from)
LENGTH      (... the length of the record in the queue)
ITEM        (... tells you which specific record in the queue)
REWRITE
END-EXEC.
```

As I said before, you want to think of temporary storage as an internally created VSAM file that uses queues to facilitate storage. In order to identify a specific record on the queue, you need to use a "pointer" such as an ITEM number, which is similar to a record key.

Thus, item 1 will correspond to the first record on the queue, while item 5 will correspond to the fifth record. The only thing that is different about these queues relative to a VSAM file is that the item number, even though it is referred to as a record key, is not part of the physical record, but merely a reference value.

Programmer-manipulated symbolic maps in BROWSE techniques

Figures 7-3 and 7-4 display a system-generated symbolic map. When you assemble a mapset, a symbolic map is created and simply moved to a copy library. In line 00370 of FIG. 7-14, I simply used a copy statement (COPY TRE6MAP) to make such a symbolic map layout available in the program. The first TRE6I is shown in line 00371 (FIG. 7-3). The other one is TRE6O, line 00437 illustrated in FIG. 7-4. The suffix "I," (TRE6I) simply refers to a mapset group used in the input operation. Likewise, "O," (alpha "O") denotes reference in an output operation. Note that each group starts with a 12-position long FILLER. This is the result of specifying TIOAPFX-YES for the mapset. As I also described in earlier chapters, the symbolic map for TRE6I has generated five fields for each element defined under DFHMDF. For example, MONTHL represents the length portion of the month field. Thus, if the terminal operator were to leave a field blank, such as the month of the year, then, the actual length of the field would be zero. The word "JANUARY," on the other hand, would yield a data length of 7 characters.

7-3 Compiler-generated symbolic map for specifying an input operation

```
00370              COPY TRE6MAP.
00371 C      01  TRE6I.
00372 C          02    FILLER PIC X(12).
00373 C          02    MONTHL      COMP    PIC  S9(4).
00374 C          02    MONTHF      PICTURE X.
00375 C          02    FILLER REDEFINES MONTHF.
00376 C            03 MONTHA    PICTURE X.
00377 C          02    MONTHI   PIC X(2).
00378 C          02    DAYL COMP  PIC   S9(4).
00379 C          02    DAYF PICTURE X.
00380 C          02    FILLER REDEFINES DAYF.
00381 C            03 DAYA    PICTURE X.
00382 C          02    DAYI  PIC X(2).
00383 C          02    YEARL       COMP  PIC  S9(4).
00384 C          02    YEARF       PICTURE X.
00385 C          02    FILLER REDEFINES YEARF.
00386 C            03 YEARA    PICTURE X.
00387 C          02    YEARI  PIC X(2).
00388 C          02    TRANIDL     COMP  PIC  S9(4).
00389 C          02    TRANIDF     PICTURE X.
00390 C          02    FILLER REDEFINES TRANIDF.
00391 C            03 TRANIDA    PICTURE X.
00392 C          02    TRANIDI  PIC X(4).
00393 C          02    CARRIERL    COMP  PIC  S9(4).
00394 C          02    CARRIERF    PICTURE X.
00395 C          02    FILLER REDEFINES CARRIERF.
```

```
00396 C            03 CARRIERA    PICTURE X.
00397 C         02    CARRIERI   PIC X(35).
00398 C         02    IMONTHL    COMP  PIC  S9(4).
00399 C         02    IMONTHF    PICTURE X.
00400 C         02    FILLER REDEFINES IMONTHF.
00401 C            03 IMONTHA    PICTURE X.
00402 C         02    IMONTHI  PIC X(2).
00403 C         02    IDAYL      COMP  PIC  S9(4).
00404 C         02    IDAYF      PICTURE X.
00405 C         02    FILLER REDEFINES IDAYF.
00406 C            03 IDAYA    PICTURE X.
00407 C         02    IDAYI  PIC X(2).
00408 C         02    IYEARL      COMP     PIC  S9(4).
00409 C         02    IYEARF      PICTURE X.
00410 C         02    FILLER REDEFINES IYEARF.
00411 C            03 IYEARA    PICTURE X.
00412 C         02    IYEARI   PIC X(2).
00413 C         02    DATAD OCCURS 11 TIMES.
00414 C            03   DATAL    COMP PIC  S9(4).
00415 C            03   DATAF    PICTURE X.
00416 C            03   DATAI  PIC X(79).
00417 C         02    MSG1L      COMP  PIC  S9(4).
00418 C         02    MSG1F      PICTURE X.
00419 C         02    FILLER REDEFINES MSG1F.
00420 C            03 MSG1A    PICTURE X.
00421 C         02    MSG1I  PIC X(79).
00422 C         02    MSGL COMP  PIC  S9(4).
00423 C         02    MSGF PICTURE X.
00424 C         02    FILLER REDEFINES MSGF.
00425 C            03 MSGA    PICTURE X.
00426 C         02    MSGI  PIC X(79).
00427 C         02    ERRORL      COMP     PIC  S9(4).
00428 C         02    ERRORF      PICTURE X.
00429 C         02    FILLER REDEFINES ERRORF.
00430 C            03 ERRORA    PICTURE X.
00431 C         02    ERRORI   PIC X(77).
00432 C         02    DUMMYL      COMP     PIC  S9(4).
00433 C         02    DUMMYF      PICTURE X.
00434 C         02    FILLER REDEFINES DUMMYF.
00435 C            03 DUMMYA    PICTURE X.
00436 C         02    DUMMYI   PIC X(1).
```

7-4 Compiler-generated symbolic map for specifying an output operation

```
00437 C      01  TRE6O REDEFINES TRE6I.
00438 C         02    FILLER PIC X(12).
00439 C         02    FILLER PICTURE X(3).
00440 C         02    MONTHO PIC 99.
00441 C         02    FILLER PICTURE X(3).
00442 C         02    DAYO PIC 99.
00443 C         02    FILLER PICTURE X(3).
00444 C         02    YEARO PIC 99.
00445 C         02    FILLER PICTURE X(3).
00446 C         02    TRANIDO  PIC X(4).
00447 C         02    FILLER PICTURE X(3).
00448 C         02    CARRIERO  PIC X(35).
00449 C         02    FILLER PICTURE X(3).
00450 C         02    IMONTHO  PIC X(2).
00451 C         02    FILLER PICTURE X(3).
00452 C         02    IDAYO  PIC X(2).
00453 C         02    FILLER PICTURE X(3).
00454 C         02    IYEARO   PIC X(2).
00455 C         02    DFHMS1 OCCURS 11 TIMES.
00456 C            03   FILLER PICTURE X(2).
00457 C            03   DATAA    PICTURE X.
00458 C            03   DATAO  PIC X(79).
00459 C         02    FILLER PICTURE X(3).
00460 C         02    MSG1O  PIC X(79).
00461 C         02    FILLER PICTURE X(3).
00462 C         02    MSGO  PIC X(79).
00463 C         02    FILLER PICTURE X(3).
00464 C         02    ERRORO   PIC X(77).
00465 C         02    FILLER PICTURE X(3).
00466 C         02    DUMMYO   PIC X(1).
```

A second version of the MONTH data field contains MONTHF. This denotes an initial input operation that sets the above field to low values.

A third version of the MONTH field contains an "A" suffix (MONTHA). This character enables the particular field to be displayed on the terminal using a number of single and combined characteristics, such as colors, intensification, protected or unprotected mode, and so on. These characteristics are referred to as attribute bytes. A fourth and fifth version simply tells CICS that the field to be moved pertains to an input (MONTHI) or to an output (MONTHO) operation.

Thus far, I've talked about computer-generated symbolic maps. Let's now focus on programmer-manipulated symbolic maps. Programmer-manipulated symbolic maps are essential when you need to use occurrences, or simply subscripts, as part of a multiline (repeating) layout. How is this done? Consider the panel shown in FIG. 7-5, which is explained in detail in the case study. When you code this map in BMS, note the following four lines in reference to the field DATA (FIG. 7-6):

```
DATA DFHMDF POS = (8,1),
             LENGTH = 79,
             ATTRB = PROT
             OCCURS = 11
```

This simply takes each repeating line on the map (rather than on a field by field basis), so you can copy the lines into the WORKING-STORAGE SECTION of your program, as highlighted in the case study. The lines are then ready for a simple "table" lookup.

```
TRE6 TRAIN OPERATING PERFORMANCE SYSTEM EQUIPMENT PROBLEM TRACKING TO DATE
                    SOUTHEASTERN COMMUTER RAILROAD
ENTER BEGINNING DATE OF INQUIRY: 01 / 01 / 89

UNIT#        DATE         TIME        CONDUCTOR NAME      CODE    DESCRIPTION

0101      04 13 89     14 09 29    McNAMARA, PAT        GR     GROUND RELAY
0111      04 13 89     13 52 03    KOWALSKI, STAN       EM     ENGINE MECHAN
0127      05 21 89     03 34 51    VARSEGI, ALEX        AC     AIR CONDITIONING
0500      05 22 89     12 08 07    MUELLER, KEN         DV     DOOR, VESTIBULE
0710      08 07 89     16 00 87    FOX, THOMAS          BW     BROKEN WINDOW




NO MORE RECORDS
PF1=MENU PF2=CANCEL ENTER=CONTINUE PF3=NEW SCREEN
```

7-5 Panel displaying equipment malfunction

```
          PRINT NOGEN
TRE6MAP   DFHMSD TYPE=&SYSPARM,                                              X
                 LANG=COBOL,                                                 X
                 MODE=INOUT,                                                 X
                 TERM=3270-2,                                                X
                 CTRL=(FREEKB,FRSET),                                        X
                 STORAGE=AUTO,                                               X
                 TIOAPFX=YES
**********************************************************************
TRE6      DFHMDI SIZE=(24,80),                                              X
                 LINE=NEXT,                                                  X
                 COLUMN=1
**********************************************************************
MONTH     DFHMDF POS=(1,63),                                                X
                 LENGTH=2,                                                   X
                 ATTRB=(ASKIP,FSET),                                         X
                 PICOUT='99'
**********************************************************************
          DFHMDF POS=(1,66),                                                X
                 LENGTH=1,                                                   X
                 ATTRB=ASKIP,                                                X
                 INITIAL=':'
**********************************************************************
DAY       DFHMDF POS=(1,68),                                                X
                 LENGTH=2,                                                   X
                 ATTRB=(ASKIP,FSET),                                         X
                 PICOUT='99'
**********************************************************************
          DFHMDF POS=(1,71),                                                X
                 LENGTH=1,                                                   X
                 ATTRB=ASKIP,                                                X
                 INITIAL=':'
**********************************************************************
YEAR      DFHMDF POS=(1,73),                                                X
                 LENGTH=2,                                                   X
                 ATTRB=(ASKIP,FSET),                                         X
                 PICOUT='99'
**********************************************************************
TRANID    DFHMDF POS=(2,1),                                                 X
                 LENGTH=4,                                                   X
                 ATTRB=(ASKIP,FSET)
**********************************************************************
          DFHMDF POS=(2,7),                                                 X
                 LENGTH=34,                                                  X
                 ATTRB=(BRT,PROT),                                           X
                 INITIAL='TRAIN OPERATION PERFORMANCE SYSTEM'
**********************************************************************
          DFHMDF POS=(2,42),                                                X
                 LENGTH=26,                                                  X
                 ATTRB=(BRT,PROT),                                           X
                 INITIAL='EQUIPMENT PROBLEM TRACKING'
**********************************************************************
          DFHMDF POS=(2,70),                                                X
                 LENGTH=8,                                                   X
                 ATTRB=(PROT,BRT),                                           X
                 INITIAL='TO DATE'
**********************************************************************
CARRIER   DFHMDF POS=(3,22),                                                X
                 LENGTH=35,                                                  X
                 ATTRB=(ASKIP,FSET)
**********************************************************************
          DFHMDF POS=(4,1),                                                 X
                 LENGTH=32,                                                  X
                 ATTRB=(BRT,PROT),                                           X
                 INITIAL='ENTER BEGINNING DATE OF INQUIRY:'
**********************************************************************
IMONTH    DFHMDF POS=(4,34),                                                X
                 LENGTH=2,                                                   X
                 ATTRB=UNPROT
**********************************************************************
          DFHMDF POS=(4,37),                                                X
                 LENGTH=1,                                                   X
                 ATTRB=ASKIP,                                                X
                 INITIAL='/'
**********************************************************************
```

Programmer-manipulated symbolic maps in BROWSE techniques **151**

```
IDAY     DFHMDF POS=(4,39),                                      X
              LENGTH=2,                                          X
              ATTRB=UNPROT
*****************************************************************
         DFHMDF POS=(4,42),                                      X
              LENGTH=1,                                          X
              ATTRB=ASKIP,                                       X
              INITIAL='/'
*****************************************************************
IYEAR    DFHMDF POS=(4,44),                                      X
              LENGTH=2,                                          X
              ATTRB=UNPROT
*****************************************************************
         DFHMDF POS=(4,47),                                      X
              LENGTH=1,                                          X
              ATTRB=ASKIP
*****************************************************************
         DFHMDF POS=(6,1),                                       X
              LENGTH=5,                                          X
              ATTRB=(PROT,BRT),                                  X
              INITIAL='UNIT#'
*****************************************************************
         DFHMDF POS=(6,10),                                      X
              LENGTH=4,                                          X
              ATTRB=(PROT,BRT),                                  X
              INITIAL='DATE'
*****************************************************************
         DFHMDF POS=(6,19),                                      X
              LENGTH=4,                                          X
              ATTRB=(PROT,BRT),                                  X
              INITIAL='TIME'
*****************************************************************
         DFHMDF POS=(6,26),                                      X
              LENGTH=16,                                         X
              ATTRB=(PROT,BRT),                                  X
              INITIAL='CONDUCTOR NAME'
*****************************************************************
         DFHMDF POS=(6,48),                                      X
              LENGTH=4,                                          X
              ATTRB=(PROT,BRT),                                  X
              INITIAL='CODE'
*****************************************************************
         DFHMDF POS=(6,54),                                      X
              LENGTH=11,                                         X
              ATTRB=(PROT,BRT),                                  X
              INITIAL='DESCRIPTION'
*****************************************************************
*    LINE 1                                                     *
*****************************************************************
DATA     DFHMDF POS=(8,1),                                       X
              LENGTH=79,                                         X
              ATTRB=PROT,                                        X
              OCCURS=11
*****************************************************************
MSG1     DFHMDF POS=(21,1),                                      X
              LENGTH=79,                                         X
              ATTRB=(BRT,PROT)
*****************************************************************
MSG      DFHMDF POS=(22,1),                                      X
              LENGTH=79,                                         X
              ATTRB=(BRT,PROT)
*****************************************************************
ERROR    DFHMDF POS=(23,1),                                      X
              LENGTH=77,                                         X
              ATTRB=(BRT,PROT)
*****************************************************************
DUMMY    DFHMDF POS=(24,79),                                     X
              LENGTH=1,                                          X
              ATTRB=(DRK,PROT,FSET),                             X
              INITIAL=' '
*****************************************************************
         DFHMSD TYPE=FINAL
         END
```

Once you have coded your map in BMS, you can assemble it. I have created a "shell" JCL for assembling the map, which is presented in FIG. 7-7. The result of your map assembly will be two types of outputs:

1. A load module.
2. A system-generated symbolic map, which can be placed in a COPY library, or whatever other library you happen to specify.

For more on this, review FIGS. 7-3 and 7-4.

7-7 Job Control (JCL) required to convert a programmer-developed BMS map to a compiler-generated symbolic map

```
//NIRLCBM7  JOB  (9000,SSOB),MSGLEVEL=(1,1),MSGCLASS=X,REGION=6144K,
//    CLASS=A,NOTIFY=VARSEGI
/*JOBPARM PROCLIB=PROC01
//MAPASM EXEC TOPSBMS,MAPNAME=TCSBMAP
//COPY.SYSUT1 DD  DSN=NIRXT.TOPS.SRCLIB(TCSBMAP),DISP=SHR
//*********************************************************
//TOPSBMS PROC INDEX='CICS17X'          FOR MACLIB
//         MAPLIB='NIRXT.TEST.CICS.LOADLIB',  TARGET MAPLIB
//         DSCTLIB='NIRXT.TEST.COPYLIB',     TARGET FOR DSECT
//         MAPNAME=,                   NAME OF MAPSET REQUIRED
//         A=,                         A=A FOR ALIGNED MAP
//         ASMBLR=IEV90,               ASSEMBLER PROGRAM NAME
//         REG=1024K,                  REGION FOR ASSEMBLY
//         OUTC=X,                     PRINT SYSOUT CLASS
//         WORK=TEMP                   WORK FILE UNIT
//COPY     EXEC PGM=IEBGENER
//SYSPRINT  DD  SYSOUT=&OUTC
//SYSUT2    DD  DSN=&&TEMPM,UNIT=&WORK,DISP=(,PASS),
//          DCB=(RECFM=FB,LRECL=8-,BLKSIZE=400),
//          SPACE=(400,(50,50))
//SYSIN     DD  DUMMY
//* SYSUT1 DD * NEEDED FOR THE MAP SOURCE
//ASMMAP    EXEC  PGM=&ASMBLR,REGION=&REG,
//    PARM='SYSPARM(&A,MAP),DECK,NOLOAD'
//SYSPRINT DD  SYSOUT=&OUTC
//SYSLIB   DD  DSN=&INDEX..MACLIB,DISP=SHR
//         DD  DSN=SYS1.MACLIB,DISP=SHR
//SYSUT1   DD  UNIT=&WORK,SPACE=(CYL,(5.5))
//SYSUT2   DD  UNIT=&WORK,SPACE=(CYL,(5,5))
//SYSUT3   DD  UNIT=&WORK,SPACE=(CYL,(5,5))
//SYSPUNCH DD  DSN=&&MAP,DISP=(,PASS),UNIT=&WORK,
//          DCB=(RECFM=FB,LRECL=80,BLKSIZE=400),
//          SPACE=(400,(50,50))
//SYSIN    DD  DSN=&&TENPM,DISP=(OLD,PASS)
//LINKMAP  EXEC  PGM=IEWL,PARM='LIST,LET,XREF',
//         COND=((5,LT,COPY),(5,LT,ASMMAP))
//SYSPRINT DD SYSOUT=&OUTC
//SYSLMOD  DD  DSN=&MAPLIB(&MAPNAME),DISP=SHR
//SYSUT1   DD  UNIT=&WORK,SPACE=(1024,(20,20))
//SYSLIN   DD  DSN=&&MAP,DISP=(OLD,PASS)
//ASMDSECT EXEC PGM=&ASMBLR,REGION=&REG,
//    PARM='SYSPARM(&A.DSECT),DECK,NOLOAD',
//    COND=((5,LT,COPY),(5,LT,ASMMAP))
//SYSPRINT  DD  SYSOUT=&OUTC
//SYSLIB    DD  DSN=&INDEX..MACLIB,DISP=SHR
//          DD  DSN=SYS1.MACLIB,DISP=SHR
//SYSUT1    DD  UNIT=&WORK,SPACE=(CYL,(5,5))
//SYSUT2    DD  UNIT=&WORK,SPACE=(CYL,(5,5))
//SYSUT3    DD  UNIT=&WORK,SPACE=(CYL,(5,5))
//SYSPUNCH  DD  DSN=&DSCTLIB(&MAPNAME),DISP=OLD
//SYSIN     DD  DSN=&&TEMP,DISP=(OLD,PASS)
```

Case study

The purpose of this BROWSE program, TRE6BRS, is to enable the user to display data on the screen one line per record, utilizing a maximum of eleven lines per "page." A screen layout of this was depicted in FIG. 7-5.

A record layout of the main master file, WS-COMPLAINT-REC, imbedded in lines 137 through 154 of the source code, is presented in FIG. 7-13, with a primary key located in the first 19 positions of the record. As you can see, it is a concatenated key, meaning that it is made up of a number of components such as a carrier code, an equipment unit number, and a problem date and time associated with a piece of equipment. Since this record layout is referenced by a number of different application programs, it has two alternate or secondary keys. The first such secondary key is the date field, which is actually used by this program for a specific inquiry located in positions 8 through 13 of the primary key. (See FIG. 7-8.)

```
---------------- File-AID VSAM INFORMATION - (PAGE 1 OF 2) -----------------
COMMAND  ===>
Catalog.. CATALOG.MVSICF1.VVSAM01
Cluster.. NIRVT.TOPS.DATEKEY.KS                  +-------------+
Data..... NIRVT.TIPS.DATEKEY.DATA                |   owner-id  |
Index.... NIRVT.TOPS.DATEKEY.INDEX               +-------------+
----------------------------------------------------------------------------
Data component information:             Current allocation options:
Volume serial:        VSAM03           RACF protected             NO
Device Type:          3380             Write Check:               NO
Organization:         AIX              Buffer Space:            9216
KSDS key length:      6                Erase on delete:           NO
KSDS key location:    7                Imbedded index:           YES
Average record size: 1000              Replicated index:          NO
Maximum record size: 1000              Reuse option:              NO
Allocated space: Unit  Primary  Secondary   Share option:        3-3
     Data  -  tracks     22        11        Spanned records:     YES
     Index -  tracks      1         1        MSS binding:      STAGED
Dataset information:                    MSS-destage wait:          NO
  Creation date:      11/10/90         Key ranges present:        NO
  Expiration date:    11/10/99         AIX-unique keys:           NO
  Modification date:  09/12/89         AIX-upgrade               YES
  Modification time:  02:27 PM         Load option:            SPEED
  >>>>>>>>>press ENTER to go to page 2; END key to return to utility menu<<<<<<<<<
```

7-8 Shows the VSAM information for the Complaint (or Problem) Master's alternate (date) key

The second such alternate key to the Problem Master (FIG. 7-9) is a two-position complaint or problem code. This is necessary for the purpose of inquiry, since other application programs need to access this file in problem code sequence, displaying all similar record types with ground relay problems, those with engine and other mechanical problems and so on. The Date of Inquiry field is the search argument that defines the duration of the search. So if you were to enter 01/01/89, as I did for the inquiry date, then, every

```
----------------- File-AID VSAM INFORMATION - (PAGE 1 OF 2) -----------------
COMMAND  ===>
Catalog.. CATALOG.MVSICF1.VVSAM01
Cluster.. NIRVT.TOPS.DATEKEY.KS
Data..... NIRVT.TIPS.DATEKEY.DATA                    +-------------+
Index.... NIRVT.TOPS.DATEKEY.INDEX                   |  owner-id   |
                                                     +-------------+
-----------------------------------------------------------------------------
Data component information:              Current allocation options:
Volume serial:       VSAM03             RACF protected            NO
Device Type:         3380               Write Check:              NO
Organization:        AIX                Buffer Space:           9216
KSDS key length:     2                  Erase on delete:          NO
KSDS key location:   27                 Imbedded index:          YES
Average record size: 1000               Replicated index          NO
Maximum record size: 1000               Reuse option:             NO
Allocated space: Unit  Primary Secondary Share option:           3-3
     Data  -    tracks   22      11      Spanned records:         YES
     Index -    tracks    1       1      MSS binding:          STAGED
Dataset information:                     MSS-destage wait:         NO
  Creation date:     11/12/90           Key ranges present:       NO
  Expiration date:   11/10/99           AIX-unique keys:          NO
  Modification date: 09/12/89           AIX-upgrade              YES
  Modification time: 02:27 PM           Load option:           SPEED
    >>>>>>>press ENTER to go to page 2; END key to return to utility menu<<<<<<<
```

7-9 Shows the VSAM information for the Complaint (or Problem) Master's alternate (complaint) key

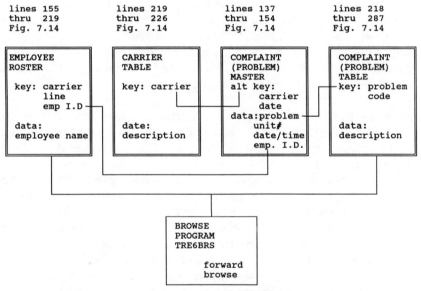

```
lines 155        lines 219        lines 137        lines 218
thru  219        thru  226        thru  154        thru  287
Fig. 7.14        Fig. 7.14        Fig. 7.14        Fig. 7.14
```

7-10 A functional overview of the TRE6BRS BROWSE program

record on the Problem Master between the inquiry and the current system dates will be displayed. The detail lines, up to a maximum of eleven to a page, are described on the symbolic map, FIG. 7-6, in the shaded area, which is part of your BMS definition. TRE6BRS has four components that are reflected in a functional overview of the program FIG. 7-10). The Complaint or Problem Master (first component) is read for extracting three data elements for a display. These are: the unit number, the employee's I.D., as well as the date and the time of the problem. The record layout of this file is presented in lines 137 through 154 in FIG. 7-13. It is called a Complaint or Problem Master because it contains pieces of equipment earmarked for repair based on a specific problem or complaint by a passenger. The above Master file contains the employee's identification or payroll number, which searches the Employee's (conductor's) name through the Employee Roster. The Employee Roster is the second component used by TRE6BRS. An extended layout of this is shown in lines 155 through 219 of FIG. 7-14. Over 95% of this layout, by the way, is not utilized by the present TRE6BRS program. (It, however, is fully utilized by other programs in the system.) Note that the Problem Master only contains a two-position alphanumeric "problem" code. To find a corresponding description you need to read a third file component, which happens to be Problem Description Table. So "GR" translates to Ground Relay problem, AC to Air Conditioning, and so on. A fourth file component refers to the Carrier table, which is not part of the detail line. Rather, it is part of the heading information (line 2: SOUTHEASTERN COMMUTER RAILROAD), which was originally entered through the main menu screen and "sent through" the path as shown in FIG. 7-11. The three function keys that appear on the bottom of FIG. 7-5 are used as follows:

- PF 1 returns the program to a previous level, which is one of the submenus for the BROWSE operation. The detail panel is actually triggered, as follows: the user signs on and invokes a panel that enables the user to describe himself or herself to the system, as a specific carrier. The carrier then passes through the COMMAREA, invoking a secondary, or functional menu. A third menu screen comes into play to further simplify the broad functional responsibilities into a more task-oriented selection criteria. Thus, if your function is "Mechanical Activities," then a more specific breakdown would include problem tracking, repair activities, problem reporting, etc. Thus, the panel shown in FIG. 7-5 is invoked. A more specific overview of the TRE6BRS path is shown in FIG. 7-11.

- PF 2 simply cancels (or voids), a transaction. It is different from merely "blanking out" a screen (PF 3) in that PF 2 also clears the search argument (inquiry date), as well. When you press the ENTER key, you are browsing forward on your file, 11 or less records at a time.

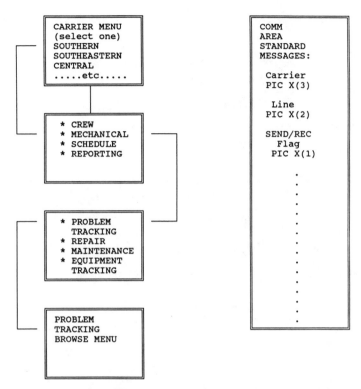

7-11 A hierarchical overview to show how TRE6BRS fits into the overall path

BMS and FCT considerations

There are two major considerations regarding your online program. The first consideration is your own BMS or Basic Mapping Support code that needs to be assembled. (See FIG. 7-6.) Your BMS map is essentially the way a screen layout is described to a CICS transaction. If you are familiar with the Basic Assembler Language (BAL), you will quickly see that the rules pertaining to an assembler language format are similar, if not identical to those governing BMS. Thus, BMS can be an effective but unsophisticated tool. Note that what is different about this BMS layout compared to those previously described is the use of the occurs clause. Occurs enables you to define multiple line, identical code without having to code each line separately. A second component of TRE6BRS is the FCT or File Control Table, which is presented in FIG. 7-12. The FCT describes to CICS the file or files and tables that need to be referenced in the program.

```
TCEMPALT   DFHFCT   TYPE=DATASET,ACCMETH=VSAM,DISP=SHR,
                    SERVREQ=(ADD,UPDATE,DELETE,BROWSE),
                    DATASET=TCEMPALT,
                    DSNAME=NIRVT.TOPS.CREMPALT.E,
                    FILSTAT=(ENABLED,CLOSED),
                    RECFORM=(FIXED),RLS=PUBLIC
>>>>>>>>>>>>>>>     EMPLOYEE ROSTER FILE   <<<<<<<<<<<<<<<

TDATEALT   DFHPCT   TYPE=DATASET,ACCMETH=VSAM,DISP=SHR,
                    SERVREQ=(BROWSE),
                    DATASET=TDATEALT,
                    DSNAME=NIRVT.TOPS.DATEKEY.E,
                    FILSTAT=(ENABLED,CLOSED),
                    RECFORM=(FIXED),RLS=PUBLIC
>>>>>>>>>>>>>>>     PROBLEM MASTER WITH THE DATE ALTERNATE KEY   <<<<<<<<

TCARRIER   DFHPCT   TYPE=DATASET,DATASET=TCARRIER,DISP=SHR,
                    FILSTAT=(ENABLED,CLOSED),RLS=PUBLIC,
                    SERVREQ=(ADD,BROWSE,DELETE,UPDATE),STRNO=4
                    ACCMETH=VSAM,
                    DSNAME=NIRVT.TOPS.CARRIER.TABLE.KS
                    BUFNO=3,BUFNI=2,RECFORM=(FIXED)
>>>>>>>>>>>>>>>     CARRIER TABLE DEFINITION   <<<<<<<<<<<<<<

TCOMPLNT   DFHFCT   TYPE=DATASET,ACCMETH=VSAM,DISP=SHR,
                    SERVREQ=(ADD,UPDATE,DELETE,BROWSE),
                    DATASET=TCOMPLNT,
                    DSNAME=NIRVT.TOPS.COMPLAIN.TABLE.KS,
                    FILSTAT=(ENABLED,CLOSED),
                    RECFORM=(FIXED),RLS=PUBLIC
>>>>>>>>>>>>>>>     PROBLEM OR COMPLAINT MASTER   <<<<<<<<<<<<<
```

Source program listing and narrative

The only output of the TRE6BRS program is an Equipment Problem Tracking to Date BROWSE screen, which is presented in FIG. 7-5. As shown in FIG. 7-13, lines 7 through 14 of the source program listing describe a number of internally set up switches to enable you to route program logic to a duplicate record routine or to procedures required when a record is not found. Lines 16 through 22 preassign corresponding values to the ENTER and function keys used in this program. Note that PENTER and PF 1 through PF 5 are defined in the DHFHAID section of the compiled program (see FIG. 7-14, lines 339 though 505). A user explanation of these function keys corresponds to the explanation given on the bottom portion of the Equipment Problem Tracking Panel To Date (FIG. 7-5). Accordingly, PF 1 will return you to the preceding menu screen, described in the case study. Note that TRE6BRS is four layers down from the main menu (see the case study) and that each menu moves vital messages back and forth among themselves, depending on the flow of communication. PF 2 merely cancels a transaction while clearing the screen. When you press the ENTER key, it enables you to continue processing by scrolling to a "second" page, provided you have sufficient data on file to continue such a multiline display. Finally PF 3 is designed to blank out a screen, but without cancelling a particular transaction.

7-13 TRE6BRS

```
1     IDENTIFICATION DIVISION.
2     PROGRAM-ID. TRE6BRS.
3     ENVIRONMENT DIVISION.
4     DATA DIVISION.
5     WORKING-STORAGE SECTION.
6  *
7     01  SWITCHES.
8         05  VALID-DATA-SW      PIC X VALUE 'Y'.
9             88  VALID-DATA     VALUE 'Y'.
10        05  DUP-RECORD-SW      PIC X VALUE SPACES.
11        05  NOT-FND-SW         PIC X VALUE 'Y'.
12            88  GOT-IT         VALUE 'Y'.
13        05  EOF-SW             PIC X  VALUE 'N'.
14            88  THE-END        VALUE 'Y'.
15 *
16    01  PF-KEYS  PIC X VALUE '0'.
17        88  PFENTER            VALUE '0'.
18        88  PF1                VALUE '1'.
19        88  PF2                VALUE '2'.
20        88  PF3                VALUE '3'.
21        88  PF4                VALUE '4'.
22        88  PF5                VALUE '5'.
23 *
24    01  MESSAGES.
25        05  MAPFAIL-MSG     PIC X(36)  VALUE
26            'MAPFAIL FOR TRANSACTION TRE6'.
27        05  NOT-OPEN-MSG    PIC X(42)  VALUE
28            'FILE NOT OPEN FOR TRANSACTION TR6B'.
29        05  PGM-NOTFND-MSG  PIC X(42)  VALUE
30            'PROGRAM NOT FOUND FOR TRANSACTION TR6B'.
31        05  GENERIC-ERROR-MSG  PIC X(39) VALUE
32            'ERROR HAS OCCURRED FOR TRANSACTION TR6B'.
33        05  INVREQ-MSG         PIC X(15) VALUE
34            'INVALID REQUEST'.
35 *
36    01  READ-SUB            PIC S9(4) COMP VALUE +0000.
37    01  HOLD-SUB            PIC S9(4) COMP.
38    01  TS-QUEUE-NAME.
39        05  TS-TERM-ID      PIC X(4).
40        05  FILLER          PIC X(4)  VALUE 'TR6B'.
41    01  TS-LENGTH           PIC S9(4)  COMP VALUE +82.
42    01  WS-DATA.
43        05  FILLER          PIC X(3).
44        05  UNIT1           PIC XXXX.
45        05  FILLER          PIC X(2).
46        05  MONTH1          PIC X(2).
47        05  FILLER          PIC X VALUE ' '.
48        05  DAY1            PIC X(2).
49        05  FILLER          PIC X  VALUE ' '.
50        05  YEAR1           PIC X(2).
51        05  FILLER          PIC X(2).
52        05  HR1             PIC X(2).
53        05  FILLER          PIC X VALUE ' '.
54        05  MIN1            PIC X(2).
55        05  FILLER          PIC X  VALUE ' '.
56        05  SEC1            PIC X(2).
57        05  FILLER          PIC X(2).
58        05  NAME1           PIC X(19).
59        05  FILLER          PIC X(3).
60        05  CODE1           PIC X(2).
61        05  FILLER          PIC X(4).
62        05  PROB1           PIC X(25).
63 *
64    01  WS-COMMAREA.
65        05  COMM-FLAG       PIC X VALUE 'I'.
66            88  INIT-MAP      VALUE 'I'.
67            88  SEND-MAP      VALUE 'S'.
68            88  RECV-MAP      VALUE 'R'.
69            88  PASS-XCTL     VALUE 'P'.
70 *
```

```
71        05  WS-COMMAREA-OUT.
72            10  COMM-CARRIER PIC X(3).
73            10  COMM-LINE    PIC XX.
74            10  WS-UNIT      PIC X(4).
75            10  E-TYPE       PIC X.
76            10  P-CODE       PIC XX.
77   *
78        05  REC-FLAG        PIC X   VALUE 'X'.
79            88  TSQ             VALUE 'T'.
80   *
81        05  TS-SUB          PIC S9(4)   COMP VALUE +1.
82        05  MOVE-CT         PIC S9(4)   COMP.
83        05  TS-ITEM         PIC S9(4)   COMP VALUE +1.
84   *
85        05  END-SESSION-SW  PIC X VALUE 'N'.
86            88  ALL-OVER        VALUE 'Y'.
87   *
88        05  DIRECTION-SW    PIC X VALUE '3'.
89            88  FIRST-TIME   VALUE '3'.
90            88  FORWARD      VALUE '1'.
91            88  BACKWARD     VALUE '2'.
92   *
93   *
94        02  TS-DATA.
95            05  FILLER      PIC X(3).
96            05  TS-UNIT1        PIC XXXX.
97            05  FILLER      PIC X(2).
98            05  TS-MONTH1       PIC X(2).
99            05  FILLER      PIC X   VALUE ' '.
100           05  TS-DAY1         PIC X(2).
101           05  FILLER      PIC X   VALUE ' '.
102           05  TS-YEAR1        PIC X(2).
103           05  FILLER      PIC X(2).
104           05  TS-HR1      PIC X(2).
105           05  FILLER      PIC X VALUE ' '.
106           05  TS-MIN1     PIC X(2).
107           05  FILLER      PIC X   VALUE ' '.
108           05  TS-SEC1     PIC X(2).
109           05  FILLER      PIC X(2).
110           05  TS-NAME1    PIC X(19).
111           05  FILLER      PIC X(3).
112           05  TS-CODE1    PIC X(2).
113           05  FILLER      PIC X(4).
114           05  TS-PROB1    PIC X(25).
115  *
116  01  ERROR-CT            PIC 99  VALUE ZEROS.
117  *
118  01  LINE-SUB           PIC S9(4) COMP.
119  *
120  01  SYS-TIME          PIC X(6).
121  01  SYS-TIME-X REDEFINES SYS-TIME.
122      05  SYS-HR        PIC X(2).
123      05  SYS-MIN       PIC X(2).
124      05  SYS-SEC       PIC X(2).
125  *
126  01  DATE-CHECK.
127      05  DATE-Y        PIC XX.
128      05  DATE-M        PIC XX.
129      05  DATE-D        PIC XX.
130  01  SYS-DATE-X REDEFINES DATE-CHECK PIC X(6).
131  01  IBM-DATE          PIC 9(6).
132  01  SYS-DATE REDEFINES IBM-DATE.
133      05  SYS-YEAR      PIC 99.
134      05  SYS-MONTH     PIC 99.
135      05  SYS-DAY       PIC 99.
136  *
137  01  WS-COMPLAINT-REC.
138      02  CO-KEY.
139          05  CO-CARRIER-CODE    PIC X(3).
140          05  CO-UNIT-NUMBER     PIC X(4).
141          05  CO-COMPLAINT-DATE.
142              10  CO-DATE-MM     PIC XX.
143              10  CO-DATE-DD     PIC XX.
144              10  CO-DATE-YY     PIC XX.
145          05  CO-TIME            PIC X(6).
146      02  CO-CONDUCTOR-ID        PIC X(7).
```

```
147        02  CO-EQ-TYPE              PIC X.
148        02  CO-COMPLAINT-CODE       PIC XX.
149        02  CO-END                  PIC X.
150        02  CO-PROBLEM              PIC X(50).
151        02  CO-COMMENT-1            PIC X(50).
152        02  CO-COMMENT-2            PIC X(50).
153        02  CO-WORK-ORDER           PIC X(6).
154        02  FILLER                  PIC X(14).
155    01  EMPLOYEE-ROSTER-REC.  COPY CCREMP.
156    01  CARRIER-TABLE.  COPY CCARRIER.
157    01  COMPLAINT-TBLE.  COPY CCOMPLNT.
158        COPY DFHAID.
159        COPY CHARACTR.
160        COPY TRE6MAP.
161  *
162    LINKAGE SECTION.
163  *
164    01  DFHCOMMAREA.
165        05  PASS-AREA               PIC X(16).
166  *
167    PROCEDURE DIVISION.
168  *
169    0000-MAIN SECTION.
170        MOVE EIBTRMID TO TS-TERM-ID.
171        EXEC CICS HANDLE AID
172            PF1(9500-RETURN-TO-MENU)
173            PF2(9000-CANCEL-RTN)
174            END-EXEC.
175        IF EIBCALEN > ZEROS
176            MOVE DFHCOMMAREA TO WS-COMMAREA
177            MOVE COMM-CARRIER TO T-CARRIER-CODE CO-CARRIER-CODE
178        IF PASS-XCTL
179            PERFORM   0115-INIT-SETUP THRU 0115-END
180            MOVE COMM-CARRIER TO T-CARRIER-CODE CO-CARRIER-CODE
181            MOVE -1 TO IMONTHL
182            PERFORM 0110-INIT-MAP
183        ELSE
184            IF INIT-MAP
185            PERFORM 0115-INIT-SETUP THRU 0115-END
186            MOVE -1 TO IMONTHL
187            PERFORM 0110-INIT-MAP
188        ELSE
189            IF SEND-MAP
190                PERFORM 0120-SEND-MAP
191        ELSE
192            IF RECV-MAP
193                PERFORM 0130-RECEIVE-MAP.
194    0000-END.
195        EXIT.
196  *
197    0110-INIT-MAP SECTION.
198        EXEC CICS HANDLE CONDITION
199            ERROR(9999-ERROR)
200            END-EXEC.
201        EXEC CICS SEND
202            MAP('TRE6')
203            MAPSET ('TRE6MAP')
204            FROM(TRE6I)
205            ERASE
206            CURSOR
207            END-EXEC.
208        MOVE 'R' TO COMM-FLAG.
209        EXEC CICS RETURN
210            TRANSID('TRE6')
211            COMMAREA(WS-COMMAREA)
212            LENGTH (16)
213            END-EXEC.
214    0110-END.
215        EXIT.
216  *
217    0115-INIT-SETUP SECTION.
218        MOVE SPACES TO ERRORO MSGO MSG1O.
219        MOVE LOW-VALUES TO TRE6I.
220        ACCEPT IBM-DATE FROM DATE.
221        MOVE SYS-MONTH TO MONTHO.
222        MOVE SYS-DAY TO DAYO.
223        MOVE SYS-YEAR TO YEARO.
224        MOVE COMM-CARRIER TO T-CARRIER-CODE CO-CARRIER-CODE.
```

```
225      IF T-CARRIER-CODE = SPACES
226          MOVE PROT-BRT TO ERRORA
227          MOVE -1 TO CARRIERL
228          MOVE 'ENTER CARRIER' TO ERRORO
229          PERFORM 0120-SEND-MAP
230      ELSE
231          MOVE UNPROT-NUM-MDT TO IMONTHA IDAYA IYEARA
232      MOVE 'TRE6' TO TRANIDO
233      MOVE 'PF1=MENU PF2=CANCEL ENTER=CONTINUE PF3=NEW SCREEN ' TO
234          MSGO
235      IF T-CARRIER-CODE NOT = SPACES
236          PERFORM 0140-READ-CARRIER THRU 0140-END.
237  0115-END.
238      EXIT.
239  *
240  0120-SEND-MAP SECTION.
241      EXEC CICS HANDLE CONDITION
242          ERROR(9999-ERROR)
243          INVREQ(9999-INVREQ)
244          END-EXEC.
245      EXEC CICS SEND
246          MAP('TRE6')
247          MAPSET('TRE6MAP')
248          FROM(TRE6I)
249          DATAONLY
250          CURSOR
251          END-EXEC.
252      MOVE 'R' TO COMM-FLAG.
253      MOVE SPACES TO ERRORO MSGO MSG1O.
254      EXEC CICS RETURN
255          TRANSID('TRE6')
256          COMMAREA(WS-COMMAREA)
257          LENGTH(16)
258          END-EXEC.
259  0120-END.
260      EXIT.
261  *
262  0126-SET-ATTRIBUTES SECTION.
263      MOVE SPACES TO DATAD(LINE-SUB).
264  0126-EXIT.
265      EXIT.
266
267  0127-SEND-NEW-MAP SECTION.
268      PERFORM 0126-SET-ATTRIBUTES VARYING LINE-SUB FROM 1 BY 1
269          UNTIL LINE-SUB > 11.
270      PERFORM 0128-RESET-ATTRIBUTES VARYING HOLD-SUB FROM 1 BY 1
271          UNTIL HOLD-SUB > 11.
272      MOVE SPACES TO MSGO ERRORO IMONTHO IYEARO IDAYO.
273      MOVE -1 TO IMONTHL.
274      MOVE 'PF1=MENU  PF2=CANCEL  ENTER=CONTINUE  PF3=NEW SCREEN'
275          TO MSGO.
276      MOVE PROT-BRT TO MSGA.
277      EXEC CICS HANDLE CONDITION
278          ERROR(9999-ERROR)
279          END-EXEC.
280          EXEC CICS SEND MAP('TRE6')
281                         MAPSET('TRE6MAP')
282                         FROM(TRE6I)
283                         ERASEAUP
284                         CURSOR
285          END-EXEC.
286      MOVE 'R' TO COMM-FLAG.
287      EXEC CICS RETURN
288          TRANSID('TRE6')
289          COMMAREA(WS-COMMAREA)
290          LENGTH(16)
291          END-EXEC.
292  0127-END.
293      EXIT.
294  *
295  0128-RESET-ATTRIBUTES SECTION.
296      MOVE PROT-MDT TO DATAA(HOLD-SUB).
297  0128-EXIT.
298      EXIT.
299  *
300  0130-RECEIVE-MAP SECTION.
```

```
301              EXEC CICS HANDLE CONDITION
302                  MAPFAIL(9999-MAPFAIL)
303                  ERROR(9999-ERROR)
304              END-EXEC.
305              EXEC CICS HANDLE AID
306                  CLEAR(9500-RETURN-TO-MENU)
307                  PF1(9500-RETURN-TO-MENU)
308                  PF3(0127-SEND-NEW-MAP)
309                  ENTER(0150-WHICH-SCENARIO)
310                  ANYKEY(9999-ANYKEY)
311              END-EXEC.
312              EXEC CICS RECEIVE
313                  MAP('TRE6')
314                  MAPSET('TRE6MAP')
315                  INTO(TRE6I)
316              END-EXEC.
317          0130-END.
318              EXIT.
319      *
320      *
321          0140-READ-CARRIER SECTION.
322              MOVE ZEROS TO ERROR-CT.
323              EXEC CICS HANDLE CONDITION
324                      NOTOPEN(9999-NOTOPEN)
325                      NOTFND(0140-NOTFND)
326                      ERROR(9999-ERROR)
327              END-EXEC.
328              EXEC CICS READ DATASET('TCARRIER')
329                  INTO(CARRIER-TABLE)
330                  RIDFLD(T-CARRIER-CODE)
331              END-EXEC.
332              MOVE T-CARRIER-DESC TO CARRIERO.
333              GO TO 0140-END.
334          0140-NOTFND.
335              MOVE 'X' TO REC-FLAG.
336              MOVE -1 TO CARRIERL.
337              MOVE SPACES TO CARRIERO.
338              MOVE PROT-BRT TO MSGA ERRORA.
339              MOVE 'YOU MUST ENTER A VALID CARRIER' TO ERRORO.
340              PERFORM 0120-SEND-MAP.
341          0140-END.
342              EXIT.
343      *
344          0150-WHICH-SCENARIO SECTION.
345              IF TSQ
346              PERFORM 0126-SET-ATTRIBUTES VARYING LINE-SUB FROM 1 BY 1
347                  UNTIL LINE-SUB > 11
348                  GO TO 1300-READ-NEXT-Q.
349                  ACCEPT IBM-DATE FROM DATE.
350                  MOVE SPACES TO TS-DATA WS-DATA.
351                  MOVE IDAYO TO CO-DATE-DD DATE-D.
352                  MOVE IMONTHO TO CO-DATE-MM DATE-M.
353                  MOVE IYEARO TO CO-DATE-YY DATE-Y.
354              PERFORM 0126-SET-ATTRIBUTES VARYING LINE-SUB FROM 1 BY 1
355                  UNTIL LINE-SUB > 11.
356              IF SYS-DATE-X < IBM-DATE OR SYS-DATE-X = IBM-DATE
357                  GO TO 0300-GOOD-DATE
358              ELSE
359              IF SYS-DATE-X > IBM-DATE
360                  MOVE 'INVALID DATE PLEASE CHECK AND REENTER' TO MSG1O
361                  MOVE PROT TO MSG1A
362              ELSE
363              IF IDAYO = SPACES OR IMONTHO = SPACES OR IYEARO = SPACES
364                  MOVE 'PLEASE ENTER A VALID DATE' TO MSG1O
365                  MOVE PROT TO MSG1A.
366              MOVE 'PF1=MENU PF2=CANCEL ENTER=CONTINUE PF3=NEW SCREEN'
367                  TO MSGO.
368              MOVE -1 TO IMONTHL.
369              MOVE PROT TO MSGA.
370              GO TO 0120-SEND-MAP.
371          0150-EXIT.
372              EXIT.
373      *
374      *
375          0300-GOOD-DATE SECTION.
376              MOVE COMM-CARRIER TO CO-CARRIER-CODE.
377              PERFORM 0600-BROWSE-CODE THRU 0600-EXIT.
378              IF GOT-IT
```

```
379             IF COMM-CARRIER = CO-CARRIER-CODE
380              IF NOT THE-END
381               IF (IDAYI < CO-DATE-DD OR IDAYI = CO-DATE-DD) AND
382                  (IMONTHI < CO-DATE-MM OR IMONTHI = CO-DATE-MM) AND
383                  (IYEARI < CO-DATE-YY OR IYEARI = CO-DATE-YY)
384           EXEC CICS
385             HANDLE CONDITION DUPKEY(0610-DUPKEY)
386           END-EXEC
387           PERFORM 0610-READ-NEXT THRU 0610-EXIT VARYING LINE-SUB FROM
388           1 BY 1 UNTIL THE-END
389           ELSE
390             IF CO-KEY = HIGH-VALUES
391               MOVE 'END OF FILE' TO MSG1O
392               MOVE PROT-BRT TO MSG1A
393               MOVE 'X' TO REC-FLAG
394           ELSE
395               MOVE 'NO MORE RECORDS FOR THIS CARRIER' TO MSG1O
396               MOVE PROT-BRT TO MSG1A
397               MOVE 'X' TO REC-FLAG.
398             IF THE-END AND
399                TS-DATA > SPACES
400                   PERFORM 1000-READ-Q VARYING TS-SUB FROM TS-SUB BY -1
401                     UNTIL READ-SUB > 11 OR THE-END.
402           MOVE 'PF1=MENU PF2=CANCEL ENTER=CONTINUE PF3=NEW SCREEN' TO
403             MSGO.
404           MOVE PROT-BRT TO MSGA.
405           MOVE -1 TO IDAYL.
406           GO TO 0120-SEND-MAP.
407       0300-EXIT.
408           EXIT.
409   *
410       0600-BROWSE-CODE SECTION.
411           EXEC CICS
412
413               HANDLE CONDITION NOTFND(0600-NOTFND)
414           END-EXEC.
415           EXEC CICS
416               STARTBR DATASET('TDATEALT')
417                       RIDFLD(CO-COMPLAINT-DATE)
418                       GTEQ
419           END-EXEC.
420           GO TO 0600-EXIT.
421       0600-NOTFND.
422           MOVE 'CONGRATULATIONS--NO PROBLEMS FOR THIS PERIOD' TO MSG1O
423           MOVE ASKIP TO MSG1A.
424           MOVE 'PF1=MENU PF2=CANCEL ENTER=CONTINUE PF3=NEW SCREEN' TO
425             MSGO.
426               MOVE PROT-BRT TO MSGA.
427                         GO TO 0120-SEND-MAP.
428       0600-EXIT.
429   *
430   *
431   *
432       0610-READ-NEXT SECTION.
433           EXEC CICS
434               HANDLE CONDITION ENDFILE(0610-ENDFILE)
435           END-EXEC.
436           EXEC CICS
437               READNEXT DATASET('TDATEALT')
438                       INTO(WS-COMPLAINT-REC)
439                       RIDFLD(CO-COMPLAINT-DATE)
440           END-EXEC.
441           IF COMM-CARRIER = CO-CARRIER-CODE
442               PERFORM 0850-MOVE-ALT-RECORD THRU 0850-EXIT
443               PERFORM 1200-WRITE-Q THRU 1200-EXIT.
444             IF TS-SUB > 11 OR THE-END
445               MOVE 'N' TO EOF-SW
446               MOVE -1 TO IMONTHL
447               MOVE 'PF1=MENU PF2=CANCEL ENTER=CONTINUE PF3=NEW SCREEN' TO
448                 MSGO
449               MOVE PROT-BRT TO MSGA.
450               GO TO 0610-EXIT.
451       0610-DUPKEY.
452           IF COMM-CARRIER = CO-CARRIER-CODE
453               PERFORM 0850-MOVE-ALT-RECORD THRU 0850-EXIT
454               PERFORM 1200-WRITE-Q THRU 1200-EXIT.
```

```
455             IF TS-SUB > 11 OR THE-END
456                MOVE -1 TO IMONTHL
457                MOVE 'PF1=MENU PF2=CANCEL ENTER=CONTINUE PF3=NEW SCREEN' TO
458                   MSGO
459                MOVE PROT-BRT TO MSGA.
460                GO TO 0610-EXIT.
461     0610-EXIT.
462             EXIT.
463     0610-ENDFILE.
464             IF TS-DATA > SPACES
465             PERFORM 1000-READ-Q THRU 1000-EXIT VARYING TS-SUB FROM
466             TS-SUB BY -1 UNTIL READ-SUB > 11
467             ELSE
468             MOVE 'NO PROBLEMS DURING THIS PERIOD' TO MSG10
469             MOVE ASKIP TO MSG1A.
470             MOVE 'PF1=MENU PF2=CANCEL ENTER=CONTINUE PF3=NEXT DATA' TO
471                MSGO.
472             MOVE PROT-BRT TO MSGA.
473             MOVE -1 TO IMONTHL.
474             GO TO 0120-SEND-MAP.
475     *
476     *
477     0850-MOVE-ALT-RECORD SECTION.
478             PERFORM 0806-CHECK-EMPLOYEE THRU 0806-EXIT.
479             PERFORM 0807-CHECK-COMPLAINT THRU 0807-EXIT.
480             MOVE CO-UNIT-NUMBER TO TS-UNIT1.
481             MOVE CO-DATE-MM TO TS-MONTH1.
482             MOVE CO-DATE-DD TO TS-DAY1.
483             MOVE CO-DATE-YY TO TS-YEAR1.
484             MOVE CO-COMPLAINT-CODE TO TS-CODE1.
485             MOVE CO-TIME TO SYS-TIME.
486             MOVE SYS-SEC TO TS-SEC1.
487             MOVE SYS-MIN TO TS-MIN1.
488             MOVE SYS-HR TO TS-HR1.
489             MOVE 'PF1=MENU PF2=CANCEL ENTER=CONTINUE PF3=NEW SCREEN' TO
490                MSGO.
491             MOVE PROT-BRT TO MSGA.
492             MOVE -1 TO IMONTHL.
493             ADD +1 TO MOVE-CT.
494     0850-EXIT.
495             EXIT.
496     *
497     0806-CHECK-EMPLOYEE SECTION.
498             MOVE CO-CONDUCTOR-ID TO CE-EMP-ID.
499             MOVE COMM-CARRIER TO CE-CARRIER-CODE.
500             EXEC CICS HANDLE CONDITION
501                     NOTFND(0806-NOTFND)
502                     NOTOPEN(9999-NOTOPEN)
503                     ERROR(9999-ERROR)
504             END-EXEC.
505             EXEC CICS READ DATASET('TCEMPLOY')
506                         INTO(EMPLOYEE-ROSTER-REC)
507                         RIDFLD(CE-KEY)
508             END-EXEC.
509             MOVE CE-EMP-NAME TO TS-NAME1.
510             GO TO 0806-EXIT.
511     0806-NOTFND.
512             MOVE 'N' TO VALID-DATA-SW.
513             MOVE PROT-BRT TO ERRORA.
514             MOVE SPACES TO TS-NAME1.
515     0806-EXIT.
516             EXIT.
517     *
518     0807-CHECK-COMPLAINT SECTION.
519             MOVE CO-COMPLAINT-CODE TO T-COMPLAINT-CODE.
520             EXEC CICS HANDLE CONDITION
521                     NOTFND(0807-NOTFND)
522                     NOTOPEN(9999-NOTOPEN)
523                     ERROR(9999-ERROR)
524             END-EXEC.
525             EXEC CICS READ DATASET('TCOMPLNT')
526                         INTO(COMPLAINT-TBLE)
527                         RIDFLD(T-COMPLAINT-CODE)
528             END-EXEC.
529             MOVE T-COMPLAINT-DESC TO TS-PROB1.
530             GO TO 0807-EXIT.
531     0807-NOTFND.
532             MOVE 'N' TO VALID-DATA-SW.
```

```
533         MOVE PROT-BRT TO ERRORA.
534         MOVE SPACES TO TS-PROB1.
535    0807-EXIT.
536         EXIT.
537  *
538  *
539  *
540    1000-READ-Q SECTION.
541         EXEC CICS HANDLE CONDITION
542                   ITEMERR(1000-ITEMERR)
543         END-EXEC.
544         EXEC CICS READQ TS QUEUE(TS-QUEUE-NAME)
545                   INTO(TS-DATA)
546                   LENGTH(TS-LENGTH)
547                   ITEM(TS-SUB)
548         END-EXEC.
549         ADD +1 TO READ-SUB.
550         PERFORM 1100-MOVE-Q THRU 1100-EXIT.
551         GO TO 1000-EXIT.
552    1000-ITEMERR.
553         EXEC CICS
554              DELETEQ TS QUEUE(TS-QUEUE-NAME)
555         END-EXEC.
556         MOVE 'Y' TO EOF-SW.
557          PERFORM 0128-RESET-ATTRIBUTES VARYING HOLD-SUB FROM
558          1 BY 1 UNTIL HOLD-SUB > 11.
559         MOVE -1 TO IMONTHL.
560         MOVE 'X' TO REC-FLAG.
561         MOVE 'NO MORE RECORDS' TO MSG10.
562         MOVE ASKIP TO MSG1A.
563         GO TO 0120-SEND-MAP.
564    1000-EXIT.
565         EXIT.
566  *
567    1100-MOVE-Q SECTION.
568         MOVE TS-DATA TO WS-DATA.
569         PERFORM 0128-RESET-ATTRIBUTES VARYING HOLD-SUB FROM
570          1 BY 1 UNTIL HOLD-SUB > 11.
571         MOVE WS-DATA TO DATAD(READ-SUB)
572         SUBTRACT +1 FROM MOVE-CT.
573         IF MOVE-CT > +0000
574            MOVE 'T' TO REC-FLAG
575            MOVE 'PRESS ENTER TO VIEW ADDITIONAL RECORDS' TO MSG10
576            MOVE ASKIP TO MSG1A.
577    1100-EXIT.
578         EXIT.
579  *
580    1200-WRITE-Q SECTION.
581         EXEC CICS
582              WRITEQ TS QUEUE(TS-QUEUE-NAME)
583                   FROM(TS-DATA)
584                   LENGTH(TS-LENGTH)
585                   ITEM(TS-SUB)
586         END-EXEC.
587    1200-EXIT.
588         EXIT.
589  *
590    1300-READ-NEXT-Q SECTION.
591         PERFORM 1400-TURN-PAGE VARYING TS-SUB FROM TS-SUB BY -1
592            UNTIL READ-SUB > 11 OR THE-END.
593         GO TO 0120-SEND-MAP.
594    1300-EXIT.
595         EXIT.
596  *
597    1400-TURN-PAGE SECTION.
598         EXEC CICS HANDLE CONDITION
599                   ITEMERR(1400-ITEMERR)
600         END-EXEC.
601         EXEC CICS READQ TS QUEUE(TS-QUEUE-NAME)
602                   INTO(TS-DATA)
603                   LENGTH(TS-LENGTH)
604                   ITEM(TS-SUB)
605         END-EXEC.
606         ADD +1 TO READ-SUB.
607         PERFORM 1500-MOVE-Q THRU 1500-EXIT.
608         GO TO 0120-SEND-MAP.
609    1400-EXIT.
```

```
610        EXEC CICS
611             DELETEQ TS QUEUE(TS-QUEUE-NAME)
612        END-EXEC.
613        MOVE 'Y' TO EOF-SW.
614        PERFORM 0128-RESET-ATTRIBUTES VARYING HOLD-SUB FROM 1 BY 1
615        UNTIL HOLD-SUB > 11.
616        MOVE -1 TO IMONTHL.
617        MOVE 'X' TO REC-FLAG.
618        MOVE 'NO MORE RECORDS' TO MSG1O.
619        MOVE ASKIP TO MSG1A.
620        GO TO 0120-SEND-MAP.
621    1400-EXIT.
622        EXIT.
623    *
624    1500-MOVE-Q SECTION.
625        MOVE TS-DATA TO WS-DATA.
626        PERFORM 0128-RESET-ATTRIBUTES VARYING HOLD-SUB FROM 1 BY 1
627        UNTIL HOLD-SUB > 11.
628        MOVE TS-DATA TO DATAD(READ-SUB).
629        SUBTRACT +1 FROM MOVE-CT.
630        IF MOVE-CT > +0000
631            MOVE 'T' TO REC-FLAG
632            MOVE 'PRESS ENTER TO VIEW ADDITIONAL RECORDS' TO MSG1O
633            MOVE ASKIP TO MSG1A.
634    1500-EXIT.
635        EXIT.
636    *
637    *
638    9000-CANCEL-RTN SECTION.
639        IF TSQ
640        EXEC CICS
641             DELETEQ TS QUEUE(TS-QUEUE-NAME)
642        END-EXEC.
643        MOVE UNPROT-NUM-MDT TO IMONTHA.
644        MOVE SPACES TO IMONTHO IDAYO IYEARO.
645        MOVE -1 TO IMONTHL.
646        MOVE PROT TO MSG1A.
647        MOVE 'TRANSACTION CANCELLED' TO MSG1O.
648        MOVE 'X' TO REC-FLAG.
649        MOVE SPACES TO ERRORO.
650         PERFORM 0127-SEND-NEW-MAP.
651    *
652    9500-RETURN-TO-MENU SECTION.
653        MOVE 'I' TO COMM-FLAG.
654        EXEC CICS HANDLE CONDITION
655             PGMIDERR(9999-NOTFND)
656             ERROR(9999-ERROR)
657        END-EXEC.
658        EXEC CICS XCTL
659             PROGRAM('TGM1MENU')
660             COMMAREA(WS-COMMAREA)
661             LENGTH(6)
662        END-EXEC.
663    *
664    9999-ANYKEY SECTION.
665        MOVE -1 TO IMONTHL.
666        MOVE PROT-BRT TO MSGA.
667        MOVE 'INVALID KEY PRESSED - VALID KEYS ARE PF1 PF2 PF3 ENTER'
668             TO MSGO
669        EXEC CICS HANDLE CONDITION
670             ERROR(9999-ERROR)
671        END-EXEC.
672        IF PASS-XCTL OR INIT-MAP
673        EXEC CICS SEND
674             MAP('TRE6')
675             MAPSET('TRE6MAP')
676             FROM(TRE6I)
677             ERASE
678             CURSOR
679        END-EXEC
680        ELSE
681        EXEC CICS SEND
682             MAP('TRE6')
683             MAPSET('TRE6MAP')
684             FROM(TRE6I)
685             DATAONLY
686             CURSOR
687        END-EXEC.
```

```
688        EXEC CICS RETURN
689            TRANSID('TRE6')
690            COMMAREA(WS-COMMAREA)
691            LENGTH(16)
692        END-EXEC.
693        IF RECV-MAP
694            GO TO 0130-END.
695  *
696    9999-MAPFAIL SECTION.
697        EXEC CICS SEND TEXT
698            FROM(MAPFAIL-MSG)
699            LENGTH(36)
700            ERASE
701            FREEKB
702        END-EXEC.
703        GO TO 9999-EXIT.
704  *
705    9999-NOTOPEN SECTION.
706        EXEC CICS SEND TEXT
707            FROM(NOT-OPEN-MSG)
708            LENGTH(42)
709            ERASE
710            FREEKB
711        END-EXEC.
712        GO TO 9999-EXIT.
713  *
714    9999-NOTFND SECTION.
715        EXEC CICS SEND TEXT
716            FROM(PGM-NOTFND-MSG)
717            LENGTH(42)
718            DATAONLY
719            FREEKB
720        END-EXEC.
721        GO TO 9999-EXIT.
722  *
723    9999-ERROR SECTION.
724        EXEC CICS SEND TEXT
725            FROM(GENERIC-ERROR-MSG)
726            LENGTH(39)
727            ERASE
728            FREEKB
729        END-EXEC.
730        EXEC CICS RETURN
731        END-EXEC.
732  *
733    9999-INVREQ SECTION.
734        EXEC CICS SEND TEXT
735            FROM(INVREQ-MSG)
736            LENGTH(15)
737            ERASE
738            FREEKB
739        END-EXEC.
740        EXEC CICS RETURN
741    9999-EXIT.
742        EXIT.
743  *
744    9999-RETURN.
745        EXEC CICS RETURN
746            TRANSID('TRE6')
747            COMMAREA(WS-COMMAREA)
748            LENGTH(16)
749        END-EXEC.
750    10000-EXIT.
751        EXIT.
752
```

01 MESSAGES correspond to lines 24 through 34 of FIG. 7-13. 01 MESSAGES are preformatted in the WORKING-STORAGE SECTION, ready to be displayed. They are triggered through the HANDLE-CON-DITION, or through problems relating to the use of temporary

queues for building a physical page. Lines 37 through 40 shows a method aimed at making the queue a unique one. These lines only represent a shell to be completed in the PROCEDURE DIVISION via the following statements:

```
EXEC CICS
      WRITEQ TS QUEUE(TS-QUEUE-NAME)
          FROM(TS-DATA)
          LENGTH(TS-LENGTH)
          ITEM(TS-SUB)
END-EXEC.
```

WS-DATA (lines 42 through 62) represents a screen layout for the repeating or recurring detail lines such as the unit number representing a piece of equipment, data and time for recording a specific problem, the name of the conductor involved in such a problem, a two-position alphanumeric "problem" code, and an explanation of that code extracted from the problem code table. Lines 64 through 69, WS-COMMAREA, enable the programmer to setup an initial (and subsequent) SEND and RECEIVE MAP procedures required for pseudoconversational processing or exit-controlling routines. Lines 71 through 76, or WS-COMMAREA-OUT, is coded in order to set up multiple carriers, similar to a multicorporate environment, as detailed in the case study.

Lines 94 through 114 define the previous detail line that I set up in temporary storage for the purpose of page building. Figure 7-10 provides a good idea of the complexity of the BROWSE program. Lines 137 through 154 of FIG. 7-13, WS-COMPLAINT-REC, represents the layout of the Problem Master imbedded in the WORKING-STORAGE, which happens to be the driver of the BROWSE. Note that other files and tables were copied into this BROWSE program through the various copy statements shown in lines 155 through 161. The physical expansion of these copied records is shown in FIG. 7-14.

Three additional copy statements are also included in lines 1620099 through 1640099. The first one is that of the DFHAID block, which is a standard CICS definition for function key assignments. An expanded format of the DFHAID block is shown in lines 303 through 339 in FIG. 7-14. A second copy statement, COPY CHARATR, refers to an internally built attribute table whose purpose is to consolidate several attribute functions into a single "character" for convenience. CHARATR provides a field with proper intensification, protection, and data tag modification function all rolled into a single definition. This is important since CICS normally does not provide you with that level of detail. Finally, there is a copy statement pertaining to the TRE6MAP, which is the actual screen layout used in this program.

The first action in the PROCEDURE DIVISION of FIG. 7-14 is to set up the individual queue so that it can be referenced uniquely. This is the function of line 170. Afterwards, HANDLE AID condition sets up the PF 1 and PF 2 assignments in lines 72 through 173. Note that the paragraph 0000-MAIN SECTION also serves two additional purposes. The first one is to move messages from the DFHCOMMAREA to determine which carrier (and line) is being inquired upon. A second purpose of this logic is to conform to pseudoconversational requirements for sending or receiving a map. As you can see, the programmer here, as in most cases, relies extensively on nested if statements.

Starting in line 197, 0110-INIT-MAP SECTION, down to line 213, procedures are being defined to send the TRE6MAP for the first time. This routine includes an error message in case the map fails, as well as a message to set up the COMM-FLAG to invoke a receive map routine ("R") the next time the cycle is repeated.

The procedure imbedded in lines 217 through 238 sets up the initial date as part of the header routine on the top of the panel shown in FIG. 7-5. Note that the procedure also verifies that the carrier field was not left blank, which would be a fatal error in the editing cycle. If an ERROR message is to be triggered, the cursor would be repositioned next to the carrier field simply by moving a – 1 into the length portion of the carrier field (CARRIERL). This is reflected in line 227 of FIG. 7-13. If there is no resulting ERROR CONDITION, you will need to set up the map as I did in lines 231 through 238. Note that I have "unprotected" the inquiry or search field to make it available for the next inquiry date. Note also the various means at your disposal to send a map. In lines 197 through 215, the TRE-6MAP is sent for the first time. It means the map is to be sent in its entirety while erasing all previous data that might still be displayed on the screen. When sending the map for the second time, lines 240 through 260, note that only the data is being sent, which, by the way, is an efficient method for handling such a procedure. DATAONLY will only send the variable or data portion of the map while retaining some of the initial title headings and systems messages from the previous cycle. Finally, in lines 267 through 293, the map is sent, erasing all unprotected data fields. This procedure is triggered via PF 3, resulting in a blanked-screen.

Through lines 312 down to 342 of FIG. 7-13, you are reading the CARRIER table, lines 220 through 227 in FIG. 7-14. If the carrier is in the table, a description corresponding to the carrier is extracted. If, however, there is no such carrier on file, a message, "YOU MUST ENTER A VALID CARRIER" will appear on the bottom of the screen in protected bright, while program logic repositions the cursor back to the original carrier field.

The paragraph 0150-WHICH-SCENARIO SECTION (lines 344 through 371 in FIG. 7-13) encompasses a set of procedures to build and clear the unused portion of the screen via subscripting the detail lines. Note that a page is made up of a maximum of 11 detail lines, which also corresponds to a physical page in temporary storage (queue). Afterwards, the inquiry date is checked for validity. This is done by comparing the inquiry date with the systems date, which always contains today, or the most current date. If the inquiry date is greater than the current date, then an error condition exists, since displaying any future transaction is disallowed. Thus, the message: "INVALID DATE, PLEASE CHECK AND REENTER" appears.

0300-GOOD-DATE SECTION, lines 375 through 408, continues with the premise that the inquiry date is either a current or a past date, while rescheduling the logic of the program through a START BROWSE routine. If there is no record for this period on file, (thus no equipment-related problem exists), a message "CONGRATULATIONS— NO PROBLEMS FOR THIS PERIOD" is to be displayed on the screen in protected mode, thus triggering a map. If the STARTBR is a successful one, then the COMM-CARRIER, line 379 is checked for validity. This needs to be done, since the COMM-CARRIER, or the carrier portion of the concatenated key stored in the COMMUNICATIONS AREA might be different from the original carrier being inquired upon. As I explained in Chapter 1, the MCRA or the Metropolitan Commuter Railway Agency keeps all equipment problems on a single file, which is qualified through a concatenated key. The highest qualifier of this concatenated key is a particular carrier.

After checking for a duplicate key, or the possibility of duplicate records on file (line 385), you need to perform a set of READNEXT instructions until you come to the end of that specific carrier. The detailed data triggering the READNEXT subroutine is shown in FIG. 7-13, lines 387 through 388.

The procedure listed in 0600-BROWSE-CODE SECTION, lines 410 through 427, represents two sets of procedures both considered TRE6BRS subroutines. The first set of code is described in lines 410 through 420, and it merely represents logic required for the BROWSE operation. The second part of this section is performed independently and is designed to inform the user that no equipment problems existed for the current accounting period.

The READ command issued in line 437 is set up to read the Problem Master via its secondary or alternate key. The program checks to see if the user is still within the same carrier. This is done for security reasons. The program TRE6BRS begins to fill the temporary queue to store up to 11 lines for a following display.

In subsequent procedures, a subroutine is accessed, lines 452 through 454, triggering the 850-MOVE-ALT-RECORD SECTION. This subroutine builds a single line of detailed data in temporary storage. Every time such a line is built, the programmer updates an internal counter, in lines 477 through 495. At that point, the logic that was invoked through a perform statement is routed back to line 444.

Paragraph 0610-ENDFILE statements 0463 through 474, is another subroutine designed to search data within a given counter. If no problem appears for a given period for a carrier, a message is to pop up on the bottom portion of the screen.

Paragraph 0806-CHECK-EMPLOYEE SECTION, lines 497 through 510, takes the employee identifier (that of a conductor in this situation) to set up an inquiry (READ) against the employee master file, EMPLOYEE-ROSTER-REC, to extract the name from it and display it on the screen as one of the required data elements. Note that a HANDLE CONDITION is specifically set for the READ instruction to redefine some of the initial error conditions. This logic also precedes a READ operation against the Problem Master, as shown in lines 518 through 524. The purpose of this read is simply to extract a problem description and move it into temporary storage (MOVE T-COMPLAINT-DESC TO TS-PROB1) for subsequent page building and display. The logic starting in 1000-ITEMERR is to delete a temporary queue once it is depleted. This particular logic is laid out in lines 552 through 587.

Finally, the purpose of 1100-MOVE-Q paragraph, starting in line 567, is to move the contents of the queue from temporary storage into WORKING-STORAGE, 11 or less detailed lines at a time. Afterward, the program will place the cursor back to the inquiry date field for a subsequent inquiry. In this process the programmer informs the terminal operator that there are no more records for display. Note that the rest of the program is made up of additional subroutines, such as page building, HANDLE CONDITION redefines, etc.

Compiler-generated source code: excerpts

This portion of the TRE6BRS program was system-generated. As shown in FIG. 7-14, the compiler expanded all copy library statements referenced in the programmer's original code. First of all, the initial copy statement, COPY CCREMP, is shown in line 156, which relates to the expansion of the Employee Roster or Personnel file as depicted in FIG. 7-10. The Employee Roster, as you can see, is a copy library member, meaning that it can be referenced either partially or in its entirety by any number of programmers. Note that although the Employee file is a 150-position record layout shown in lines 157 through 219 of FIG. 7-14, the current program, TRE6BRS, only utilizes a couple of data fields out of the file, specifically the employee number (CE-EMP-ID) and the employee name (CE-EMP-NAME). The employee ID is also part of the Complaint Master, which is then matched against the Employee Roster in order to extract the employee's name. Everything else is ignored by the program.

A second copy statement, line 221 COPY CARRIER, is the expansion of a small VSAM file, with the key being the carrier. This record contains a mere 48 positions. The third copy library member for TRE6BRS is shown in lines 281 through 286. The key to this VSAM table is the problem code that relates to a specific piece of equipment. These records contain a total of 40 bytes. Their sole purpose is to translate a given problem code into a more meaningful description.

Note that the fourth file is expanded by the programmer under WS-COMPLAINT-REC in the original program, lines 1370099 through 1540099. The key to this (driver) file is made up of the carrier and equipment unit number, date and time, which are system-supplied and a specific problem code. TRE6BRS uses an alternate key, which is the Date field.

Line 302 contains a copy statement for the DFHAID, block which is expanded at compile time by the system. This expansion is shown in lines 303 through 339, and it contains all 24 function key references, the ENTER and the CLEAR keys, a light pen and other valuable information.

A copy statement for CHARATR, or attribute byte definition, was done specifically for shop use and placed into a copy library for future references by the programming staff. The names are self explanatory and their value lies mainly in combining a number of attribute functions into a single and specific reference field such as UNPROT-NUM-BRT-MDT (value "R"), meaning that a field is to be displayed on the screen as an unprotected, numeric field. Note that the field will also be intensified with its modified data tag turned on. This attribute expansion scheme is shown in lines 342 through 366.

Next, the compiler generated symbolic map is presented (both input and output versions), starting in lines 370 through lines 366. This is the compiled version of the BMS MAP described earlier in FIG. 7-6. Finally, the DFHEIBLK block is expanded in the LINKAGE SECTION in lines 516 through 547. Note that the DFHEIBLK does not require a copy statement, because DFHEIBLK is automatically expanded by the compiler.

```
00001      IDENTIFICATION DIVISION.
00002          PROGRAM-ID. TRE6BRS.
00003          ENVIRONMENT DIVISION.
00004          DATA DIVISION.
00005          WORKING-STORAGE SECTION.
00006          *
         •
         •
         •
00155          01  EMPLOYEE-ROSTER-REC.
00156                      COPY CCREMP.
00157 C        05   CE-KEY.
00158 C        10   CE-CARRIER-CODE  PIC XXX.
00159 C        10   CE-LINE-CODE     PIC XX.
00160 C        10   CE-EMP-ID        PIC 9(7).
00161 C        10   CE-EMP-ID-X REDEFINES CE-EMP-ID    PIC X(7).
00162 C        10   CE-EMP-ID1 REDEFINES CE-EMP-ID     PIC 9(7).
00163 C        10   CE-EMP-ID2 REDEFINES CE-EMP-ID     PIC 9(7).
00164 C        10   CE-EMP-ID3 REDEFINES CE-EMP-ID     PIC 9(7).
00165 C        05   CE-EMP-NAME        PIC X(25).
00166 C        05   CE-EMP-NAME1 REDEFINES CE-EMP-NAME   PIC X(25).
00167 C        05   CE-EMP-NAME2 REDEFINES CE-EMP-NAME   PIC X(25).
00168 C        05   CE-EMP-NAME3 REDEFINES CE-EMP-NAME   PIC X(25).
00169 C        05   CE-CREW-TYPE        PIC X.
00170 C        05   CE-EMPOCC-CODE      PIC X.
00171 C        05   CE-EMPOCC-CODE1 REDEFINES CE-EMPOCC-CODE    PIC X.
00172 C        05   CE-EMPOCC-CODE2 REDEFINES CE-EMPOCC-CODE    PIC X.
00173 C        05   CE-EMPOCC-CODE3 REDEFINES CE-EMPOCC-CODE    PIC X.
00174 C        05   CE-PHONE-NO1        PIC  X(10).
00175 C        05   CE-PHONE-NO1X REDEFINES CE-PHONE-NO1.
00176 C        10   CE-PHONE-NO1A    PIC 999.
00177 C        10   CE-PHONE-NO1B    PIC 999.
00178 C        10   CE-PHONE-NO1C    PIC 9(4).
00179 C        05   CE-PHONE-NO2.
00180 C        10   CE-PHONE-NO2A    PIC 999.
00181 C        10   CE-PHONE-NO2B    PIC 999.
00182 C        10   CE-PHONE-NO2C    PIC 9(4).
00183 C        05   CE-PHONE-NO2-X REDEFINES CE-PHONE-NO2.
00184 C        10   CE-PHONE-NO2A-X  PIC XXX.
00185 C        10   CE-PHONE-NO2B-X  PIC XXX.
00186 C        10   CE-PHONE-NO2C-X  PIC X(4).
00187 C        05   CE-PAGER-NO         PIC X(4).
00188 C        05   CE-CR-SENDST-DATE.
00189 C        10   CE-CR-SENIORITY-YY    PIC 99.
00190 C        10   CE-CR-SENIORITY-YYX REDEFINES CE-CR-SENIORITY-YY
00191 C                      PIC XX.
00192 C        10   CE-CR-SENIORITY-MM    PIC 99.
00193 C        10   CE-CR-SENIORITY-MMX REDEFINES CE-CR-SENIORITY-MM
00194 C                      PIC XX.
00195 C        10   CE-CR-SENIORITY-DD    PIC 99.
00196 C        10   CE-CR-SENIORITY-DDX REDEFINES CE-CR-SENIORITY-DD
00197 C                      PIC XX.
00198 C        05   CE-EXTRA-BOARD        PIC X.
00199 C        05   CE-EXTRA-BOARD-ORDER     PIC 999.
00200 C        05   CE-QUALIFICATION1    PIC X.
00201 C        05   CE-QUALIFICATION2    PIC X.
00202 C        05   CE-QUALIFICATION3    PIC X.
00203 C        05   CE-QUALIFICATION4    PIC X.
00204 C        05   CE-QUALIFICATION5    PIC X.
00205 C        05   CE-QUALIFICATION6    PIC X.
00206 C        05   CE-PRIORITY-RIGHT    PIC XX.
00207 C        05   CE-CR-RANK           PIC XX.
00208 C        05   CE-CREW-NO1          PIC 9(4).
00209 C        05   CE-CREW-NO1-X REDEFINES CE-CREW-NO1   PIC X(4).
00210 C        05   CE-CREW-NO2          PIC 9(4).
00211 C        05   CE-CREW-NO2-X REDEFINES CE-CREW-NO2   PIC X(4).
00212 C        05   CE-CREW-NO3          PIC 9(4).
00213 C        05   CE-CREW-NO3-X REDEFINES CE-CREW-NO3   PIC X(4).
00214 C        05   CE-CREW-NO4          PIC 9(4).
00215 C        05   CE-CREW-NO4-X REDEFINES CE-CREW-NO4   PIC X(4).
00216 C        05   CE-CREW-NO5          PIC 9(4).
00217 C        05   CE-CREW-NO5-X REDEFINES CE-CREW-NO5   PIC X(4).
00218 C        05   FILLER             PIC X(47).
00219 C      *  RECORD LENGTH = 150
00220          01  CARRIER-TABLE.
00221                      COPY CCARRIER.
```

```
00222 C       05      T-CARRIER-CODE       PIC XXX.
00223 C       05      FILLER               PIC X(4).
00224 C       05      T-CARRIER-DESC       PIC X(35).
00225 C       05      FILLER               PIC X(2).
00226 C       05      HOLD-CODE       PIC X(4).
00227 C    *    RECORD LENGTH = 48
00281         01  COMPLAINT-TBLE.
00282                   COPY CCOMPLNT.
00283 C       05      T-COMPLAINT-CODE     PIC XX.
00284 C       05      FILLER               PIC X(5)    VALUE SPACES.
00285 C       05      T-COMPLAINT-DESC     PIC X(32).
00286 C       05      T-EQUIPMENT-CODE     PIC X       VALUE SPACES.
00287 C    *    RECORD LENGTH = 40
00302               COPY DFHAID.
00303 C  01    DFHAID.
00304 C       02  DFHNULL     PIC  X     VALUE IS ''.
00305 C       02  DFHENTER    PIC  X     VALUE IS QUOTE.
00306 C       02  DFHCLEAR    PIC  X     VALUE IS ' '.
00307 C       02  DFHCLRP     PIC  X     VALUE IS 'T'.
00308 C       02  DFHPEN PIC  X     VALUE IS '='.
00309 C       02  DFHOPID     PIC  X     VALUE IS 'W'.
00310 C       02  DFHMSRE     PIC  X     VALUE IS 'X'.
00311 C       02  DFHSTRF     PIC  X     VALUE IS 'h'.
00312 C       02  DFHTRIG     PIC  X     VALUE IS '"'.
00313 C       02  DFHPA1 PIC  X     VALUE IS '%'.
00314 C       02  DFHPA2 PIC  X     VALUE IS '>'.
00315 C       02  DFHPA3 PIC  X     VALUE IS ','.
00316 C       02  DFHPF1 PIC  X     VALUE IS '1'.
00317 C       02  DFHPF2 PIC  X     VALUE IS '2'.
00318 C       02  DFHPF3 PIC  X     VALUE IS '3'.
00319 C       02  DFHPF4 PIC  X     VALUE IS '4'.
00320 C       02  DFHPF5 PIC  X     VALUE IS '5'.
00321 C       02  DFHPF6 PIC  X     VALUE IS '6'.
00322 C       02  DFHPF7 PIC  X     VALUE IS '7'.
00323 C       02  DFHPF8 PIC  X     VALUE IS '8'.
00324 C       02  DFHPF9 PIC  X     VALUE IS '9'.
00325 C       02  DFHPF10     PIC  X     VALUE IS ':'.
00326 C       02  DFHPF11     PIC  X     VALUE IS '#'.
00327 C       02  DFHPF12     PIC  X     VALUE IS '@'.
00328 C       02  DFHPF13     PIC  X     VALUE IS 'A'.
00329 C       02  DFHPF14     PIC  X     VALUE IS 'B'.
00330 C       02  DFHPF15     PIC  X     VALUE IS 'C'.
00331 C       02  DFHPF16     PIC  X     VALUE IS 'D'.
00332 C       02  DFHPF17     PIC  X     VALUE IS 'E'.
00333 C       02  DFHPF18     PIC  X     VALUE IS 'F'.
00334 C       02  DFHPF19     PIC  X     VALUE IS 'G'.
00335 C       02  DFHPF20     PIC  X     VALUE IS 'H'.
00336 C       02  DFHPF21     PIC  X     VALUE IS 'I'.
00337 C       02  DFHPF22     PIC  X     VALUE IS '['.
00338 C       02  DFHPF23     PIC  X     VALUE IS '.'.
00339 C       02  DFHPF24     PIC  X     VALUE IS '<'.
00340               COPY CHARATR.
00341 C    *------------*  ATTRIBUTE-BYTES    *-------------------------------
00342 C  01    CHARATR.
00343 C       05      UNPROT-ALPHA            PIC X   VALUE SPACE.
00344 C       05      UNPROT-ALPHA-MDT        PIC X   VALUE 'A'.
00345 C       05      UNPROT-ALPHA-BRT        PIC X   VALUE 'H'.
00346 C       05      UNPROT-ALPHA-BRT-MDT    PIC X   VALUE 'I'.
00347 C       05      UNPROT-ALPHA-DRK        PIC X   VALUE '<'.
00348 C       05      UNPROT-ALPHA-DRK-MDT    PIC X   VALUE '('.
00349 C       05      UNPROT-NUM              PIC X   VALUE '&'.
00350 C       05      UNPROT-NUM-MDT          PIC X   VALUE 'J'.
00351 C       05      UNPROT-NUM-BRT          PIC X   VALUE 'Q'.
00352 C       05      UNPROT-NUM-BRT-MDT      PIC X   VALUE 'R'.
00353 C       05      UNPROT-NUM-DRK          PIC X   VALUE '*'.
00354 C       05      UNPROT-NUM-DRK-MDT      PIC X   VALUE ')'.
00355 C       05      PROT            PIC X   VALUE '-'.
00356 C       05      PROT-MDT        PIC X   VALUE '/'.
00357 C       05      PROT-BRT        PIC X   VALUE 'Y'.
00358 C       05      PROT-BRT-MDT            PIC X   VALUE 'Z'.
00359 C       05      PROT-DRK        PIC X   VALUE '%'.
00360 C       05      PROT-DRK-MDT            PIC X   VALUE ' '.
00361 C       05      ASKIP           PIC X   VALUE '0'.
00362 C       05      ASKIP-MDT       PIC X   VALUE '1'.
00363 C       05      ASKIP-BRT       PIC X   VALUE '8'.
00364 C       05      ASKIP-BRT-MDT           PIC X   VALUE '9'.
00365 C       05      ASKIP-DRK       PIC X   VALUE '@'.
00366 C       05      ASKIP-DRK-MDT           PIC X   VALUE QUOTE.
```

7-14 Continued

```
00367 C        *---------------* LENGTH BYTES   *------------------------------
00368 C   01  LENGTH-BYTES.
00369 C       05   CSR-REPO        PIC S9(4) COMP VALUE -1.
00370              COPY TRE6MAP.
00371 C   01  TRE6I.
00372 C       02   FILLER PIC X(12).
00373 C       02   MONTHL      COMP   PIC  S9(4).
00374 C       02   MONTHF      PICTURE X.
00375 C       02   FILLER REDEFINES MONTHF.
00376 C          03 MONTHA   PICTURE X.
00377 C       02   MONTHI   PIC X(2).
00378 C       02   DAYL COMP  PIC  S9(4).
00379 C       02   DAYF PICTURE X.
00380 C       02   FILLER REDEFINES DAYF.
00381 C          03 DAYA   PICTURE X.
00382 C       02   DAYI   PIC X(2).
00383 C       02   YEARL       COMP  PIC  S9(4).
00384 C       02   YEARF       PICTURE X.
00385 C       02   FILLER REDEFINES YEARF.
00386 C          03 YEARA   PICTURE X.
00387 C       02   YEARI  PIC X(2).
00388 C       02   TRANIDL    COMP  PIC  S9(4).
00389 C       02   TRANIDF    PICTURE X.
00390 C       02   FILLER REDEFINES TRANIDF.
00391 C          03 TRANIDA    PICTURE X.
00392 C       02   TRANIDI  PIC X(4).
00393 C       02   CARRIERL    COMP  PIC  S9(4).
00394 C       02   CARRIERF    PICTURE X.
00395 C       02   FILLER REDEFINES CARRIERF.
00396 C          03 CARRIERA   PICTURE X.
00397 C       02   CARRIERI  PIC X(35).
00398 C       02   IMONTHL    COMP  PIC  S9(4).
00399 C       02   IMONTHF    PICTURE X.
00400 C       02   FILLER REDEFINES IMONTHF.
00401 C          03 IMONTHA    PICTURE X.
00402 C       02   IMONTHI  PIC X(2).
00403 C       02   IDAYL       COMP  PIC  S9(4).
00404 C       02   IDAYF       PICTURE X.
00405 C       02   FILLER REDEFINES IDAYF.
00406 C          03 IDAYA   PICTURE X.
00407 C       02   IDAYI  PIC X(2).
00408 C       02   IYEARL      COMP   PIC  S9(4).
00409 C       02   IYEARF      PICTURE X.
00410 C       02   FILLER REDEFINES IYEARF.
00411 C          03 IYEARA   PICTURE X.
00412 C       02   IYEARI   PIC X(2).
00413 C       02   DATAD OCCURS 11 TIMES.
00414 C          03  DATAL   COMP  PIC  S9(4).
00415 C          03  DATAF   PICTURE X.
00416 C          03  DATAI  PIC X(79).
00417 C       02   MSG1L       COMP  PIC  S9(4).
00418 C       02   MSG1F       PICTURE X.
00419 C       02   FILLER REDEFINES MSG1F.
00420 C          03 MSG1A   PICTURE X.
00421 C       02   MSG1I  PIC X(79).
00422 C       02   MSGL COMP  PIC  S9(4).
00423 C       02   MSGF PICTURE X.
00424 C       02   FILLER REDEFINES MSGF.
00425 C          03 MSGA   PICTURE X.
00426 C       02   MSGI  PIC X(79).
00427 C       02   ERRORL      COMP    PIC  S9(4).
00428 C       02   ERRORF      PICTURE X.
00429 C       02   FILLER REDEFINES ERRORF.
00430 C          03 ERRORA    PICTURE X.
00431 C       02   ERRORI   PIC X(77).
00432 C       02   DUMMYL      COMP    PIC  S9(4).
00433 C       02   DUMMYF      PICTURE X.
00434 C       02   FILLER REDEFINES DUMMYF.
00435 C          03 DUMMYA    PICTURE X.
00436 C       02   DUMMYI   PIC X(1).
00437 C   01  TRE6O REDEFINES TRE6I.
00438 C       02   FILLER PIC X(12).
00439 C       02   FILLER PICTURE X(3).
00440 C       02   MONTHO PICTURE 99.
00441 C       02   FILLER PICTURE X(3).
```

```
00442 C      02    DAYO PIC 99.
00443 C      02    FILLER PICTURE X(3).
00444 C      02    YEARO PIC 99.
00445 C      02    FILLER PICTURE X(3).
00446 C      02    TRANIDO  PIC X(4).
00447 C      02    FILLER PICTURE X(3).
00448 C      02    CARRIERO  PIC X(35).
00449 C      02    FILLER PICTURE X(3).
00450 C      02    IMONTHO   PIC X(2).
00451 C      02    FILLER PICTURE X(3).
00452 C      02    IDAYO  PIC X(2).
00453 C      02    FILLER PICTURE X(3).
00454 C      02    IYEARO    PIC X(2).
00455 C      02    DFHMS1 OCCURS 11 TIMES.
00456 C        03  FILLER PICTURE X(2).
00457 C        03  DATAA      PICTURE X.
00458 C        03  DATAO  PIC X(79).
00459 C      02    FILLER PICTURE X(3).
00460 C      02    MSG1O  PIC X(79).
00461 C      02    FILLER PICTURE X(3).
00462 C      02    MSGO   PIC X(79).
00463 C      02    FILLER PICTURE X(3).
00464 C      02    ERRORO    PIC X(77).
00465 C      02    FILLER PICTURE X(3).
00466 C      02    DUMMYO    PIC X(1).
00467        *
00468        01  DFHLDVER PIC X(22) VALUE 'LD TABLE DFHEITAB 170.'.
00469        01  DFHEIDO PICTURE S9(7) COMPUTATIONAL-3 VALUE ZERO.
00470        01  DFHEIBO PICTURE S9(4) COMPUTATIONAL VALUE ZERO.
00471        01  DFHEICB  PICTURE X(8) VALUE IS '        '.
00472
00473        01  DFHEIV16  COMP PIC S9(8).
00474        01  DFHB0041  COMP PIC S9(8).
00475        01  DFHB0042  COMP PIC S9(8).
00476        01  DFHB0043  COMP PIC S9(8).
00477        01  DFHB0044  COMP PIC S9(8).
00478        01  DFHB0045  COMP PIC S9(8).
00479        01  DFHB0046  COMP PIC S9(8).
00480        01  DFHB0047  COMP PIC S9(8).
00481        01  DFHB0048  COMP PIC S9(8).
00482        01  DFHEIV11  COMP PIC S9(4).
00483        01  DFHEIV12  COMP PIC S9(4).
00484        01  DFHEIV13  COMP PIC S9(4).
00485        01  DFHEIV14  COMP PIC S9(4).
00486        01  DFHEIV15  COMP PIC S9(4).
00487        01  DFHB0025  COMP PIC S9(4).
00488        01  DFHEIV5   PIC X(4).
00489        01  DFHEIV6   PIC X(4).
00490        01  DFHEIV17  PIC X(4).
00491        01  DFHEIV18  PIC X(4).
00492        01  DFHEIV19  PIC X(4).
00493        01  DFHEIV1   PIC X(8).
00494        01  DFHEIV2   PIC X(8).
00495        01  DFHEIV3   PIC X(8).
00496        01  DFHEIV20  PIC X(8).
00497        01  DFHC0084  PIC X(8).
00498        01  DFHC0085  PIC X(8).
00499        01  DFHC0320  PIC X(32).
00500        01  DFHEIV7   PIC X(2).
00501        01  DFHEIV8   PIC X(2).
00502        01  DFHC0022  PIC X(2).
00503        01  DFHC0023  PIC X(2).
00504        01  DFHEIV10  PIC S9(7) COMP-3.
00505        01  DFHEIV9   PIC X(1).
00506        01  DFHC0011  PIC X(1).
00507        01  DFHEIV4   PIC X(6).
00508        01  DFHC0070  PIC X(7).
00509        01  DFHC0071  PIC X(7).
00510        01  DFHC0440  PIC X(44).
00511        01  DFHC0441  PIC X(44).
00512        01  DFHDUMMY COMP PIC S9(4).
00513        01  DFHEIV0  PICTURE X(29).
00514        LINKAGE SECTION.
00515        *
00516        01  DFHEIBLK.
00517            02    EIBTIME  PIC S9(7) COMP-3.
00518            02    EIBDATE  PIC S9(7) COMP-3.
00519            02    EIBTRNID PIC X(4).
```

```
00520              02   EIBTASKN PIC S9(7) COMP-3.
00521              02   EIBTRMID PIC X(4).
00522              02   DFHEIGDI COMP PIC S9(4).
00523              02   EIBCPOSN COMP PIC S9(4).
00524              02   EIBCALEN COMP PIC S9(4).
00525              02   EIBAID   PIC X(1).
00526              02   EIBFN    PIC X(2).
00527              02   EIBRCODE PIC X(6).
00528              02   EIBDS    PIC X(8).
00529              02   EIBREQID PIC X(8).
00530              02   EIBRSRCE PIC X(8).
00531              02   EIBSYNC  PIC X(1).
00532              02   EIBFREE  PIC X(1).
00533              02   EIBRECV  PIC X(1).
00534              02   EIBFIL01 PIC X(1).
00535              02   EIBATT   PIC X(1).
00536              02   EIBEOC   PIC X(1).
00537              02   EIBFMH   PIC X(1).
00538              02   EIBCOMPL PIC X(1).
00539              02   EIBSIG   PIC X(1).
00540              02   EIBCONF  PIC X(1).
00541              02   EIBERR   PIC X(1).
00542              02   EIBERRCD PIC X(4).
00543              02   EIBSYNRB PIC X(1).
00544              02   EIBNODAT PIC X(1).
00545              02   EIBRESP  COMP PIC S9(8).
00546              02   EIBRESP2 COMP PIC S9(8).
00547              02   EIBRLDBK PIC X(1).
00548          01  DFHCOMMAREA.
00549              05   PASS-AREA        PIC X(16).
00550          *
00551          01  DFHBLLSLOT1 PICTURE X(1).
00552          01  DFHBLLSLOT2 PICTURE X(1).
00553          PROCEDURE DIVISION USING DFHEIBLK DFHCOMMAREA.
```

8

BROWSE capabilities using extended attribute features

This chapter describes a complex environment in which to BROWSE and DISPLAY a dataset based on a number of mandatory and optional requirements. The sample program used in this chapter, unlike the one presented in Chapter 7, performs a BROWSE operation in a forward or backward fashion, including the ability to locate the first and the last record on file.

Case study

This case study is a logical extension of the techniques used in Chapter 7. In this chapter, however, I introduce a great deal more operational complexities by enhancing the role of several search arguments, and by providing the ability to BROWSE forward or backward. A comprehensive scenario of this particular environment is reflected in FIG. 8-1.

It is the terminal operator who initiates the INQUIRY, based on certain processing requirements. These processing requirements are entered on the menu screen shown in FIG. 8-2, which includes the carrier and the starting date for the INQUIRY, as well as some optional information. This menu then triggers the TLT1BRS BROWSE program shown in step 2 of the system flow presented in FIG. 8-1.

This BROWSE program essentially relies on three files: a TRIP Master file, which drives this inquiry, and two additional VSAM tables, such as a carrier and a delay code table. A programmer-defined layout of each one of the above files is shown in FIG. 8-7.

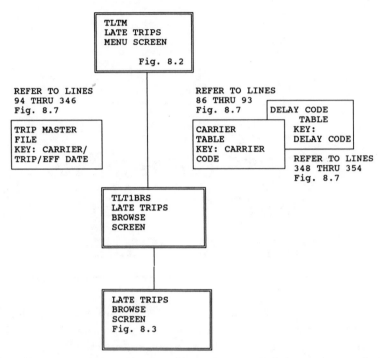

8-1 A logical flow of the TLT1BRS BROWSE program and the menu screen that triggers it

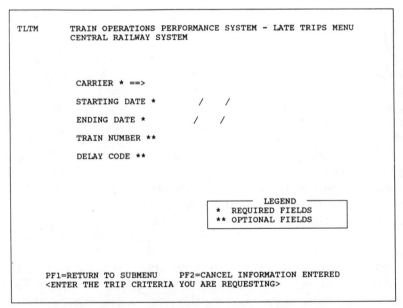

8-2 Menu screen to trigger a multisearch key BROWSE program

With regards to the TRIP Master, note the following characteristics. The TRIP Master represents an historical overview of a database. It contains all the necessary data relating to a TRIP, including approximately 18 months worth of activities. Since it is referenced by at least a dozen or so programmers in the overall system, the TRIP Master has a total record length of some 780 characters, which are accessed and brought in from a standard copy library. Interestingly enough, in this INQUIRY program only a few selected data fields are referenced, which are presented in two separate shaded areas in FIG. 8-7. Thus, the train number and the effective date fields are shown in lines 98 through 107. In addition, a delay code and associated description fields are laid out in lines 145 through 150.

The carrier table is required since the user only needs to enter a 3-position carrier identifier, such as CEN, which is then translated into CENTRAL RAILWAYS by the system. (See Chapter 1 for more detail.) The final product of this inquiry is illustrated in FIG. 8-3.

```
TLT1              TRAIN OPERATIONS PERFORMANCE SYSTEM
                  CENTRAL RAILWAY SYSTEM
                       LATE TRIPS BROWSE


TRAIN#   DATE   MINUTES LATE    DELAY CODE    DESCRIPTION

0600    113090      7              G          SIGNAL MALFUNCTION

0601    112290     13              K          DESTRUCTION ON TRACKS

0609    110190     10              J          REMOVAL OF PASSENGER

0619    110790     17              J          REMOVAL OF PASSENGER

0611    110990     39              E          LOCOMOTIVE MALFUNCTION

0611    111990      6              D          FREIGHT TRAIN INTERFERENCE

0618    113090      7              H          INTERLOCKING MECHANISM MALF

0620    110290     20              K          DESTRUCTION ON TRACKS



PF1=MENU   PF2=CANCEL   PF6=FORWARD   PF7=PREVIOUS   PF8=FIRST   PF9=LAST
<PRESS ENTER OR PF6 TO SE NEXT PAGE>
```

8-3 Display screen generated by a multicriteria search

Chapter 1 explained that, for security reasons, it is necessary to identify yourself as a specific carrier in order to lock into a predefined path, unless you are representing one of the users from the parent company having simultaneous access to the entire system. Note that this is all done through the menu screen shown in FIG. 8-2.

There are five data fields on the Late Trip Menu shown in FIG. 8-2. Three of these are mandatory fields (*) while the latter two (**) are simply optional. These are:

1. A three-position carrier code matched against the key in the carrier code table to verify that such a code exists and was entered correctly. If the code cannot be located or was entered with an incorrect syntax, a corresponding error message will be generated by the system.
2. The security software, which is an independently driven systems software, will check your initial logon I.D. to determine whether to allow or deny you access to the requested database.

Two other dates are also mandatory on the INQUIRY screen shown in FIG. 8-2. These are the starting and the ending dates. Proper format for the data field is MMYYDD where MM denotes the month of the inquiry, DD stands for the day and YY represents the particular year in question. Thus, by entering:

STARTING DATE: 01/01/90
ENDING DATE: 12/31/90

I have instructed the system to search the entire database and extract those records that conform to the STARTING DATE and END-ING DATE requirements, which encompass the entire calendar year of 1990. This can be further qualified by additional requirements. From FIG. 8-2 you can see that both the train number and the delay code are optional fields. This means that in defining your initial search parameters, you can enter the TRAIN DATE and/or the DELAY CODE or you can altogether omit them.

In identifying the different search types available in the sample program, note the following:

1. You can enter any legitimate carrier, including a valid beginning and ending date for the search.
2. You can also request a specific train number. This will cut down on the physical size of the database, since now you are only interested in a particular train that ran within a specific time frame.
3. You can further associate a train with a delay code. There are several delay code types, meaning that the train was late due to the malfunction of one of the signals directing traffic (code G) or due to an obstruction on the tracks, (code K), or due to a failure by the interlocking mechanism, and

so forth. Thus, you might be interested in displaying only a specific train with delay code "G."

4. Finally, you might want to inquire about a specific delay code in conjunction with a carrier and a time frame. For example, you could inquire about delays caused by a failure in the interlocking mechanism of a locomotive.

Once you have defined a set of search parameters for your program and have pressed ENTER, a display screen, such as the one shown in FIG. 8-3 will be triggered. On the bottom of the screen is a message bearing standard information such as PF key assignments and prompts as to the next course of action. Several aspects of this program, TLT1BRS, are different from the one reviewed in Chapter 7. For example, in TLT1BRS, you have the ability to BROWSE backward. You also have access to the first and the last record on file by utilizing PF 8 and PF 9, respectively. These functions are especially helpful when dealing with high-volume datasets.

As you can see in FIG. 8-3, four pieces of information come from the so-called TRIP Master, the term "trip" being synonymous with a particular train. The following information is taken from the TRIP master: a four-position long train number, a date field associated with that train, and minutes of delay computed from the scheduled arrival time. A fourth element, which is the delay code, extracts a description field from a VSAM table. The volume of the material displayed on the screen depends on your search parameters.

Figure 8-1 gives you an overview of how this particular segment of the system is put together and the datasets utilized in the TLT1BRS program. Accordingly, step 1 is the menu program where you need to select a particular set of criteria that will trigger the search. This will invoke the TCL1BRS BROWSE program, as shown in step 2. TLT1BRS essentially relies on three files, two of which are small tables or VSAM datasets, (i.e., a carrier and a delay code table) and a third one, the TRIP file, which is the driver of this inquiry process.

FCT and map considerations

As shown in FIG. 8-4, I used extended attributes mainly for accommodating colors over and above those used in a conventional sense. The File Control Table definition for the TRIP Master is shown in FIG. 8-5. Actually, colors are not the only thing you can utilize in an extended environment. You can also use extended highlighting capabilities in a particular display such as blinking, underlining, or even reverse video.

8-4 BMS map for the BROWSE program

```
      PRINT  NOGEN                                                    TRE10001
*                                                                     TRE10002
TLT1MAP DFHMSD TYPE=&SYSPARM,MODE=INOUT,LANG=COBOL,CTRL=(FREEKB),    CTRE10005
               TIOAPFX=YES,EXTATT=YES                                 TRE10006
*                                                                     TRE10007
TLT1   DFHMDI SIZE=(24,80),COLUMN=1,LINE=1,JUSTIFY=(LEFT,FIRST)       TRE10010
*                                                                     TRE10011
TRANSID DFHMDF POS=(1,1),LENGTH=4,ATTRB=(PROT),COLOR=YELLOW           TRE10014
        DFHMDF POS=(1,6),LENGTH=1,ATTRB=(ASKIP)                       TRE10015
        DFHMDF POS=(1,21),LENGTH=35,INITIAL='TRAIN OPERATIONS PERFORMANCTRE10016
               CE SYSTEM',ATTRB=(ASKIP,BRT),COLOR=BLUE                TRE10017
*                                                                     TRE10020
HDATE   DFHMDF POS=(1,71),LENGTH=8,ATTRB=(PROT),COLOR=YELLOW          TRE1002
        DFHMDF POS=(1,80),LENGTH=1,ATTRB=(ASKIP)                      TRE1002
*                                                                     TRE1002
CARDESC DFHMDF POS=(2,25),LENGTH=35,ATTRB=(PROT),COLOR=PINK           TRE1002
        DFHMDF POS=(2,62),LENGTH=1,ATTRB=(ASKIP)                      TRE1002
*                                                                     TRE1002
        DFHMDF POS=(03,30),LENGTH=18,INITIAL='LATE TRIPS BROWSE',    CTRE1003
               COLOR=BLUE,ATTRB=(PROT,BRT)
        DFHMDF POS=(03,57),LENGTH=1,ATTRB=(ASKIP)                     TRE1002
*                                                                     TRE1003
        DFHMDF POS=(05,01),LENGTH=79,INITIAL='TRAIN#  DATE   MINUTES LACTRE1003
               TE DELAY CODE  DESCRIPTION',ATTRB=(ASKIP),COLOR=BLUE
*                                                                     TRE1003
TRAIN1  DFHMDF POS=(07,02),LENGTH=04,ATTRB=(PROT,BRT),COLOR=YELLOW    TRE1003
DATE1   DFHMDF POS=(07,08),LENGTH=08,ATTRB=PROT,COLOR=YELLOW,        CTRE1003
               PICOUT='ZZ/ZZ/ZZ'
MINLAT1 DFHMDF POS=(07,21),LENGTH=03,ATTRB=(PROT,BRT),COLOR=YELLOW,  CTRE1003
               PICOUT='ZZZ'
LATECD1 DFHMDF POS=(07,34),LENGTH=02,ATTRB=PROT,COLOR=YELLOW          TRE1003
LATDES1 DFHMDF POS=(07,42),LENGTH=30,ATTRB=(PROT,BRT),COLOR=YELLOW    TRE1003
        DFHMDF POS=(07,73),LENGTH=1,ATTRB=(ASKIP)                     TRE1003
*                                                                     TRE1020
TRAIN2  DFHMDF POS=(09,02),LENGTH=04,ATTRB=(PROT,BRT),COLOR=YELLOW    TRE1003
DATE2   DFHMDF POS=(09,08),LENGTH=08,ATTRB=PROT,COLOR=YELLOW,        CTRE1003
               PICOUT='ZZ/ZZ/ZZ'
MINLAT2 DFHMDF POS=(09,21),LENGTH=03,ATTRB=(PROT,BRT),COLOR=YELLOW,  CTRE1003
               PICOUT='ZZZ'
LATECD2 DFHMDF POS=(09,34),LENGTH=02,ATTRB=PROT,COLOR=YELLOW          TRE1003
LATDES2 DFHMDF POS=(09,42),LENGTH=30,ATTRB=(PROT,BRT),COLOR=YELLOW    TRE1003
        DFHMDF POS=(09,73),LENGTH=1,ATTRB=(ASKIP)                     TRE1003
*                                                                     TRE1020
TRAIN3  DFHMDF POS=(11,02),LENGTH=04,ATTRB=(PROT,BRT),COLOR=YELLOW    TRE1003
DATE3   DFHMDF POS=(11,08),LENGTH=08,ATTRB=PROT,COLOR=YELLOW,        CTRE1003
               PICOUT='ZZ/ZZ/ZZ'
MINLAT3 DFHMDF POS=(11,21),LENGTH=03,ATTRB=(PROT,BRT),COLOR=YELLOW,  CTRE1003
               PICOUT='ZZZ'
LATECD3 DFHMDF POS=(11,34),LENGTH=02,ATTRB=PROT,COLOR=YELLOW          TRE1003
LATDES3 DFHMDF POS=(11,42),LENGTH=30,ATTRB=(PROT,BRT),COLOR=YELLOW    TRE1003
        DFHMDF POS=(11,73),LENGTH=1,ATTRB=(ASKIP)                     TRE1003
*                                                                     TRE1020
TRAIN4  DFHMDF POS=(13,02),LENGTH=04,ATTRB=(PROT,BRT),COLOR=YELLOW    TRE1003
DATE4   DFHMDF POS=(13,08),LENGTH=08,ATTRB=PROT,COLOR=YELLOW,        CTRE1003
               PICOUT='ZZ/ZZ/ZZ'
MINLAT4 DFHMDF POS=(13,21),LENGTH=03,ATTRB=(PROT,BRT),COLOR=YELLOW,  CTRE1003
               PICOUT='ZZZ'
LATECD4 DFHMDF POS=(13,34),LENGTH=02,ATTRB=PROT,COLOR=YELLOW          TRE1003
LATDES4 DFHMDF POS=(13,42),LENGTH=30,ATTRB=(PROT,BRT),COLOR=YELLOW    TRE1003
        DFHMDF POS=(13,73),LENGTH=1,ATTRB=(ASKIP)                     TRE1003
*                                                                     TRE1020
TRAIN5  DFHMDF POS=(15,02),LENGTH=04,ATTRB=(PROT,BRT),COLOR=YELLOW    TRE1003
DATE5   DFHMDF POS=(15,08),LENGTH=08,ATTRB=PROT,COLOR=YELLOW,        CTRE1003
               PICOUT='ZZ/ZZ/ZZ'
MINLAT5 DFHMDF POS=(15,21),LENGTH=03,ATTRB=(PROT,BRT),COLOR=YELLOW,  CTRE1003
               PICOUT='ZZZ'
LATECD5 DFHMDF POS=(15,34),LENGTH=02,ATTRB=PROT,COLOR=YELLOW          TRE1003
LATDES5 DFHMDF POS=(15,42),LENGTH=30,ATTRB=(PROT,BRT),COLOR=YELLOW    TRE1003
        DFHMDF POS=(15,73),LENGTH=1,ATTRB=(ASKIP)                     TRE1003
*                                                                     TRE1020
TRAIN6  DFHMDF POS=(17,02),LENGTH=04,ATTRB=(PROT,BRT),COLOR=YELLOW    TRE1003
DATE6   DFHMDF POS=(17,08),LENGTH=08,ATTRB=PROT,COLOR=YELLOW,        CTRE1003
               PICOUT='ZZ/ZZ/ZZ'
```

```
MINLAT6 DFHMDF POS=(17,21),LENGTH=03,ATTRB=(PROT,BRT),COLOR=YELLOW,        CTRE1003
               PICOUT='ZZZ'
LATECD6 DFHMDF POS=(17,34),LENGTH=02,ATTRB=PROT,COLOR=YELLOW                TRE1003
LATDES6 DFHMDF POS=(17,42),LENGTH=30,ATTRB=(PROT,BRT),COLOR=YELLOW          TRE1003
        DFHMDF POS=(17,73),LENGTH=1,ATTRB=(ASKIP)                           TRE1003
*                                                                          TRE1020
TRAIN7  DFHMDF POS=(19,02),LENGTH=04,ATTRB=(PROT,BRT),COLOR=YELLOW          TRE1003
DATE7   DFHMDF POS=(19,08),LENGTH=08,ATTRB=PROT,COLOR=YELLOW,              CTRE1003
               PICOUT='ZZ/ZZ/ZZ'
MINLAT7 DFHMDF POS=(19,21),LENGTH=03,ATTRB=(PROT,BRT),COLOR=YELLOW,        CTRE1003
               PICOUT='ZZZ'
LATECD7 DFHMDF POS=(19,34),LENGTH=02,ATTRB=PROT,COLOR=YELLOW                TRE1003
LATDES7 DFHMDF POS=(19,42),LENGTH=30,ATTRB=(PROT,BRT),COLOR=YELLOW          TRE1003
        DFHMDF POS=(19,73),LENGTH=1,ATTRB=(ASKIP)                           TRE1003
*                                                                          TRE1020
TRAIN8  DFHMDF POS=(21,02),LENGTH=04,ATTRB=(PROT,BRT),COLOR=YELLOW          TRE1003
DATE8   DFHMDF POS=(21,08),LENGTH=08,ATTRB=PROT,COLOR=YELLOW,              CTRE1003
               PICOUT='ZZ/ZZ/ZZ'
MINLAT8 DFHMDF POS=(21,21),LENGTH=03,ATTRB=(PROT,BRT),COLOR=YELLOW,        CTRE1003
               PICOUT='ZZZ'
LATECD8 DFHMDF POS=(21,34),LENGTH=02,ATTRB=PROT,COLOR=YELLOW                TRE1003
LATDES8 DFHMDF POS=(21,42),LENGTH=30,ATTRB=(PROT,BRT),COLOR=YELLOW          TRE1003
        DFHMDF POS=(21,73),LENGTH=1,ATTRB=(ASKIP)                           TRE1003
*                                                                          TRE1020
MSG1    DFHMDF POS=(23,1),LENGTH=75,ATTRB=(PROT),COLOR=YELLOW               TRE1020
        DFHMDF POS=(23,77),LENGTH=1,ATTRB=(ASKIP)                           TRE1020
MSG2    DFHMDF POS=(24,1),LENGTH=75,ATTRB=(PROT,BRT),COLOR=BLUE             TRE1020
        DFHMDF POS=(24,77),LENGTH=1,ATTRB=(ASKIP)                           TRE1020
*                                                                          TRE1020
TLT1MAP DFHMSD TYPE=FINAL                                                   TRE1020
        END                                                                TRE1020
```

```
TRIPI   DFHFCT   TYPE=DATASET,ACCMETH=VSAM,DISP=SHR,              C
                 SERVREQ=(READ,ADD,UPDATE,DELETE,BROWSE),         C
                 DATASET=TRIPI,                                   C
                 DSNAME=NIRVT.TOPS.INC.TRIP.KS,                   C
                 FILSTAT=(ENABLED,CLOSED),                        C
                 RECFORM=(FIXED),RSL=PUBLIC
```

8-5   File Control Table for the trip file, driver of the TLT1BRS BROWSE

As soon as an extended color attribute is received in your transaction, the display treats the whole image as an extended color image. Fields that have no color attribute adopt the default colors (i.e., green for normal intensity and white for bright). If the color control switch is set to base color, the part of the image that has already been displayed will change from base color to default color.

Source program listing and narrative

The switches shown in FIG. 8-6, lines 21 through 25, are primarily set up, as you will see throughout this program, to monitor the flow and the display of each TRIP record on the screen. The COMMUNICA-TIONS AREA, which is defined in the LINKAGE SECTION in line 100, contains a 44-character data string, part of which is laid out in a

```
1              IDENTIFICATION DIVISION.
2              PROGRAM-ID.        LATETRIP.
3
4              REMARKS.  THIS PROGRAM WILL BROWSE THE COMPLETE TRIPS FILE
5                        & DISPLAY THE LATE TRIPS.
6
7
8              DATE-WRITTEN.    JAN 16, 1990.
9              DATE-REVISED.
10             DATE-COMPILED.
11
12             ENVIRONMENT DIVISION.
13             CONFIGURATION SECTION.
14             SOURCE-COMPUTER.    IBM-370.
15             OBJECT-COMPUTER.    IBM-370.
16
17             DATA DIVISION.
18
19             WORKING-STORAGE SECTION.
20
21             01  SWITCHES.
22                 05  MORE-RECS-SW        PIC X  VALUE 'Y'.
23                 88  MORE-RECS              VALUE 'Y'.
24                 05  MORE-PREV-RECS-SW  PIC X  VALUE 'Y'.
25                 88  MORE-PREV-RECS         VALUE 'Y'.
26
27             01  LINE-SUB          PIC 9(4) COMP.
28
29             ****    COMM AREA      ****
30             01  WS-COMMAREA.
31                 05  COMM-FLAG      PIC X     VALUE 'I'.
32                 88  INIT-MAP          VALUE 'I'.
33                 88  SEND-MAP          VALUE 'S'.
34                 88  RECV-MAP          VALUE 'R'.
35                 05  WS-COMMAREA-OUT.
36                 10  COMM-CARRIER   PIC XXX.
37                 10  COMM-LINE      PIC XX.
38                 05  WS-COMMAREA-TRIP.
39                 10  CARRIER-ENTERED PIC XXX.
40                 10  COMM-BEG-DATE.
41                     15  COMM-BEG-YR    PIC XX.
42                     15  COMM-BEG-MO    PIC XX.
43                     15  COMM-BEG-DA    PIC XX.
44                 10  COMM-END-DATE.
45                     15  COMM-END-YR    PIC XX.
46                     15  COMM-END-MO    PIC XX.
47                     15  COMM-END-DA    PIC XX.
48                 10  COMM-TRAIN-NO    PIC XXXX.
49                 10  COMM-DELAY-CODE  PIC XX.
50                 05  WORK-TR-KEY.
51                 10  WK-CARRIER-CODE PIC X(3).
52                 10  WK-LINE         PIC XX.
53                 10  WK-TRAIN-NO    PIC X(4).
54                 10  WK-TR-DATE.
55                     15  WK-TR-DATEY    PIC XX.
56                     15  WK-TR-DATEM    PIC XX.
57                     15  WK-TR-DATED    PIC XX.
58                 05  DIRECTION-FLAG     PIC X.
59                 88  FORW-DIR          VALUE 'F'.
60                 88  PREV-DIR          VALUE 'P'.
61                 05  END-SEARCH-SW       PIC X  VALUE 'N'.
62                 88  SEARCH-ENDED        VALUE 'Y'.
63             *******************************************
64             ****    DATA-AREA FOR TRIP-KEY     ****
65             *******************************************
66             01  TRIP-KEY       PIC X(15) VALUE IS SPACES.
67
68             01  DATE-DISPLAY.
69                 05  DATE-MO      PIC XX.
70                 05  FILLER       PIC X VALUE '/'.
71                 05  DATE-DA      PIC XX.
72                 05  FILLER       PIC X VALUE '/'.
73                 05  DATE-YR      PIC XX.
```

```
74
75         01  WS-ERROR-MESSAGES.
76             05  MAPFAIL-MSG          PIC X(36) VALUE
77             '*** MAPFAIL FOR TRANSACTION TLT1 ***'.
78             05  FILE-NOTOPEN-MSG     PIC X(42) VALUE
79             '*** FILE NOT OPEN FOR TRANSACTION TLT1 ***'.
80             05  PGM-NOTFND-MSG       PIC X(46) VALUE
81             '*** PROGRAM NOT FOUND FOR TRANSACTION TLT1 ***'.
82             05  ERROR-MSG       PIC X(42) VALUE
83             '*** UNKNOWN ERROR FOR TRANSACTION TLT1 ***'.
84             EJECT
85
86         ******************************************
87         *******   FILE RECORDS DESCRIPTION   ******
88         ******************************************
89
90         01  CARRIER-TABLE.      COPY CCARRIER.
91         01  TRIP-REC.           COPY CTRIP.
92         01  DELAY-TABLE.        COPY CDELAY.
93         01  STATION-TABLE.      COPY CSTATION.
94             COPY TLT1MAP.
95             COPY DFHAID.
96             COPY DFHBMSCA.
97             COPY CHARATR.
98
99         LINKAGE SECTION.
100        01  DFHCOMMAREA        PIC X(44).
101
102        PROCEDURE DIVISION.
103        0000-MAIN.
104            EXEC CICS HANDLE AID
105            PF1   (9500-RETURN-TO-MENU-RTN)
106            PF2   (9500-RETURN-TO-MENU-RTN)
107            PF6   (0145-NEXT-PAGE)
108            PF7   (0140-PREVIOUS-PAGE)
109            PF8   (0150-FIRST-PAGE)
110            PF9   (0155-LAST-PAGE)
111            CLEAR (9500-RETURN-TO-MENU-RTN)
112            ANYKEY(9000-ANYKEY-ROUTINE)
113            END-EXEC.
114        ***********************************************
115        *    TEST FOR RECEIVED TRANSACTION            *
116        *    CHECK INPUT DATA AND MOVE KEY TO START   *
117        ***********************************************
118            IF EIBCALEN > ZEROS
119            MOVE DFHCOMMAREA TO WS-COMMAREA.
120            IF INIT-MAP
121            MOVE CSR-REPO  TO  LT-L-TRAIN(1)
122            PERFORM 0115-INIT-SETUP THRU 0115-END
123            MOVE LOW-VALUES TO TRIP-KEY
124            PERFORM 0200-FIND-RECORD
125            PERFORM 0110-INIT-MAP
126            ELSE
127            IF SEND-MAP
128               PERFORM 0120-SEND-MAP
129            ELSE
130               PERFORM 0130-RECEIVE-MAP THRU 0130-END.
131
132        0000-END.
133            EXIT.
134
135        0110-INIT-MAP.
136            EXEC CICS HANDLE CONDITION
137            ERROR     (9999-ERROR-RTN)
138            END-EXEC.
139            EXEC CICS SEND
140            MAP ('TLT1')
141            MAPSET ('TLT1MAP')
142            FROM (LATEMAP)
143            ERASE
144            CURSOR
145            END-EXEC.
146            MOVE 'R'  TO  COMM-FLAG.
147            EXEC CICS RETURN
148            TRANSID ('TLT1')
149            COMMAREA (WS-COMMAREA)
150            LENGTH (44)
151            END-EXEC.
```

```
152
153          0115-INIT-SETUP.
154              MOVE CARRIER-ENTERED TO WK-CARRIER-CODE.
155              MOVE 'TLT1' TO LT-D-TRANS.
156              MOVE CURRENT-DATE TO LT-D-HDATE.
157              MOVE 'PF1=MENU  PF2=CANCEL  PF6=FORWARD  PF7=PREVIOUS
158     PF8=
159        -RST PF9=LAST'      TO LT-D-PFMSG.
160              MOVE PROT-MDT TO LT-A-PFMSG.
161              MOVE PROT-BRT TO LT-A-ERMSG.
162              PERFORM 0310-FIND-CARRIER THRU 0310-END.
163
164          0115-END.
165              EXIT.
166
167          0120-SEND-MAP.
168              EXEC CICS HANDLE CONDITION
169                ERROR      (9999-ERROR-RTN)
170              END-EXEC.
171              EXEC CICS SEND
172                MAP ('TLT1')
173                MAPSET ('TLT1MAP')
174                FROM (LATEMAP)
175                DATAONLY
176                CURSOR
177              END-EXEC.
178              MOVE 'R'  TO  COMM-FLAG.
179              EXEC CICS RETURN
180                TRANSID ('TLT1')
181                COMMAREA (WS-COMMAREA)
182                LENGTH (44)
183              END-EXEC.
184
185          0120-END.
186              EXIT.
187
188          0130-RECEIVE-MAP.
189              EXEC CICS HANDLE CONDITION
190                MAPFAIL (9999-MAPFAIL-RTN)
191                ERROR      (9999-ERROR-RTN)
192              END-EXEC.
193              EXEC CICS RECEIVE
194                MAP ('TLT1')
195                MAPSET ('TLT1MAP')
196                INTO(LATEMAP)
197              END-EXEC.
198              MOVE WORK-TR-KEY TO TRIP-KEY.
199              IF DIRECTION-FLAG = 'P'
200              PERFORM 0240-PAGE-BACKWARD
201              ELSE
202              PERFORM 0200-FIND-RECORD.
203
204          0130-END.
205              EXIT.
206
207          0140-PREVIOUS-PAGE.
208              MOVE 'P' TO DIRECTION-FLAG.
209              MOVE SPACES TO LT-D-ERMSG.
210              MOVE WORK-TR-KEY TO TRIP-KEY.
211              PERFORM 0240-PAGE-BACKWARD.
212
213          0145-NEXT-PAGE.
214              MOVE 'F' TO DIRECTION-FLAG.
215              MOVE SPACES TO LT-D-ERMSG.
216              MOVE WORK-TR-KEY TO TRIP-KEY.
217              PERFORM 0200-FIND-RECORD.
218
219          0150-FIRST-PAGE.
220              MOVE LOW-VALUES TO TRIP-KEY.
221              PERFORM 0200-FIND-RECORD.
222
223          0155-LAST-PAGE.
224              MOVE HIGH-VALUES TO WORK-TR-KEY.
225              PERFORM 0240-PAGE-BACKWARD.
226
```

```
227              0200-FIND-RECORD.
228                  EXEC CICS HANDLE CONDITION
229                          NOTOPEN(9999-FILE-NOTOPEN)
230                          ENDFILE(0280-TOOHIGH)
231                          NOTFND(0205-RESET-BROWSE)
232                  END-EXEC.
233              ***********************************************
234              *     SET/ESTABLISH STARTING POINT           *
235              ***********************************************
236                  EXEC CICS STARTBR DATASET('TTRIP')
237                          RIDFLD(TRIP-KEY)
238                  END-EXEC.
239                  IF TRIP-KEY NOT EQUAL HIGH-VALUES
240                  PERFORM 0210-PAGE-FORWARD
241                  ELSE
242                  PERFORM 0240-PAGE-BACKWARD.
243
244              0205-RESET-BROWSE.
245                  MOVE LOW-VALUES TO TRIP-KEY.
246                  GO TO 0200-FIND-RECORD.
247
248              0210-PAGE-FORWARD.
249                  PERFORM 0300-CLEAR-MAPAREA VARYING LINE-SUB
250                    FROM 1 BY 1 UNTIL LINE-SUB > 8.
251                  MOVE CSR-REPO TO LT-L-TRAIN(1).
252                  MOVE 'N' TO END-SEARCH-SW.
253                  MOVE 1 TO LINE-SUB.
254                  PERFORM 0220-READ-NEXT-TRIP THRU 0225-CHECK-CRITERIA.
255              *
256              0220-READ-NEXT-TRIP.
257                  EXEC CICS READNEXT INTO(TRIP-REC)
258                          DATASET('TTRIP')
259                          RIDFLD(TRIP-KEY)
260                  END-EXEC.
261              *
262              0225-CHECK-CRITERIA.
263                  IF CARRIER-ENTERED NOT = TR-CARRIER-CODE
264                  PERFORM 0220-READ-NEXT-TRIP THRU 0225-CHECK-CRITERIA.
265
266                  IF TR-DATE-EFFECT < COMM-BEG-DATE OR
267                  TR-DATE-EFFECT > COMM-END-DATE
268                  PERFORM 0220-READ-NEXT-TRIP THRU 0225-CHECK-CRITERIA.
269
270                  IF COMM-TRAIN-NO NOT = LOW-VALUES AND SPACES
271                  IF COMM-TRAIN-NO = TR-TRAIN-NO
272                    NEXT SENTENCE
273                  ELSE
274                       PERFORM    0220-READ-NEXT-TRIP    THRU
275          0225-CHECK-CRITERIA.
276
277                  IF COMM-DELAY-CODE NOT = LOW-VALUES AND SPACES
278                  IF COMM-DELAY-CODE = TR-DELAY-CODE
279                    NEXT SENTENCE
280                  ELSE
281                       PERFORM    0220-READ-NEXT-TRIP    THRU
282          0225-CHECK-CRITERIA.              IF TR-DELAY-MIN < 6
283                  PERFORM 0220-READ-NEXT-TRIP THRU 0225-CHECK-CRITERIA
284                  ELSE
285                  MOVE TRIP-KEY TO WORK-TR-KEY
286                  PERFORM 0230-MOVE-TO-MAP.
287              0230-MOVE-TO-MAP.
288                  MOVE TR-TRAIN-NO TO LT-D-TRAIN(LINE-SUB).
289                  MOVE TR-DATE-EFFECT-M TO DATE-MO.
290                  MOVE TR-DATE-EFFECT-D TO DATE-DA.
291                  MOVE TR-DATE-EFFECT-Y TO DATE-YR.
292                  MOVE DATE-DISPLAY TO LT-D-DATE(LINE-SUB).
293                  MOVE TR-DELAY-MIN-X TO LT-D-MINUTES(LINE-SUB).
294                  IF TR-DELAY-CODE NOT = LOW-VALUES AND SPACES
295                  MOVE TR-DELAY-CODE TO LT-D-LATECODE(LINE-SUB)
296                                  T-DELAY-CODE
297                  PERFORM 0320-FIND-DELAY-DESC THRU 0320-END
298                  MOVE T-DELAY-DESC TO LT-D-LATEDESC(LINE-SUB).
299                  ADD 1 TO LINE-SUB.
300                  IF LINE-SUB  < 9
301                  PERFORM 0220-READ-NEXT-TRIP THRU 0225-CHECK-CRITERIA.
302                  MOVE TRIP-KEY TO WORK-TR-KEY.
303                  MOVE '< PRESS ENTER OR PF6 TO SEE NEXT PAGE >'
304                    TO LT-D-ERMSG.
```

```
305                     MOVE 'F' TO DIRECTION-FLAG.
306                     IF INIT-MAP
307                     PERFORM 0110-INIT-MAP
308                     ELSE
309                     PERFORM 0120-SEND-MAP.
310
311             ****************************************************
312             *           BUILD PREVIOUS BACK PAGE              *
313             ****************************************************
314             0240-PAGE-BACKWARD.
315                     EXEC CICS HANDLE CONDITION
316                               ENDFILE(0290-TOOLOW)
317                               NOTFND (0250-RESET-BROWSE)
318                     END-EXEC.
319                     PERFORM 0300-CLEAR-MAPAREA VARYING LINE-SUB
320                     FROM 1 BY 1 UNTIL LINE-SUB > 8.
321                     MOVE 1 TO LINE-SUB.
322                     MOVE WORK-TR-KEY TO TRIP-KEY.
323                     EXEC CICS STARTBR DATASET('TTRIP')
324                               RIDFLD(TRIP-KEY)
325                     END-EXEC.
326                     IF TRIP-KEY NOT = HIGH-VALUES
327                     IF END-SEARCH-SW = 'N'
328                         PERFORM 0220-READ-NEXT-TRIP
329                         PERFORM 0260-READ-PREV-TRIP.
330                     PERFORM 0260-READ-PREV-TRIP THRU 0260-CHECK-CRITERIA.
331
332             0250-RESET-BROWSE.
333                     MOVE HIGH-VALUES TO TRIP-KEY.
334                     GO TO 0240-PAGE-BACKWARD.
335
336             0260-READ-PREV-TRIP.
337                     EXEC CICS READPREV INTO(TRIP-REC)
338                             DATASET('TTRIP')
339                             RIDFLD(TRIP-KEY)
340                     END-EXEC.
341
342             0260-CHECK-CRITERIA.
343                     MOVE CSR-REPO TO LT-L-TRAIN(1).
344                     MOVE 'N' TO END-SEARCH-SW.
345
346                     IF CARRIER-ENTERED NOT = TR-CARRIER-CODE
347                     PERFORM 0260-READ-PREV-TRIP THRU 0260-CHECK-CRITERIA.
348
349                     IF TR-DATE-EFFECT < COMM-BEG-DATE OR
350                     TR-DATE-EFFECT > COMM-END-DATE
351                     PERFORM 0260-READ-PREV-TRIP THRU 0260-CHECK-CRITERIA.
352
353                     IF COMM-TRAIN-NO NOT = LOW-VALUES AND SPACES
354                     IF COMM-TRAIN-NO = TR-TRAIN-NO
355                         NEXT SENTENCE
356                     ELSE
357                         PERFORM    0260-READ-PREV-TRIP    THRU
358             0260-CHECK-CRITERIA.
359
360                     IF COMM-DELAY-CODE NOT = LOW-VALUES AND SPACES
361                     IF COMM-DELAY-CODE = TR-DELAY-CODE
362                         NEXT SENTENCE
363                     ELSE
364                         PERFORM    0260-READ-PREV-TRIP    THRU
365             0260-CHECK-CRITERIA.
366
367                     IF TR-DELAY-MIN < 6
368                     PERFORM 0260-READ-PREV-TRIP THRU 0260-CHECK-CRITERIA
369                     ELSE
370                     MOVE TRIP-KEY TO WORK-TR-KEY
371                     PERFORM 0270-MOVE-TO-MAP.
372
373             0270-MOVE-TO-MAP.
374                     MOVE TR-TRAIN-NO TO LT-D-TRAIN(LINE-SUB).
375                     MOVE TR-DATE-EFFECT-M TO DATE-MO.
376                     MOVE TR-DATE-EFFECT-D TO DATE-DA.
377                     MOVE TR-DATE-EFFECT-Y TO DATE-YR.
378                     MOVE DATE-DISPLAY TO LT-D-DATE(LINE-SUB).
379                     MOVE TR-DELAY-MIN-X TO LT-D-MINUTES(LINE-SUB).
```

```
380                     IF TR-DELAY-CODE NOT = LOW-VALUES AND SPACES
381                        MOVE TR-DELAY-CODE TO LT-D-LATECODE(LINE-SUB)
382                                   T-DELAY-CODE
383                        PERFORM 0320-FIND-DELAY-DESC THRU 0320-END
384                        MOVE T-DELAY-DESC TO LT-D-LATEDESC(LINE-SUB).
385                     ADD 1 TO LINE-SUB.
386                 IF LINE-SUB < 9
387                     PERFORM 0260-READ-PREV-TRIP THRU 0260-CHECK-CRITERIA.
388                 MOVE TRIP-KEY TO WORK-TR-KEY.
389                 MOVE '< PRESS PF7 OR ENTER TO SEE NEXT PAGE >'
390                     TO LT-D-ERMSG.
391                 MOVE 'P' TO DIRECTION-FLAG.
392                 IF INIT-MAP
393                     PERFORM 0110-INIT-MAP
394                 ELSE
395                     PERFORM 0120-SEND-MAP.
396
397          0280-TOOHIGH.
398                 MOVE TRIP-KEY TO WORK-TR-KEY.
399                 MOVE 'Y' TO END-SEARCH-SW.
400                 MOVE 'P' TO DIRECTION-FLAG.
401                 MOVE '< HIGH-END OF THE FILE HAS BEEN REACHED >'
402                     TO LT-D-ERMSG.
403                 MOVE PROT-BRT TO LT-A-ERMSG.
404                 IF INIT-MAP
405                     PERFORM 0110-INIT-MAP
406                 ELSE
407                     PERFORM 0120-SEND-MAP.
408
409          0290-TOOLOW.
410                 MOVE TRIP-KEY TO WORK-TR-KEY.
411                 MOVE 'F' TO DIRECTION-FLAG.
412                 MOVE 'Y' TO END-SEARCH-SW.
413                 MOVE '< BEGINNING OF THE FILE HAS BEEN REACHED >'
414                     TO LT-D-ERMSG.
415                 MOVE PROT-BRT TO LT-A-ERMSG.
416                 IF INIT-MAP
417                     PERFORM 0110-INIT-MAP
418                 ELSE
419                     PERFORM 0120-SEND-MAP.
420
421          0300-CLEAR-MAPAREA.
422                 MOVE SPACES TO LT-D-TRAIN(LINE-SUB)
423                               LT-D-LATECODE(LINE-SUB)
424                               LT-D-LATEDESC(LINE-SUB)
425                               LT-D-MINUTES(LINE-SUB)
426                               LT-D-DATE(LINE-SUB).
427
428          0310-FIND-CARRIER.
429                 EXEC CICS HANDLE CONDITION
430                   NOTOPEN (9999-FILE-NOTOPEN)
431                   NOTFND  (0310-CARRIER-NOTFND)
432                   ERROR   (9999-ERROR-RTN)
433                 END-EXEC.
434                 EXEC CICS READ DATASET('TCARRIER')
435                   INTO(CARRIER-TABLE)
436                   RIDFLD(WK-CARRIER-CODE)
437                 END-EXEC.
438                 MOVE T-CARRIER-DESC TO LT-D-CAR-DESC.
439
440          0310-END.
441                 EXIT.
442
443          0310-CARRIER-NOTFND.
444                 MOVE UNPROT-ALPHA-BRT TO LT-A-ERMSG.
445                 MOVE 'CARRIER DESC NOT FOUND' TO LT-D-ERMSG.
446                 PERFORM 0120-SEND-MAP.
447
448          0320-FIND-DELAY-DESC.
449                 EXEC CICS HANDLE CONDITION
450                   NOTOPEN (9999-FILE-NOTOPEN)
451                   NOTFND  (0320-DELAY-DESC-NOTFND)
452                   ERROR   (9999-ERROR-RTN)
453                 END-EXEC.
454                 EXEC CICS READ DATASET('TDELAY')
455                   INTO(DELAY-TABLE)
456                   RIDFLD(T-DELAY-CODE)
457                 END-EXEC.
```

```
458
459              0320-END.
460                  EXIT.
461
462              0320-DELAY-DESC-NOTFND.
463                  MOVE UNPROT-ALPHA-BRT TO LT-A-ERMSG.
464                  MOVE UNPROT-ALPHA-BRT TO LT-A-LATECODE(LINE-SUB).
465                  MOVE 'AN INVALID DELAY CODE WAS ENTERED INTO THE TRIP
466      FILE'
467                      TO LT-D-ERMSG.
468                  PERFORM 0120-SEND-MAP.
469
470              9000-ANYKEY-ROUTINE.
471                  MOVE PROT-BRT TO LT-A-ERMSG.
472                  MOVE 'WRONG KEY PRESSED'  TO LT-D-ERMSG.
473                  PERFORM 0120-SEND-MAP.
474
475              9200-WRONG-KEY.
476                  MOVE CSR-REPO TO  LT-L-TRAIN(1).
477                  MOVE 'PRESS PF KEYS AS STATED ABOVE ' TO LT-D-PFMSG.
478                  MOVE UNPROT-ALPHA-BRT TO LT-A-ERMSG.
479                  PERFORM 0120-SEND-MAP.
480
481              9500-RETURN-TO-MENU-RTN.
482                  MOVE SPACES TO WS-COMMAREA-TRIP
483                              WORK-TR-KEY
484                              DIRECTION-FLAG.
485                  MOVE  'I' TO  COMM-FLAG.
486                  EXEC CICS HANDLE CONDITION
487                  PGMIDERR(9999-PGM-NOTFND)
488                  ERROR      (9999-ERROR-RTN)
489                  END-EXEC.
490                  EXEC CICS XCTL
491                  PROGRAM ('TLT1MENU')
492                  COMMAREA (WS-COMMAREA)
493                  LENGTH (44)
494                  END-EXEC.
495
496              9999-MAPFAIL-RTN.
497                  EXEC CICS SEND TEXT
498                  FROM(MAPFAIL-MSG)
499                  LENGTH(36)
500                  ERASE
501                  FREEKB
502                  END-EXEC.
503                  EXEC CICS RETURN
504                  END-EXEC.
505
506              9999-FILE-NOTOPEN.
507                  EXEC CICS SEND TEXT
508                  FROM(FILE-NOTOPEN-MSG)
509                  LENGTH(42)
510                  ERASE
511                  FREEKB
512                  END-EXEC.
513                  EXEC CICS RETURN
514                  END-EXEC.
515
516              9999-PGM-NOTFND.
517                  EXEC CICS SEND TEXT
518                  FROM(PGM-NOTFND-MSG)
519                  LENGTH(46)
520                  ERASE
521                  FREEKB
522                  END-EXEC.
523                  EXEC CICS RETURN
524                  END-EXEC.
525
526              9999-ERROR-RTN.
527                  EXEC CICS SEND TEXT
528                  FROM(ERROR-MSG)
529                  LENGTH(42)
530                  ERASE
531                  FREEKB
532                  END-EXEC.
533                  EXEC CICS RETURN
```

```
534          END-EXEC.
535          STOP RUN.
536          GOBACK.
537          ************************************************************
538
539
```

standardized format. Actually, the layout of the COMMAREA is shown in detail in the WORKING-STORAGE-SECTION under WS-COMMAREA, incorporating lines 30 through 62. The first three fields (6 positions) in the COMMAREA area are standard occurrences.

The PROCEDURE DIVISION starts out showing standard function key assignments through a standard HANDLE CONDITION statement, which closely resembles the instruction on the bottom of the LATE TRIPS BROWSE panel shown in FIG. 8-3. Accordingly, by pressing PF 1 or PF 2, lines 105 through 106, TLT1BRS branches to the subroutine 9500-RETURN-TO-MENU-RTN. Note that the same procedure is triggered when pressing the CLEAR key (line 111). The reason these keys are dedicated to an identical routine, which is the invocation of the previous submenu screen shown in FIG. 8-2, is the way initial standards are observed in this system. (For more on this, refer to Chapter 1.) For example, by pressing CLEAR once, a previous submenu panel is displayed. By pressing the CLEAR key for a second time, and this procedure is not an integral part of the TLT1BRS process, you will have invoked a previous screen, which happens to be the "parent" or the predecessor of that panel. So, if you are four levels deep into the hierarchical path of the system, by pressing the CLEAR key a total of four times, you will have invoked the main system directory screen. PF 2, on the other hand, is a standard "cancel" function, part of the set up, but not necessarily a useful procedure in this particular application.

PF 6 and PF 7, lines 107 through 108, are designed to provide BROWSE forward and backward mobility, while PF 8 and PF 9 enable you to fetch the first and the last record on the TRIP Master. In addition to these initial PF key definitions, an ANYKEY routine has been coded to notify the terminal operator that pressing any other key in the program is not a legitimate procedure.

Let me elaborate on each paragraph or procedure associated with a particular function key. The first procedure takes place when you press PF 1, PF 2, or the CLEAR key. The response is described in paragraph 9500-RETURN-TO-MENU-RTN, which is merely an exit control statement to the previous selection menu, shown in lines 428 through 438. The second procedure is initiated once you have pressed PF 6. This procedure will take you to the 0145-NEXT-PAGE paragraph, line 213, a routine subdivided into two major components. The first component requires some additional branching or the invocation of other subroutines, such as those presented in paragraph 0200-FIND-RECORD. These subroutines can be summarized as follows:

1. Redefine or simply requalify your earlier HANDLE CONDITION, this time to provide for additional ERROR CONDITIONS, such as when files are not open (lines 506 through 514), in case of an end-of-file routine (lines 397 through 407), or when a specific record on file cannot be located (lines 244 through 246). Incidentally, this last condition will reset the inquiry key to low values and retrigger the BROWSE apparatus.

2. Once the HANDLE CONDITION is redefined, a BROWSE of the TRIP Master will be initiated. This part of the program is actually set up as a standard or generic set of procedures allowing you to branch to a page forward or to a page backward routine, depending on your place (and timing) in a given transaction. For the time being, though, we only need to concern ourselves with forward paging procedures, for which logic was developed in lines 248 through 254 under the 0210-PAGE-FORWARD paragraph.

As you can see in FIG. 8-6, I set up a line counter known as a "subscript" to produce eight lines of TRIP data on the screen just after executing a procedure referred to as 0300-CLEAR-MAPAREA. This is shown in lines 421 through 426. 0300-CLEAR-MAPAREA is designed to clear the entire screen in front of you, line by line, using subscripts. In this paragraph, you need to invoke a series of consecutive read operations (READNEXT), starting in line 256. Note that although this logic was set up as part of the main logic in your program to trigger certain additional subroutines, there is a visible fragmentation in TLT1BRS that enables the programmer to perform a subroutine from other hierarchically higher level subroutines. A typical example of this philosophy is reflected in paragraph 0225-CHECK-CRITERIA (line 262), where during all the initial edit requirements some half a dozen or so subroutines are invoked and executed.

During this edit processing, you need to check whether or not the proper train number was accessed (or possibly left blank), check the proper ranges in regards to the inquiry date carried in the communications area, and check whether the inquiry date matches a specific record on file, as in lines 271 through 274. If your response to these criteria is positive, TLT1BRS will continue to perform some additional editing. The validation of < 6 minutes for a train delay is also performed, since only those trains that exceed the six minute mark are considered late (for reporting and display efficiency).

Note that the execution of two sets of paragraphs hinge upon the success or failure of meeting the < 6 criterion. Greater than six minutes of delay is designed to generate a line by performing the 0230-MOVE-TO-MAP paragraph, lines 287 through 310, where you have provided logic for the transfer of your data from storage to a terminal display through subscripts. In this process, an entire map is developed up to eight lines of display, including some of the necessary constant information, i.e., <PRESS ENTER OR PF 6 TO SEE THE NEXT PAGE>, etc.

When sending the map, the programmer needs to determine through the current value of an 88 level data field, such as the INIT-MAP (line 32), whether the map should be sent for the first time or for subsequent activities. When it is sent for the first time, the programmer references the 0110-INIT-MAP paragraph, a set of procedures highlighted in lines 135 through 151. There are a couple of things that are different about a map that is being sent for the first time.

When sending a map for the first time, you need to send an entire map "unabridged," that is both the constant and the variable portions of it. In subsequent sends, however, lines 167 through 183, only the data portion of the map is relayed to the terminal, which is to improve on the overall transmission speed of the data. Also, in the initial send map you want to erase the screen prior to any data transmission, whereas under dissimilar circumstances an erase would actually delete the constant portion of the map already on display at your terminal.

If you were to press PF 7 any time during this transaction, you would invoke a "PREVIOUS PAGE" routine, initially defined in line 108 as part of a HANDLE CONDITION. This is the place where paragraph 0140-PREVIOUS-PAGE routine kicks in. First of all, you need to set a field I refer to as a "direction flag" simply to indicate the flow of the BROWSE, "P" meaning previous or backward, and "F" meaning forward browsing. Having set up the key for the BROWSE operation you are now ready to perform it starting in 0240-PAGE-BACKWARD paragraph, highlighted in detail in lines 314 through 374.

First of all, you need to redefine your HANDLE CONDITION to provide for an end of file, as well as for a file not found routine. Let me explain the end of file routine first. When you display data on the screen and thereafter continue browsing forward (or backward) on that screen, your program calculates the number of lines that need to appear simultaneously. For example, if you were to display ten lines of data on the screen, then every time you were to send a map, you would, in fact, be repositioning yourself on the corresponding file by the above number of records. So if you were on record number 79 and pressed PF 7 (BROWSE BACKWARD), the program would fetch the next 10 records, bring them into buffer, and stop on record number 69. If you were to press the above function key repeatedly, it would loop around to stop on record 59, followed by record number 49 and by record number 39, then 29, 19, and 09. If you were to press PF 7 one more time, and since there are now less than ten records remaining on file when in a previous BROWSE mode, you need to have in place a routine in your program to handle that eventuality, which is exactly what I did in paragraph 0290-TOOLOW, lines 409 through 419.

A second element in the above HANDLE CONDITION has to do with a situation when the requested record cannot be located. A reference to this is made in paragraph 0250-RESET-BROWSE, which resets the key with high values while reinvoking the "build previous back page" routine starting in line 314. The map is then cleared, as before, through subscripting, until all 8 detail lines are readied for the next display. Accordingly, a STARTBR operation is set up in line 323. Depending now on the status of the END-SEARCH-SW data field, a read forward or a read previous operation is triggered. Along with the 0260-READ-PREVIOUS routine, the TRIP Master is read while performing a number of edit criteria starting in line 336 through 371. Again, the 6 minute delay indicator comes into play. If there has been less than a 6 minute delay, overall, you are simply to issue another previous, or "backward" read relative to the TRIP Master. If the duration of delay exceeds 6 minutes, you need to display a corresponding detail line on the CRT, such as the one under 0270-MOVE-TO-MAP paragraph.

Note that you need to build every detail line to be displayed on the screen using subscripts until all 8 lines are satisfied. The perform statement in lines 393 through 396 is merely for the purpose of differentiating between initial and subsequent map operations.

Every BROWSE operation in this program is triggered through the 0130-RECEIVE-MAP paragraph, lines 188 through 206, just as soon as the map becomes available to the terminal operator, telling him or her whether to BROWSE forward or backward, whether to invoke the first or the last record on file, etc. Forward or backward BROWSE is essentially dependent on the value of an indicator. Starting in line 428 and virtually until the end of the PROCEDURE DIVISION, I have laid out for you a number of subroutines that are also integral parts of TLT1BRS. To mention them one by one, the first one of these procedures is the 0310-FIND-CARRIER paragraph, lines 428 through 438, which consists of two components. These are a

HANDLE CONDITION routine, and a CARRIER TABLE routine. The HANDLE CONDITION routine is set up to provide you with procedures when the record on the carrier code table cannot be located or when the above file is physically closed. In addition there is a generalized ERROR ROUTINE (9999-ERROR-RTN), which is a catch-all procedure for all other ERROR CONDITIONS. Note that the "NOT FOUND" routine is laid out in lines 516 through 524 and similarly, a generalized ERROR ROUTINE is shown in lines 526 through 536.

The READ CARRIER TABLE routine, which I have referenced as a second component, builds the VSAM key and reads the carrier code table. If the record is found, a carrier description (i.e., CEN-CENTRAL RAILWAYS) is extracted. A similar routine is laid out in 0320-FIND-DELAY-DESC, in an effort to attain a delay code description.

An invalid delay code will set off a "CARRIER NOT FOUND" condition, and the operator, as a result, is informed of that through program logic. There are three additional conditions requiring some clarification in this program. The first one is an ANYKEY CONDITION, which is merely a response to a HANDLE AID. This procedure is highlighted in lines 470 through 473.

A second condition is caused by pressing an undefined key, such as a function key, since the program does not have any logic set up for that, except an ERROR CONDITION referenced in 9200-WRONG-KEY paragraph. A third condition is triggered during a mapfail operation, and procedures to handle such an eventuality are highlighted in lines 496 through 504 under 9999-MAPFAIL-RTN.

Compiler-generated source code: excerpts

As shown in FIG. 8-7, the compiler-generated source list contains the expansion of a number of copy statements initiated by the programmer. The first one of these statements concerns the carrier table in line 90 (FIG. 8-6), which is expanded in detail in lines 86 through 93 of FIG. 8-7. Again, the primary purpose of the carrier table is to provide a description to a specific carrier. It is also there for security reasons. If you were to enter the wrong carrier code on the inquiry screen, you would not attain a description, and your inquiry code would be rejected by the system as an invalid transaction.

The second copy statement in the programmer-written source code refers to the TRIP record or Master shown in line 91 (FIG. 8-6). This historical file is some 780 bytes long, although for all practical purposes TLT1BRS only utilizes relatively few data fields. Fields that are utilized in this program are denoted in two separate shaded areas in FIG. 8-7. The first one of these areas is shown in lines 94 through 107, while the second area is expanded in lines 144 through 149.

A third copy statement, line 92 (FIG. 8-6), refers to a delay code table, which gives you an explanation for each code entered into the system. An expanded layout of this record is shown in lines 339 through 345 of FIG. 8-7. Note that a fourth copy statement, the so-called station code table, is also part of the source list, even though this table is not utilized in this program. The station code table is in the program for a number of reasons. Primarily, it is there in case you need to enhance the current panel to include station codes, and explanation-related display. Another reason is that this program was modified from an earlier "shell" that has utilized station codes, thus the procedure remained imbedded in the original logic.

8-7 LATETRIP compiler version

```
1       IDENTIFICATION DIVISION.
2       PROGRAM-ID.      LATETRIP.
3
4       REMARKS.  THIS PROGRAM WILL BROWSE THE COMPLETE TRIPS FILE    &
5                       DISPLAY THE LATE TRIPS.
6
7       DATE-REVISED.
8       DATE-COMPILED. JAN 26,1990.
9       ENVIRONMENT DIVISION.
10      CONFIGURATION SECTION.
11      SOURCE-COMPUTER.      IBM-370.
12      OBJECT-COMPUTER.      IBM-370.
13
14      DATA DIVISION.
15
16      WORKING-STORAGE SECTION.
17
18      01  SWITCHES.
19          05  MORE-RECS-SW         PIC X  VALUE 'Y'.
20          88  MORE-RECS           VALUE 'Y'.
21          05  MORE-PREV-RECS-SW  PIC X  VALUE 'Y'.
22          88  MORE-PREV-RECS      VALUE 'Y'.
23
24      01  LINE-SUB             PIC 9(4) COMP.
25
26      ****    COMM AREA       ****
27      01  WS-COMMAREA.
28          05  COMM-FLAG       PIC X   VALUE 'I'.
29          88  INIT-MAP        VALUE 'I'.
30          88  SEND-MAP        VALUE 'S'.
31          88  RECV-MAP        VALUE 'R'.
32          05  WS-COMMAREA-OUT.
33          10  COMM-CARRIER    PIC XXX.
34          10  COMM-LINE       PIC XX.
35          05  WS-COMMAREA-TRIP.
36          10  CARRIER-ENTERED PIC XXX.
37          10  COMM-BEG-DATE.
38              15  COMM-BEG-YR     PIC XX.
39              15  COMM-BEG-MO     PIC XX.
40              15  COMM-BEG-DA     PIC XX.
41          10  COMM-END-DATE.
42              15  COMM-END-YR     PIC XX.
43              15  COMM-END-MO     PIC XX.
44              15  COMM-END-DA     PIC XX.
45          10  COMM-TRAIN-NO      PIC XXXX.
46          10  COMM-DELAY-CODE    PIC XX.
47          05  WORK-TR-KEY.
48          10  WK-CARRIER-CODE PIC X(3).
49          10  WK-LINE         PIC XX.
50          10  WK-TRAIN-NO      PIC X(4).
```

```
51              10  WK-TR-DATE.
52                  15  WK-TR-DATEY    PIC XX.
53                  15  WK-TR-DATEM    PIC XX.
54                  15  WK-TR-DATED    PIC XX.
55          05  DIRECTION-FLAG      PIC X.
56              88  FORW-DIR        VALUE 'F'.
57              88  PREV-DIR        VALUE 'P'.
58          05  END-SEARCH-SW       PIC X  VALUE 'N'.
59              88  SEARCH-ENDED     VALUE 'Y'.
60      ******************************************
61      ****   DATA-AREA FOR TRIP-KEY      ****
62      ******************************************
63          01  TRIP-KEY        PIC X(15) VALUE IS SPACES.
64
65          01  DATE-DISPLAY.
66              05  DATE-MO     PIC XX.
67              05  FILLER      PIC X VALUE '/'.
68              05  DATE-DA     PIC XX.
69              05  FILLER      PIC X VALUE '/'.
70              05  DATE-YR     PIC XX.
71
72          01  WS-ERROR-MESSAGES.
73              05  MAPFAIL-MSG         PIC X(36) VALUE
74          '*** MAPFAIL FOR TRANSACTION TLT1 ***'.
75              05  FILE-NOTOPEN-MSG   PIC X(42) VALUE
76          '*** FILE NOT OPEN FOR TRANSACTION TLT1 ***'.
77              05  PGM-NOTFND-MSG     PIC X(46) VALUE
78          '*** PROGRAM NOT FOUND FOR TRANSACTION TLT1 ***'.
79              05  ERROR-MSG       PIC X(42) VALUE
80          '*** UNKNOWN ERROR FOR TRANSACTION TLT1 ***'.
81
82      ********************************************
83      *******   FILE RECORDS DESCRIPTION    ******
84      ********************************************
85
86          01  CARRIER-TABLE.
87                  COPY CCARRIER.
88              05  T-CARRIER-CODE    PIC XXX.
89              05  FILLER          PIC X(4).
90              05  T-CARRIER-DESC    PIC X(35).
91              05  FILLER          PIC X(2).
92              05  HOLD-CODE        PIC X(4).
93      * RECORD LENGTH = 48
94      01  TRIP-REC.
95                  COPY CTRIP.
96          05  TR-KEY.
97              10  TR-CARRIER-CODE   PIC XXX.
98              10  TR-LINE-CODE      PIC XX.
99              10  TR-TRAIN-NO       PIC X(4).
100             10  TR-DATE-EFFECT.
101                 15  TR-DATE-EFFECT-Y  PIC 99.
102                 15  TR-DATE-EFFECT-M  PIC 99.
103                 15  TR-DATE-EFFECT-D  PIC 99.
104             10  TR-DATE-EFFECT-X REDEFINES TR-DATE-EFFECT.
105                 15  TR-DATE-EFFECT-Y-X PIC XX.
106                 15  TR-DATE-EFFECT-M-X PIC XX.
107                 15  TR-DATE-EFFECT-D-M PIC XX.
108         05  FILLER          PIC X.
109         05  TR-CYCLE        PIC XXX.
110         05  TR-DAY-IND      PIC XX.
111         05  TR-PEAK-IND         PIC X.
112         05  TR-AM-PM-IND        PIC X.
113         05  TR-SPECIAL-IND   PIC X.
114         05  TR-ANNULLED-IND  PIC X.
115         05  TR-DEADHEAD-IND  PIC X.
116         05  FILLER          PIC X.
117         05  TR-PASSENGERS         PIC 9(4).
118         05  TR-STANDEES          PIC 9(4).
119         05  TR-TOTAL-COACHES     PIC 99.
120         05  TR-OPEN-COACHES  PIC 99.
121         05  TR-SEAT-CAP          PIC 9(4).
122         05  FILLER          PIC X.
123         05  TR-TRAIN-MILES   PIC S9(2)V9 COMP-3 VALUE ZERO
124         05  FILLER          PIC X.
125         05  TR-REV-TRAIN-MILES      PIC S9(2)V9 COMP-3 VALUE ZERO
126         05  FILLER          PIC X.
127         05  TR-SCHED-DEPART-TIME.
128             10  TR-SCHED-DEPART-H    PIC 99.
```

```
129          10  TR-SCHED-DEPART-M      PIC 99.
130          05  TR-SCHED-ARRIV-TIME.
131          10  TR-SCHED-ARRIV-H       PIC 99.
132          10  TR-SCHED-ARRIV-M       PIC 99.
133          05  TR-ACTUAL-DEPART-TIME.
134          10  TR-ACTUAL-DEPART-H     PIC 99.
135          10  TR-ACTUAL-DEPART-M     PIC 99.
136          05  TR-ACTUAL-ARRIV-TIME.
137          10  TR-ACTUAL-ARRIV-H      PIC 99.
138          10  TR-ACTUAL-ARRIV-M      PIC 99.
139          05  TR-DEPART-STA-CODE     PIC 999.
140          05  TR-DEPART-STA-DESC     PIC X(20).
141          05  TR-ARRIV-STA-CODE      PIC 999.
142          05  TR-ARRIV-STA-DESC      PIC X(20).
143          05  FILLER            PIC X.
144          05  TR-DELAY-MIN      PIC 9(3).
145          05  TR-DELAY-MIN-X REDEFINES TR-DELAY-MIN   PIC XXX.
146          05  TR-DELAY-CODE.
147          10  TR-DELAY-PRIMARY      PIC X.
148          10  TR-DELAY-SECONDARY   PIC X.
149          10  TR-DELAY-WEATHER     PIC X.
150          05  TR-DELAY-LOCATION      PIC XXX.
151          05  TR-DELAY-UNIT-NO       PIC X(4).
152          05  TR-DELAY-EXPLANATION.
153          10  TR-EXPLAIN1       PIC X(63).
154          10  TR-EXPLAIN2       PIC X(77).
155          05  FILLER            PIC X.
156          05  TR-LOCO-NO1            PIC X(4).
157          05  TR-LOCO-NO2            PIC X(4).
158          05  TR-LOCOMOTIVE-CYCLE   PIC XXX.
159          05  TR-LOCO-OVERRIDE      PIC X.
160          05  TR-COACHES-X          PIC X(96).
161          05  TR-COACH-N  REDEFINES TR-COACHES-X
162              OCCURS 16 TIMES.
163          10  TR-COACH-NO       PIC 9(4).
164          10  TR-COACH-TYPE-CODE    PIC X.
165          10  TR-COACH-FLAG-CODE    PIC X.
166          05  TR-COACH     REDEFINES TR-COACHES-X.
167          10  TR-COACH-NO1          PIC X(4).
168          10  TR-COACH-TYPE-CODE1      PIC X.
169          10  TR-COACH-FLAG-CODE1      PIC X.
170          10  TR-COACH-NO2          PIC X(4).
171          10  TR-COACH-TYPE-CODE2      PIC X.
172          10  TR-COACH-FLAG-CODE2      PIC X.
173          10  TR-COACH-NO3          PIC X(4).
174          10  TR-COACH-TYPE-CODE3      PIC X.
175          10  TR-COACH-FLAG-CODE3      PIC X.
176          10  TR-COACH-NO4          PIC X(4).
177          10  TR-COACH-TYPE-CODE4      PIC X.
178          10  TR-COACH-FLAG-CODE4      PIC X.
179          10  TR-COACH-NO5          PIC X(4).
180          10  TR-COACH-TYPE-CODE5      PIC X.
181          10  TR-COACH-FLAG-CODE5      PIC X.
182          10  TR-COACH-NO6          PIC X(4).
183          10  TR-COACH-TYPE-CODE6      PIC X.
184          10  TR-COACH-FLAG-CODE6      PIC X.
185          10  TR-COACH-NO7          PIC X(4).
186          10  TR-COACH-TYPE-CODE7      PIC X.
187          10  TR-COACH-FLAG-CODE7      PIC X.
188          10  TR-COACH-NO8          PIC X(4).
189          10  TR-COACH-TYPE-CODE8      PIC X.
190          10  TR-COACH-FLAG-CODE8      PIC X.
191          10  TR-COACH-NO9          PIC X(4).
192          10  TR-COACH-TYPE-CODE9      PIC X.
193          10  TR-COACH-FLAG-CODE9      PIC X.
194          10  TR-COACH-NO10         PIC X(4).
195          10  TR-COACH-TYPE-CODE10     PIC X.
196          10  TR-COACH-FLAG-CODE10     PIC X.
197          10  TR-COACH-NO11         PIC X(4).
198          10  TR-COACH-TYPE-CODE11     PIC X.
199          10  TR-COACH-FLAG-CODE11     PIC X.
200          10  TR-COACH-NO12         PIC X(4).
201          10  TR-COACH-TYPE-CODE12     PIC X.
202          10  TR-COACH-FLAG-CODE12     PIC X.
203          10  TR-COACH-NO13         PIC X(4).
204          10  TR-COACH-TYPE-CODE13     PIC X.
```

```
205        10   TR-COACH-FLAG-CODE13      PIC X.
206        10   TR-COACH-NO14         PIC X(4).
207        10   TR-COACH-TYPE-CODE14      PIC X.
208        10   TR-COACH-FLAG-CODE14      PIC X.
209        10   TR-COACH-NO15         PIC X(4).
210        10   TR-COACH-TYPE-CODE15      PIC X.
211        10   TR-COACH-FLAG-CODE15      PIC X.
212        10   TR-COACH-NO16         PIC X(4).
213        10   TR-COACH-TYPE-CODE16      PIC X.
214        10   TR-COACH-FLAG-CODE16      PIC X.
215     05   FILLER               PIC X.
216     05   TR-ENG-CREW-NO    PIC X(4).
217     05   TR-ENG-X          PIC X(72).
218     05   TR-ENG-CREW REDEFINES TR-ENG-X
219             OCCURS   2 TIMES.
220        10   TR-ENG-ID-1          PIC X(7).
221        10   TR-ENG-NAME-1        PIC X(25).
222        10   TR-ENG-OCC-CODE-1        PIC X.
223        10   TR-ENG-TEMP-IND-1        PIC X.
224        10   TR-ENG-REAS-CODE-1       PIC X.
225        10   FILLER               PIC X.
226     05   TR-ENGINE    REDEFINES TR-ENG-X.
227        10   TR-ENG-ID            PIC 9(7).
228        10   TR-ENG-ID-X REDEFINES TR-ENG-ID    PIC X(7).
229        10   TR-ENG-NAME          PIC X(25).
230        10   TR-ENG-OCC-CODE         PIC X.
231        10   TR-ENG-TEMP-IND         PIC X.
232        10   TR-ENG-REAS-CODE        PIC X.
233        10   FILLER               PIC X.
234        10   TR-FIR-ID            PIC 9(7).
235        10   TR-FIR-ID-X REDEFINES TR-FIR-ID    PIC X(7).
236        10   TR-FIR-NAME          PIC X(25).
237        10   TR-FIR-OCC-CODE         PIC X.
238        10   TR-FIR-TEMP-IND         PIC X.
239        10   TR-FIR-REAS-CODE        PIC X.
240        10   FILLER               PIC X.
241     05   TR-TRA-CREW-NO    PIC X(4).
242     05   TR-TRA-CREW-X            PIC X(108).
243     05   TR-TRA-CREW REDEFINES TR-TRA-CREW-X
244             OCCURS   3 TIMES.
245        10   TR-TRA-ID            PIC X(7).
246        10   TR-TRA-NAME          PIC X(25).
247        10   TR-TRA-OCC-CODE         PIC X.
248        10   TR-TRA-TEMP-IND         PIC X.
249        10   TR-TRA-REAS-CODE        PIC X.
250        10   FILLER               PIC X.
251     05   TR-TRAIN-CR REDEFINES TR-TRA-CREW-X.
252        10   TR-CON-ID            PIC 9(7).
253        10   TR-CON-ID-X REDEFINES TR-CON-ID    PIC X(7).
254        10   TR-CON-NAME          PIC X(25).
255        10   TR-CON-OCC-CODE         PIC X.
256        10   TR-CON-TEMP-IND         PIC X.
257        10   TR-CON-REAS-CODE        PIC X.
258        10   FILLER               PIC X.
259        10   TR-COL-ID1           PIC 9(7).
260        10   TR-COL-ID1-X REDEFINES TR-COL-ID1    PIC X(7).
261        10   TR-COL-NAME1         PIC X(25).
262        10   TR-COL-OCC-CODE1        PIC X.
263        10   TR-COL-TEMP-IND1        PIC X.
264        10   TR-COL-REAS-CODE1       PIC X.
265        10   FILLER               PIC X.
266        10   TR-COL-ID2           PIC 9(7).
267        10   TR-COL-ID2-X REDEFINES TR-COL-ID2    PIC X(7).
268        10   TR-COL-NAME2         PIC X(25).
269        10   TR-COL-OCC-CODE2        PIC X.
270        10   TR-COL-TEMP-IND2        PIC X.
271        10   TR-COL-REAS-CODE2       PIC X.
272        10   FILLER               PIC X.
273     05   TR-SWING-X              PIC X(138).
274     05   TR-SWI-CREW   REDEFINES TR-SWING-X
275             OCCURS 3 TIMES.
276        10   TR-SWI-CREW-NO       PIC X(4).
277        10   TR-SWI-ID            PIC X(7).
278        10   TR-SWI-NAME          PIC X(25).
279        10   TR-SWI-OCC-CODE         PIC X.
280        10   TR-SWI-TEMP-IND         PIC X.
281        10   TR-SWI-REAS-CODE        PIC X.
282        10   TR-SWI-BGN-STA-CODE     PIC XXX.
```

```
283              10  TR-SWI-END-STA-CODE        PIC XXX.
284              10  FILLER               PIC X.
285          05  TR-SWING-CREW     REDEFINES  TR-SWING-X.
286              10  TR-SWI-CREW-NO1            PIC X(4).
287              10  TR-SWI-ID1           PIC 9(7).
288              10  TR-SWI-ID1-X REDEFINES TR-SWI-ID1    PIC X(7).
289              10  TR-SWI-NAME1         PIC X(25).
290              10  TR-SWI-OCC-CODE1           PIC X.
291              10  TR-SWI-TEMP-IND1           PIC X.
292              10  TR-SWI-REAS-CODE1          PIC X.
293              10  TR-SWI-BGN-STA-CODE1       PIC XXX.
294              10  TR-SWI-END-STA-CODE1       PIC XXX.
295              10  FILLER               PIC X.
296              10  TR-SWI-CREW-NO2            PIC X(4).
297              10  TR-SWI-ID2           PIC 9(7).
298              10  TR-SWI-ID2-X REDEFINES TR-SWI-ID2    PIC X(7).
299              10  TR-SWI-NAME2         PIC X(25).
300              10  TR-SWI-OCC-CODE2           PIC X.
301              10  TR-SWI-TEMP-IND2           PIC X.
302              10  TR-SWI-REAS-CODE2          PIC X.
303              10  TR-SWI-BGN-STA-CODE2       PIC XXX.
304              10  TR-SWI-END-STA-CODE2       PIC XXX.
305              10  FILLER               PIC X.
306              10  TR-SWI-CREW-NO3            PIC X(4).
307              10  TR-SWI-ID3           PIC 9(7).
308              10  TR-SWI-ID3-X REDEFINES TR-SWI-ID3    PIC X(7).
309              10  TR-SWI-NAME3         PIC X(25).
310              10  TR-SWI-OCC-CODE3           PIC X.
311              10  TR-SWI-TEMP-IND3           PIC X.
312              10  TR-SWI-REAS-CODE3          PIC X.
313              10  TR-SWI-BGN-STA-CODE3       PIC XXX.
314              10  TR-SWI-END-STA-CODE3       PIC XXX.
315              10  FILLER               PIC X.
316          05  TR-DH-ENG-CREW-NO    PIC X(4).
317          05  TR-DH-TRA-CREW-NO    PIC X(4).
318          05  TR-DH-SWI-CREW-NO1   PIC X(4).
319          05  TR-DH-SWI-CREW-NO2   PIC X(4).
320          05  TR-DH-SWI-CREW-NO3   PIC X(4).
321          05  TR-HIST-ENG-ID                PIC 9(7).
322          05  TR-HIST-ENG-ID-X REDEFINES TR-HIST-ENG-ID    PIC X(7).
323          05  TR-HIST-FIR-ID                PIC 9(7).
324          05  TR-HIST-FIR-ID-X REDEFINES TR-HIST-FIR-ID    PIC X(7).
325          05  TR-HIST-CON-ID                PIC 9(7).
326          05  TR-HIST-CON-ID-X REDEFINES TR-HIST-CON-ID    PIC X(7).
327          05  TR-HIST-COL1-ID               PIC 9(7).
328          05  TR-HIST-COL1-ID-X REDEFINES TR-HIST-COL1-ID PIC X(7).
329          05  TR-HIST-COL2-ID               PIC 9(7).
330          05  TR-HIST-COL2-ID-X REDEFINES TR-HIST-COL2-ID PIC X(7).
331          05  TR-HIST-SWI1-ID               PIC 9(7).
332          05  TR-HIST-SWI1-ID-X REDEFINES TR-HIST-SWI1-ID PIC X(7).
333          05  TR-HIST-SWI2-ID               PIC 9(7).
334          05  TR-HIST-SWI2-ID-X REDEFINES TR-HIST-SWI2-ID PIC X(7).
335          05  TR-HIST-SWI3-ID               PIC 9(7).
336          05  TR-HIST-SWI3-ID-X REDEFINES TR-HIST-SWI3-ID PIC X(7).
337          05  FILLER              PIC X(02).
338     * RECORD LENGTH = 780
339       01  DELAY-TABLE.
340                   COPY CDELAY.
341          05  T-DELAY-CODE         PIC XX.
342          05  FILLER          PIC X(5).
343          05  T-DELAY-DESC         PIC X(30).
344          05  FILLER          PIC XXX.
345     * RECORD LENGTH = 40
346       01  STATION-TABLE.
347                   COPY CSTATION.
348          05  T-STATION-CODE.
349             10  TS-CARRIER-CODE PIC XXX.
350             10  TS-LINE-CODE    PIC XX.
351             10  TS-MILE-MARKER  PIC XXX.
352          05  T-STATION-DESC      PIC X(20).
353          05  FILLER          PIC X(12).
354     * RECORD LENGTH = 40
355             COPY TLT1MAP.
356       01  LATEMAP.
357          02  FILLER              PIC X(12).
358     ************************************************************
```

```
359          02  LT-L-TRANS       PIC S9(4)    COMP.
360          02  LT-A-TRANS       PIC X.
361          02  LT-C-TRANS       PIC X.
362          02  LT-P-TRANS       PIC X.
363          02  LT-H-TRANS       PIC X.
364          02  LT-V-TRANS       PIC X.
365          02  LT-D-TRANS       PIC X(4).
366     ********************************************************
367          02  LT-L-HDATE       PIC S9(4)    COMP.
368          02  LT-A-HDATE       PIC X.
369          02  LT-C-HDATE       PIC X.
370          02  LT-P-HDATE       PIC X.
371          02  LT-H-HDATE       PIC X.
372          02  LT-V-HDATE       PIC X.
373          02  LT-D-HDATE       PIC X(8).
374     ********************************************************
375          02  LT-L-CAR-DESC        PIC S9(4)    COMP.
376          02  LT-A-CAR-DESC        PIC X.
377          02  LT-C-CAR-DESC        PIC X.
378          02  LT-P-CAR-DESC        PIC X.
379          02  LT-H-CAR-DESC        PIC X.
380          02  LT-V-CAR-DESC        PIC X.
381          02  LT-D-CAR-DESC        PIC X(35).
382     ********************************************************
383          02  LT-TRIP-LINE              OCCURS 8.
384          05  LT-L-TRAIN       PIC S9(4)    COMP.
385          05  LT-A-TRAIN       PIC X.
386          05  LT-C-TRAIN       PIC X.
387          05  LT-P-TRAIN       PIC X.
388          05  LT-H-TRAIN       PIC X.
389          05  LT-V-TRAIN       PIC X.
390          05  LT-D-TRAIN       PIC XXXX.
391     ********************************************************
392          05  LT-L-DATE        PIC S9(4)    COMP.
393          05  LT-A-DATE        PIC X.
394          05  LT-C-DATE        PIC X.
395          05  LT-P-DATE        PIC X.
396          05  LT-H-DATE        PIC X.
397          05  LT-V-DATE        PIC X.
398          05  LT-D-DATE        PIC X(8).
399     ********************************************************
400          05  LT-L-MINUTES     PIC S9(4)    COMP.
401          05  LT-A-MINUTES     PIC X.
402          05  LT-C-MINUTES     PIC X.
403          05  LT-P-MINUTES     PIC X.
404          05  LT-H-MINUTES     PIC X.
405          05  LT-V-MINUTES     PIC X.
406          05  LT-D-MINUTES     PIC XXX.
407     ********************************************************
408          05  LT-L-LATECODE    PIC S9(4)    COMP.
409          05  LT-A-LATECODE    PIC X.
410          05  LT-C-LATECODE    PIC X.
411          05  LT-P-LATECODE    PIC X.
412          05  LT-H-LATECODE    PIC X.
413          05  LT-V-LATECODE    PIC X.
414          05  LT-D-LATECODE    PIC XX.
415     ********************************************************
416          05  LT-L-LATEDESC    PIC S9(4)    COMP.
417          05  LT-A-LATEDESC    PIC X.
418          05  LT-C-LATEDESC    PIC X.
419          05  LT-P-LATEDESC    PIC X.
420          05  LT-H-LATEDESC    PIC X.
421          05  LT-V-LATEDESC    PIC X.
422          05  LT-D-LATEDESC    PIC X(30).
423     ********************************************************
424          02  LT-L-PFMSG       PIC S9(4)    COMP.
425          02  LT-A-PFMSG       PIC X.
426          02  LT-C-PFMSG       PIC X.
427          02  LT-P-PFMSG       PIC X.
428          02  LT-H-PFMSG       PIC X.
429          02  LT-V-PFMSG       PIC X.
430          02  LT-D-PFMSG       PIC X(75).
431     ********************************************************
432          02  LT-L-ERMSG       PIC S9(4)    COMP.
433          02  LT-A-ERMSG       PIC X.
434          02  LT-C-ERMSG       PIC X.
435          02  LT-P-ERMSG       PIC X.
436          02  LT-H-ERMSG       PIC X.
```

```
437              02  LT-V-ERMSG      PIC X.
438              02  LT-D-ERMSG      PIC X(75).
439           COPY DFHAID.
440       01    DFHAID.
441          02  DFHNULL   PIC  X  VALUE IS ' '.
442          02  DFHENTER  PIC  X  VALUE IS QUOTE.
443          02  DFHCLEAR  PIC  X  VALUE IS ' '.
444          02  DFHCLRP   PIC  X  VALUE IS '|T'.
445          02  DFHPEN    PIC  X  VALUE IS '='.
446          02  DFHOPID   PIC  X  VALUE IS 'W'.
447          02  DFHMSRE   PIC  X  VALUE IS 'X'.
448          02  DFHSTRF   PIC  X  VALUE IS 'h'.
449          02  DFHTRIG   PIC  X  VALUE IS '"'.
450          02  DFHPA1    PIC  X  VALUE IS '%'.
451          02  DFHPA2    PIC  X  VALUE IS '>'.
452          02  DFHPA3    PIC  X  VALUE IS ','.
453          02  DFHPF1    PIC  X  VALUE IS '1'.
454          02  DFHPF2    PIC  X  VALUE IS '2'.
455          02  DFHPF3    PIC  X  VALUE IS '3'.
456          02  DFHPF4    PIC  X  VALUE IS '4'.
457          02  DFHPF5    PIC  X  VALUE IS '5'.
458          02  DFHPF6    PIC  X  VALUE IS '6'.
459          02  DFHPF7    PIC  X  VALUE IS '7'.
460          02  DFHPF8    PIC  X  VALUE IS '8'.
461          02  DFHPF9    PIC  X  VALUE IS '9'.
462          02  DFHPF10   PIC  X  VALUE IS ':'.
463          02  DFHPF11   PIC  X  VALUE IS '#'.
464          02  DFHPF12   PIC  X  VALUE IS '@'.
465          02  DFHPF13   PIC  X  VALUE IS 'A'.
466          02  DFHPF14   PIC  X  VALUE IS 'B'.
467          02  DFHPF15   PIC  X  VALUE IS 'C'.
468          02  DFHPF16   PIC  X  VALUE IS 'D'.
469          02  DFHPF17   PIC  X  VALUE IS 'E'.
470          02  DFHPF18   PIC  X  VALUE IS 'F'.
471          02  DFHPF19   PIC  X  VALUE IS 'G'.
472          02  DFHPF20   PIC  X  VALUE IS 'H'.
473          02  DFHPF21   PIC  X  VALUE IS 'I'.
474          02  DFHPF22   PIC  X  VALUE IS '['.
475          02  DFHPF23   PIC  X  VALUE IS '.'.
476          02  DFHPF24   PIC  X  VALUE IS '<'.
477           COPY DFHBMSCA.
478       01    DFHBMSCA.
479          02      DFHBMPEM  PICTURE X    VALUE  IS   ' '.
480          02      DFHBMPNL  PICTURE X    VALUE  IS   ' '.
481          02      DFHBMASK  PICTURE X    VALUE  IS   '0'.
482          02      DFHBMUNP  PICTURE X    VALUE  IS   ' '.
483          02      DFHBMUNN  PICTURE X    VALUE  IS   '&'.
484          02      DFHBMPRO  PICTURE X    VALUE  IS   '-'.
485          02      DFHBMBRY  PICTURE X    VALUE  IS   'H'.
486          02      DFHBMDAR  PICTURE X    VALUE  IS   '<'.
487          02      DFHBMFSE  PICTURE X    VALUE  IS   'A'.
488          02      DFHBMPRF  PICTURE X    VALUE  IS   '/'.
489          02      DFHBMASF  PICTURE X    VALUE  IS   '1'.
490          02      DFHBMASB  PICTURE X    VALUE  IS   '8'.
491          02      DFHBMEOF  PICTURE X    VALUE  IS   ' '.
492          02      DFHBMDET  PICTURE X    VALUE  IS   ' '.
493          02      DFHBMPSO  PICTURE X    VALUE  IS   ' '.
494          02      DFHBMPSI  PICTURE X    VALUE  IS   ' '.
495          02      DFHSA       PICTURE X     VALUE  IS   ' '.
496          02      DFHCOLOR  PICTURE X    VALUE  IS   ' '.
497          02      DFHPS       PICTURE X     VALUE  IS   ' '.
498          02      DFHHLT    PICTURE X    VALUE  IS   ' '.
499          02      DFH3270   PICTURE X    VALUE  IS   '{'.
500          02      DFHVAL    PICTURE X    VALUE  IS   'A'.
501          02      DFHOUTLN  PICTURE X    VALUE  IS   'B'.
502          02      DFHBKTRN  PICTURE X    VALUE  IS   ' '.
503          02      DFHALL    PICTURE X    VALUE  IS   ' '.
504          02      DFHERROR  PICTURE X    VALUE  IS   ' '.
505          02      DFHDFT    PICTURE X    VALUE  IS   ' '.
506          02      DFHDFCOL  PICTURE X    VALUE  IS   ' '.
507          02      DFHBLUE   PICTURE X    VALUE  IS   '1'.
508          02      DFHRED    PICTURE X    VALUE  IS   '2'.
509          02      DFHPINK   PICTURE X    VALUE  IS   '3'.
510          02      DFHGREEN  PICTURE X    VALUE  IS   '4'.
511          02      DFHTURQ   PICTURE X    VALUE  IS   '5'.
512          02      DFHYELLO  PICTURE X    VALUE  IS   '6'.
```

```
513        02      DFHNEUTR  PICTURE X    VALUE  IS  '7'.
514        02      DFHBASE   PICTURE X    VALUE  IS  ' '.
515        02      DFHDFHI   PICTURE X    VALUE  IS  ' '.
516        02      DFHBLINK  PICTURE X    VALUE  IS  '1'.
517        02      DFHREVRS  PICTURE X    VALUE  IS  '2'.
518        02      DFHUNDLN  PICTURE X    VALUE  IS  '4'.
519        02      DFHMFIL   PICTURE X    VALUE  IS  ' '.
520        02      DFHMENT   PICTURE X    VALUE  IS  ' '.
521        02      DFHMFE    PICTURE X    VALUE  IS  ' '.
522        02      DFHUNNOD  PICTURE X    VALUE  IS  '('.
523        02      DFHUNIMD  PICTURE X    VALUE  IS  'I'.
524        02      DFHUNNUM  PICTURE X    VALUE  IS  'J'.
525        02      DFHUNINT  PICTURE X    VALUE  IS  'R'.
526        02      DFHUNNON  PICTURE X    VALUE  IS  ')'.
527        02      DFHPROTI  PICTURE X    VALUE  IS  'Y'.
528        02      DFHPROTN  PICTURE X    VALUE  IS  '%'.
529        02      DFHMT           PICTURE X    VALUE  IS  ' '.
530        02      DFHMFT    PICTURE X    VALUE  IS  ' '.
531        02      DFHMET    PICTURE X    VALUE  IS  ' '.
532        02      DFHMFET   PICTURE X    VALUE  IS  ' '.
533        02      DFHDFFR   PICTURE X    VALUE  IS  ' '.
534        02      DFHLEFT   PICTURE X    VALUE  IS  ' '.
535        02      DFHOVER   PICTURE X    VALUE  IS  ' '.
536        02      DFHRIGHT  PICTURE X    VALUE  IS  ' '.
537        02      DFHUNDER  PICTURE X    VALUE  IS  ' '.
538        02      DFHBOX    PICTURE X    VALUE  IS  ' '.
539        02      DFHSOSI   PICTURE X    VALUE  IS  ' '.
540        02      DFHTRANS  PICTURE X    VALUE  IS  '0'.
541        02      DFHOPAQ   PICTURE X    VALUE  IS  ' '.
542        COPY CHARATR.
543    *------------* ATTRIBUTE-BYTES  *--------------------------
544    01  CHARATR.
545        05   UNPROT-ALPHA             PIC X    VALUE SPACE.
546        05   UNPROT-ALPHA-MDT         PIC X    VALUE 'A'.
547        05   UNPROT-ALPHA-BRT         PIC X    VALUE 'H'.
548        05   UNPROT-ALPHA-BRT-MDT     PIC X    VALUE 'I'.
549        05   UNPROT-ALPHA-DRK         PIC X    VALUE '<'.
550        05   UNPROT-ALPHA-DRK-MDT     PIC X    VALUE '('.
551        05   UNPROT-NUM         PIC X    VALUE '&'.
552        05   UNPROT-NUM-MDT           PIC X    VALUE 'J'.
553        05   UNPROT-NUM-BRT           PIC X    VALUE 'Q'.
554        05   UNPROT-NUM-BRT-MDT       PIC X    VALUE 'R'.
555        05   UNPROT-NUM-DRK           PIC X    VALUE '*'.
556        05   UNPROT-NUM-DRK-MDT       PIC X    VALUE ')'.
557        05   PROT              PIC X    VALUE '-'.
558        05   PROT-MDT          PIC X    VALUE '/'.
559        05   PROT-BRT          PIC X    VALUE 'Y'.
560        05   PROT-BRT-MDT          PIC X    VALUE 'Z'.
561        05   PROT-DRK          PIC X    VALUE '%'.
562        05   PROT-DRK-MDT          PIC X    VALUE '_'.
563        05   ASKIP             PIC X    VALUE '0'.
564        05   ASKIP-MDT         PIC X    VALUE '1'.
565        05   ASKIP-BRT         PIC X    VALUE '8'.
566        05   ASKIP-BRT-MDT         PIC X    VALUE '9'.
567        05   ASKIP-DRK         PIC X    VALUE '@'.
568        05   ASKIP-DRK-MDT         PIC X    VALUE QUOTE.
569    *---------------* LENGTH BYTES  *--------------------------
570    01  LENGTH-BYTES.
571        05   CSR-REPO         PIC S9(4) COMP VALUE -1.
572
573    01  DFHLDVER PIC X(22) VALUE 'LD TABLE DFHEITAB 170.'.
574    01  DFHEID0 PICTURE S9(7) COMPUTATIONAL-3 VALUE ZERO.
575    01  DFHEIB0 PICTURE S9(4) COMPUTATIONAL VALUE ZERO.
576    01  DFHEICB  PICTURE X(8) VALUE IS '        '.
577
578    01  DFHEIV16 COMP PIC S9(8).
579    01  DFHB0041 COMP PIC S9(8).
580    01  DFHB0042 COMP PIC S9(8).
581    01  DFHB0043 COMP PIC S9(8).
582    01  DFHB0044 COMP PIC S9(8).
583    01  DFHB0045 COMP PIC S9(8).
584    01  DFHB0046 COMP PIC S9(8).
585    01  DFHB0047 COMP PIC S9(8).
586    01  DFHB0048 COMP PIC S9(8).
587    01  DFHEIV11 COMP PIC S9(4).
588    01  DFHEIV12 COMP PIC S9(4).
589    01  DFHEIV13 COMP PIC S9(4).
590    01  DFHEIV14 COMP PIC S9(4).
```

```
591        01   DFHEIV15 COMP PIC S9(4).
592        01   DFHB0025 COMP PIC S9(4).
593        01   DFHEIV5  PIC X(4).
594        01   DFHEIV6  PIC X(4).
595        01   DFHEIV17 PIC X(4).
596        01   DFHEIV18 PIC X(4).
597        01   DFHEIV19 PIC X(4).
598        01   DFHEIV1  PIC X(8).
599        01   DFHEIV2  PIC X(8).
600        01   DFHEIV3  PIC X(8).
601        01   DFHEIV20 PIC X(8).
602        01   DFHC0084 PIC X(8).
603        01   DFHC0085 PIC X(8).
604        01   DFHC0320 PIC X(32).
605        01   DFHEIV7  PIC X(2).
606        01   DFHEIV8  PIC X(2).
607        01   DFHC0022 PIC X(2).
608        01   DFHC0023 PIC X(2).
609        01   DFHEIV10 PIC S9(7) COMP-3.
610        01   DFHEIV9  PIC X(1).
611        01   DFHC0011 PIC X(1).
612        01   DFHEIV4  PIC X(6).
613        01   DFHC0070 PIC X(7).
614        01   DFHC0071 PIC X(7).
615        01   DFHC0440 PIC X(44).
616        01   DFHC0441 PIC X(44).
617        01   DFHDUMMY COMP PIC S9(4).
618        01   DFHEIV0  PICTURE X(29).
619   LINKAGE SECTION.
620        01   DFHEIBLK.
621        02      EIBTIME PIC S9(7) COMP-3.
622        02      EIBDATE PIC S9(7) COMP-3.
623        02      EIBTRNID PIC X(4).
624        02      EIBTASKN PIC S9(7) COMP-3.
625        02      EIBTRMID PIC X(4).
626        02      DFHEIGDI COMP PIC S9(4).
627        02      EIBCPOSN COMP PIC S9(4).
628        02      EIBCALEN COMP PIC S9(4).
629        02      EIBAID  PIC X(1).
630        02      EIBFN   PIC X(2).
631        02      EIBRCODE PIC X(6).
632        02      EIBDS   PIC X(8).
633        02      EIBREQID PIC X(8).
634        02      EIBRSRCE PIC X(8).
635        02      EIBSYNC PIC X(1).
636        02      EIBFREE PIC X(1).
637        02      EIBRECV PIC X(1).
638        02      EIBFIL01 PIC X(1).
639        02      EIBATT  PIC X(1).
640        02      EIBEOC  PIC X(1).
641        02      EIBFMH  PIC X(1).
642        02      EIBCOMPL PIC X(1).
643        02      EIBSIG  PIC X(1).
644        02      EIBCONF PIC X(1).
645        02      EIBERR  PIC X(1).
646        02      EIBERRCD PIC X(4).
647        02      EIBSYNRB PIC X(1).
648        02      EIBNODAT PIC X(1).
649        02      EIBRESP  COMP PIC S9(8).
650        02      EIBRESP2 COMP PIC S9(8).
651        02      EIBRLDBK PIC X(1).
652        01   DFHCOMMAREA      PIC X(44).
653
654        01   DFHBLLSLOT1 PICTURE X(1).
655        01   DFHBLLSLOT2 PICTURE X(1).
656   ^Z
```

A fourth copy statement, shown in line 94 (of FIG. 8-6) is the TLT1MAP or BMS module I talked about before, which is the programmer's layout of the LATE TRIPS BROWSE panel. At compile time, the statement copies into the program an expanded map, which I referred to earlier as the symbolic map. Because of the use of extended colors, (EXTATT=YES, in FIG. 8-4), I have developed my own symbolic map, a process illustrated in lines 356 through 438 in FIG. 8-7. This methodology, however, is slightly different from previous procedures. Because of the extended nature of the map, the user-written symbolic map relies on positional values or definitions. Let's look at the example shown in lines 359 through 365 of FIG. 8-7. The first field definition, regardless of the specific field name, refers to the length portion of a field. Thus, 02 LT-L-TRANS, line 359 can be called FIELD-LENGTH-TRANSACT. Likewise, the second field on this symbolic definition is always the attribute byte, the third field defines the color, and so on.

A fifth copy statement refers to the DFHAID block, line 95 (FIG. 8-6), necessary for the identification of all function (both PF and PA) keys, as well as the ENTER key, the CLEAR key, a light pen, and so on. This block is further expanded in detail in lines 440 through 476 of FIG. 8-7. Two additional copy statements are also extracted, seemingly in conflict with one another. These are the DFHBMSCA and the CHARATR block. The first is an IBM, while the latter is an in-house provision for defining attribute bytes. DFDMSCBA is shown in lines 478 through 541 of FIG. 8-7, and this block is required to handle additional colors. The second block, lines 543 through 568, is used to invoke some of the necessary combined attributes—a table that was built in-house. The reason for utilizing both tables is that it will now give you access to a number of extended attributes in your program, while allowing you to have access to consolidated functions built for specific shop requirements.

9

How to develop and code your own HELP subsystem

Tutorial subsystems provide a variety of users with the online, interactive capabilities to identify, clarify, or diagnose a specific problem that might otherwise require substantial research or reference to user manuals. The development of tutorial subsystems entails some fundamental design considerations in two separate areas. The first one of these is the actual building and maintenance of such a system through a set of dedicated programs and panels. A second area is where such procedures are physically referenced or invoked by the user in order to attain information from a file, a data field, an edit rule or an ERROR message. All this is normally triggered through function key action. Figure 9-1 highlights an entire tutorial mechanism.

The economy of developing a subsystem lies in its generic value to many departments within a company. Comprehensive tutorial subsystems need to be developed only once, due to their generic nature. Once developed, such a system can fully satisfy a variety of corporate users. All you need to do is to define exit points in the individual application programs. From these exit points, you can easily leave the current transaction and enter its associated HELP module. In this process, it is essential that you retain the current position of the cursor, so that once you return to the original panel, you can resume processing at the same point.

As stated before, the purpose of the tutorial (HELP) module is to enable the user to build customized panels, thereby assisting the user in learning the system in a relatively brief period and resolving some of the potential problems during that interactive session.

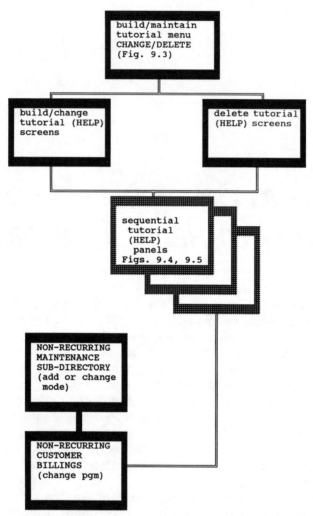

9-1 Interaction between HELP screens and tutorial programs

The tutorial cycle allows the user to enter approximately six pages of information, while assisting and advising him or her in a step-by-step fashion. Clearly, the advantage of such a system remains in its customized ability to describe each data field the way it appears on the screen, including complex edit rules, computations, path information, and an ability to branch back and forth between the various panels without "losing place" in the exercise.

To initiate the tutorial module, enter task 6 on the main systems directory, FIG. 9-2, which is essentially designed to trigger the HELP screen directory panel shown in FIG. 9-3. In building a HELP

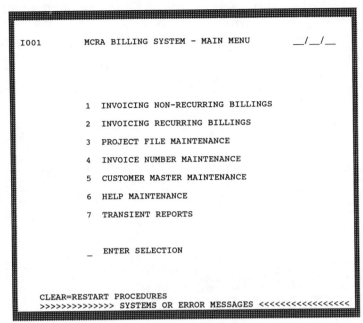

```
    I001          MCRA BILLING SYSTEM - MAIN MENU        __/__/__




               1   INVOICING NON-RECURRING BILLINGS

               2   INVOICING RECURRING BILLINGS

               3   PROJECT FILE MAINTENANCE

               4   INVOICE NUMBER MAINTENANCE

               5   CUSTOMER MASTER MAINTENANCE

               6   HELP MAINTENANCE

               7   TRANSIENT REPORTS


               _   ENTER SELECTION



        CLEAR=RESTART PROCEDURES
        >>>>>>>>>>>>>> SYSTEMS OR ERROR MESSAGES <<<<<<<<<<<<<<<<<
```

9-2 Main systems directory for invoking a HELP subsystem

```
    AR80                  HELP SCREEN DIRECTORY              09/10/90


    RECURRING CUSTOMERS                   NON RECURRING CUSTOMERS

    01  INVOICE HEADER                    04   INVOICE HEADER
    02  INVOICE DESCRIPTION               05   INVOICE DESWCRIPTION
    03  INVOICE DISTRIBUTION              06   INVOICE DISTRIBUTION

    PROJECT FILE MAINTENANCE              PREFIX TABLE MAINTENANCE

    07  ADD A NEW PROJECT                 11   ADD CHANGE DELETE MAINTENANCE
    08  CHANGE A PROJECT
    09  DELETE A PROJECT
    10  BROWSE A PROJECT


              ENTER TASK SELECTION      (1 THROUGH 11 )
              ENTER MAINTENANCE CODE    ( C=CHANGE D=DELETE )


        PF1: RETURN TO MENU
    ENTER TASK AND MAINTENANCE MODE
    >>>>>>>>>>>>>>> systems or error messages <<<<<<<<<<<<<<<<<<<<<<<<
```

9-3 Subdirectory for invoking a HELP module

screen, the system allows you to perform one of two tasks. These
are:

- Changing an existing task (enter the code C).
- Deleting an existing task (enter the code D).

CHANGE mode in reality refers to both adding a new or changing an existing text on the system. When invoking a tutorial for the first time, a blank panel, like the one shown in FIG. 9-4, appears on the screen.

```
AR81           DEVELOP YOUR OWN HELP SCREEN              09/10/90

   01
   02
   03
   04
   05
   06
   07
   08
   09
   10
   11
   12
   13
   14
   15
   16

   PF1: RETURN TO TUTORIAL MENU   PF3: TO VIEW UPDATE
   PF6: NEXT PAGE   PF7: PREV PAGE
 >>>>>>>>>>>> SYSTEMS OR ERROR MESSAGES <<<<<<<<<<<<<<<<<<<<<<<<
```

9-4 Initial HELP screen for entering text

If no such panel was created earlier, the program is to display the initial layout, allowing you to enter 16 lines of messages per page in a free form. Each line is numbered for your convenience, with the cursor initially positioned in line 01, ready to receive tutorial instructions. Following the two-digit sequence numbers corresponding to each line, the system also allows you to enter a single character designating the color in which a specific line is to appear. The four characters used in this program are:

- W, meaning text appearing in high-intensity, protected white.
- R, meaning text in high-intensity, unprotected red
- B, meaning low-intensity, protected blue
- G, meaning low-intensity, unprotected green.

Since green is the standard default color used in the system, you do not need to specify it to the computer. Rather, you can simply leave it blank. Once the attribute color is defined, you can commence entering the text in a free form within the framework of those sixteen lines. This screen is highlighted in FIG. 9-5.

In order to verify previously entered colors, press PF 3, and each line will appear in the specific color requested. You can continue to enter additional text at this point, pressing PF 3 at your

```
  AR81        DEVELOP YOUR OWN HELP SCREEN              09/10/90

01 R THE CUSTOMER NUMBER IS A FOUR POSITION LONG NUMERIC FIELD.
02 R THIS FIELD IS USED TO REFERENCE ANY DEMOGRAPHIC DATA, I.E.
03 R THE CUSTOMERS FULL ADDRESS, TELEPHONE NUMBER, ACCOUNT NUMBER,
04 R ETC. THIS FIELD IS MANDATORY AND IT CANNOT BE OMITTED.
05
06 W THE PROJECT NUMBER IS A 6 POSITION LONG ALPHANUMERIC FIELD
07 W AND IT IS USED PRIMARILY TO VERIFY AGAINST THE PROJECT MASTER
08 W AND TO RETRIEVE A PARTICULAR PREFIX FOR DETERMINING THE
09 W INVOICE NUMBER. THIS FIELD IS ALSO A MANDATORY DATA COMPONENT.
10
11
12
13
14
15
16
   PF1: RETURN TO TUTORIAL MENU  PF3: TO VIEW UPDATE
   PF6: NEXT PAGE  PF7: PREV PAGE
>>>>>>>>>>>> SYSTEMS OR ERROR MESSAGES <<<<<<<<<<<<<<<<<<<<<<<<
```

9-5 Entering partial text on a tutorial ADD/CHANGE panel

convenience to verify a proper attribute scheme or to make sure
that the format and the color of the text is acceptable to you. To
suggest some standard attribute scheme, use RED to denote critical
instructions, the omission of which can result in an ERROR CONDI-
TION. Use GREEN simply for describing a procedure. Protected or
intensified colors (i.e., BLUE and WHITE) should be used for referencing data from other files (i.e., a name field that is part of the customer master). In any case, these are just some of the suggestions
to emphasize that colors need to be used consistently.

Deleting a line does not refer to deleting a line on the HELP
screen, since this can be done by blanking out a particular line
when in CHANGE mode, or by using the erase (EOF) key. A DELETE
function is selected in order to erase an entire set of tutorial
instructions associated with a particular transaction. To invoke
such a routine, select any task on the screen from 01 through 11
and a "D," denoting a delete operation for a required maintenance
code. As in most standard DELETE transactions, you need to press
PF 3 twice before physically deleting a record. A record, by definition, stands for each line of text that appears on each page.

If you were to press PF 6 (next page routine) at this point, a new
panel containing lines 17 through 32 will appear. Every time you
press PF 6, you will, in fact, create a following page on the HELP file,
provided that such a page is currently not in existence. PF 7
enables you to return to a previously created page. In pressing PF 1,
you can return to a HELP screen directory, which is essentially a
second-level menu function from the main systems directory on.

Assume you are in the middle of entering data on a screen and
you need some assistance in deciding what to do next. To initiate a

HELP function, press PF 3, which will invoke the first page of the associated tutorial panel. If you are satisfied with the text that appears on the first page, you can press the ENTER key to return to the previous panel exactly where you left it. If the information you seek is not on the first page, you can press PF 6 one more time to attain the second or subsequent page as well. Likewise, moving backward on these customized HELP panels only requires you to press PF 7, one page at a time. (Note that a page is equal to 16 lines of text.)

If no tutorials are available for a particular transaction, the message "TUTORIAL HAS NOT BEEN DEVELOPED FOR THIS MODEL" will appear in line 24 of the HELP screen.

Field sensitivity versus page sensitivity

In developing sophisticated, user-driven HELP modules, you might want to employ one of two types of HELP apparatus. These are:

1. A field-sensitive HELP apparatus.
2. A page-sensitive HELP apparatus.

By now you realize that this HELP system is built on the premise that it will be the responsibility of some of the more knowledgeable users to develop and maintain information for the rest of the user community. After all, who is more knowledgeable with a particular customer database, for example, than those in the accounts receivable or customer billing departments?

Field sensitivity is a method that enables the terminal operator to position the cursor on or next to a particular data field and, by pressing a function key, (or the ENTER key, for that matter) invoke an explanation of the use, format and disposition of the field in question). Thus, if you were to position the cursor next to the customer header, a panel similar to the one shown in FIG. 9-6 would be invoked. This panel, as you can see, is totally dedicated to doing one thing—to explain to you all the rules, requirements and references relative to a single data field, such as the customer name. A cursor-sensitive screen requires that you define every cell on your 80 by 24 panel, a total of 1,920 positions for your reference. Once you have invoked this field-related panel, you can BROWSE it in a forward or backward fashion, provided you have sufficient information encompassing more than a single page. To reenter the initial detail screen, all you need to do is press the ENTER key.

A second apparatus is characterized by page sensitivity. In this sort of tutorial environment, your goal is to provide the user with

```
CUSTOMER NAME: THE BROWNLY WALTER INTERNATIONAL CO.

MAXIMUM FIELD LENGTH:    35 POSITIONS
                         ALPHANUMERIC

DISPOSITION:             MANDATORY
                         CANNOT BE LEFT BLANK

MAINTENANCE:             THIS FIELD IS NOT PART OF THE CUSTOMER MASTER.
                         IT IS LOCATED AND MAINTAINED ON A SEPARATE TABLE
                         THAT CAN BE ACCESSED FOR DISPLAY OR CHANGES
                         (INCLUDING A DELETE OPERATION) VIA A CUSTOMER
                         REFERENCE NUMBER.

SCREEN REFERENCE NO:     THIS FIELD OCCURS ON THE FOLLOWING PANELS:
                         AR21, AR72,AR87, AR89, AR90, AR93




    PRESS ENTER TO RETURN TO THE INITIAL SCREEN
    PF6: BROWSE FORWARD    PF7  BROWSE BACKWARD
```

9-6 "Component" screen presented on a data field level and invoked through cursor sensitivity

more generic information in which you might or might not want to deal with data on an individual field level. Page sensitive HELP will enable you to invoke an entire HELP screen, one page at a time, and reference as many as a dozen or so data elements on a concurrent display. It is possible that the information you require resides on a subsequent page, which means you need to scan sometimes two or more pages before finding the requested data. The HELP subsystem described in this chapter relies on this latter technique.

Case study

Figure 9-1 highlights the individual components of our tutorial subsystem and how these components work in unison. Thus, the primary purpose of this module is to provide a vehicle through which you can enter your own explanation of an error. This section also explains countermeasures you can take to correct an error. These procedures are accessed through the HELP subdirectory screen shown in FIG. 9-3

This menu program has access to all the operational pieces in the Billing system, such as an invoice header for the recurring customers, invoice description, invoice distribution and so on. Note that HELP is only available for the ADD and CHANGE transactions because of their relative complexity when used for editing a record and validating a criterion.

When selecting task 04, (Invoice Header for Nonrecurring customers) and a maintenance code, such as a CHANGE, the program takes the transaction identifier of all requested modules (AR21), which is part of the concatenated key necessary to access the ARA81C program. ARA81C, as you'll soon see, is the program that allows you to build a tutorial text for the nonrecurring customer header. This screen, incidentally, was described in FIG. 3-1 in Chapter 3. Once you have pressed ENTER along with the appropriate selection criteria (i.e., 04 and "C"), a blank panel is invoked, displaying line numbers (01 through 16 on the first screen) as depicted in FIG. 9-4.

Note that the maintenance mode does not differentiate between a CHANGE or an ADD transaction type. If you have already developed text for a particular panel, the system is now going to display all that for you using lines or a number of consecutive panels. If no text was developed relating to that screen, the second program, a so-called HELP development program enables you to start building the required tutorial. This screen is shown in FIG. 9-4 and again in FIG. 9-5, reflecting the completion of the first page. The total number of lines available to display tutorial text for a single panel, of course, is limited to 6 pages, representing a total of 96 lines. (This ought to be plenty for all practical purposes.)

In navigating through this program, note that we have consolidated certain EDIT and BROWSE features, which unfortunately happen to substantially complicate program logic. This method of using multiple transaction types was necessary to create a new page in memory simply through browsing, while retaining the capability of maintaining the required text on a line by line basis.

Once you have completed the viewing of a certain panel, you should be able to invoke that panel and request tutorial assistance through PF 3. In doing so, you need to reference a fourth module that is not an integral part of the HELP maintenance scheme, but one that is integrated into the application. This program, which is merely a BROWSE program, accesses the same file you have just created and makes it available for the terminal operator in case there is a question about a certain procedure, an EDIT rule, or a data field. An overview of the HELP maintenance operation is depicted in FIG. 9-7

When pressing PF 3 in FIG. 9-8, the program builds a concatenated key in block 5, where the transaction identifier of a procedure is coupled with an individual line number for reference. Every record on the tutorial file (block 4) is treated as a record, thus six pages of tutorial information might be the result of as many as 96 records on file, or as few as 1.

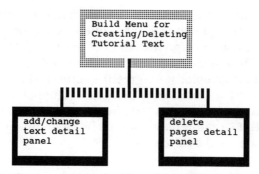

9-7 Components required to maintain a HELP subsystem

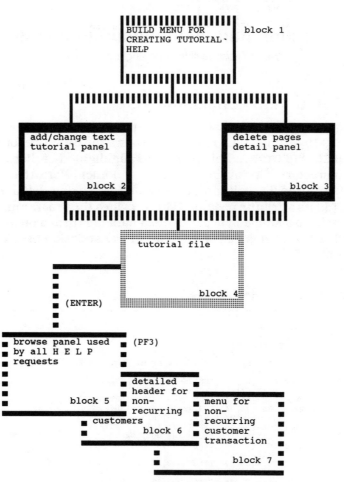

9-8 Interaction between the HELP maintenance module and a specific operational module, such as the header screen for billing nonrecurring customers

Every line on the tutorial files is made up of two data fields (apart from the previously mentioned concatenated key fields). These are: a color designator and the actual tutorial text depicted in FIG. 9-9. The color designators are designed to transform a "standard" data entry color (i.e., green) to one of the additional colors depicted in FIG. 9-9 such as W (white), B (blue) or R (red). When initially defining a line with a specific color, you need to press PF 3 on the initial HELP maintenance screen (view update) to see the actual color scheme used by the system.

trans I.D.	sequenc number	color W/B/ R/G	TUTORIAL TEXT
AR21	01		...in order to access the name field..

9-9 "Cross section" of a single HELP record

FCT and map considerations

The three BMS or Basic Mapping Support definitions are shown in FIGS. 9-10 through 9-12. Figure 9-10 shows the BMS code for the HELP SCREEN DIRECTORY. This panel was highlighted earlier in FIG. 9-3 (subdirectory for invoking a HELP module). Note that the field DUMMY, (line 24, column 79 in FIG. 9-10) is being defined with an FSET in its attribute position. This provides the programmer a vehicle to keep a single byte of modified data tag turned on at all times while this panel is displayed to avoid transmission problems such as a MAPFAIL.

9-10 Basic mapping for the tutorial submenu panel

```
          PRINT NOGEN
ARM80M    DFHMSD   TYPE=&SYSPARM,MODE=INOUT,CTRL=FREEKB,LANG=COBOL,        C
                   TIOAPFX=YES
ARM80M6   DFHMDI   SIZE=(24,80)
          DFHMDF POS=(01,01),LENGTH=04,ATTRB=(BRT,ASKIP),                  C
                   INITIAL='AR80'
          DFHMDF POS=(01,23),LENGTH=35,ATTRB=ASKIP,                        C
                   INITIAL='HELP SCREEN DIRECTORY'
DATE      DFHMDF POS=(01,68),LENGTH=08,ATTRB=(BRT,ASKIP)
          DFHMDF POS=(06,04),LENGTH=19,ATTRB=ASKIP,                        C
                   INITIAL='RECURRING CUSTOMERS'
          DFHMDF POS=(06,36),LENGTH=23,ATTRB=(BRT,ASKIP),                  C
                   INITIAL='NON-RECURRING CUSTOMERS'
          DFHMDF POS=(07,04),LENGTH=02,ATTRB=(ASKIP),                      C
                   INITIAL='01'
          DFHMDF POS=(07,07),LENGTH=20,ATTRB=(BRT,ASKIP),                  C
                   INITIAL='INVOICE HEADER       '
          DFHMDF POS=(07,36),LENGTH=02,ATTRB=(BRT,ASKIP),                  C
                   INITIAL='04'
          DFHMDF POS=(07,39),LENGTH=20,ATTRB=(ASKIP),                      C
                   INITIAL='INVOICE HEADER       '
          DFHMDF POS=(08,04),LENGTH=02,ATTRB=(BRT,ASKIP),                  C
                   INITIAL='02'
```

```
        DFHMDF POS=(08,07),LENGTH=20,ATTRB=(ASKIP),            c
              INITIAL='INVOICE DESCRIPTION'
        DFHMDF POS=(08,36),LENGTH=02,ATTRB=ASKIP,              c
              INITIAL='05'
        DFHMDF POS=(08,39),LENGTH=20,ATTRB=(BRT,ASKIP),        c
              INITIAL='INVOICE DESCRIPTION'
        DFHMDF POS=(09,04),LENGTH=02,ATTRB=ASKIP,              c
              INITIAL='03'
        DFHMDF POS=(09,07),LENGTH=20,ATTRB=(BRT,ASKIP),        c
              INITIAL='INVOICE DISTRIBUTION'
        DFHMDF POS=(09,36),LENGTH=02,ATTRB=(BRT,ASKIP),        c
              INITIAL='06'
        DFHMDF POS=(09,39),LENGTH=20,ATTRB=(ASKIP),            c
              INITIAL='INVOICE DISTRIBUTION'
        DFHMDF POS=(11,04),LENGTH=24,ATTRB=ASKIP,              c
              INITIAL='PROJECT FILE MAINTENANCE'
        DFHMDF POS=(11,36),LENGTH=24,ATTRB=(BRT,ASKIP),        c
              INITIAL='PREFIX TABLE MAINTENANCE'
        DFHMDF POS=(12,04),LENGTH=02,ATTRB=ASKIP,              c
              INITIAL='07'
        DFHMDF POS=(12,07),LENGTH=20,ATTRB=(BRT,ASKIP),        c
              INITIAL='ADD TO PROJECT FILE'

        DFHMDF POS=(12,36),LENGTH=02,ATTRB=(BRT,ASKIP),        c
              INITIAL='09'
        DFHMDF POS=(12,39),LENGTH=20,ATTRB=(ASKIP),            c
              INITIAL='ADD TO PREFIX TABLE'
        DFHMDF POS=(13,04),LENGTH=02,ATTRB=(BRT,ASKIP),        c
              INITIAL='08'
        DFHMDF POS=(13,07),LENGTH=20,ATTRB=ASKIP,              c
              INITIAL='UPDATE PROJECT FILE'
        DFHMDF POS=(13,36),LENGTH=02,ATTRB=ASKIP,              c
              INITIAL='10'
        DFHMDF POS=(13,39),LENGTH=20,ATTRB=(BRT,ASKIP),        c
              INITIAL='UPDATE PREFIX TABLE'
TASK    DFHMDF POS=(17,04),LENGTH=02,ATTRB=(UNPROT,FSET)
        DFHMDF POS=(17,07),LENGTH=01,ATTRB=ASKIP,              c
              INITIAL=' '
        DFHMDF POS=(17,10),LENGTH=22,ATTRB=(BRT,PROT),         c
              INITIAL='ENTER TASK SELECTION  '
        DFHMDF POS=(17,33),LENGTH=01,ATTRB=(BRT,ASKIP),        c
              INITIAL='('
        DFHMDF POS=(17,35),LENGTH=12,ATTRB=ASKIP,              c
              INITIAL='1 THROUGH 10'
        DFHMDF POS=(17,48),LENGTH=01,ATTRB=(BRT,ASKIP),        c
              INITIAL=')'
CODE    DFHMDF POS=(18,04),LENGTH=01,ATTRB=(UNPROT,FSET)
        DFHMDF POS=(18,06),LENGTH=01,ATTRB=ASKIP,              c
              INITIAL=' '
        DFHMDF POS=(18,10),LENGTH=22,ATTRB=ASKIP,              c
              INITIAL='ENTER MAINTENANCE CODE'
        DFHMDF POS=(18,33),LENGTH=01,ATTRB=(ASKIP),            c
              INITIAL='('
        DFHMDF POS=(18,35),LENGTH=17,ATTRB=(BRT,ASKIP),        c
              INITIAL='C=CHANGE D=DELETE'
        DFHMDF POS=(18,53),LENGTH=01,ATTRB=(ASKIP),            c
              INITIAL=')'
        DFHMDF POS=(22,01),LENGTH=25,ATTRB=ASKIP,              c
              INITIAL='PF1: RETURN TO MAIN MENU'
ERMSG   DFHMDF POS=(24,01),LENGTH=77,ATTRB=(BRT,PROT),         c
              INITIAL='                     '
DUMMY   DFHMDF POS=(24,79),LENGTH=1,INITIAL=' ',               c
              ATTRB=(DRK,PROT,FSET)
        DFHMSD TYPE=FINAL
        END
```

9-11 Basic mapping for the CHANGE tutorial CHANGE panel

```
        PRINT NOGEN
ARC81M  DFHMSD  TYPE=&SYSPARM,MODE=INOUT,CTRL=FREEKB,LANG=COBOL,
              TIOAPFX=YES
ARC81M6 DFHMDI  SIZE=(24,80)
TRANS   DFHMDF POS=(01,03),LENGTH=04,ATTRB=(BRT,PROT),
HEDR    DFHMDF POS=(01,18),LENGTH=32,ATTRB=ASKIP,              c
              INITIAL='DEVELOP YOUR OWN HELP SCREEN(S) '
```

```
DATE       DFHMDF POS=(01,60),LENGTH=08,ATTRB=(BRT,PROT),
SEQ1       DFHMDF POS=(05,01),LENGTH=02,ATTRB=(BRT,ASKIP,FSET)
COL1       DFHMDF POS=(05,04),LENGTH=01,ATTRB=(UNPROT,FSET)
           DFHMDF POS=(05,06),LENGTH=01,ATTRB=ASKIP,                       C
              INITIAL=' '
LINE1      DFHMDF POS=(05,08),LENGTH=70,ATTRB=(UNPROT,FSET)
           DFHMDF POS=(05,79),LENGTH=01,INITIAL=' ',ATTRB=ASKIP
SEQ2       DFHMDF POS=(06,01),LENGTH=02,ATTRB=(BRT,ASKIP,FSET)
COL2       DFHMDF POS=(06,04),LENGTH=01,ATTRB=(UNPROT,FSET)
           DFHMDF POS=(06,06),LENGTH=01,ATTRB=ASKIP,                       C
              INITIAL=' '
LINE2      DFHMDF POS=(06,08),LENGTH=70,ATTRB=(UNPROT,FSET)
           DFHMDF POS=(06,79),LENGTH=01,INITIAL=' ',ATTRB=ASKIP
SEQ3       DFHMDF POS=(07,01),LENGTH=02,ATTRB=(BRT,ASKIP,FSET)
COL3       DFHMDF POS=(07,04),LENGTH=01,ATTRB=(UNPROT,FSET)
           DFHMDF POS=(07,06),LENGTH=01,ATTRB=ASKIP,                       C
              INITIAL=' '
LINE3      DFHMDF POS=(07,08),LENGTH=70,ATTRB=(UNPROT,FSET)
           DFHMDF POS=(07,79),LENGTH=01,INITIAL=' ',ATTRB=ASKIP
SEQ4       DFHMDF POS=(08,01),LENGTH=02,ATTRB=(BRT,ASKIP,FSET)
COL4       DFHMDF POS=(08,04),LENGTH=01,ATTRB=(UNPROT,FSET)
           DFHMDF POS=(08,06),LENGTH=01,ATTRB=ASKIP,                       C
              INITIAL=' '
LINE4      DFHMDF POS=(08,08),LENGTH=70,ATTRB=(UNPROT,FSET)
           DFHMDF POS=(08,79),LENGTH=01,INITIAL=' ',ATTRB=ASKIP
SEQ5       DFHMDF POS=(09,01),LENGTH=02,ATTRB=(BRT,ASKIP,FSET)
COL5       DFHMDF POS=(09,04),LENGTH=01,ATTRB=(UNPROT,FSET)
           DFHMDF POS=(09,06),LENGTH=01,ATTRB=ASKIP,                       C
              INITIAL=' '
LINE5      DFHMDF POS=(09,08),LENGTH=70,ATTRB=(UNPROT,FSET)
           DFHMDF POS=(09,79),LENGTH=01,INITIAL=' ',ATTRB=ASKIP
SEQ6       DFHMDF POS=(10,01),LENGTH=02,ATTRB=(BRT,ASKIP,FSET)
COL6       DFHMDF POS=(10,04),LENGTH=01,ATTRB=(UNPROT,FSET)
           DFHMDF POS=(10,06),LENGTH=01,ATTRB=ASKIP,                       C
              INITIAL=' '
LINE6      DFHMDF POS=(10,08),LENGTH=70,ATTRB=(UNPROT,FSET)
           DFHMDF POS=(10,79),LENGTH=01,INITIAL=' ',ATTRB=ASKIP
SEQ7       DFHMDF POS=(11,01),LENGTH=02,ATTRB=(BRT,ASKIP,FSET)
COL7       DFHMDF POS=(11,04),LENGTH=01,ATTRB=(UNPROT,FSET)
           DFHMDF POS=(11,06),LENGTH=01,ATTRB=ASKIP,                       C
              INITIAL=' '
LINE7      DFHMDF POS=(11,08),LENGTH=70,ATTRB=(UNPROT,FSET)
           DFHMDF POS=(11,79),LENGTH=01,INITIAL=' ',ATTRB=ASKIP
SEQ8       DFHMDF POS=(12,01),LENGTH=02,ATTRB=(BRT,ASKIP,FSET)
COL8       DFHMDF POS=(12,04),LENGTH=01,ATTRB=(UNPROT,FSET)
           DFHMDF POS=(12,06),LENGTH=01,ATTRB=ASKIP,                       C
              INITIAL=' '
LINE8      DFHMDF POS=(12,08),LENGTH=70,ATTRB=(UNPROT,FSET)
           DFHMDF POS=(12,79),LENGTH=01,INITIAL=' ',ATTRB=ASKIP
SEQ9       DFHMDF POS=(13,01),LENGTH=02,ATTRB=(BRT,ASKIP,FSET)
COL9       DFHMDF POS=(13,04),LENGTH=01,ATTRB=(UNPROT,FSET)
           DFHMDF POS=(13,06),LENGTH=01,ATTRB=ASKIP,                       C
              INITIAL=' '
LINE9      DFHMDF POS=(13,08),LENGTH=70,ATTRB=(UNPROT,FSET)
           DFHMDF POS=(13,79),LENGTH=01,INITIAL=' ',ATTRB=ASKIP
SEQ10      DFHMDF POS=(14,01),LENGTH=02,ATTRB=(BRT,ASKIP,FSET)
COL10      DFHMDF POS=(14,04),LENGTH=01,ATTRB=(UNPROT,FSET)
           DFHMDF POS=(14,06),LENGTH=01,ATTRB=ASKIP,                       C
              INITIAL=' '
LINE10     DFHMDF POS=(14,08),LENGTH=70,ATTRB=(UNPROT,FSET)
           DFHMDF POS=(14,79),LENGTH=01,INITIAL=' ',ATTRB=ASKIP
SEQ11      DFHMDF POS=(15,01),LENGTH=02,ATTRB=(BRT,ASKIP,FSET)
COL11      DFHMDF POS=(15,04),LENGTH=01,ATTRB=(UNPROT,FSET)
           DFHMDF POS=(15,06),LENGTH=01,ATTRB=ASKIP,                       C
              INITIAL=' '
LINE11     DFHMDF POS=(15,08),LENGTH=70,ATTRB=(UNPROT,FSET)
           DFHMDF POS=(15,79),LENGTH=01,INITIAL=' ',ATTRB=ASKIP
SEQ12      DFHMDF POS=(16,01),LENGTH=02,ATTRB=(BRT,ASKIP,FSET)
COL12      DFHMDF POS=(16,04),LENGTH=01,ATTRB=(UNPROT,FSET)
           DFHMDF POS=(16,06),LENGTH=01,ATTRB=ASKIP,                       C
              INITIAL=' '
LINE12     DFHMDF POS=(16,08),LENGTH=70,ATTRB=(UNPROT,FSET)
           DFHMDF POS=(16,79),LENGTH=01,INITIAL=' ',ATTRB=ASKIP
SEQ13      DFHMDF POS=(17,01),LENGTH=02,ATTRB=(BRT,ASKIP,FSET)
COL13      DFHMDF POS=(17,04),LENGTH=01,ATTRB=(UNPROT,FSET)
           DFHMDF POS=(17,06),LENGTH=01,ATTRB=ASKIP,                       C
              INITIAL=' '
```

```
LINE13    DFHMDF POS=(17,08),LENGTH=70,ATTRB=(UNPROT,FSET)
          DFHMDF POS=(17,79),LENGTH=01,INITIAL=' ',ATTRB=ASKIP
SEQ14     DFHMDF POS=(18,01),LENGTH=02,ATTRB=(BRT,ASKIP,FSET)
COL14     DFHMDF POS=(18,04),LENGTH=01,ATTRB=(UNPROT,FSET)
          DFHMDF POS=(18,06),LENGTH=01,ATTRB=ASKIP,                 C
             INITIAL=' '
LINE14    DFHMDF POS=(18,08),LENGTH=70,ATTRB=(UNPROT,FSET)
          DFHMDF POS=(18,79),LENGTH=01,INITIAL=' ',ATTRB=ASKIP
SEQ15     DFHMDF POS=(19,01),LENGTH=02,ATTRB=(BRT,ASKIP,FSET)
COL15     DFHMDF POS=(19,04),LENGTH=01,ATTRB=(UNPROT,FSET)
          DFHMDF POS=(19,06),LENGTH=01,ATTRB=ASKIP,                 C
             INITIAL=' '
LINE15    DFHMDF POS=(19,08),LENGTH=70,ATTRB=(UNPROT,FSET)
          DFHMDF POS=(19,79),LENGTH=01,INITIAL=' ',ATTRB=ASKIP
SEQ16     DFHMDF POS=(20,01),LENGTH=02,ATTRB=(BRT,ASKIP,FSET)
COL16     DFHMDF POS=(20,04),LENGTH=01,ATTRB=(UNPROT,FSET)
          DFHMDF POS=(20,06),LENGTH=01,ATTRB=ASKIP,                 C
             INITIAL=' '
LINE16    DFHMDF POS=(20,08),LENGTH=70,ATTRB=(UNPROT,FSET)
          DFHMDF POS=(20,79),LENGTH=01,INITIAL=' ',ATTRB=ASKIP
          DFHMDF POS=(22,02),LENGTH=28,ATTRB=(BRT,ASKIP),          C
             INITIAL='PF1: RETURN TO TUTORIAL MENU'
PFK       DFHMDF POS=(22,36),LENGTH=19,ATTRB=ASKIP,                C
             INITIAL='PF3: TO VIEW UPDATE'
          DFHMDF POS=(23,02),LENGTH=28,ATTRB=ASKIP,                C
             INITIAL='PF7: NEXT PAGE              '
          DFHMDF POS=(23,36),LENGTH=19,ATTRB=(BRT,ASKIP),          C
             INITIAL='PF8: PREVIOUS PAGE'
ERMSG     DFHMDF POS=(24,05),LENGTH=60,ATTRB=(BRT,ASKIP)
          DFHMSD TYPE=FINAL
          END
```

9-12 Basic mapping for the tutorial DELETE panel

```
          PRINT NOGEN
ARD82M    DFHMSD  TYPE=&SYSPARM,MODE=INOUT,CTRL=FREEKB,LANG=COBOL,   C
             TIOAPFX=YES
ARD82M6   DFHMDI   SIZE=(24,80)
TRANS     DFHMDF POS=(01,03),LENGTH=04,ATTRB=(BRT,PROT),            C
             INITIAL='AR82'
          DFHMDF POS=(01,18),LENGTH=32,ATTRB=(ASKIP,FSET),         C
             INITIAL='DELETE YOUR OWN HELP SCREEN(S)'
DATE      DFHMDF POS=(01,60),LENGTH=08,ATTRB=(BRT,PROT),
SEQ1      DFHMDF POS=(05,01),LENGTH=02,ATTRB=ASKIP
LINE1     DFHMDF POS=(05,06),LENGTH=70,ATTRB=(BRT,ASKIP)
          DFHMDF POS=(05,77),LENGTH=01,INITIAL=' ',ATTRB=ASKIP
SEQ2      DFHMDF POS=(06,01),LENGTH=02,ATTRB=(BRT,ASKIP)
LINE2     DFHMDF POS=(06,06),LENGTH=70,ATTRB=ASKIP
          DFHMDF POS=(06,77),LENGTH=01,INITIAL=' ',ATTRB=ASKIP
SEQ3      DFHMDF POS=(07,01),LENGTH=02,ATTRB=ASKIP
LINE3     DFHMDF POS=(07,06),LENGTH=70,ATTRB=(BRT,ASKIP)
          DFHMDF POS=(07,77),LENGTH=01,INITIAL=' ',ATTRB=ASKIP
SEQ4      DFHMDF POS=(08,01),LENGTH=02,ATTRB=(BRT,ASKIP)
LINE4     DFHMDF POS=(08,06),LENGTH=70,ATTRB=ASKIP
          DFHMDF POS=(08,77),LENGTH=01,INITIAL=' ',ATTRB=ASKIP
SEQ5      DFHMDF POS=(09,01),LENGTH=02,ATTRB=ASKIP
LINE5     DFHMDF POS=(09,06),LENGTH=70,ATTRB=(BRT,ASKIP)
          DFHMDF POS=(09,77),LENGTH=01,INITIAL=' ',ATTRB=ASKIP
SEQ6      DFHMDF POS=(10,01),LENGTH=02,ATTRB=(BRT,ASKIP)
LINE6     DFHMDF POS=(10,06),LENGTH=70,ATTRB=ASKIP
          DFHMDF POS=(10,77),LENGTH=01,INITIAL=' ',ATTRB=ASKIP
SEQ7      DFHMDF POS=(11,01),LENGTH=02,ATTRB=ASKIP
LINE7     DFHMDF POS=(11,06),LENGTH=70,ATTRB=(BRT,ASKIP)
          DFHMDF POS=(11,77),LENGTH=01,INITIAL=' ',ATTRB=ASKIP
SEQ8      DFHMDF POS=(12,01),LENGTH=02,ATTRB=(BRT,ASKIP)
LINE8     DFHMDF POS=(12,06),LENGTH=70,ATTRB=ASKIP
          DFHMDF POS=(12,77),LENGTH=01,INITIAL=' ',ATTRB=ASKIP
SEQ9      DFHMDF POS=(13,01),LENGTH=02,ATTRB=ASKIP
LINE9     DFHMDF POS=(13,06),LENGTH=70,ATTRB=(BRT,ASKIP)
          DFHMDF POS=(13,77),LENGTH=01,INITIAL=' ',ATTRB=ASKIP
SEQ10     DFHMDF POS=(14,01),LENGTH=02,ATTRB=(BRT,ASKIP)
LINE10    DFHMDF POS=(14,06),LENGTH=70,ATTRB=ASKIP
          DFHMDF POS=(14,77),LENGTH=01,INITIAL=' ',ATTRB=ASKIP
SEQ11     DFHMDF POS=(15,01),LENGTH=02,ATTRB=ASKIP
```

9-12 Continued

```
LINE11    DFHMDF POS=(15,06),LENGTH=70,ATTRB=(BRT,ASKIP)
          DFHMDF pos=(15,77),LENGTH=01,INITIAL=' ',ATTRB=ASKIP
EQ12      DFHMDF POS=(16,01),LENGTH=02,ATTRB=(BRT,ASKIP)
LINE12    DFHMDF POS=(16,06),LENGTH=70,ATTRB=ASKIP
          DFHMDF POS=(16,77),LENGTH=01,INITIAL=' ',ATTRB=ASKIP
EQ13      DFHMDF POS=(17,01),LENGTH=02,ATTRB=ASKIP
LINE13    DFHMDF POS=(17,06),LENGTH=70,ATTRB=(BRT,ASKIP)
          DFHMDF POS=(17,77),LENGTH=01,INITIAL=' ',ATTRB=ASKIP
SEQ14     DFHMDF POS=(18,01),LENGTH=02,ATTRB=(BRT,ASKIP)
LINE14    DFHMDF POS=(18,06),LENGTH=70,ATTRB=ASKIP
          DFHMDF POS=(18,77),LENGTH=01,INITIAL=' ',ATTRB=ASKIP
SEQ15     DFHMDF POS=(19,01),LENGTH=02,ATTRB=ASKIP
LINE15    DFHMDF POS=(19,06),LENGTH=70,ATTRB=(BRT,ASKIP)
          DFHMDF POS=(19,77),LENGTH=01,INITIAL=' ',ATTRB=ASKIP
SEQ16     DFHMDF POS=(20,01),LENGTH=02,ATTRB=(BRT,ASKIP)
LINE16    DFHMDF POS=(20,06),LENGTH=70,ATTRB=ASKIP
          DFHMDF POS=(20,77),LENGTH=01,INITIAL=' ',ATTRB=ASKIP
          DFHMDF POS=(23,02),LENGTH=28,ATTRB=(BRT,ASKIP),            C
               INITIAL='PF1: RETURN TO TUTORIAL MENU'
          DFHMDF POS=(23,31),LENGTH=14,ATTRB=ASKIP,                  C
               INITIAL='PF6: NEXT PAGE'
          DFHMDF POS=(23,46),LENGTH=18,ATTRB=(BRT,ASKIP),            C
               INITIAL='PF7: PREVIOUS PAGE'
ERMSG     DFHMDF POS=(24,05),LENGTH=60,ATTRB=(BRT,PROT,FSET)
          DFHMSD TYPE=FINAL
          END
```

The second map, or BMS, is taken from FIGS. 9-4 and 9-5 (DEVELOP YOUR OWN HELP SCREEN). The BMS for FIGS. 9-4 and 9-5 is laid out in FIG. 9-11. Note three fields of primary importance here. These are:

1. A sequence indicator that assigns a physical pointer and reference number to each line.
2. A single position field (i.e., column 1 through 16) that enables you to enter one of four specific colors you want to use to highlight the contents of your message.
3. A message field for the total length of 70 positions.

A third BMS layout is in reference to a DELETE (or "generic" DELETE) panel shown in FIG. 9-12. The only thing that is different about this panel is the missing color indicator, which is nonessential when deleting a set of records.

Source program listing and narrative

While reviewing the HELP Menu program (ARM80C, shown in FIG. 9-13), keep FIG. 9-13 handy for a continuous reference. As shown in FIG. 9-13, paragraph 0000-MAIN (line 21) starts out in a conventional fashion by examining the length of the COMMUNICATIONS AREA before "dumping" its contents into an area in WORKING-STORAGE. This is followed by examining the EIBTRNID for the transaction identifier of the current program. At first, paragraph 0900-START SESSION (line 25) will be executed, since the transaction identifier

```
1    IDENTIFICATION DIVISION.
2    PROGRAM-ID.     ARM80C.
3    DATE-COMPILED. JUNE 13 1990.
4    ENVIRONMENT DIVISION.
5    DATA DIVISION.
6
7    WORKING-STORAGE SECTION.
8    01  COMM-AREA.
9        05  ENTRY-SW            PIC X VALUE '0'.
10           88  INITIAL-ENTRY          VALUE '0'.
11       05  HELP-KEY.
12           10  HELP-TRANS         PIC X(4).
13
14       COPY ARM80M.
15
16   LINKAGE SECTION.
17   01  DFHCOMMAREA         PIC X(5).
18
19   PROCEDURE DIVISION.
20
21   0000-MAIN.
22       IF EIBCALEN > ZERO
23           MOVE DFHCOMMAREA TO COMM-AREA.
24       IF EIBTRNID NOT = 'AR80'
25           GO TO 0900-START-SESSION.
26       EXEC CICS
27           HANDLE AID
28               CLEAR(0100-PF1-EXIT)
29               PF1(0100-PF1-EXIT)
30               ANYKEY(0400-INVALID-KEY)
31       END-EXEC.
32       EXEC CICS
33           RECEIVE MAP('ARM80M6')
34                   MAPSET('ARM80M')
35       END-EXEC
36       GO TO 0300-SELECT-OPTION.
37
38   0100-PF1-EXIT.
39           EXEC CICS
40               XCTL PROGRAM('ARM10C')
41           END-EXEC
42
43   0300-SELECT-OPTION.
44       EXEC CICS
45           HANDLE CONDITION
46               PGMIDERR(0400-PGM-NOT-FOUND)
47       END-EXEC.
48       MOVE ' ' TO ERMSGA.
49       MOVE 'A' TO TASKA CODEA ERMSGA.
50       IF CODEI = 'C' OR 'D'
51           NEXT SENTENCE
52       ELSE
53         GO TO 0400-INVALID-CODE.
54       IF (TASKI = '1 ' OR TASKI = ' 1' OR TASKI = '01')
55           AND (CODEI = 'C')
56           MOVE 'AR41' TO HELP-TRANS
57           EXEC CICS
58               XCTL PROGRAM('ARA81C')
59               COMMAREA(COMM-AREA)
60               LENGTH(5)
61               END-EXEC.
62       IF (TASKI = '1 ' OR TASKI = ' 1' OR TASKI = '01')
63           AND (CODEI = 'D')
64           MOVE 'AR41' TO HELP-TRANS
65           EXEC CICS
66               XCTL PROGRAM('ARD82C')
67               COMMAREA(COMM-AREA)
68               LENGTH(5)
69               END-EXEC.
70       IF (TASKI = '2 ' OR TASKI = ' 2' OR TASKI = '02')
71           AND (CODEI = 'C')
72           MOVE 'AR42' TO HELP-TRANS
73           EXEC CICS
74               XCTL PROGRAM('ARA81C')
```

```
 75                         COMMAREA(COMM-AREA)
 76                         LENGTH(5)
 77                         END-EXEC.
 78          IF (TASKI = '2 ' OR TASKI = ' 2' OR TASKI = '02')
 79              AND (CODEI = 'D')
 80               MOVE 'AR42' TO HELP-TRANS
 81               EXEC CICS
 82                    XCTL PROGRAM('ARD82C')
 83                    COMMAREA(COMM-AREA)
 84                    LENGTH(5)
 85                    END-EXEC.
 86          IF (TASKI = '3 ' OR TASKI = ' 3' OR TASKI = '03')
 87              AND (CODEI = 'C')
 88               MOVE 'AR43' TO HELP-TRANS
 89               EXEC CICS
 90                    XCTL PROGRAM('ARA81C')
 91                    COMMAREA(COMM-AREA)
 92                    LENGTH(5)
 93                    END-EXEC.
 94          IF (TASKI = '3 ' OR TASKI = ' 3' OR TASKI = '03')
 95              AND (CODEI = 'D')
 96               MOVE 'AR43' TO HELP-TRANS
 97               EXEC CICS
 98                    XCTL PROGRAM('ARD82C')
 99                    COMMAREA(COMM-AREA)
100                    LENGTH(5)
101                    END-EXEC.
102          IF (TASKI = '4 ' OR TASKI = ' 4' OR TASKI = '04')
103              AND (CODEI = 'C')
104               MOVE 'AR21' TO HELP-TRANS
105               EXEC CICS
106                    XCTL PROGRAM('ARA81C')
107                    COMMAREA(COMM-AREA)
108                    LENGTH(5)
109                    END-EXEC.
110          IF (TASKI = '4 ' OR TASKI = ' 4' OR TASKI = '04')
111              AND (CODEI = 'D')
112               MOVE 'AR21' TO HELP-TRANS
113               EXEC CICS
114                    XCTL PROGRAM('ARD82C')
115                    COMMAREA(COMM-AREA)
116                    LENGTH(5)
117                    END-EXEC.
118          IF (TASKI = '5 ' OR TASKI = ' 5' OR TASKI = '05')
119              AND (CODEI = 'C')
120               MOVE 'AR22' TO HELP-TRANS
121               EXEC CICS
122                    XCTL PROGRAM('ARA81C')
123                    COMMAREA(COMM-AREA)
124                    LENGTH(5)
125                    END-EXEC.
126          IF (TASKI = '5 ' OR TASKI = ' 5' OR TASKI = '05')
127              AND (CODEI = 'D')
128               MOVE 'AR22' TO HELP-TRANS
129               EXEC CICS
130                    XCTL PROGRAM('ARD82C')
131                    COMMAREA(COMM-AREA)
132                    LENGTH(5)
133                    END-EXEC.
134          IF (TASKI = '6 ' OR TASKI = ' 6' OR TASKI = '06')
135              AND (CODEI = 'C')
136               MOVE 'AR23' TO HELP-TRANS
137               EXEC CICS
138                    XCTL PROGRAM('ARA81C')
139                    COMMAREA(COMM-AREA)
140                    LENGTH(5)
141                    END-EXEC.
142          IF (TASKI = '6 ' OR TASKI = ' 6' OR TASKI = '06')
143              AND (CODEI = 'D')
144               MOVE 'AR23' TO HELP-TRANS
145               EXEC CICS
146                    XCTL PROGRAM('ARD82C')
147                    COMMAREA(COMM-AREA)
148                    LENGTH(5)
149                    END-EXEC.
150          IF (TASKI = '7 ' OR TASKI = ' 7' OR TASKI = '07')
```

```
151              AND (CODEI = 'C')
152              MOVE 'AR61' TO HELP-TRANS
153              EXEC CICS
154                  XCTL PROGRAM('ARA81C')
155                  COMMAREA(COMM-AREA)
156                  LENGTH(5)
157                  END-EXEC.
158          IF (TASKI = '7 ' OR TASKI = ' 7' OR TASKI = '07')
159              AND (CODEI = 'D')
160              MOVE 'AR61' TO HELP-TRANS
161              EXEC CICS
162                  XCTL PROGRAM('ARD82C')
163                  COMMAREA(COMM-AREA)
164                  LENGTH(5)
165                  END-EXEC.
166          IF (TASKI = '8 ' OR TASKI = ' 8' OR TASKI = '08')
167              AND (CODEI = 'C')
168              MOVE 'AR62' TO HELP-TRANS
169              EXEC CICS
170                  XCTL PROGRAM('ARA81C')
171                  COMMAREA(COMM-AREA)
172                  LENGTH(5)
173                  END-EXEC.
174          IF (TASKI = '8 ' OR TASKI = ' 8' OR TASKI = '08')
175              AND (CODEI = 'D')
176              MOVE 'AR62' TO HELP-TRANS
177              EXEC CICS
178                  XCTL PROGRAM('ARD82C')
179                  COMMAREA(COMM-AREA)
180                  LENGTH(5)
181                  END-EXEC.
182          IF (TASKI = '9 ' OR TASKI = ' 9' OR TASKI = '09')
183              AND (CODEI = 'C')
184              MOVE 'AR71' TO HELP-TRANS
185              EXEC CICS
186                  XCTL PROGRAM('ARA81C')
187                  COMMAREA(COMM-AREA)
188                  LENGTH(5)
189                  END-EXEC.
190          IF (TASKI = '9 ' OR TASKI = ' 9' OR TASKI = '09')
191              AND (CODEI = 'D')
192              MOVE 'AR71' TO HELP-TRANS
193              EXEC CICS
194                  XCTL PROGRAM('ARD82C')
195                  COMMAREA(COMM-AREA)
196                  LENGTH(5)
197                  END-EXEC.
198          IF (TASKI = '10') AND (CODEI = 'C')
199              MOVE 'AR72' TO HELP-TRANS
200              EXEC CICS
201                  XCTL PROGRAM('ARA81C')
202                  COMMAREA(COMM-AREA)
203                  LENGTH(5)
204                  END-EXEC.
205          IF (TASKI = '10') AND (CODEI = 'D')
206              MOVE 'AR72' TO HELP-TRANS
207              EXEC CICS
208                  XCTL PROGRAM('ARD82C')
209                  COMMAREA(COMM-AREA)
210                  LENGTH(5)
211                  END-EXEC.
212          IF TASKI = LOW-VALUES OR TASKI = SPACES
213              MOVE -1 TO TASKL
214              MOVE 'I' TO ERMSGA TASKA
215              MOVE 'ENTER TASK' TO ERMSGO
216              GO TO 0910-SEND-MAP-DATAONLY.
217          IF CODEI = LOW-VALUES OR CODEI = SPACES
218              MOVE -1 TO CODEL
219              MOVE 'I' TO ERMSGA CODEA
220              MOVE 'ENTER CODE' TO ERMSGO
221              GO TO 0910-SEND-MAP-DATAONLY.
222
223      0400-INVALID-KEY.
224          MOVE 'I' TO TASKA ERMSGA.
225          MOVE -1 TO TASKL.
226          MOVE 'INVALID TASK SELECTION' TO ERMSGO.
227          GO TO 0910-SEND-MAP-DATAONLY.
```

```
228
229    0400-INVALID-CODE.
230        MOVE 'I' TO CODEA ERMSGA.
231        MOVE -1 TO CODEL.
232        MOVE 'INVALID MAINTENANCE CODE' TO ERMSGO.
233        GO TO 0910-SEND-MAP-DATAONLY.
234
235    0400-PGM-NOT-FOUND.
236        MOVE 'I' TO ERMSGA.
237        MOVE -1 TO TASKL.
238        MOVE 'PROGRAM NOT IN PRODUCTION AT THIS TIME' TO ERMSGO.
239        GO TO 0910-SEND-MAP-DATAONLY.
240
241    0900-START-SESSION.
242        MOVE -1 TO TASKL.
243        MOVE 'ENTER TASK AND MAINTENANCE CODE' TO ERMSGO.
244        MOVE CURRENT-DATE TO DATEO.
245
246    0900-SEND-MAP.
247        EXEC CICS
248                SEND MAP('ARM80M6')
249                     MAPSET('ARM80M')
250                     ERASE
251                     CURSOR
252        END-EXEC.
253        GO TO 0920-RETURN-TRANSID.
254
255    0910-SEND-MAP-DATAONLY.
256        EXEC CICS
257                SEND MAP('ARM80M6')
258                     MAPSET('ARM80M')
259                     DATAONLY
260                     CURSOR
261        END-EXEC.
262        GO TO 0920-RETURN-TRANSID.
263
264    0920-RETURN-TRANSID.
265        EXEC CICS
266            RETURN TRANSID('AR80')
267            COMMAREA(COMM-AREA)
268            LENGTH(5)
269        END-EXEC.
270        STOP RUN. GOBACK.
```

of the current session has not yet been defined to the program through a RETURN statement. Note that 0900-START-SESSION is detailed in line 241 through 244, and it encompasses the initial sending of the map (lines 246 through 253) and a RETURN (lines 264 through 270), triggering the reinvocation of the current (AR80) session.

Once the map is sent (and subsequently received) program logic describes a set of selection criteria beginning in line 43 part of 0300-SELECT-OPTION. Since there are two positions assigned to a TASK number (see FIG. 9-3), the program provides a way for such a field to be entered in a two-position long field. Thus, you can enter a 1 in the first position, while leaving the second position blank or simply by leaving the first position blank and entering 1 in the second position.

Each selection made by the user builds a record using a particular transaction identifier in reference. Thus, when you select task 1 and the maintenance code "C," one or a set of records are to be referenced using the transaction identifier of AR41. Likewise, task 2 relates to a transaction identifier of AR42, task 3 to AR43 and so on. This logic is laid out in lines 43 through 211. (Note that we have not developed a HELP routine for task 11 because of the relative simplicity of the prefix table maintenance operation.)

The following tasks, clearly subroutines, were coded with a number of objectives in mind. As shown in FIG. 9-13, statements 212 through 216 checks the individual task to see if it contains any spaces or low values. If it does, it means that the operator neglected to enter any value in that field, legitimate or illegitimate, thus no further editing will be performed by the program until this is resolved. A same type of code evaluation takes place in line 217 through 220. This time, however, the maintenance code is being checked for spaces or low values.

The invalid key option (line 223 through 227) and the invalid code option (lines 229 through 233) are invoked upon entering erroneous date (i.e., tasks ranging from 1 through 10 and a maintenance code corresponding to a "C" or to a "D").

HELP development

The purpose of this development module was discussed earlier in the case study. Allow me to start my review with the PROCEDURE DIVISION and refer back to the DATA DIVISION, as required. As shown in FIG. 9-14, 000-MAIN opens with a standard inquiry routine (line 78) to verify the contents of the COMMUNICATIONS AREA before moving it to the WORKING-STORAGE area. Afterwards, the EIBTRNID is checked for the presence of the transaction identifier of the current session. If it (AR81) is not available, the session is in its initial stage (i.e., no RETURN was issued so far that would have recorded the new transaction identifier), so the program will branch to 0800-START-SESSION, shown in statements 391 through 429.

9-14 ARA81C

```
1    IDENTIFICATION DIVISION.
2    PROGRAM-ID.      ARA81C.
3    DATE-COMPILED.   JUNE 14 1990.
4    ENVIRONMENT DIVISION.
5    DATA DIVISION.
6    WORKING-STORAGE SECTION.
7    01  COMM-AREA.
8        05  BROWSE-SW               PIC X      VALUE '0'.
9            88  INITIAL-ENTRY                  VALUE '0'.
10           88  BROWSE-FORWARD                 VALUE '7'.
11           88  BROWSE-BACKWARD                VALUE '8'.
12       05  TASK-TRANS              PIC X(4)   VALUE SPACES.
13       05  REC-KEY.
14           10  HELP-TRANS          PIC X(4)   VALUE SPACES.
15           10  HELP-SEQ            PIC X(2).
16       05  FIRST-REC-KEY.
17           10  F-HELP-TRANS        PIC X(4)   VALUE SPACES.
```

```
18               10  F-HELP-SEQ                PIC X(2).
19          05  LAST-REC-KEY.
20               10  L-HELP-TRANS              PIC X(4)  VALUE SPACES.
21               10  L-HELP-SEQ               PIC X(2).
22          05  SAVE-REC-KEY.
23               10  S-HELP-TRANS              PIC X(4)  VALUE SPACES.
24               10  S-HELP-SEQ               PIC X(2).
25          05  RECORD-UPDATED-SW             PIC X     VALUE 'N'.
26               88  RECORD-UPDATED                     VALUE 'Y'.
27          05  ATTRIB-CHANGED-SW             PIC X     VALUE 'N'.
28               88  ATTRIB-CHANGED                     VALUE 'Y'.
29          05  PAGE-NUM                      PIC 9(2).
30          05  PAGE-NUMX REDEFINES PAGE-NUM  PIC X(2).
31          05  LINE-NUM                      PIC 9(2).
32          05  LINE-NUMX REDEFINES LINE-NUM  PIC X(2).
33
34   01  SUB                                  PIC S9(4) COMP SYNC VALUE +0.
35   01  SUB2                                 PIC S9(4) COMP SYNC VALUE +0.
36
37   01  BROWSE-END-SW                        PIC X     VALUE 'N'.
38       88  BROWSE-END                                 VALUE 'Y'.
39
40   01  COLOR-FOUND-SW                       PIC X     VALUE 'N'.
41       88  COLOR-FOUND                                VALUE 'Y'.
42
43   01  HELP-RECORD.                         COPY HELP.
44
45   01  HELPMAP.
46       05  FILLER                           PIC X(12).
47       05  IM-L-TRAN                        PIC S9(4)    COMP.
48       05  IM-A-TRAN                        PIC X.
49       05  IM-D-TRAN                        PIC X(4).
50       05  IM-L-HDR                         PIC S9(4)    COMP.
51       05  IM-A-HDR                         PIC X.
52       05  IM-D-HDR                         PIC X(32).
53       05  IM-L-DATE                        PIC S9(4)    COMP.
54       05  IM-A-DATE                        PIC X.
55       05  IM-D-DATE                        PIC X(8).
56       05  IM-D-OCCURS                      OCCURS 16.
57            10  IM-L-SEQNUM                 PIC S9(4)    COMP.
58            10  IM-A-SEQNUM                 PIC X.
59            10  IM-D-SEQNUM                 PIC X(2).
60            10  IM-L-COLOR                  PIC S9(4)    COMP.
61            10  IM-A-COLOR                  PIC X.
62            10  IM-D-COLOR                  PIC X(1).
63            10  IM-L-TEXT                   PIC S9(4)    COMP.
64            10  IM-A-TEXT                   PIC X.
65            10  IM-D-TEXT                   PIC X(70).
66       05  IM-L-PFMSG                       PIC S9(4)    COMP.
67       05  IM-A-PFMSG                       PIC X.
68       05  IM-D-PFMSG                       PIC X(19).
69       05  IM-L-ERMSG                       PIC S9(4)    COMP.
70       05  IM-A-ERMSG                       PIC X.
71       05  IM-D-ERMSG                       PIC X(60).
72
73   LINKAGE SECTION.
74   01  DFHCOMMAREA                          PIC X(35).
75
76   PROCEDURE DIVISION.
77   0000-MAIN.
78       MOVE DFHCOMMAREA TO COMM-AREA.
79       IF EIBTRNID NOT = 'AR81'
80           GO TO 0800-START-SESSION.
81       EXEC CICS
82           HANDLE AID
83                   CLEAR(0100-RETURN-TO-MENU)
84                   PF1(0100-RETURN-TO-MENU)
85                   PF3(0105-SET-ATTRIBUTES)
86                   PF7(0110-PF7-NEXT-REC)
87                   PF8(0120-PF8-PREV-REC)
88                   ANYKEY(0120-INVALID-KEY)
89       END-EXEC.
90       EXEC CICS
91           RECEIVE MAP('ARC81M6')
92                   MAPSET('ARC81M')
                     INTO(HELPMAP)
```

```
93
94          END-EXEC.
95          GO TO 0910-SEND-MAP-DATAONLY.
96
97   0100-RETURN-TO-MENU.
98          EXEC CICS
99          XCTL PROGRAM('ARM80C')
100         END-EXEC.
101
102  0105-SET-ATTRIBUTES.
103         PERFORM 0540-DISPLAY-ATTRIBUTES
104             VARYING SUB FROM 1 BY 1
105                 UNTIL SUB > 16.
106         MOVE 'Y' TO ATTRIB-CHANGED-SW.
107         GO TO 0910-SEND-MAP-DATAONLY.
108
109  0110-PF7-NEXT-REC.
110         MOVE '7' TO BROWSE-SW.
111         IF ATTRIB-CHANGED
112             MOVE 'HIT PF7 TO UPDATE RECORD AND GO TO NEXT PAGE'
113                 TO IM-D-ERMSG
114             MOVE 'N' TO ATTRIB-CHANGED-SW
115             PERFORM 0560-RESTORE-ATTRIBUTES
116                 VARYING SUB FROM 1 BY 1
117                     UNTIL SUB > 16
118             GO TO 0910-SEND-MAP-DATAONLY.
119         ADD 1 TO PAGE-NUM.
120         IF PAGE-NUM > 6
121             MOVE 6 TO PAGE-NUM
122             GO TO 0720-LAST-UPDATE.
123         GO TO 0700-UPDATE-RECORD.
124
125  0120-PF8-PREV-REC.
126         MOVE '8' TO BROWSE-SW.
127         IF PAGE-NUM > 0
128             SUBTRACT 1 FROM PAGE-NUM
129         ELSE
130             MOVE 1 TO PAGE-NUM
131             GO TO 0605-LAST-PAGE.
132         MOVE FIRST-REC-KEY TO REC-KEY.
133         GO TO 0410-BROWSE-BACKWARD.
134
135  0120-INVALID-KEY.
136         MOVE 'I' TO IM-A-ERMSG.
137         MOVE 'KEY IS NOT FUNCTIONAL IN TUTORIAL MODE'
138             TO IM-D-ERMSG.
139         GO TO 0910-SEND-MAP-DATAONLY.
140
141  0400-BROWSE-FORWARD.
142         EXEC CICS
143             HANDLE CONDITION
144                 NOTFND (0600-WRITE-PAGE)
145                 ENDFILE (0600-WRITE-PAGE)
146         END-EXEC.
147         MOVE '7' TO BROWSE-SW.
148         PERFORM 0500-START-BROWSE.
149         PERFORM 0505-NULL-READ-NEXT.
150         IF BROWSE-END
151             MOVE SAVE-REC-KEY TO LAST-REC-KEY
152             GO TO 0600-WRITE-PAGE.
153         MOVE REC-KEY TO SAVE-REC-KEY.
154         PERFORM 0510-READ-NEXT-RECORD
155             THRU 0510-READ-NEXT-EXIT
156                 VARYING SUB FROM 1 BY 1
157                     UNTIL (SUB > 16) OR (BROWSE-END).
158         IF BROWSE-END
159             MOVE SAVE-REC-KEY TO LAST-REC-KEY
160             GO TO 0600-WRITE-PAGE.
161         GO TO 0910-SEND-MAP-DATAONLY.
162
163  0410-BROWSE-BACKWARD.
164         EXEC CICS
165             HANDLE CONDITION
166                 NOTFND (0605-LAST-PAGE)
167                 ENDFILE (0605-LAST-PAGE)
168         END-EXEC.
169         MOVE '8' TO BROWSE-SW.
```

```
170          PERFORM 0500-START-BROWSE.
171          MOVE 16 TO SUB.
172          PERFORM 0505-NULL-READ-NEXT.
173          IF BROWSE-END
174              GO TO 0605-LAST-PAGE.
175          MOVE REC-KEY TO FIRST-REC-KEY SAVE-REC-KEY.
176          MOVE 16 TO SUB.
177          PERFORM 0515-NULL-READ-PREV.
178          IF BROWSE-END
179              GO TO 0605-LAST-PAGE.
180          MOVE REC-KEY TO FIRST-REC-KEY SAVE-REC-KEY.
181          MOVE 16 TO SUB.
182          PERFORM 0520-READ-PREV-RECORD
183              THRU 0520-READ-PREV-EXIT
184                  UNTIL (SUB = 0) OR (BROWSE-END).
185          IF BROWSE-END
186              GO TO 0605-LAST-PAGE.
187          MOVE REC-KEY TO FIRST-REC-KEY.
188          GO TO 0910-SEND-MAP-DATAONLY.
189
190      0500-START-BROWSE.
191          MOVE ' ' TO IM-D-ERMSG.
192          MOVE 'A' TO IM-A-ERMSG.
193          EXEC CICS
194              STARTBR DATASET ('ARA81C')
195                      RIDFLD (REC-KEY)
196          END-EXEC.
197
198      0505-NULL-READ-NEXT.
199          EXEC CICS
200              READNEXT DATASET ('ARA81C')
201                       INTO (HELP-RECORD)
202                       RIDFLD (REC-KEY)
203          END-EXEC.
204          IF H-TRANS NOT = TASK-TRANS
205              MOVE 'Y' TO BROWSE-END-SW.
206
207      0510-READ-NEXT-RECORD.
208          EXEC CICS
209              READNEXT DATASET ('ARA81C')
210                       INTO (HELP-RECORD)
211                       RIDFLD (REC-KEY)
212          END-EXEC.
213          IF H-TRANS NOT = TASK-TRANS
214              MOVE 'Y' TO BROWSE-END-SW
215              GO TO 0510-READ-NEXT-EXIT.
216          PERFORM 0530-MOVE-DATA-TO-MAP.
217      0510-READ-NEXT-EXIT.
218
219      0515-NULL-READ-PREV.
220          EXEC CICS
221              READPREV DATASET('ARA81C')
222                       INTO (HELP-RECORD)
223                       RIDFLD (REC-KEY)
224          END-EXEC.
225          IF H-TRANS NOT = TASK-TRANS
226              MOVE 'Y' TO BROWSE-END-SW.
227
228      0520-READ-PREV-RECORD.
229          EXEC CICS
230              READPREV DATASET('ARA81C')
231                       INTO (HELP-RECORD)
232                       RIDFLD (REC-KEY)
233          END-EXEC.
234          IF H-TRANS NOT = TASK-TRANS
235              MOVE 'Y' TO BROWSE-END-SW
236              GO TO 0520-READ-PREV-EXIT.
237          PERFORM 0530-MOVE-DATA-TO-MAP.
238      0520-READ-PREV-EXIT.
239
240      0530-MOVE-DATA-TO-MAP.
241          IF SUB = 1
242              MOVE REC-KEY TO FIRST-REC-KEY.
243          IF SUB = 16
244              MOVE REC-KEY TO LAST-REC-KEY.
245          MOVE REC-KEY TO SAVE-REC-KEY.
```

```
246          MOVE H-MSG TO IM-D-TEXT(SUB).
247          MOVE H-SEQ TO IM-D-SEQNUM(SUB) LINE-NUMX.
248          MOVE H-COLOR TO IM-D-COLOR(SUB).
249          IF BROWSE-BACKWARD
250              SUBTRACT 1 FROM SUB
251          ELSE
252              MOVE H-SEQ TO LINE-NUMX.
253
254
255      0540-DISPLAY-ATTRIBUTES.
256          IF IM-D-COLOR(SUB) = 'R'
257              MOVE 'I' TO IM-A-TEXT(SUB)
258          ELSE IF IM-D-COLOR(SUB) = 'G'
259              MOVE 'A' TO IM-A-TEXT(SUB)
260          ELSE IF IM-D-COLOR(SUB) = 'W'
261              MOVE 'Y' TO IM-A-TEXT(SUB)
262          ELSE IF IM-D-COLOR(SUB) = 'B'
263              MOVE '-' TO IM-A-TEXT(SUB)
264          ELSE
265              COMPUTE SUB2 = SUB - 1
266              PERFORM 0545-CHECK-COLOR UNTIL
267                  COLOR-FOUND OR SUB2 = 0.
268          MOVE 'N' TO COLOR-FOUND-SW.
269
270      0545-CHECK-COLOR.
271          IF IM-D-TEXT(SUB) = SPACES OR LOW-VALUES
272              MOVE 'Y' TO COLOR-FOUND-SW
273          ELSE
274              PERFORM 0550-FIND-COLOR.
275
276      0550-FIND-COLOR.
277          IF IM-D-COLOR(SUB2) = 'R' OR 'W' OR 'B'
278              MOVE IM-D-COLOR(SUB2) TO IM-D-COLOR(SUB)
279              PERFORM 0555-SET-COLOR
280          ELSE
281              SUBTRACT 1 FROM SUB2.
282
283      0555-SET-COLOR.
284          IF IM-D-COLOR(SUB) = 'R'
285              MOVE 'I' TO IM-A-TEXT(SUB)
286          ELSE IF IM-D-COLOR(SUB) = 'G'
287              MOVE 'A' TO IM-A-TEXT(SUB)
288          ELSE IF IM-D-COLOR(SUB) = 'W'
289              MOVE 'Y' TO IM-A-TEXT(SUB)
290          ELSE IF IM-D-COLOR(SUB) = 'B'
291              MOVE '-' TO IM-A-TEXT(SUB).
292          MOVE 'Y' TO COLOR-FOUND-SW.
293
294      0560-RESTORE-ATTRIBUTES.
295          MOVE 'A' TO IM-A-TEXT(SUB).
296
297      0600-WRITE-PAGE.
298          IF NOT INITIAL-ENTRY
299              EXEC CICS
300                  ENDBR DATASET ('ARA81C')
301              END-EXEC.
302          IF BROWSE-FORWARD OR INITIAL-ENTRY
303              IF PAGE-NUM < 7
304                  MOVE TASK-TRANS TO HELP-TRANS
305                  MOVE SPACES TO HELP-SEQ
306                  EXEC CICS
307                      UNLOCK DATASET ('ARA81C')
308                  END-EXEC
309                  PERFORM 0820-CREATE-HELP-RECS
310                      VARYING SUB FROM 1 BY 1
311                          UNTIL SUB > 16
312                  GO TO 0900-SEND-MAP.
313
314      0605-LAST-PAGE.
315          IF BROWSE-FORWARD
316              MOVE SAVE-REC-KEY TO LAST-REC-KEY
317              MOVE 'THIS IS THE END OF THE FILE' TO IM-D-ERMSG.
318          IF BROWSE-BACKWARD
319              MOVE SAVE-REC-KEY TO FIRST-REC-KEY
320              MOVE 'THIS IS THE START OF THE FILE' TO IM-D-ERMSG.
321          MOVE 'I' TO IM-A-ERMSG.
322          GO TO 0910-SEND-MAP-DATAONLY.
323
```

```
324    0700-UPDATE-RECORD.
325        EXEC CICS
326            HANDLE CONDITION
327                    NOTFND (0710-UPDATE-OVER)
328                    ENDFILE (0710-UPDATE-OVER)
329        END-EXEC.
330        MOVE TASK-TRANS TO HELP-TRANS.
331        PERFORM 0710-UPDATE-RECORD THRU 0710-UPDATE-OVER
332        VARYING SUB FROM 1 BY 1 UNTIL
333            (RECORD-UPDATED) OR (SUB > 16).
334        MOVE 'RECORD UPFDATED HERE IS NEXT PAGE'
335            TO IM-D-ERMSG.
336        MOVE 'N' TO RECORD-UPDATED-SW.
337        MOVE 'A' TO IM-A-ERMSG.
338        MOVE LAST-REC-KEY TO REC-KEY.
339        GO TO 0400-BROWSE-FORWARD.
340    0710-UPDATE-RECORD.
341        IF IM-D-SEQNUM(SUB) NOT NUMERIC
342            MOVE 'Y' TO RECORD-UPDATED-SW
343            GO TO 0710-UPDATE-OVER.
344        MOVE IM-D-SEQNUM(SUB) TO HELP-SEQ.
345        EXEC CICS
346            READ DATASET ('ARA81C')
347                    INTO (HELP-RECORD)
348                    RIDFLD (REC-KEY)
349                    UPDATE
350        END-EXEC.
351        MOVE IM-D-TEXT(SUB) TO H-MSG.
352        MOVE IM-D-COLOR(SUB) TO H-COLOR.
353        EXEC CICS
354            REWRITE DATASET ('ARA81C')
355                    FROM (HELP-RECORD)
356        END-EXEC.
357    0710-UPDATE-OVER.
358
359    0720-LAST-UPDATE.
360        EXEC CICS
361            HANDLE CONDITION
362                    NOTFND (0740-UPDATE-END)
363                    ENDFILE (0740-UPDATE-END)
364        END-EXEC.
365        MOVE TASK-TRANS TO HELP-TRANS.
366        PERFORM 0730-UPDATE-LAST THRU 0740-UPDATE-END
367        VARYING SUB FROM 1 BY 1 UNTIL
368            (RECORD-UPDATED) OR (SUB > 16).
369        MOVE 'N' TO RECORD-UPDATED-SW.
370        MOVE 'A' TO IM-A-ERMSG.
371        GO TO 0605-LAST-PAGE.
372    0730-UPDATE-LAST.
373        IF IM-D-SEQNUM(SUB) NOT NUMERIC
374            MOVE 'Y' TO RECORD-UPDATED-SW
375            GO TO 0710-UPDATE-OVER.
376        MOVE IM-D-SEQNUM(SUB) TO HELP-SEQ.
377        EXEC CICS
378            READ DATASET ('ARA81C')
379                    INTO (HELP-RECORD)
380                    RIDFLD (REC-KEY)
381                    UPDATE
382        END-EXEC.
383        MOVE IM-D-TEXT(SUB) TO H-MSG.
384        MOVE IM-D-COLOR(SUB) TO H-COLOR.
385        EXEC CICS
386            REWRITE DATASET ('ARA81C')
387                    FROM (HELP-RECORD)
388        END-EXEC.
389    0740-UPDATE-END.
390
391    0800-START-SESSION.
392        EXEC CICS
393            HANDLE CONDITION
394                    NOTFND (0600-WRITE-PAGE)
395                    ENDFILE (0600-WRITE-PAGE)
396        END-EXEC.
397        EXEC CICS
398            UNLOCK DATASET ('ARA81C')
399        END-EXEC.
```

```
400        MOVE 'AR81' TO IM-D-TRAN.
401        MOVE CURRENT-DATE TO IM-D-DATE.
402        MOVE 1 TO PAGE-NUM.
403        MOVE 0 TO LINE-NUM.
404        MOVE '0' TO BROWSE-SW.
405        MOVE TASK-TRANS TO HELP-TRANS F-HELP-TRANS.
406        MOVE SPACES TO HELP-SEQ.
407        PERFORM 0500-START-BROWSE.
408        PERFORM 0510-READ-NEXT-RECORD
409            THRU 0510-READ-NEXT-EXIT
410                VARYING SUB FROM 1 BY 1
411                    UNTIL (SUB > 16) OR (BROWSE-END).
412        IF (SUB < 16) AND (BROWSE-END)
413            MOVE 0 TO LINE-NUM
414            EXEC CICS
415                ENDBR DATASET ('ARA81C')
416            END-EXEC
417            EXEC CICS
418                UNLOCK DATASET ('ARA81C')
419            END-EXEC
420            PERFORM 0820-CREATE-HELP-RECS
421                VARYING SUB FROM 1 BY 1
422                    UNTIL SUB > 16.
423        MOVE 16 TO LINE-NUM.
424        MOVE '01' TO F-HELP-SEQ.
425        MOVE REC-KEY TO LAST-REC-KEY.
426        GO TO 0900-SEND-MAP.
427
428    0820-CREATE-HELP-RECS.
429        IF LINE-NUM NOT NUMERIC
430            MOVE 1 TO LINE-NUM.
431        ADD 1 TO LINE-NUM.
432        MOVE SPACES TO IM-D-TEXT(SUB) IM-D-COLOR(SUB).
433        MOVE SPACES TO IM-D-SEQNUM(SUB).
434        MOVE TASK-TRANS TO HELP-TRANS H-TRANS.
435        MOVE LINE-NUMX TO HELP-SEQ H-SEQ IM-D-SEQNUM(SUB).
436        MOVE IM-D-TEXT(SUB) TO H-MSG.
437        MOVE IM-D-COLOR(SUB) TO H-COLOR.
438        EXEC CICS
439            WRITE DATASET ('ARA81C')
440                FROM (HELP-RECORD)
441                RIDFLD(REC-KEY)
442        END-EXEC.
443        IF SUB = 1
444            MOVE REC-KEY TO FIRST-REC-KEY.
445        IF SUB = 16
446            MOVE REC-KEY TO LAST-REC-KEY.
447
448    0900-SEND-MAP.
449        IF NOT INITIAL-ENTRY
450            GO TO 0910-SEND-MAP-DATAONLY.
451        MOVE '7' TO BROWSE-SW.
452        MOVE -1 TO IM-L-COLOR(1).
453        EXEC CICS
454            SEND MAP('ARC81M6')
455                MAPSET('ARC81M')
456                FROM(HELPMAP)
457            ERASE
458            CURSOR
459        END-EXEC.
460        GO TO 0920-RETURN-TRANSID.
461
462    0910-SEND-MAP-DATAONLY.
463        MOVE -1 TO IM-L-COLOR(1).
464        EXEC CICS
465            SEND MAP('ARC81M6')
466                MAPSET('ARC81M')
467                FROM(HELPMAP)
468            DATAONLY
469            CURSOR
470        END-EXEC.
471        GO TO 0920-RETURN-TRANSID.
472
473    0920-RETURN-TRANSID.
474        EXEC CICS
475            RETURN TRANSID('AR81')
476                COMMAREA(COMM-AREA)
477                LENGTH(35)
```

```
478        END-EXEC.
479        STOP RUN.
480        GOBACK.
481
```

If a return has been issued, program logic will continue with statement 81. CLEAR and PF 1 enables the operator to return to the previous subdirectory from which this transaction was invoked in the first place. This logic is related to paragraph 0100-RETURN-TO-MENU, as shown in lines 97 through 100.

PF 3 enables you to view a requested color scheme for each of the 16 lines. This logic is provided in statement 102 through 123. Note that the maximum number of pages accessible to the operator is 6. This number is roughly the limit you can attain using a two-digit line counter at 16 lines a page.

Paragraph 0150-SET-ATTRIBUTES (lines 102 through 123) "colorizes," so to speak, each line of text according to a user specification. This, in turn, triggers a chain of events, the first one of which is paragraph 0540-DISPLAY-ATTRIBUTES. This paragraph (see lines 255 through 274) sets the proper color for each line of text according to what is specified in the line/color indictor field, IM-D-COLOR. Thus, an "R" (short for RED) will result in moving the attribute character "I," (an unprotected, intensified alpha character with its modified data tag turned on) into the IM-A-TEXT portion of the field, while subscripting through 16 lines of data.

Paragraph 0550-FIND-COLOR utilizes a scheme (sub2, meaning a second array routine) to compare current and previous lines for color consistency. For example, if you have used blue for displaying line number 1 by entering the character "B," and if you do not indicate a specific color in entering line number 2, then the second line will also be displayed, utilizing an identical color to that of line number 1.

PF 7 and PF 8 allows you to BROWSE forward and backward by invoking paragraph 0110-PF 7-NEXT-REC and 0120-PF 8-PREV-REC, respectively. Finally, the ANYKEY option is designed to provide a summary routine should you decide to use any other (undefined) function key(s) in the program. This is laid out in paragraph 0210-INVALID-KEY (lines 135 through 139).

After this initial setup, the ARC81M6 map is received, triggering a number of events. Having displayed the initial line number, the cursor stops next to the field that designates the color in which a particular line of text is to appear. This logic is now highlighted in lines 462 through 471. Note that when you subscript the field, IM-L-COLOR, program logic will reference the IM-D-OCCURS subset (lines

57 through 65 in the DATA DIVISION) which describes each one of the 16 lines to be displayed. Let me elaborate on this a bit.

There are essentially three data fields highlighted on each HELP panel. These are a sequence or line number, a color indicator, and the actual (tutorial) text. IM-D-OCCURS utilizes three separate definitions for the same field (very much like typical BMS or Basic Mapping Support definition does) to denote field length (L), field attribute (A), and the display field, as defined in the program. Once the map is set (statement 462), the transaction is reinvoked (lines 473 through 480). The logic involved in browsing forward is initiated in paragraph 0400-BROWSE-FORWARD, (statements 141 through 188) and in a subsequent paragraph, such as 0500-START-BROWSE (lines 190 through 205) and 0510-READ-NEXT-RECORD (lines 207 through 216).

Compiler-generated source code: excerpts

This section briefly reviews the compiler version of the HELP Development program, since the DELETE is part of that program. As shown in FIG. 9-15, the COMMUNICATIONS AREA is laid out in the WORKING-STORAGE SECTION in statements 0005 through 00032. This storage area enables the programmer to monitor forward and backward BROWSE operations, including access to the first or the last record on file. The COMMUNICATIONS AREA is also the mechanism through which updates, page and line control and color (attribute) definitions are provided.

9-15 ARA81C compiler version

```
00001      IDENTIFICATION DIVISION.
00002      PROGRAM-ID.      ARA81C.
00003      DATE-COMPILED. JUN 15,1990.
00004      ENVIRONMENT DIVISION.
00005      DATA DIVISION.
00006      WORKING-STORAGE SECTION.
00007      01  COMM-AREA.
00008          05  BROWSE-SW              PIC X      VALUE '0'.
00009              88  INITIAL-ENTRY                 VALUE '0'.
00010              88  BROWSE-FORWARD                VALUE '7'.
00011              88  BROWSE-BACKWARD               VALUE '8'.
00012          05  TASK-TRANS            PIC X(4)    VALUE SPACES.
00013          05  REC-KEY.
00014              10  HELP-TRANS        PIC X(4)    VALUE SPACES.
00015              10  HELP-SEQ          PIC X(2).
00016          05  FIRST-REC-KEY.
00017              10  F-HELP-TRANS      PIC X(4)    VALUE SPACES.
00018              10  F-HELP-SEQ        PIC X(2).
00019          05  LAST-REC-KEY.
00020              10  L-HELP-TRANS      PIC X(4)    VALUE SPACES.
00021              10  L-HELP-SEQ        PIC X(2).
00022          05  SAVE-REC-KEY.
00023              10  S-HELP-TRANS      PIC X(4)    VALUE SPACES.
00024              10  S-HELP-SEQ        PIC X(2).
00025          05  RECORD-UPDATED-SW    PIC X       VALUE 'N'.
00026              88  RECORD-UPDATED                VALUE 'Y'.
00027          05  ATTRIB-CHANGED-SW    PIC X       VALUE 'N'.
```

```
00028                        88   ATTRIB-CHANGED                        VALUE 'Y'.
00029                   05   PAGE-NUM                      PIC 9(2).
00030                   05   PAGE-NUMX REDEFINES PAGE-NUM  PIC X(2).
00031                   05   LINE-NUM                      PIC 9(2).
00032                   05   LINE-NUMX REDEFINES LINE-NUM  PIC X(2).
00033
00034        01   SUB                      PIC S9(4) COMP SYNC VALUE +0
00035        01   SUB2                     PIC S9(4) COMP SYNC VALUE +0
00036
00037        01   BROWSE-END-SW                 PIC X       VALUE 'N'.
00038             88   BROWSE-END                           VALUE 'Y'.
00039
00040        01   COLOR-FOUND-SW                PIC X       VALUE 'N'.
00041             88   COLOR-FOUND                          VALUE 'Y'.
00042
00043        01   HELP-RECORD.
00044                                          COPY HELP.
00045 C   ***** HELP THE TUTORIAL RECORD
00046 C         05   HELP-KEY.
00047 C              10   H-TRANS            PIC X(4).
00048 C              10   H-SEQ              PIC X(2).
00049 C         05   H-COLOR                 PIC X.
00050 C         05   H-MSG                   PIC X(70).
00051 C         05   FILLER                  PIC X(3).
00052
00053        01   HELPMAP.
00054             05   FILLER                 PIC X(12).
00055             05   IM-L-TRAN              PIC S9(4)    COMP.
00056             05   IM-A-TRAN              PIC X.
00057             05   IM-D-TRAN              PIC X(4).
00058             05   IM-L-HDR               PIC S9(4)    COMP.
00059             05   IM-A-HDR               PIC X.
00060             05   IM-D-HDR               PIC X(32).
00061             05   IM-L-DATE              PIC S9(4)    COMP.
00062             05   IM-A-DATE              PIC X.
00063             05   IM-D-DATE              PIC X(8).
00064             05   IM-D-OCCURS            OCCURS 16.
00065                  10   IM-L-SEQNUM       PIC S9(4)    COMP.
00066                  10   IM-A-SEQNUM       PIC X.
00067                  10   IM-D-SEQNUM       PIC X(2).
00068                  10   IM-L-COLOR        PIC S9(4)    COMP.
00069                  10   IM-A-COLOR        PIC X.
00070                  10   IM-D-COLOR        PIC X(1).
00071                  10   IM-L-TEXT         PIC S9(4)    COMP.
00072                  10   IM-A-TEXT         PIC X.
00073                  10   IM-D-TEXT         PIC X(70).
00074             05   IM-L-PFMSG             PIC S9(4)    COMP.
00075             05   IM-A-PFMSG             PIC X.
00076             05   IM-D-PFMSG             PIC X(19).
00077             05   IM-L-ERMSG             PIC S9(4)    COMP.
00078             05   IM-A-ERMSG             PIC X.
00079             05   IM-D-ERMSG             PIC X(60).
00080
00081        01   DFHLDVER PIC X(22) VALUE 'LD TABLE DFHEITAB 210.'.
00082        01   DFHEID0 PICTURE S9(7) COMPUTATIONAL-3 VALUE ZERO.
00083        01   DFHEIB0 PICTURE S9(4) COMPUTATIONAL VALUE ZERO.
00084        01   DFHEICB  PICTURE X(8) VALUE IS '        '.
00085
00086        01   DFHEIV16  COMP PIC S9(8).
00087        01   DFHB0041  COMP PIC S9(8).
00088        01   DFHB0042  COMP PIC S9(8).
00089        01   DFHB0043  COMP PIC S9(8).
00090        01   DFHB0044  COMP PIC S9(8).
00091        01   DFHB0045  COMP PIC S9(8).
00092        01   DFHB0046  COMP PIC S9(8).
00093        01   DFHB0047  COMP PIC S9(8).
00094        01   DFHB0048  COMP PIC S9(8).
00095        01   DFHEIV11  COMP PIC S9(4).
00096        01   DFHEIV12  COMP PIC S9(4).
00097        01   DFHEIV13  COMP PIC S9(4).
00098        01   DFHEIV14  COMP PIC S9(4).
00099        01   DFHEIV15  COMP PIC S9(4).
00100        01   DFHB0025  COMP PIC S9(4).
00101        01   DFHEIV5   PIC X(4).
00102        01   DFHEIV6   PIC X(4).
00103        01   DFHEIV17  PIC X(4).
```

```
00104          01   DFHEIV18  PIC X(4).
00105          01   DFHEIV19  PIC X(4).
00106          01   DFHEIV1   PIC X(8).
00107          01   DFHEIV2   PIC X(8).
00108          01   DFHEIV3   PIC X(8).
00109          01   DFHEIV20  PIC X(8).
00110          01   DFHC0084  PIC X(8).
00111          01   DFHC0085  PIC X(8).
00112          01   DFHC0320  PIC X(32).
00113          01   DFHEIV7   PIC X(2).
00114          01   DFHEIV8   PIC X(2).
00115          01   DFHC0022  PIC X(2).
00116          01   DFHC0023  PIC X(2).
00117          01   DFHEIV10  PIC S9(7)  COMP-3.
00118          01   DFHEIV9   PIC X(1).
00119          01   DFHC0011  PIC X(1).
00120          01   DFHEIV4   PIC X(6).
00121          01   DFHC0070  PIC X(7).
00122          01   DFHC0071  PIC X(7).
00123          01   DFHC0440  PIC X(44).
00124          01   DFHDUMMY COMP PIC S9(4).
00125          01   DFHEIV0   PICTURE X(29).
00126          LINKAGE SECTION.
00127          01   DFHEIBLK.
00128          02     EIBTIME  PIC S9(7)  COMP-3.
00129          02     EIBDATE  PIC S9(7)  COMP-3.
00130          02     EIBTRNID PIC X(4).
00131          02     EIBTASKN PIC S9(7)  COMP-3.
00132          02     EIBTRMID PIC X(4).
00133          02     DFHEIGDI COMP PIC S9(4).
00134          02     EIBCPOSN COMP PIC S9(4).
00135          02     EIBCALEN COMP PIC S9(4).
00136          02     EIBAID   PIC X(1).
00137          02     EIBFN    PIC X(2).
00138          02     EIBRCODE PIC X(6).
00139          02     EIBDS    PIC X(8).
00140          02     EIBREQID PIC X(8).
00141          02     EIBRSRCE PIC X(8).
```

The HELP Development program only utilizes a single record layout, which is attained through the system's COPY library. This layout is shown in lines 45 through 51. As you recall, the key is made up of a four-position transaction identifier and a two-position long sequence number. There are two other fields in this record: one representing the color in which a particular message is to appear, and the text of the message.

Data structure highlighted as part of the "HELPMAP" definition is designed to provide heading or title information, plus 16 lines of variable data for a display. Each of these fields are redefined a total of three times to provide length attribute and an overall definition in handling the data. This is laid out in statements 53 through 79.

10
Developing online transient reports

Online transient reporting capabilities are important in a CICS environment for several reasons:

1. Batch reports cannot be submitted without closing and disabling CICS (VSAM) files.
2. Batch reports are inefficient with frequently requested documents, where turnaround time tends to be substantial.

Online reports are usually short ones, a few pages in volume. Some of them do not use sophisticated formatting with headers and other requirements. Actually, most transient reports are designed with a great deal of simplicity in mind. They print in a continuous flow without skipping, and they space only a single line.

The example shown in FIG. 10-1 highlights a fairly extensive report utilizing a two-step mechanism. In step 1, the program creates a report in a transient data queue. The queue contains print images to be extracted by a subsequent program that physically prints from the transient data queue. Printing continues until the entire transient data queue is depleted, based on a predefined trigger level entered in the destination control table (DCT). For example, if you were to define your trigger level as 100, CICS will print in blocks of 100 records each record corresponding to any number of lines of print images. Thus, if you only accumulated 82 records on the transient queue, no action would be taken by CICS until the queue is once again filled up as defined by the initial trigger level.

```
DB01PRT        EQUIPMENT AND MECHANICAL REPORTING           PAGE 1
               DAILY OUT OF SERVICE ON LINE REPORT
               REPORT DATE: 11/01/90      RUN DATE: 12/14/90


      ┌─────────────────────────────────────┐
      │  CARRIER: SOUTHEASTERN               │
      └─────────────────────────────────────┘


      ORIG  TEMP    UNIT#   DATE IN    DATE OUT  REPAIR CODE COMMENT

      CE    SOI 1344   08/30/90   10/09/90     10      TRUCK REPAIR
                                               25      MODIFICATION
                                               21      DIAPHRAM REPAIR
                                               29      UPHOLSTERY REPAIR
                                               31      DOORS
                                               32      PAINT
      CE    SOI 2209   09/27/90   10/31/90     10      TRUCK REPAIR
                                               05      COUPLER REPAIR
                                               24      CLEANING/HEADLINING
                                               25      MODIFICATION
                                               31      DOORS
                                               32      PAINT
      CE    SOI 2400   09/13/90   10/20/90     10      TRUCK REPAIR
                                               21      DIAPHRAM REPAIR
                                               23      GLAZING REPLACEMENT
                                               25      MODIFICATION
                                               29      UPHOLSTERY REPAIR
                                               31      DOORS
      CE        3000   06/12/90               10      TRUCK REPAIR
                                               16      CARBODY REPAIR
                                               24      CLEANING/HEADLINING
      CE        4077   04/21/90   04/31/90     17      AIR SYSTEM REPAIR
```

10-1 Transient data report, the output of the actual print program that reads the transient queue

The destination control table

Using CICS terminology, each transient data queue can be referred to as a destination. Thus, the term destination control table or DCT. There are essentially two types of transient data queues: the first one is called an *extrapartition destination*, and it allows you to use non VSAM datasets regardless of the particular device. The second type of transient queue is called *intrapartition destination*, which is, by far, a more widely used vehicle. This type of destination is used only by tasks that are CICS partition-related.

Figure 10-2 shows entries made in the destination control table associated with the DB01PRT program. In addition to extra-partition and intrapartition destination, I need to talk about indirect destinations. An *indirect destination* enables a transient data queue to be referenced by more than a single destination identifier. Thus, an entry made in the DCT associates a particular queue with one or a number of devices such as an online printer, or a CRT-type terminal.

Consider the diagram and the associated entries in the DCT as shown in FIG. 10-2. A device defined as a CRT in the terminal control table (TCT) (and referred to as LS01) writes print images to a transient data queue for a report presented in FIG. 10-1, LS01 in the DCT is associated with LS16, which is shown as the first printer through

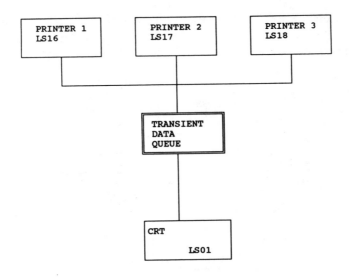

```
LS01   DFHDCT   TYPE=INDIRECT,DESTID=LS01,INDDEST=LS16
LS01   DFHDCT   TYPE=INDIRECT,DESTID=LD01,INDDEST=LS17
LS01   DFHDCT   TYPE=INDIRECT,DESTID=LD01,INDDEST=LS18


LS16   DFHDCT   TYPE=INTRA,DESTID=LS16,DESTFAC=TERMINAL,
                TRANSID=PRT1,TRIGLEV=10,RSL=PUBLIC
LS17   DFHDCT   TYPE=INTRA,DESTID=LS17,DESTFAC=TERMINAL,
                TRANSID=PRT2,TRIGLEV=10,RLS=PUBLIC
LS18   DFHDCT   TYPE=INTRA,DESTID=LS18,DESTFAC=TERMINAL,
                TRANSID=PRT3,TRIGLEV=10,RLS=PUBLIC
```

10-2 Transient data queue and its link with three physical printers

an indirect destination or INDDEST parameter. Likewise, a second entry for LS01 is associated with a second physical printer, as well as with a third such printer referred to as LS17 and LS18 respectively. Note that in those three entries the three satellite printers show a corresponding transaction identifier (i.e., PRT1, PRT2, and PRT3) arranged in an intrapartition destination setting.

Using the indirect destination scheme, you can attach just about any number of physical printers to a transient data queue to give you added capabilities in enhancing your environment. The indirect destination scheme also gives you a great deal of flexibility so that when you need to change an existing configuration, you won't have to do it through the logic of your application program.

Case study

The purpose of this case study is to show you techniques necessary to develop and print a "transient" report triggered in an online environment. Figure 10-3 is an overview of this three-step process. The first step is to invoke a menu program necessary to define the type of transient report you need to generate.

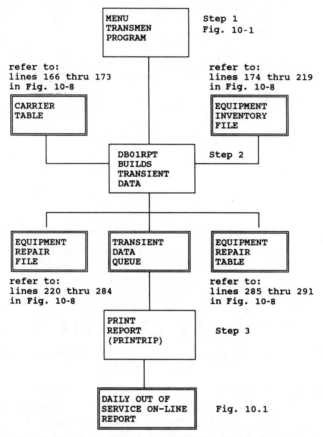

10-3 Transient data flow presented in three logical steps

The menu program enables you to bring up a menu screen such as the one presented in FIG. 10-4, allowing you to make a proper selection. By selecting a valid task from the menu, you are in fact issuing two separate requirements. For example, by entering the character "H" on this panel, you are simply telling the program that:

1. You need a report keyed on the Southeastern Commuter Railway carrier.
2. The report has to be a cumulative, month-to-date report.

```
DB01   TRAIN SCHEDULE PERFORMANCE SYSTEM - OUT OF SERVICE ON-LINE RPTS
       NORTHEASTERN ILLINOIS


       OUT OF SERVICE ON-LINE REPORTS MENU

              A   CENTRAL - DAILY
              B   SOUTHEASTERN - DAILY
              C   SOUTHEAST INDIANA - DAILY
              D   CENTRAL MICHIGAN - DAILY
              E   NORTHEASTERN ILLINOIS - DAILY
              F   ALL CARRIERS-DAILY - DAILY
              G   CENTRAL - MONTHLY - MONTHLY
              H   SOUTHEASTERN - MONTHLY
              I   SOUTHEAST INDIANA - MONTHLY
              J   CENTRAL MICHIGAN - MONTHLY
              K   NORTHEASTERN ILLINOIS - MONTHLY
              L   ALL CARRIERS - MONTHLY

                  OPTION: CHOOSE ONE OF THE ABOVE OPTIONS
               7   /     ENTER DATE (MMDDYY)
       PF1=RETURN TO EQUIPMENT STATUS REPAIR MENU
```

10-4 Shows prior menu selection screen that triggers the transient data processing

Since you are combining month-to-date and daily capabilities
in the same transient program, a report requested on the 10th of
October can represent a report specifically for that day or one
reflecting the month of October to the present.

The menu screen shown in FIG. 10-4 comes into play several
hierarchical levels down from the main systems. Every time a
lower menu selection is triggered, the program utilizes informative
messages passed along the COMMUNICATIONS AREA.

Note that I have standardized a layout for the COMMUNICATIONS
AREA in regards to three elements. These are the carrier, the line,
and an indicator differentiating first and subsequent MAP procedures, as well as differentiating a SEND from a RECEIVE MAP cycle.
Once you have made your selection and pressed ENTER, you have
activated the transient program, shown in step 2, DB01RPT, which
builds the queue for subsequent report generation. DB01RPT utilizes four VSAM files using a KSDS key structure: two of these are
simple look-up tables describing a repair code table and a carrier
code table. The other two are major files representing an Equipment Inventory File and a Repair File. From this data, a temporary
queue is written, which is fed into step 3. As the contents of the
queue are printed, they are promptly erased from the transient
storage until the entire dataset is depleted. This transient report
was initially shown in FIG. 10-1.

A programmer-defined layout of the Equipment Inventory File
extracted from the copy library is shown in lines 174 through 219

in FIG. 10-8. The key to this file is a three-position carrier code and an equipment identification or unit number. This record is 160 positions long.

A second file being read by DB01RPT is a Repair File laid out in lines 220 through 284, in FIG. 10-8. This record is 260 positions long and has a concatenated key that is made up of the following elements: Equipment Identification Number (Unit#), a two-position long Repair Code and a Date field denoting equipment removal from active service for repair.

A third file shown in FIG. 10-3 is the Carrier Table. This table contains a three-position carrier code, which is the sole key, and an associated description field. A layout of this table is presented in lines 166 through 173 of FIG. 10-8.

Finally, an additional table containing all the repair codes is specified in lines 285 through 291. This 40-byte long dataset has the same structure as the carrier table, except that in this instance the key happens to be a two-position long repair code corresponding to a particular description.

A programmer coded map (BMS) layout is described in detail in FIG. 10-5, representing step 1 of the above case study. This panel, by the way, utilizes extended colors. Note that the equipment repair table is only searched if the COMMENT field on the equipment repair master contains blanks or low values. The reason for that is because the user might want to override a standard repair code and description, using his or her own explanation. A simple way of entering a number of different repair codes corresponding to a piece of equipment is by using repair code 99. This code essentially overrides the initial premise, whereby only one repair code at a time can be assigned to an equipment.

10-5 Programmer-coded BMS map

```
        PRINT  NOGEN                                                    TRE10001
*                                                                       TRE10002
DB01MAP DFHMSD TYPE=&SYSPARM,MODE=INOUT,LANG=COBOL,CTRL=(FREEKB),      CTRE10005
               TIOAPFX=YES,EXTATT=YES                                   TRE10006
*                                                                       TRE10007
DB01    DFHMDI SIZE=(24,80),COLUMN=1,LINE=1,JUSTIFY=(LEFT,FIRST)        TRE10010
*                                                                       TRE10011
TRANSID DFHMDF POS=(1,1),LENGTH=4,ATTRB=(PROT),COLOR=YELLOW             TRE10014
        DFHMDF POS=(1,6),LENGTH=35,INITIAL='TRAIN OPERATIONS PERFORMANCCTRE10016
               E SYSTEM',ATTRB=(ASKIP,BRT),HILIGHT=UNDERLINE,COLOR=BLUE TRE10017
        DFHMDF POS=(1,42),LENGTH=28,INITIAL='-OUT OF SERVICE ON-LINE RPCTRE10018
               TS',ATTRB=(ASKIP),HILIGHT=UNDERLINE,COLOR=YELLOW         TRE10019
*                                                                       TRE10020
HDATE   DFHMDF POS=(1,71),LENGTH=8,ATTRB=(PROT,BRT),COLOR=BLUE          TRE10023
        DFHMDF POS=(1,80),LENGTH=1,ATTRB=(ASKIP)                        TRE10024
*                                                                       TRE10025
CARDESC DFHMDF POS=(2,09),LENGTH=35,ATTRB=(PROT),COLOR=PINK             TRE10028
        DFHMDF POS=(2,45),LENGTH=1,ATTRB=(ASKIP)                        TRE10029
*                                                                       TRE10025
LINE    DFHMDF POS=(2,50),LENGTH=15,ATTRB=(PROT,BRT)                    TRE10028
        DFHMDF POS=(2,66),LENGTH=1,ATTRB=(ASKIP)                        TRE10029
*
```

```
                                                                    TRE10032
      DFHMDF POS=(04,15),LENGTH=35,INITIAL='OUT OF SERVICE ON-LINE RECTRE10030
             PORTS MENU',ATTRB=(ASKIP),COLOR=BLUE                    TRE10031
*     DFHMDF POS=(4,57),LENGTH=1,ATTRB=(ASKIP)                       TRE10029
                                                                    TRE10032
      DFHMDF POS=(06,20),LENGTH=02,INITIAL='A ',                   CTRE10030
             ATTRB=(ASKIP),COLOR=YELLOW                             TRE10031
      DFHMDF POS=(06,23),LENGTH=40,INITIAL='CENTRAL               CTRE10030
             DAILY',ATTRB=(ASKIP,BRT),COLOR=BLUE                    TRE10031
*     DFHMDF POS=(06,64),LENGTH=1,ATTRB=(ASKIP)                     TRE10036
                                                                    TRE10032
      DFHMDF POS=(07,20),LENGTH=02,INITIAL='B ',                   CTRE10030
             ATTRB=(ASKIP,BRT),COLOR=BLUE                           TRE10031
      DFHMDF POS=(07,23),LENGTH=40,INITIAL='SOUTHEASTERN          CTRE10030
                 DAILY',ATTRB=(ASKIP),COLOR=YELLOW                  TRE10031
*     DFHMDF POS=(07,64),LENGTH=1,ATTRB=(ASKIP)                     TRE10036
                                                                    TRE10032
      DFHMDF POS=(08,20),LENGTH=02,INITIAL='C ',                   CTRE10030
             ATTRB=(ASKIP),COLOR=YELLOW                             TRE10031
      DFHMDF POS=(08,23),LENGTH=30,INITIAL='SOUTHEAST INDIANA    DCTRE10030
             AILY',ATTRB=(ASKIP,BRT),COLOR=BLUE                     TRE10031
*     DFHMDF POS=(08,54),LENGTH=1,ATTRB=(ASKIP)                     TRE10036
                                                                    TRE10032
      DFHMDF POS=(09,20),LENGTH=02,INITIAL='D ',                   CTRE10030
             ATTRB=(ASKIP,BRT),COLOR=BLUE                           TRE10031
      DFHMDF POS=(09,23),LENGTH=30,INITIAL='CENTRAL MICHIGAN     DCTRE10030
             AILY',ATTRB=(ASKIP),COLOR=YELLOW                       TRE10031
      DFHMDF POS=(09,54),LENGTH=1,ATTRB=(ASKIP)                     TRE10036
                                                                    TRE10032
      DFHMDF POS=(10,20),LENGTH=02,INITIAL='E ',                   CTRE10030
             ATTRB=(ASKIP),COLOR=YELLOW                             TRE10031
      DFHMDF POS=(10,23),LENGTH=30,INITIAL='NORTHEASTERN ILL    DAILCTRE10030
             Y',ATTRB=(ASKIP,BRT),COLOR=BLUE                        TRE10031
      DFHMDF POS=(10,54),LENGTH=1,ATTRB=(ASKIP)                     TRE10036
                                                                    TRE10032
      DFHMDF POS=(11,20),LENGTH=02,INITIAL='F ',                   CTRE10030
             ATTRB=(ASKIP,BRT),COLOR=BLUE                           TRE10031
      DFHMDF POS=(11,23),LENGTH=18,INITIAL='ALL CARRIERS-DAILY',  CTRE10030
             ATTRB=(ASKIP),COLOR=YELLOW                             TRE10031
      DFHMDF POS=(11,48),LENGTH=1,ATTRB=(ASKIP)                     TRE10036
                                                                    TRE10032
      DFHMDF POS=(12,20),LENGTH=02,INITIAL='G ',                   CTRE10030
             ATTRB=(ASKIP),COLOR=YELLOW                             TRE10031
      DFHMDF POS=(12,23),LENGTH=40,INITIAL='CENTRAL              CTRE10030
                 MONTHLY',ATTRB=(ASKIP,BRT),COLOR=BLUE              TRE10031
      DFHMDF POS=(12,64),LENGTH=1,ATTRB=(ASKIP)                     TRE10036
                                                                    TRE10032
      DFHMDF POS=(13,20),LENGTH=02,INITIAL='H ',                   CTRE10030
             ATTRB=(ASKIP,BRT),COLOR=BLUE                           TRE10031
      DFHMDF POS=(13,23),LENGTH=41,INITIAL='SOUTHEASTERN         CTRE10030
             DISTRICT-MONTHLY',ATTRB=(ASKIP),COLOR=YELLOW           TRE10031
      DFHMDF POS=(13,65),LENGTH=1,ATTRB=(ASKIP)                     TRE10036
                                                                    TRE10032
      DFHMDF POS=(14,20),LENGTH=02,INITIAL='I ',                   CTRE10030
             ATTRB=(ASKIP),COLOR=YELLOW                             TRE10031
      DFHMDF POS=(14,23),LENGTH=31,INITIAL='SOUTHEAST INDIANA    MCTRE10030
             ONTHLY',ATTRB=(ASKIP,BRT),COLOR=BLUE                   TRE10031
      DFHMDF POS=(14,55),LENGTH=1,ATTRB=(ASKIP)                     TRE10036
                                                                    TRE10032
      DFHMDF POS=(15,20),LENGTH=02,INITIAL='J ',                   CTRE10030
             ATTRB=(ASKIP,BRT),COLOR=BLUE                           TRE10031
      DFHMDF POS=(15,23),LENGTH=31,INITIAL='CENTRAL MICHIGAN     MCTRE10030
             ONTHLY',ATTRB=(ASKIP),COLOR=YELLOW                     TRE10031
      DFHMDF POS=(15,55),LENGTH=1,ATTRB=(ASKIP)                     TRE10036
                                                                    TRE10032
      DFHMDF POS=(16,20),LENGTH=02,INITIAL='K ',                   CTRE10030
             ATTRB=(ASKIP),COLOR=YELLOW                             TRE10031
      DFHMDF POS=(16,23),LENGTH=30,INITIAL='NORTHEASTERN ILL    MONTCTRE10030
             HLY',ATTRB=(ASKIP,BRT),COLOR=BLUE                      TRE10031
      DFHMDF POS=(16,54),LENGTH=1,ATTRB=(ASKIP)                     TRE10036

      DFHMDF POS=(17,20),LENGTH=02,INITIAL='L ',                   CTRE10030
             ATTRB=(ASKIP,BRT),COLOR=BLUE                           TRE10031
      DFHMDF POS=(17,23),LENGTH=20,INITIAL='ALL CARRIERS-MONTHLY', CTRE10030
             ATTRB=(ASKIP),COLOR=YELLOW                             TRE10031
      DFHMDF POS=(17,48),LENGTH=1,ATTRB=(ASKIP)                     TRE10036
```

```
*                                                                      TRE10032
OPTION  DFHMDF POS=(19,20),LENGTH=01,ATTRB=(UNPROT,IC),COLOR=BLUE       TRE10030
        DFHMDF POS=(19,22),LENGTH=41,INITIAL=' OPTION: CHOOSE ONE OF THCTRE10030
               E ABOVE OPTIONS',ATTRB=(ASKIP),COLOR=YELLOW              TRE10031
*       DFHMDF POS=(19,64),LENGTH=1,ATTRB=(ASKIP)                       TRE10036
*                                                                      TRE10032
DATEMO  DFHMDF POS=(20,20),LENGTH=02,ATTRB=(UNPROT),COLOR=BLUE          TRE10030
        DFHMDF POS=(20,23),LENGTH=1,INITIAL='/',ATTRB=ASKIP            TRE10036
DATEDA  DFHMDF POS=(20,25),LENGTH=02,ATTRB=(UNPROT),COLOR=BLUE          TRE10030
        DFHMDF POS=(20,28),LENGTH=1,INITIAL='/',ATTRB=ASKIP            TRE10036
DATEYR  DFHMDF POS=(20,30),LENGTH=02,ATTRB=(UNPROT),COLOR=BLUE          TRE10030
        DFHMDF POS=(20,33),LENGTH=19,INITIAL='ENTER DATE (MMDDYY)',    CTRE10030
               ATTRB=(ASKIP),COLOR=YELLOW                              TRE10031
        DFHMDF POS=(20,53),LENGTH=1,ATTRB=(ASKIP)                       TRE10036
*                                                                      TRE10032
MSG1    DFHMDF POS=(23,1),LENGTH=75,ATTRB=(PROT,BRT),COLOR=YELLOW       TRE10204
        DFHMDF POS=(23,77),LENGTH=1,ATTRB=(ASKIP)                       TRE10205
*                                                                      TRE10201
MSG2    DFHMDF POS=(24,1),LENGTH=75,ATTRB=(PROT,BRT),COLOR=BLUE         TRE10204
        DFHMDF POS=(24,77),LENGTH=1,ATTRB=(ASKIP)                       TRE10205
*                                                                      TRE10201
DB01MAP DFHMSD TYPE=FINAL                                               TRE10206
        END                                                            TRE10207
```

Once the transient data queue (TD) is built by the DB01RPT program, the information becomes available in step 3 of FIG. 10-3 for a subsequent print routine. Printing is triggered by certain control statements in the destination control table until the entire database is depleted or the trigger level is temporarily exhausted. The actual printout of the third step (PRINTRIP) is illustrated to you in FIG. 10-1.

The purpose of the Daily Out of Service Online report shown in FIG. 10-1 is to show equipment taken out of service for a specific repair job, such as cleaning, headlining, painting, repairing upholstery, and an array of other activities. Figure 10-1 also shows original and temporary carriers, since a piece of equipment owned by Central Railroad, for example, might have to be transferred to Southeastern for certain specialized repair facilities unavailable at Central. Thus, the two dates denote when such an equipment was taken out of service for repair and when repair is expected to be completed. Each work order has one or more associated repair codes that are matched against the repair table for description.

ORIG or original owner refers to the carrier the specific equipment is assigned to. TEMP or temporary facilities tells you where the equipment is being temporarily transferred for the necessary repair. For example, line 1 on the Daily Out of Service Report simply refers to a piece of equipment, such as unit 1344, that was transferred from Central to Southeastern Illinois for any number of repair activities. In the first entry on the "DAILY OUT OF SERVICE ONLINE REPORT," a truck was moved to the Southeastern Illinois workshop on August 30, 1990 to be repaired by no later than October 9. The truck will have a number of repair jobs done: some general and diaphragm repair, miscellaneous engine work, upholstery work, door repair and a paint job. At that point the equipment is to be transferred back to Central, the carrier that has full ownership of the repaired equipment. Note that in the fourth detail line (unit 3000), the equipment does not have a target date for completing the repair, but that information will be supplied sometime in the near future.

Source program listing and narrative

As shown in FIG. 10-6, DB01RPT is the program responsible for creating transient data (TD) that is fed into a separate print program, PRINTRIP. In the case study, I mentioned that there is a standardized approach to the layout of the COMMUNICATIONS AREA. By standardization, I simply mean the presence of certain data fields that are constantly being passed along the path for the purpose of equipment identification and carrier verification.

10-6 DB01RPT

```
 1 IDENTIFICATION DIVISION.
 2 PROGRAM-ID.     DB01RPT.
 3 DATE-COMPILED.
 4
 5 ENVIRONMENT DIVISION.
 6
 7 DATA DIVISION.
 8 WORKING-STORAGE SECTION.
 9 01  SWITCHES.
10     05  EQUIP-EOF-SWPIC X  VALUE 'N'.
11     88  EQUIP-EOF  VALUE 'Y'.
12
13 01  WORK-FIELDS.
14     05  RECORD-COUNT PIC S9(5) VALUE ZERO COMP-3.
15
16 01  COMPARE-AREA.
17     05  MAIN-CARRIER PIC XXX.
18
19 01  COMM-AREA.
20     05  COMM-FLAG.
21         10  PF-KEYS     PIC X     VALUE '0'.
22     05  WS-COMMAREA-OUT.
23         10  COMM-CARRIER     PIC XXX.
24         10  COMM-LINE    PIC XX.
25         10  COMM-DATE.
26             15  COMM-YR    PIC XX   VALUE SPACES.
27             15  COMM-MO    PIC XX   VALUE SPACES.
28             15  COMM-DA    PIC XX   VALUE SPACES.
29
30 01  PRINT-FIELDS.
31     05  LINE-COUNT PIC S99    VALUE 0     COMP-3.
32     05  LINES-ON-PAGE PIC S99    VALUE +43  COMP-3.
33     05  PAGE-NO PIC S999  VALUE +1   COMP-3.
34     88  FIRST-PAGE    VALUE +1.
35     05  PRINT-AREA PIC X(132).
36     05  LINE-LENGTH PIC S9(4)   COMP.
37
38 01  FILE-NOTOPEN-MSG    PIC X(17) VALUE '**FILE NOT OPEN**'.
39 01  ERROR-MSG       PIC X(22) VALUE '**ERROR HAS OCCURED**'.
40 01  HDG-LINE-1.
41     05  FILLER PIC X(6)   VALUE SPACES.
42     05  FILLER PIC X(08)  VALUE 'DB01RPT '.
43     05  FILLER PIC X(24)  VALUE SPACES.
```

```
44      05  FILLER PIC X(17) VALUE 'TRAIN OPERATIONS '.
45      05  FILLER PIC X(18) VALUE 'PERFORMANCE SYSTEM'.
46      05  FILLER PIC X(33) VALUE SPACES.
47      05  FILLER PIC X(5)  VALUE 'PAGE:'.
48      05  HDG-PAGE  PIC ZZZ9.
49      05  FILLER PIC X(17) VALUE SPACES.
50      05  HDG1-CC PIC XX    VALUE '15'.
51 01  HDG-LINE-2.      05  FILLER PIC X(38) VALUE SPACES.
52      05  FILLER PIC X(20) VALUE 'DAILY OUT OF SERVICE'.
53      05  FILLER PIC X(15) VALUE ' ON-LINE REPORT'.
54      05  FILLER PIC X(33) VALUE SPACES.
55      05  FILLER PIC X(10) VALUE 'RUN DATE: '.
56      05  RPT-DATE  PIC X(8).
57      05  FILLER PIC X(08) VALUE SPACES.
58      05  HDG2-CC PIC XX    VALUE '15'.
59
60 01  HDG-LINE-3.
61      05  FILLER PIC X(46) VALUE SPACES.
62      05  FILLER PIC X(13) VALUE 'REPORT DATE: '.
63      05  RE-MO PIC XX.
64      05  FILLER PIC X    VALUE '/'.
65      05  RE-DAPIC XX.
66      05  FILLER PIC X    VALUE '/'.
67      05  RE-YR PIC XX.
68      05  FILLER PIC X(65) VALUE SPACES.
69      05  HDG3-CC PIC XX    VALUE '15'.
70
71 01  HDG-LINE-4.
72      05  FILLER PIC X(9)  VALUE SPACES.
73      05  FILLER PIC X(18) VALUE '+-----------------'.
74      05  FILLER PIC X(18) VALUE '------------------'.
75      05  FILLER PIC X(12) VALUE '-----------+'.
76      05  FILLER PIC X(75) VALUE SPACES.
77      05  HDG4-C PIC XX    VALUE '15'.
78
79 01  HDG-LINE-5.
80      05  FILLER PIC X(9)  VALUE SPACES.
81      05  FILLER PIC X(12) VALUE '] CARRIER: '.
82      05  CARRIER-DESC PIC X(35).
83      05  FILLER PIC X       VALUE ']'.
84      05  FILLER PIC X(75) VALUE SPACES.
85      05  HDG5-CC PIC XX    VALUE '15'.
86
87 01  HDG-LINE-6.
88      05  FILLER PIC X(9)  VALUE SPACES.
89      05  FILLER PIC X(18) VALUE '+-----------------'.
90      05  FILLER PIC X(18) VALUE '------------------'.
91      05  FILLER PIC X(12) VALUE '-----------+'.
92      05  FILLER PIC X(75) VALUE SPACES.
93      05  HDG6-CC PIC XX    VALUE '15'.
94 01  HDG-LINE-7.
95      05  FILLER PIC X(08) VALUE SPACES.
96      05  FILLER PIC X(08) VALUE 'CARRIERS'.
97      05  FILLER PIC X(05) VALUE SPACES.
98      05  FILLER PIC X(04) VALUE 'UNIT'.
99      05  FILLER PIC X(05) VALUE SPACES.
100     05  FILLER PIC X(07) VALUE 'DATE IN'.
101     05  FILLER PIC X(05) VALUE SPACES.
102     05  FILLER PIC X(07) VALUE 'DUE OUT'.
103     05  FILLER PIC X(05) VALUE SPACES.
104     05  FILLER PIC X(11) VALUE 'REPAIR CODE'.
105     05  FILLER PIC X(03) VALUE SPACES.
106     05  FILLER PIC X(07) VALUE 'COMMENT'.
107     05  FILLER PIC X(57) VALUE SPACES.
108     05  HDG7-CC PIC XX    VALUE '15'.
109
110 01  HDG-LINE-8.
111     05  FILLER PIC X(07) VALUE SPACES.
112     05  FILLER PIC X(10) VALUE 'ORIG  TEMP'.
113     05  FILLER PIC X(115) VALUE SPACES.
114     05  HDG8-CC PIC XX    VALUE '15'.
115 01  HDG-LINE-9.
116     05  FILLER PIC X(132) VALUE SPACES.
117     05  HDG9-CC PIC XX    VALUE '15'.
118
```

```
119 01  EQUIP-LINE-1.
120     05  FILLER PIC X(08) VALUE SPACES.
121     05  ORIG-CARRIER PIC XXX.
122     05  FILLER PIC XX    VALUE SPACES.
123     05  TEMP-CARRIER PIC XXX.
124     05  FILLER PIC X(05) VALUE SPACES.
125     05  UNIT-NO PIC XXXX.
126     05  FILLER PIC X(04) VALUE SPACES.
127     05  DATE-IN.
128         10  DATE-IN-MO PIC XX.
129         10  SLASH1 PIC XVALUE '/'.
130         10  DATE-IN-DA PIC XX.
131         10  SLASH1A PIC XVALUE '/'.
132         10  DATE-IN-YR PIC XX.
133     05  FILLER PIC X(04) VALUE SPACES.
134     05  DUE-OUT.
135         10  DUE-OUT-MO PIC XX.
136         10  SLASH2 PIC XVALUE '/'.
137         10  DUE-OUT-DA PIC XX.
138         10  SLASH2A PIC XVALUE '/'.
139         10  DUE-OUT-YR PIC XX.
140     05  FILLER PIC X(09) VALUE SPACES.
141     05  REPAIR-CODE PIC XX.
142     05  FILLER PIC X(08) VALUE SPACES.
143     05  COMMENT PIC X(64).
144     05  EL-CC PIC XX    VALUE SPACES.
145
146 01  EQUIP-LINE-2.
147     05  FILLER PIC X(132) VALUE SPACES.
148     05  EL2-CC PIC XX    VALUE SPACES.
149 01  DESTINATION-ID PIC X(4)    VALUE '    '.
150 01  EOJ-MSG.
151     05  FILLER PIC X(20) VALUE 'DAILY OUT OF SERVICE'.
152     05  FILLER PIC X(09) VALUE ' ON-LINE '.
153     05  FILLER PIC X(14) VALUE 'REPORT PRINTED'.
154     05  FILLER PIC X(05) VALUE SPACES.
155     05  FILLER PIC X(15) VALUE 'PRESS CLEAR KEY'.
156     05  FILLER PIC X(14) VALUE ' TO START OVER'.
157     05  FILLER PIC X(07) VALUE SPACES.
158
159 01  CARRIER-TABLE. COPY CCARRIER.
160 01  EQUIP-REC. COPY CEQUIP.
161 01  REPAIR-REC. COPY CREPAIR.
162 01  EQ-REPAIR-TABLE. COPY CEQREPAR.
163
164
165 LINKAGE SECTION.
166 01  DFHCOMMAREA        PIC X(12).
167 PROCEDURE DIVISION.
168
169 0000-PRODUCE-INCOMPLETE-TRIPS.
170     MOVE DFHCOMMAREA TO COMM-AREA.
171     MOVE COMM-CARRIER TO MAIN-CARRIER.
172     MOVE SPACES TO RE-KEY  EQ-KEY.
173     EXEC CICS HANDLE CONDITION ENDFILE(1100-ENDFILE)
174     END-EXEC.
175     MOVE COMM-CARRIER TO T-CARRIER-CODE.
176     IF COMM-CARRIER NOT = LOW-VALUES AND SPACES
177     PERFORM 2000-READ-CARRIER THRU 2000-CARRIER-END
178                 ELSE
179     MOVE 'ALL CARRIERS' TO CARRIER-DESC.
180     PERFORM 1000-START-EQUIP-BROWSE THRU 1000-BROWSE-EXIT.
181     MOVE EIBTRMID TO DESTINATION-ID.
182         EXEC CICS
183         ENQ RESOURCE(DESTINATION-ID)
184         LENGTH(4)
185         END-EXEC.
186     PERFORM 3000-PRODUCE-EQUIP-LINE
187     UNTIL EQUIP-EOF.
188
189 0000-END-OF-FILE-ROUTINE.
190         EXEC CICS
191         DEQ RESOURCE(DESTINATION-ID)
192         LENGTH(4)
193         END-EXEC.
194         EXEC CICS SEND TEXT FROM (EOJ-MSG)
195         LENGTH(80)
196         ERASE
```

```
197              FREEKB
198           END-EXEC.
199        MOVE 'I' TO PF-KEYS.
200        MOVE MAIN-CARRIER TO COMM-CARRIER.
201              EXEC CICS
202              RETURN TRANSID('DB01')
203              COMMAREA(COMM-AREA)
204              LENGTH(6)
205              END-EXEC.
206
207 1000-START-EQUIP-BROWSE.
208              EXEC CICS
209              HANDLE CONDITION NOTFND(1000-BROWSE-NOTFND)
210              END-EXEC.
211        MOVE LOW-VALUES TO EQ-CARRIER-CODE.
212        MOVE LOW-VALUES TO EQ-UNIT-NO.
213              EXEC CICS
214              STARTBR DATASET('TEQUIP')
215              RIDFLD (EQ-KEY)
216              END-EXEC.
217        GO TO 1000-BROWSE-EXIT.
218
219 1000-BROWSE-NOTFND.
220        MOVE 'Y' TO EQUIP-EOF-SW.
221        GO TO 0000-END-OF-FILE-ROUTINE.
222
223 1000-BROWSE-EXIT.
224        EXIT.
225
226 1100-START-REPAIR-BROWSE.
227              EXEC CICS
228              STARTBR DATASET('TREPAIR')
229              RIDFLD (RE-KEY)
230              END-EXEC.
231        GO TO 1100-END.
232
233 1100-BROWSE-NOTFND.
234        MOVE HIGH-VALUES TO RE-KEY.
235        GO TO 1100-START-REPAIR-BROWSE.
236
237 1100-ENDFILE.
238        MOVE 'Y' TO EQUIP-EOF-SW.
239        GO TO 0000-END-OF-FILE-ROUTINE.
240
241 1100-END.
242        EXIT.
243
244 1200-END-BROWSE-REPAIR.
245              EXEC CICS
246              ENDBR DATASET('TREPAIR')
247              END-EXEC.
248        GO TO 1200-END.
249
250 1200-END.
251        EXIT.
252
253 2000-READ-CARRIER.
254        EXEC CICS READ DATASET('TCARRIER')
255        INTO (CARRIER-TABLE)
256        RIDFLD(T-CARRIER-CODE)
257        END-EXEC.
258        MOVE T-CARRIER-DESC TO CARRIER-DESC.
259        GO TO 2000-CARRIER-END.
260
261 2000-CARRIER-END.
262        EXIT.
263
264 2100-READ-NEXT-EQUIP-REC.
265              EXEC CICS
266              READNEXT DATASET('TEQUIP')
267              INTO (EQUIP-REC)
268              RIDFLD(EQ-KEY)
269              END-EXEC.
270        IF COMM-CARRIER = EQ-CARRIER-CODE OR EQ-TEMP-CARRIER
```

```
271         GO TO 2100-READ-NEXT-END.
272                    ELSE
273         GO TO 3000-PRODUCE-EQUIP-LINE.
274
275 2100-READ-ENDFILE.
276         MOVE 'Y' TO EQUIP-EOF-SW.
277         GO TO 0000-END-OF-FILE-ROUTINE.
278
279 2100-READ-NEXT-END.
280         EXIT.
281
282 2200-READ-NEXT-REPAIR-REC.
283             EXEC CICS
284             HANDLE CONDITION NOTFND(2200-BROWSE-NOTFND)
285             END-EXEC.
286             EXEC CICS
287             READNEXT DATASET('TREPAIR')
288             INTO (REPAIR-REC)
289             RIDFLD(RE-KEY)
290             END-EXEC.
291         GO TO 2200-END.
292
293 2200-BROWSE-NOTFND.
294         PERFORM 1200-END-BROWSE-REPAIR.
295         GO TO 3000-PRODUCE-EQUIP-LINE.
296
297 2200-READ-ENDFILE.
298         MOVE 'Y' TO EQUIP-EOF-SW.
299         GO TO 0000-END-OF-FILE-ROUTINE.
300
301 2200-END.
302         EXIT.
303
304 3000-PRODUCE-EQUIP-LINE.
305         PERFORM 2100-READ-NEXT-EQUIP-REC THRU 2100-READ-NEXT-END.
306         IF EQ-STCND-CODE NOT = 'B' AND 'C' AND 'D' AND
307         'M' AND 'W'
308         GO TO 3000-PRODUCE-EQUIP-LINE
309                    ELSE
310         MOVE EQ-UNIT-NO TO RE-UNIT-NO-X
311         MOVE LOW-VALUES TO RE-EQ-REPAIR-CODE
312         RE-DATE-OUT-SERV-X
313         PERFORM 1100-START-REPAIR-BROWSE THRU 1100-END
314         PERFORM 2200-READ-NEXT-REPAIR-REC THRU 2200-END
315         IF RE-UNIT-NO-X = EQ-UNIT-NO
316         IF RE-EQ-STCND-CODE NOT = 'B' AND 'C' AND 'D'
317         AND 'M' AND 'W'
318         PERFORM 2200-READ-NEXT-REPAIR-REC THRU 2200-END
319         UNTIL (RE-UNIT-NO-X = EQ-UNIT-NO) AND
320         (RE-EQ-STCND-CODE = 'B' OR 'C' OR 'D'
321         OR 'M' OR 'W') AND
322         (RE-DATE-IN-SERV-X = LOW-VALUES OR SPACES)
323         PERFORM 3500-CHECK-OUT-DATE THRU 3500-END
324         PERFORM 1200-END-BROWSE-REPAIR THRU 1200-END
325         PERFORM 3100-MOVE-TO-OUTPUT
326         PERFORM 5000-PRINT-EQUIP-LINES
327                    ELSE
328         IF RE-DATE-IN-SERV-X = LOW-VALUES OR SPACES
329         PERFORM 3500-CHECK-OUT-DATE THRU 3500-END
330         PERFORM 1200-END-BROWSE-REPAIR THRU 1200-END
331         PERFORM 3100-MOVE-TO-OUTPUT
332         PERFORM 5000-PRINT-EQUIP-LINES
333                    ELSE
334         PERFORM 2200-READ-NEXT-REPAIR-REC THRU 2200-END
335         UNTIL (RE-UNIT-NO-X = EQ-UNIT-NO)    AND
336         (RE-EQ-STCND-CODE = 'B' OR 'C' OR 'D'
337         OR 'M' OR 'W') AND
338         (RE-DATE-IN-SERV-X = LOW-VALUES OR SPACES)
339         PERFORM 3500-CHECK-OUT-DATE THRU 3500-END
340         PERFORM 1200-END-BROWSE-REPAIR THRU 1200-END
341         PERFORM 3100-MOVE-TO-OUTPUT
342         PERFORM 5000-PRINT-EQUIP-LINES
343                    ELSE
344         PERFORM 1200-END-BROWSE-REPAIR THRU 1200-END
345         GO TO 3000-PRODUCE-EQUIP-LINE.
346
```

```
347 3100-MOVE-TO-OUTPUT.
348     MOVE '/' TO SLASH1 SLASH1A SLASH2 SLASH2A.
349     MOVE RE-TEMP-CARRIER TO TEMP-CARRIER.
350     MOVE EQ-CARRIER-CODE TO ORIG-CARRIER.
351     MOVE RE-UNIT-NO-X TO UNIT-NO.
352     MOVE RE-DATE-OUT-SERV-M-X TO DATE-IN-MO.
353     MOVE RE-DATE-OUT-SERV-D-X TO DATE-IN-DA.
354     MOVE RE-DATE-OUT-SERV-Y-X TO DATE-IN-YR.
355     IF RE-DUE-OUT-DATE-X NOT = LOW-VALUES AND SPACES
356     MOVE RE-DUE-OUT-DATE-M-X TO DUE-OUT-MO
357     MOVE RE-DUE-OUT-DATE-D-X TO DUE-OUT-DA
358     MOVE RE-DUE-OUT-DATE-Y-X TO DUE-OUT-YR
359                 ELSE
360     MOVE SPACES TO DUE-OUT.
361     IF RE-PROBLEM NOT = LOW-VALUES AND SPACES
362     MOVE RE-PROBLEM TO COMMENT
363                 ELSE
364     IF RE-EQ-REPAIR-CODE NOT = '99'
365     MOVE RE-EQ-REPAIR-CODE TO REPAIR-CODE
366     PERFORM 3300-READ-REPCODE THRU 3300-END.
367     IF RE-EQ-REPAIR-CODE = '99'
368     PERFORM 3200-CHECK-REPAIR-CODE
369                 ELSE
370     MOVE RE-EQ-REPAIR-CODE TO REPAIR-CODE.
371
372 3200-CHECK-REPAIR-CODE.
373     IF RE-EQ-REPAIR-CODE1 NOT = LOW-VALUES AND SPACES
374     IF RE-PROBLEM NOT = LOW-VALUES AND SPACES
375     MOVE RE-EQ-REPAIR-CODE1 TO REPAIR-CODE
376     MOVE RE-PROBLEM TO COMMENT
377     PERFORM 5000-PRINT-EQUIP-LINES
378                 ELSE
379     MOVE RE-EQ-REPAIR-CODE1 TO REPAIR-CODE
380     PERFORM 3300-READ-REPCODE THRU 3300-END
381     PERFORM 5000-PRINT-EQUIP-LINES
382                 ELSE
383     GO TO 3000-PRODUCE-EQUIP-LINE.
384     IF RE-EQ-REPAIR-CODE2 NOT = LOW-VALUES AND SPACES
385     MOVE SPACES TO ORIG-CARRIER UNIT-NO DATE-IN DUE-OUT
386     TEMP-CARRIER
387     MOVE RE-EQ-REPAIR-CODE2 TO REPAIR-CODE
388     PERFORM 3300-READ-REPCODE THRU 3300-END
389     PERFORM 5000-PRINT-EQUIP-LINES
390                 ELSE
391     GO TO 3000-PRODUCE-EQUIP-LINE.
392     IF RE-EQ-REPAIR-CODE3 NOT = LOW-VALUES AND SPACES
393     MOVE SPACES TO ORIG-CARRIER UNIT-NO DATE-IN DUE-OUT
394     TEMP-CARRIER
395     MOVE RE-EQ-REPAIR-CODE3 TO REPAIR-CODE
396     PERFORM 3300-READ-REPCODE THRU 3300-END
397     PERFORM 5000-PRINT-EQUIP-LINES
398                 ELSE
399     GO TO 3000-PRODUCE-EQUIP-LINE.
400     IF RE-EQ-REPAIR-CODE4 NOT = LOW-VALUES AND SPACES
401     MOVE SPACES TO ORIG-CARRIER UNIT-NO DATE-IN DUE-OUT
402     TEMP-CARRIER
403     MOVE RE-EQ-REPAIR-CODE4 TO REPAIR-CODE
404     PERFORM 3300-READ-REPCODE THRU 3300-END
405     PERFORM 5000-PRINT-EQUIP-LINES
406                 ELSE
407     GO TO 3000-PRODUCE-EQUIP-LINE.
408     IF RE-EQ-REPAIR-CODE5 NOT = LOW-VALUES AND SPACES
409     MOVE SPACES TO ORIG-CARRIER UNIT-NO DATE-IN DUE-OUT
410     TEMP-CARRIER
411     MOVE RE-EQ-REPAIR-CODE5 TO REPAIR-CODE
412     PERFORM 3300-READ-REPCODE THRU 3300-END
413     PERFORM 5000-PRINT-EQUIP-LINES
414                 ELSE
415     GO TO 3000-PRODUCE-EQUIP-LINE.
416     IF RE-EQ-REPAIR-CODE6 NOT = LOW-VALUES AND SPACES
417     MOVE SPACES TO ORIG-CARRIER UNIT-NO DATE-IN DUE-OUT
418     TEMP-CARRIER
419     MOVE RE-EQ-REPAIR-CODE6 TO REPAIR-CODE
420     PERFORM 3300-READ-REPCODE THRU 3300-END
421     PERFORM 5000-PRINT-EQUIP-LINES
```

```
422                        ELSE
423        GO TO 3000-PRODUCE-EQUIP-LINE.
424        IF RE-EQ-REPAIR-CODE7 NOT = LOW-VALUES AND SPACES
425        MOVE SPACES TO ORIG-CARRIER UNIT-NO DATE-IN DUE-OUT
426        TEMP-CARRIER
427        MOVE RE-EQ-REPAIR-CODE7 TO REPAIR-CODE
428        PERFORM 3300-READ-REPCODE THRU 3300-END
429        PERFORM 5000-PRINT-EQUIP-LINES
430                        ELSE
431        GO TO 3000-PRODUCE-EQUIP-LINE.
432        IF RE-EQ-REPAIR-CODE8 NOT = LOW-VALUES AND SPACES
433        MOVE SPACES TO ORIG-CARRIER UNIT-NO DATE-IN DUE-OUT
434        TEMP-CARRIER
435        MOVE RE-EQ-REPAIR-CODE8 TO REPAIR-CODE
436        PERFORM 3300-READ-REPCODE THRU 3300-END
437        PERFORM 5000-PRINT-EQUIP-LINES
438                        ELSE
439        GO TO 3000-PRODUCE-EQUIP-LINE.
440        IF RE-EQ-REPAIR-CODE9 NOT = LOW-VALUES AND SPACES
441        MOVE SPACES TO ORIG-CARRIER UNIT-NO DATE-IN DUE-OUT
442        TEMP-CARRIER
443        MOVE RE-EQ-REPAIR-CODE9 TO REPAIR-CODE
444        PERFORM 3300-READ-REPCODE THRU 3300-END
445        PERFORM 5000-PRINT-EQUIP-LINES
446                        ELSE
447        GO TO 3000-PRODUCE-EQUIP-LINE.
448        IF RE-EQ-REPAIR-CODE10 NOT = LOW-VALUES AND SPACES
449        MOVE SPACES TO ORIG-CARRIER UNIT-NO DATE-IN DUE-OUT
450        TEMP-CARRIER
451        MOVE RE-EQ-REPAIR-CODE10 TO REPAIR-CODE
452        PERFORM 3300-READ-REPCODE THRU 3300-END
453        PERFORM 5000-PRINT-EQUIP-LINES
454                        ELSE
455        GO TO 3000-PRODUCE-EQUIP-LINE.
456
457 3300-READ-REPCODE.
458        EXEC CICS HANDLE CONDITION
459        NOTOPEN(1100-ENDFILE)
460        ERROR  (1100-ENDFILE)
461        END-EXEC.
462            EXEC CICS READ DATASET('TEQREPAR')
463            INTO (EQ-REPAIR-TABLE)
464            RIDFLD(REPAIR-CODE)
465            END-EXEC.
466        MOVE T-EQ-REPAIR-DESC TO COMMENT.
467
468 3300-END.
469        EXIT.
470
471 3500-CHECK-OUT-DATE.
472        IF RE-DATE-OUT-SERV-X NOT > COMM-DATE
473        NEXT SENTENCE
474                        ELSE
475        PERFORM 1200-END-BROWSE-REPAIR THRU 1200-END
476        GO TO 3000-PRODUCE-EQUIP-LINE.
477 3500-END.
478        EXIT.
479
480 5000-PRINT-EQUIP-LINES.
481        IF LINE-COUNT = LINES-ON-PAGE OR
482        IS GREATER THAN LINES-ON-PAGE OR
483        FIRST-PAGE
484        PERFORM 5100-PRINT-HEADING-LINES.
485        MOVE EQUIP-LINE-1 TO PRINT-AREA.
486        MOVE 132 TO LINE-LENGTH.
487        PERFORM 6000-WRITE-QUEUE-RECORD.
488        ADD 1 TO LINE-COUNT.
489 5100-PRINT-HEADING-LINES.
490        MOVE PAGE-NO TO HDG-PAGE.
491        MOVE CURRENT-DATE TO RPT-DATE.
492        MOVE COMM-MO TO RE-MO.
493        MOVE COMM-DA TO RE-DA.
494        MOVE COMM-YR TO RE-YR.
495        MOVE HDG-LINE-9 TO PRINT-AREA.
496        MOVE 132 TO LINE-LENGTH.
497        PERFORM 6000-WRITE-QUEUE-RECORD.
498        MOVE '15' TO HDG9-CC.
```

```
499          MOVE HDG-LINE-9 TO PRINT-AREA.
500          MOVE 132 TO LINE-LENGTH.
501          PERFORM 6000-WRITE-QUEUE-RECORD.
502          MOVE '15' TO HDG9-CC.
503          MOVE HDG-LINE-1 TO PRINT-AREA.
504          MOVE 132 TO LINE-LENGTH.
505          PERFORM 6000-WRITE-QUEUE-RECORD.
506          ADD 1 TO PAGE-NO.
507          MOVE HDG-LINE-9 TO PRINT-AREA.
508          MOVE 132 TO LINE-LENGTH.
509          PERFORM 6000-WRITE-QUEUE-RECORD.
510          MOVE HDG-LINE-2 TO PRINT-AREA.
511          MOVE 132 TO LINE-LENGTH.
512          PERFORM 6000-WRITE-QUEUE-RECORD.
513          MOVE HDG-LINE-3 TO PRINT-AREA.
514          MOVE 132 TO LINE-LENGTH.
515          PERFORM 6000-WRITE-QUEUE-RECORD.
516          MOVE HDG-LINE-9 TO PRINT-AREA.
517          MOVE 132 TO LINE-LENGTH.
518          PERFORM 6000-WRITE-QUEUE-RECORD.
519          MOVE HDG-LINE-4 TO PRINT-AREA.
520          MOVE 132 TO LINE-LENGTH.
521          PERFORM 6000-WRITE-QUEUE-RECORD.
522          MOVE HDG-LINE-5 TO PRINT-AREA.
523          MOVE 132 TO LINE-LENGTH.
524          PERFORM 6000-WRITE-QUEUE-RECORD.
525          MOVE HDG-LINE-6 TO PRINT-AREA.
526          MOVE 132 TO LINE-LENGTH.
527          PERFORM 6000-WRITE-QUEUE-RECORD.
528          MOVE HDG-LINE-9 TO PRINT-AREA.
529          MOVE 132 TO LINE-LENGTH.
530          PERFORM 6000-WRITE-QUEUE-RECORD.
531          MOVE HDG-LINE-7 TO PRINT-AREA.
532          MOVE 132 TO LINE-LENGTH.
533          PERFORM 6000-WRITE-QUEUE-RECORD.
534          MOVE HDG-LINE-8 TO PRINT-AREA.
535          MOVE 132 TO LINE-LENGTH.
536          PERFORM 6000-WRITE-QUEUE-RECORD.
537          MOVE HDG-LINE-9 TO PRINT-AREA.
538          MOVE 132 TO LINE-LENGTH.
539          PERFORM 6000-WRITE-QUEUE-RECORD.
540          MOVE '15' TO EL-CC.
541          MOVE ZERO TO LINE-COUNT.
542 6000-WRITE-QUEUE-RECORD.
543              EXEC CICS
544              WRITEQ TD QUEUE(DESTINATION-ID)
545              FROM (PRINT-AREA)
546              LENGTH(LINE-LENGTH)
547              END-EXEC.
548
549
```

In lines 19 through 28 of FIG. 10-6, this standardized layout of the COMMUNICATIONS AREA is defined. The first element using a PIC clause (PF-KEYS PIC VALUE "0"), is an indicator segregating first and subsequent SEND and RECEIVE procedures. This layout then continues with a carrier and a line definition. Note that the COMM-DATE is not part of the COMMAREA's standardized format, but that this is an extra field tacked onto it for repair purposes.

Under the PRINT-FIELD subheading, lines 20 through 36, there are a number of useful data fields, such as a line and a page counter, a print area definition for storing and/or reformatting transient data for the report. Corresponding to the report, a series of header information is being defined from HDG-LINE-1, line 41 of

FIG. 10-8, through the tail-end of the ninth heading line, HDG-LINE-9, shown in line 121.

Note that the last field of each header definition, HDG1-CC, HDG2-CC, HDG3-CC, etc. has an assigned value of 15 that causes the printer to space a single line. The value 15 in this particular situation happens to be a hexadecimal, EBCDIC value for a new line, part of IBM's printer character order for the 3270 data stream. The data stream is as follows:

. . . . . .Order . . . . . .EBCDIC . . . . . .ASCII . . .		
(Hex)	(Hex)	
New Line (NL)	15	0A
End of Message (EM)	19	19
Format Feed (FF)	0C	0C
Press Index (SI)	BF	
Carriage Return (CR)	0D	

You might recognize EQUIP-LINE-1 as a repeat format for the detail line definition. The COMMENT field that appears in line 1490099, can be used as the actual description for a specific repair job. If the comment field, RE-COMMENT1, (line 252 of FIG. 10-8) is left blank, a table search is triggered by the program, as shown in lines 285 through 291, to extract a corresponding program narrative. If, however, the above RE-COMMENT1 field is filled in, a truncated or "chopped off" version of the field is used in place of the table description.

In line 153 of FIG. 10-8, I have defined a destination identifier (DESTINATION-ID) designed to route the printing of the queue to a particular physical location such as R465, denoting an online printer. This methodology might be too simplistic, especially if you do not want to hardcode certain hardware restrictions into your source program and you have any number of terminals to route your printing to. Thus, a preferable way to handle a practical situation such as that is through indirect destinations as in section 10.2 using the destination control table (DCT), as explained earlier.

Finally, a number of copy statements need to be highlighted for each one of the four file components used in this program. These are:

- A carrier table, line 64.
- An Equipment inventory file, line 165.
- A repair service file, line 166.
- An equipment repair table, line 167.

Note that in the LINKAGE-SECTION, lines 170 through 171, the program is to receive external or self invoked messages. These messages all conform to a 12-position long alphanumeric field, of which the first 6 positions are standardized throughout the system (i.e., a SEND/RECEIVE flag, a carrier and a line field, excluding some minor exceptions). The other 6 positions represent the date of inquiry for the particular report requested via the previous task.

The PROCEDURE DIVISION, line 173 of FIG. 10-8, starts with a number of necessary "house-keeping" activities required to set up the transient data for printing the daily/monthly report. Once the contents of the COMMUNICATIONS AREA are loaded into WORKING-STORAGE, they are checked for validity to see whether the message contains any low values or spaces. Afterwards, a carrier code is extracted and a VSAM key is set up (T-CARRIER-CODE) to search the carrier code table for a valid description. Note that the T-CARRIER-CODE is defined in lines 166 through 173 of FIG. 10-8 through a copy statement. Once the record key is developed in this fashion, the carrier table is read and processed, followed by a BROWSE against the Equipment Inventory File.

The statement in lines 188 through 191 of FIG. 10-8 re-ensures the operator of his or her exclusive use of the transient data by simply "enqueuing" it. ENQ should be coded in your program if you need to write more than a single record to a destination. This will prevent other tasks writing to it concurrently. Once this process is complete, you should release the record via a process called dequeueing (DEQ).

At this point the START BROWSE operation continues with a read-next instruction by checking the repair status code as shown in lines 270 through 275 of FIG. 10-6. This is done primarily to select those records whose status is equal to a "B", (meaning out of service), or a "C", (equipment in need of some sort of repair), or a "D", (equipment requiring rebuilding), or an "M", (equipment awaiting material) or a "W" (equipment defective, but still in service). If status code does not equal any one of the above values, the record does not get processed. Rather, a new read statement is issued. In a positive situation (i.e., the search key equals one of the previously explained values), the file is to be processed in the following manner:

1. Issue a STARTBR on the equipment repair file as highlighted in statement 319 (PERFORM-110-START-REPAIR-BROWSE THRU 1100-END).
2. Process and extract a number of valid records through paragraph 320-S, PERFORM-2200-READ-NEXT-REC THRU 2200-

END. To reiterate, the term "valid" means that the status code needs to be a "B," or a "C," or a "D," or an "M," or a "W", and there must be a match between the equipment inventory and the equipment repair masters.

If one of these conditions is met, the program transfers you to the 3500-CHECK-OUT-DATE paragraph, shown in statement 477, which examines the inquiry date carried forward from step 1 FIG. 10-3.

If the date in the communications area is equal to the one shown on the equipment repair file, the record is to be further processed. Otherwise:

1. The BROWSE is to be terminated. This will return you to main program logic, reflected in lines 232 through 237 of FIG. 10-6.
2. Once the BROWSE is over, the program will invoke a set of procedures starting with 300-PRODUCE-EQUIP-LINE, line 310, which is mostly a simple rehash or revalidation that indeed the record to be extracted conforms to the selection criteria described earlier.

Otherwise, the program will branch to line 353, as shown in paragraph 3100-MOVE-TO-OUTPUT. In this paragraph, a transient data queue is being built with exact print images to be physically printed in step 3, utilizing the PRINTRIP program.

As you have probably noticed by now, in producing a viable output for a transient print program, you need to build every line, including header and detail lines, that make up the report. Thus, the data to be printed is moved to a mask in the WORKING-STORAGE SECTION, which is the actual print format. Note that the procedures making up repair code 99 maintain a number of different repair operations. As you recall from the case study explained earlier, to simplify data entry you can enter up to 10 different repair problems associated with a piece of equipment. This process is reflected in lines 376 through 459.

The queue is now updated with valid data, and a description is extracted from the repair code table and inserted into the COMMENT line on the report, as shown in FIG. 10-1. The building process continues moving exact print images and placing them into the transient data queue via the WORKING-STORAGE SECTION.

Note that another way to handle the multiple occurrence of repair code 99, is through subscripting them, the way I have done in the TRE6BRS program, for example, in Chapter 7. This would require an "occur" clause built into your own BMS map, which is a relatively simple process. When testing for multirepair codes, (lines 378 through line 459 of FIG. 10-6), a valid code will be matched against the repair code table to extract a corresponding description.

As you develop print lines in the WORKING-STORAGE SECTION, the program will move each line into the transient data queue. A single write statement to the queue is shown in paragraph 600-WRITE-QUEUE-RECORD, lines 551 through 557. What is interesting about this process is that print lines are basically developed the same way you develop them for a print routine in a batch report. Thus, you need to check the page number, set up a header based on line counts, etc. In paragraph 5100-PRINT-HEADING-LINES, I used a value of "15," which is now also part of the transient queue. This value is assigned to trigger spacing on the printed report.

Once the transient queue is built in this fashion, a second program, PRINTRIP, takes over, as shown in the system flow diagram in FIG. 10-3. The sole purpose of PRINTRIP, shown in FIG. 10-7, is to physically list print images off the transient queue and route them to a specific remote printer. I hardcoded a terminal printer into my program to simplify the process. Note that you can also use indirect destinations explained earlier in this chapter, in order to define multiple print facilities for the same program.

I used a destination I.D. in this PRINTRIP program, such as R415, merely relying on a simple destination for the print. Thus, to set up multiple indirect destinations is not a programming, but a table function in CICS. As you can see, the only consideration of the WORKING-STORAGE-SECTION deals with setting up print requirements with regards to spacing, identifying print characters and write control characters, setting up print queue switches, and so on. These activities are coded in lines 1 through 4 of FIG. 10-7.

The entire PROCEDURE DIVISION of the PRINTRIP program is made up of a total of 91 lines. This is due to the fact that all you have to do now is to list images built in the prior DB01PRT program. Transient printing has a destructive read mechanism. Thus, as a particular line is printed, it gets promptly deleted from the transient queue.

As shown in FIG. 10-7, printing is invoked via lines 46 through 47, while triggering paragraph 1100-READ-QUEUE SECTION. In issuing a READQ statement, you need to associate the transient data queue with a particular terminal identifier. PRINT-QUEUE-RECORD, line 17 was set up in the DATA DIVISION to define a print line. The print line is made up of control character values for form feeding or for the various spacing requirements. A print line is defined on a character by character basis, limited to 132 bytes in this particular

```
1     IDENTIFICATION DIVISION.
2     PROGRAM-ID. PRINTRIP.
3     DATE-COMPILED.
4     ENVIRONMENT DIVISION.
5     DATA DIVISION.
6     WORKING-STORAGE SECTION.
7     COPY DFHBMSCA.
8
9     01  SWITCHES.
10        05  PRINT-QUEUE-EOF-SW PIC X    VALUE 'N'.
11        88  PRINT-QUEUE-EOF             VALUE 'Y'.
12    01  WORK-FIELDS.
13        05  NEW-LINE-COUNT     PIC 9.
14        05  SET-CHAR           PIC X.
15
16    01  PRINT-QUEUE-RECORD.
17        05  PRINT-CC           PIC X.
18        88  FORM-FEED                   VALUE '1'.
19        88  SINGLE-SPACE               VALUE ' '.
20        88  DOUBLE-SPACE               VALUE '0'.
21        88  TRIPLE-SPACE               VALUE '-'.
22        05  PRINT-CHAR     OCCURS 132
23        INDEXED BY PRINT-INDEX
24                           PIC X
25    01  PRINT-RECORD-LENGTH   PIC S9(4) COMP.
26    01  BUFFER-AREA.
27        05  BUFFER-CHAR    OCCURS 1920
28        INDEXED BY BUFFER-INDEX
29                           PIC X.
30
31    01  PRINT-ORDERS.
32        05  NEW-LINE-ORDER    PIC X    VALUE ' '.
33        05  FORM-FEED-ORDER   PIC X    VALUE ' '.
34        05  CAR-RTN-ORDER     PIC X    VALUE ' '.
35
36    01  WRITE-CONTROL-CHAR    PIC X    VALUE 'H'.
37    01  DESTINATION-ID        PIC X(4) VALUE 'R415'.
38
39    PROCEDURE DIVISION.
40    FORMAT-QUEUE-RECORDS SECTION.
41        EXEC CICS
42        HANDLE CONDITION QZERO(1100-QZERO)
43        END-EXEC.
44        MOVE LOW-VALUE TO BUFFER-AREA.
45        SET BUFFER-INDEX TO 1.
46        PERFORM 1000-PRINT-QUEUE-RECORD
47        UNTIL PRINT-QUEUE-EOF.
48        EXEC CICS
49        RETURN
50        END-EXEC.
51
52    1000-PRINT-QUEUE-RECORD SECTION.
53        PERFORM 1100-READ-QUEUE-RECORD.
54        IF PRINT-QUEUE-EOF
55        PERFORM 1240-PRINT-RPT
56               ELSE
57        PERFORM 1200-MASK-DATA.
58
59    1100-READ-QUEUE-RECORD SECTION.
60        MOVE 132 TO PRINT-RECORD-LENGTH.
61        EXEC CICS
62        READQ TD QUEUE(EIBTRMID)
63        INTO(PRINT-QUEUE-RECORD)
64        LENGTH(PRINT-RECORD-LENGTH)
65        END-EXEC.
66        SET PRINT-INDEX TO 1.
67        GO TO 1100-EXIT.
68
69    1100-QZERO.
70        MOVE 'Y' TO PRINT-QUEUE-EOF-SW.
71
72    1100-EXIT.
73        EXIT.
74
```

```
75   1200-MASK-DATA SECTION.
76       IF BUFFER-INDEX > 1916 - PRINT-RECORD-LENGTH
77       PERFORM 1240-PRINT-RPT
78       MOVE LOW-VALUE TO BUFFER-AREA
79       SET BUFFER-INDEX TO 1.
80       PERFORM 1210-MASK-DATA.
81       PERFORM 1230-MOVE-PRINT-CHARACTER
82       VARYING PRINT-INDEX FROM 1 BY 1
83       UNTIL PRINT-INDEX = PRINT-RECORD-LENGTH.
84
85   1210-PRINT-IMAGE SECTION.
86       IF NOT (     FORM-FEED
87       OR SINGLE-SPACE
88       OR DOUBLE-SPACE
89       OR TRIPLE-SPACE)
90       MOVE ' ' TO PRINT-CC.
91       IF FORM-FEED
92       MOVE CAR-RTN-ORDER TO SET-CHAR
93       PERFORM 1220-SET-BUFFER-CHARACTER
94       MOVE FORM-FEED-ORDER TO SET-CHAR
95       PERFORM 1220-SET-BUFFER-CHARACTER
96       MOVE CAR-RTN-ORDER TO SET-CHAR
97       PERFORM 1220-SET-BUFFER-CHARACTER
98           ELSE
99       IF SINGLE-SPACE
100      MOVE 1 TO NEW-LINE-COUNT
101          ELSE
102      IF DOUBLE-SPACE
103      MOVE 2 TO NEW-LINE-COUNT
104          ELSE
105      IF TRIPLE-SPACE
106      MOVE 3 TO NEW-LINE-COUNT.
107      IF NOT FORM-FEED
108      IF BUFFER-INDEX = 1
109      SUBTRACT 1 FROM NEW-LINE-COUNT.
110      IF NOT FORM-FEED
111      MOVE NEW-LINE-ORDER TO SET-CHAR
112      PERFORM 1220-SET-BUFFER-CHARACTER
113      NEW-LINE-COUNT TIMES.
114
115  1220-SET-BUFFER-CHARACTER SECTION.
116      MOVE SET-CHAR TO BUFFER-CHAR(BUFFER-INDEX).
117      SET BUFFER-INDEX UP BY 1.
118
119  1230-MOVE-PRINT-CHARACTER SECTION.
120      MOVE PRINT-CHAR(PRINT-INDEX) TO SET-CHAR.
121      PERFORM 1220-SET-BUFFER-CHARACTER.
122
123  1240-PRINT-RPT SECTION.
124      EXEC CICS
125      SEND FROM (BUFFER-AREA)
126      LENGTH(1920)
127      CTLCHAR(WRITE-CONTROL-CHAR)
128      ERASE
129      END-EXEC.
130
```

instance. This, by the way, also corresponds to a physical print line. The length of the line is defined in PRINT-RECORD-LENGTH, at which time the queue is read and processed. This reading process is active until the end of the file, line 54, just like in a batch program. If there are still more records available in the transient data queue, PRINTRIP is going to format the next record into a print mask (1200-MASK-DATA), otherwise, paragraph 1240-PRINT-RPT will be executed, which physically sends the contents of the "buffer" containing the print images for actual printing. This procedure is described in lines 123 through 129.

The subroutine 1200-MASK-DATA SECTION treats the contents of the storage area you have developed for printing on a character by character basis. Printing is initiated or "triggered" as soon as the buffer area is full. A BUFFER-INDEX of 1920 (80 by 24) is used, indicating the next available record buffer minus the length of the record just processed in packed decimals.

Compiler-generated source code: excerpts

As shown in FIG. 10-8, this program is a compiler-derived expansion of the DB01RPT program, (step 2 in FIG. 10-3) responsible for building a transient data queue. The first file to be expanded by the compiler is that of the carrier code table, presented in lines 166 through 173 of FIG. 10-8. The key to the carrier table is the carrier code that enables you to find and extract a description corresponding to a specific carrier (i.e., Central, Southeast Indiana, etc.).

10-8 DB01RPT compiler version

```
1PP 5740-CB1 RELEASE 2.4              IBM OS/VS COBOL   JULY  1, 1990

00001  IDENTIFICATION DIVISION.
00002  PROGRAM-ID.    DB01RPT.
00004  DATE-COMPILED. DEC 13,1989.
00006  ENVIRONMENT DIVISION.
00007   DATA DIVISION.
00009      WORKING-STORAGE SECTION.
00010  01  SWITCHES.
00011          05       EQUIP-EOF-SW      PIC X          VALUE 'N'.
00012          88  EQUIP-EOF             VALUE 'Y'.
00013
00014  01  WORK-FIELDS.
00015          05       RECORD-COUNT      PIC S9(5) VALUE ZERO COMP-3.
00016
00017  01  COMPARE-AREA.
00018          05       MAIN-CARRIER      PIC XXX.
00019
00020  01  COMM-AREA.
00021          05       COMM-FLAG.
00022          10  PF-KEYS        PIC X     VALUE '0'.
00023          05       WS-COMMAREA-OUT.
00024          10  COMM-CARRIER     PIC XXX.
00025          10  COMM-LINE        PIC XX.
00026          10  COMM-DATE.
00027              15       COMM-YR      PIC XX   VALUE SPACES.
00028              15       COMM-MO      PIC XX   VALUE SPACES.
00029              15       COMM-DA      PIC XX   VALUE SPACES.
00030
00031  01  PRINT-FIELDS.
00032          05       LINE-COUNT    PIC S99   VALUE 0     COMP-3.
00033          05       LINES-ON-PAGE     PIC S99   VALUE +43  COMP-3.
00034          05       PAGE-NO       PIC S999  VALUE +1    COMP-3.
00035          88  FIRST-PAGE             VALUE +1.
00036          05       PRINT-AREA    PIC X(132).
00037          05       LINE-LENGTH   PIC S9(4)  COMP.
00038
00039  01  FILE-NOTOPEN-MSG     PIC X(17) VALUE '**FILE NOT OPEN**'.
00040  01  ERROR-MSG            PIC X(22) VALUE '**ERROR HAS OCCURED**'.
00041
00042  01  HDG-LINE-1.
00043          05       FILLER               PIC X(6)  VALUE SPACES.
00044          05       FILLER               PIC X(08) VALUE 'DB01RPT '.
```

```
00045        05     FILLER              PIC X(24) VALUE SPACES.
00046        05     FILLER              PIC X(17) VALUE 'TRAIN OPERATIONS '.
00047        05     FILLER              PIC X(18) VALUE 'PERFORMANCE SYSTEM'.
00048        05     FILLER              PIC X(33) VALUE SPACES.
00049        05     FILLER              PIC X(5)  VALUE 'PAGE:'.
00050        05     HDG-PAGE     PIC ZZZ9.
00051        05     FILLER              PIC X(17) VALUE SPACES.
00052        05     HDG1-CC      PIC XX    VALUE '15'.
00053
00054  01  HDG-LINE-2.
00055        05     FILLER              PIC X(38) VALUE SPACES.
00056        05     FILLER              PIC X(20) VALUE 'DAILY OUT OF SERVICE'
00057        05     FILLER              PIC X(15) VALUE ' ON-LINE REPORT'.
00058        05     FILLER              PIC X(33) VALUE SPACES.
00059        05     FILLER              PIC X(10) VALUE 'RUN DATE: '.
00060        05     RPT-DATE     PIC X(8).
00061        05     FILLER              PIC X(08) VALUE SPACES.
00062        05     HDG2-CC      PIC XX    VALUE '15'.
00063
00064  01  HDG-LINE-3.
00065        05     FILLER              PIC X(46) VALUE SPACES.
00066        05     FILLER              PIC X(13) VALUE 'REPORT DATE: '.
00067        05     RE-MO        PIC XX.
00068        05     FILLER              PIC X     VALUE '/'.
00069        05     RE-DA        PIC XX.
00070        05     FILLER              PIC X     VALUE '/'.
00071        05     RE-YR        PIC XX.
00072        05     FILLER              PIC X(65) VALUE SPACES.
00073        05     HDG3-CC      PIC XX    VALUE '15'.
00074
00075  01  HDG-LINE-4.
00076        05     FILLER              PIC X(9)  VALUE SPACES.
00077        05     FILLER              PIC X(18) VALUE '+----------------'.
00078        05     FILLER              PIC X(18) VALUE '------------------'.
00079        05     FILLER              PIC X(12) VALUE '-----------+'.
00080        05     FILLER              PIC X(75) VALUE SPACES.
00081        05     HDG4-CC      PIC XX    VALUE '15'.
00082
00083  01  HDG-LINE-5.
00084        05     FILLER              PIC X(9)  VALUE SPACES.
00085        05     FILLER              PIC X(12) VALUE '] CARRIER: '.
00086        05     CARRIER-DESC        PIC X(35).
00087        05     FILLER              PIC X     VALUE ']'.
00088        05     FILLER              PIC X(75) VALUE SPACES.
00089        05     HDG5-CC      PIC XX    VALUE '15'.
00090
00091  01  HDG-LINE-6.
00092        05     FILLER              PIC X(9)  VALUE SPACES.
00093        05     FILLER              PIC X(18) VALUE '+----------------'.
00094        05     FILLER              PIC X(18) VALUE '------------------'.
00095        05     FILLER              PIC X(12) VALUE '-----------+'.
00096        05     FILLER              PIC X(75) VALUE SPACES.
00097        05     HDG6-CC      PIC XX    VALUE '15'.
00098
00099  01  HDG-LINE-7.
00100        05     FILLER              PIC X(08) VALUE SPACES.
00101        05     FILLER              PIC X(08) VALUE 'CARRIERS'.
00102        05     FILLER              PIC X(05) VALUE SPACES.
00103        05     FILLER              PIC X(04) VALUE 'UNIT'.
00104        05     FILLER              PIC X(05) VALUE SPACES.
00105        05     FILLER              PIC X(07) VALUE 'DATE IN'.
00106        05     FILLER              PIC X(05) VALUE SPACES.
00107        05     FILLER              PIC X(07) VALUE 'DUE OUT'.
00108        05     FILLER              PIC X(05) VALUE SPACES.
00109        05     FILLER              PIC X(11) VALUE 'REPAIR CODE'.
00110        05     FILLER              PIC X(03) VALUE SPACES.
00111        05     FILLER              PIC X(07) VALUE 'COMMENT'.
00112        05     FILLER              PIC X(57) VALUE SPACES.
-00113        05     HDG7-CC      PIC XX    VALUE '15'.
00114
00115  01  HDG-LINE-8.
00116        05     FILLER              PIC X(07) VALUE SPACES.
00117        05     FILLER              PIC X(10) VALUE 'ORIG  TEMP'.
00118        05     FILLER              PIC X(115) VALUE SPACES.
00119        05     HDG8-CC      PIC XX    VALUE '15'.
00120
```

```
00121  01  HDG-LINE-9.
00122         05      FILLER                  PIC X(132) VALUE SPACES.
00123         05      HDG9-CC        PIC XX     VALUE '15'.
00124
00125  01  EQUIP-LINE-1.
00126         05      FILLER                  PIC X(08) VALUE SPACES.
00127         05      ORIG-CARRIER            PIC XXX.
00128         05      FILLER                  PIC XX   VALUE SPACES.
00129         05      TEMP-CARRIER            PIC XXX.
00130         05      FILLER                  PIC X(05) VALUE SPACES.
00131         05      UNIT-NO        PIC XXXX.
00132         05      FILLER                  PIC X(04) VALUE SPACES.
00133         05      DATE-IN.
00134            10   DATE-IN-MO     PIC XX.
00135            10   SLASH1    PIC X  VALUE '/'.
00136            10   DATE-IN-DA     PIC XX.
00137            10   SLASH1A   PIC X  VALUE '/'.
00138            10   DATE-IN-YR     PIC XX.
00139         05      FILLER                  PIC X(04) VALUE SPACES.
00140         05      DUE-OUT.
00141            10   DUE-OUT-MO     PIC XX.
00142            10   SLASH2    PIC X  VALUE '/'.
00143            10   DUE-OUT-DA     PIC XX.
00144            10   SLASH2A   PIC X  VALUE '/'.
00145            10   DUE-OUT-YR     PIC XX.
00146         05      FILLER                  PIC X(09) VALUE SPACES.
00147         05      REPAIR-CODE    PIC XX.
00148         05      FILLER                  PIC X(08) VALUE SPACES.
00149         05      COMMENT        PIC X(64).
00150         05      EL-CC          PIC XX    VALUE SPACES.
00151
00152  01  EQUIP-LINE-2.
00153         05      FILLER                  PIC X(132) VALUE SPACES.
00154         05      EL2-CC         PIC XX      VALUE SPACES.
00155  01  DESTINATION-ID    PIC X(4) VALUE 'R465'.
00156
00157  01  EOJ-MSG.
00158         05      FILLER                  PIC X(20) VALUE 'DAILY OUT OF SERVICE'
00159         05      FILLER                  PIC X(09) VALUE ' ON-LINE '.
00160         05      FILLER                  PIC X(14) VALUE 'REPORT PRINTED'.
00161         05      FILLER                  PIC X(05) VALUE SPACES.
00162         05      FILLER                  PIC X(15) VALUE 'PRESS CLEAR KEY'.
00163         05      FILLER                  PIC X(14) VALUE ' TO START OVER'.
00164         05      FILLER                  PIC X(07) VALUE SPACES.
00165
00166        01  CARRIER-TABLE.
00167                        COPY CCARRIER.
00168 C      05      T-CARRIER-CODE          PIC XXX.
00169 C      05      FILLER                  PIC X(4).
00170 C      05      T-CARRIER-DESC          PIC X(35).
00171 C      05      FILLER                  PIC X(2).
00172 C      05      HOLD-CODE      PIC X(4).
00173 C      * RECORD LENGTH = 48
00174  01  EQUIP-REC.
00175                        COPY CEQUIP.
00176 C      05      EQ-KEY.
00177 C         10   EQ-CARRIER-CODE         PIC XXX.
00178 C         10   EQ-UNIT-NO              PIC X(4).
00179 C      05      FILLER                  PIC X VALUE SPACES.
00180 C      05      EQ-TYPE-CODE            PIC X.
00181 C      05      EQ-SEAT-CAP    PIC 999.
00182 C      05      EQ-STCND-CODE           PIC X.
00183 C      05      EQ-DATE-IN-OUT-SERV.
00184 C         10   EQ-DATE-IN-OUT-SERV-Y  PIC 99.
00185 C         10   EQ-DATE-IN-OUT-SERV-M  PIC 99.
00186 C         10   EQ-DATE-IN-OUT-SERV-D  PIC 99.
00187 C      05      EQ-TRACK-END            PIC XXX.
00188 C      05      EQ-YARD        PIC X(5).
00189 C      05      FILLER                  PIC X VALUE SPACES.
00190 C      05      EQ-BUFFER-STRENGTH      PIC X.
00191 C      05      EQ-SEAT-TYPE            PIC X.
00192 C      05      EQ-RESTROOMS            PIC X.
00193 C      05      EQ-PROPULSION           PIC X.
00194 C      05      EQ-E-H-ACCESS           PIC X.
00195 C      05      FILLER                  PIC X VALUE SPACES.
00196 C      05      EQ-MODEL-NO    PIC X(7).
00197 C      05      EQ-OWNER-CODE           PIC X(7).
00198 C      05      EQ-SERIAL-NO            PIC X(25).
```

```
00199 C    05      EQ-DATE-FIRST-SERV.
00200 C      10  EQ-DATE-FIRST-SERV-Y   PIC 99.
00201 C      10  EQ-DATE-FIRST-SERV-M   PIC 99.
00202 C    05      EQ-BUILD-CODE            PIC X.
00203 C    05      EQ-YEAR-BUILT            PIC 99.
00204 C    05      FILLER                   PIC X VALUE SPACES.
00205 C    05      EQ-GRANT-PROJECT-ID      PIC X(6).
00206 C    05      EQ-GRANT-NO      PIC X(10).
00207 C    05      EQ-GRANT-EQUIP-STATUS    PIC X.
00208 C    05      EQ-FUEL-CAPACITY    PIC 9(4).
00209 C    05      FILLER                   PIC X VALUE SPACES.
00210 C    05      EQ-YTD-DELAY-MILES       PIC 9(6).
00211 C    05      EQ-YTD-MECH-DELAYS       PIC 9(4).
00212 C    05      EQ-REBUILD-CODE     PIC X.
00213 C    05      EQ-DATE-REBUILD.
00214 C      10  EQ-DATE-REBUILD-Y      PIC 99.
00215 C      10  EQ-DATE-REBUILD-M      PIC 99.
00216 C    05      FILLER                   PIC X VALUE SPACES.
00217 C    05      EQ-TEMP-CARRIER     PIC X(3) VALUE SPACES.
00218 C    05      FILLER                   PIC X(38) VALUE SPACES.
00219 C      * RECORD LENGTH = 160
00220   01  REPAIR-REC.
00221                           COPY CREPAIR.
00222 C    05      RE-KEY.
00223 C      10  RE-UNIT-NO-X      PIC X(4).
00224 C      10  RE-UNIT-NO REDEFINES RE-UNIT-NO-X PIC 9(4).
00225 C      10  RE-EQ-REPAIR-CODE      PIC XX.
00226 C      10  RE-DATE-OUT-SERV.
00227 C        15    RE-DATE-OUT-SERV-Y  PIC 99.
00228 C        15    RE-DATE-OUT-SERV-M  PIC 99.
00229 C        15    RE-DATE-OUT-SERV-D  PIC 99.
00230 C      10  RE-DATE-OUT-SERV-X REDEFINES RE-DATE-OUT-SERV.
00231 C        15    RE-DATE-OUT-SERV-Y-X  PIC XX.
00232 C        15    RE-DATE-OUT-SERV-M-X  PIC XX.
00233 C        15    RE-DATE-OUT-SERV-D-X  PIC XX.
00234 C    05      FILLER              PIC X VALUE SPACES.
00235 C    05      RE-DATE-IN-SERV.
00236 C      10  RE-DATE-IN-SERV-Y      PIC 99.
00237 C      10  RE-DATE-IN-SERV-M      PIC 99.
00238 C      10  RE-DATE-IN-SERV-D      PIC 99.
00239 C    05      RE-DATE-IN-SERV-X REDEFINES RE-DATE-IN-SERV.
00240 C      10  RE-DATE-IN-SERV-Y-X   PIC XX.
00241 C      10  RE-DATE-IN-SERV-M-X   PIC XX.
00242 C      10  RE-DATE-IN-SERV-D-X   PIC XX.
00243 C    05      FILLER                   PIC X VALUE SPACES.
00244 C    05      RE-CARRIER-CODE     PIC XXX.
00245 C    05      RE-EQ-TYPE-CODE     PIC X.
00246 C    05      RE-UNIT-END         PIC X.
00247 C    05      RE-WORK-ORDER-NO    PIC X(6).
00248 C    05      RE-EQ-STCND-CODE    PIC X.
00249 C    05      RE-TRACK-END             PIC XXX.
00250 C    05      RE-YARD             PIC X(5).
00251 C    05      RE-PROBLEM          PIC X(50).
00252 C    05      RE-COMMENT1         PIC X(50).
00253 C    05      RE-COMMENT2         PIC X(50).
00254 C    05      FILLER                   PIC X VALUE SPACES.
00255 C    05      RE-EQ-RBUILD-CODE   PIC X.
00256 C    05      RE-GRANT-PROJECT-ID      PIC X(6).
00257 C    05      RE-GRANT-NO         PIC X(10).
00258 C    05      FILLER                   PIC X(2) VALUE SPACES.
00259 C    05      RE-EQ-REP-CODE-X    PIC X(20).
00260 C    05      RE-EQ-REPCODE   REDEFINES  RE-EQ-REP-CODE-X
00261 C        OCCURS 10 TIMES      PIC X(2).
00262 C    05      RE-EQ-REP-CODE    REDEFINES  RE-EQ-REP-CODE-X.
00263 C      10  RE-EQ-REPAIR-CODE1    PIC X(2).
00264 C      10  RE-EQ-REPAIR-CODE2    PIC X(2).
00265 C      10  RE-EQ-REPAIR-CODE3    PIC X(2).
00266 C      10  RE-EQ-REPAIR-CODE4    PIC X(2).
00267 C      10  RE-EQ-REPAIR-CODE5    PIC X(2).
00268 C      10  RE-EQ-REPAIR-CODE6    PIC X(2).
00269 C      10  RE-EQ-REPAIR-CODE7    PIC X(2).
00270 C      10  RE-EQ-REPAIR-CODE8    PIC X(2).
00271 C      10  RE-EQ-REPAIR-CODE9    PIC X(2).
00272 C      10  RE-EQ-REPAIR-CODE10   PIC X(2).
00273 C    05      FILLER                   PIC X VALUE SPACES.
```

```
00274 C    05    RE-TEMP-CARRIER        PIC X(3).
00275 C    05    RE-DUE-OUT-DATE.
00276 C      10  RE-DUE-OUT-DATE-Y      PIC 99.
00277 C      10  RE-DUE-OUT-DATE-M      PIC 99.
00278 C      10  RE-DUE-OUT-DATE-D      PIC 99.
00279 C    05    RE-DUE-OUT-DATE-X REDEFINES RE-DUE-OUT-DATE.
00280 C      10  RE-DUE-OUT-DATE-Y-X    PIC XX.
00281 C      10  RE-DUE-OUT-DATE-M-X    PIC XX.
00282 C      10  RE-DUE-OUT-DATE-D-X    PIC XX.
00283 C    05    FILLER                      PIC X(20) VALUE SPACES.
00284 C    * RECORD LENGTH = 260
00285  01  EQ-REPAIR-TABLE.
00286                          COPY CEQREPAR.
00287 C    05    T-EQ-REPAIR-CODE   PIC XX.
00288 C    05    FILLER             PIC X(5).
00289 C    05    T-EQ-REPAIR-DESC   PIC X(25).
00290 C    05    FILLER             PIC X(8).
00291 C    * RECORD LENGTH = 40
00292
00293
00294  01  DFHLDVER PIC X(22) VALUE 'LD TABLE DFHEITAB 170.'.
00295  01  DFHEIDO PICTURE S9(7) COMPUTATIONAL-3 VALUE ZERO.
00296  01  DFHEIBO PICTURE S9(4) COMPUTATIONAL VALUE ZERO.
00297  01  DFHEICB  PICTURE X(8) VALUE IS '        '.
00298
00299  01  DFHEIV16  COMP PIC S9(8).
00300  01  DFHB0041  COMP PIC S9(8).
00301  01  DFHB0042  COMP PIC S9(8).
00302  01  DFHB0043  COMP PIC S9(8).
00303  01  DFHB0044  COMP PIC S9(8).
00304  01  DFHB0045  COMP PIC S9(8).
00305  01  DFHB0046  COMP PIC S9(8).
00306  01  DFHB0047  COMP PIC S9(8).
00307  01  DFHB0048  COMP PIC S9(8).
00308  01  DFHEIV11  COMP PIC S9(4).
00309  01  DFHEIV12  COMP PIC S9(4).
00310  01  DFHEIV13  COMP PIC S9(4).
00311  01  DFHEIV14  COMP PIC S9(4).
00312  01  DFHEIV15  COMP PIC S9(4).
00313  01  DFHB0025  COMP PIC S9(4).
00314  01  DFHEIV5   PIC X(4).
00315  01  DFHEIV6   PIC X(4).
00316  01  DFHEIV17  PIC X(4).
00317  01  DFHEIV18  PIC X(4).
00318  01  DFHEIV19  PIC X(4).
00319  01  DFHEIV1   PIC X(8).
00320  01  DFHEIV2   PIC X(8).
00321  01  DFHEIV3   PIC X(8).
00322  01  DFHEIV20  PIC X(8).
00323  01  DFHC0084  PIC X(8).
00324  01  DFHC0085  PIC X(8).
00325  01  DFHC0320  PIC X(32).
00326  01  DFHEIV7   PIC X(2).
00327  01  DFHEIV8   PIC X(2).
00328  01  DFHC0022  PIC X(2).
00329  01  DFHC0023  PIC X(2).
00330  01  DFHEIV10  PIC S9(7) COMP-3.
00331  01  DFHEIV9   PIC X(1).
00332  01  DFHC0011  PIC X(1).
00333  01  DFHEIV4   PIC X(6).
00334  01  DFHC0070  PIC X(7).
00335  01  DFHC0071  PIC X(7).
00336  01  DFHC0440  PIC X(44).
00337  01  DFHC0441  PIC X(44).
00338  01  DFHDUMMY COMP PIC S9(4).
00339  01  DFHEIV0  PICTURE X(29).
00340 LINKAGE SECTION.
00341  01  DFHEIBLK.
00342       02    EIBTIME  PIC S9(7) COMP-3.
00343       02    EIBDATE  PIC S9(7) COMP-3.
00344       02    EIBTRNID PIC X(4).
00345       02    EIBTASKN PIC S9(7) COMP-3.
00346       02    EIBTRMID PIC X(4).
00347       02    DFHEIGDI COMP PIC S9(4).
00348       02    EIBCPOSN COMP PIC S9(4).
00349       02    EIBCALEN COMP PIC S9(4).
00350       02    EIBAID   PIC X(1).
00351       02    EIBFN    PIC X(2).
```

```
00352        02   EIBRCODE PIC X(6).
00353        02   EIBDS    PIC X(8).
00354        02   EIBREQID PIC X(8).
00355        02   EIBRSRCE PIC X(8).
00356        02   EIBSYNC  PIC X(1).
00357        02   EIBFREE  PIC X(1).
00358        02   EIBRECV  PIC X(1).
00359        02   EIBFIL01 PIC X(1).
00360        02   EIBATT   PIC X(1).
00361        02   EIBEOC   PIC X(1).
00362        02   EIBFMH   PIC X(1).
00363        02   EIBCOMPL PIC X(1).
00364        02   EIBSIG   PIC X(1).
00365        02   EIBCONF  PIC X(1).
00366        02   EIBERR   PIC X(1).
00367        02   EIBERRCD PIC X(4).
00368        02   EIBSYNRB PIC X(1).
00369        02   EIBNODAT PIC X(1).
00370        02   EIBRESP  COMP PIC S9(8).
00371        02   EIBRESP2 COMP PIC S9(8).
00372        02   EIBRLDBK PIC X(1).
00373   01  DFHCOMMAREA      PIC X(12).
00375   01  DFHBLLSLOT1 PICTURE X(1).
00376   01  DFHBLLSLOT2 PICTURE X(1).
```

A second copy routine is a compiler-expanded record layout of the Equipment File that was copied into this program through the COPY EQUIP statement. This layout is presented in its entirety in lines 174 through 219. The concatenated key to the Equipment File is made up of two elements. These are a carrier identifier and a unit number, which is, in fact, a numeric identifier of a particular piece of equipment. Note that a file definition of the equipment record is also shown in FIG. 10-9 through a productivity tool called File-AID.

```
--------------- File-AID VSAM INFORMATION - (PAGE 1 OF 2) -----------------
COMMAND  ===>
Catalog.. CATALOG.MVSICF1.VVSAM01
Cluster.. NIRVT.TOPS.EQUIP.KS                    +-------------+
Data..... NIRVT.TOPS.EQUIP.KS.DATA               |             |
Index.... NIRVT.TOPS.EQUIP.KS.INDEX              |  owner-id   |
                                                 |             |
                                                 +-------------+
---------------------------------------------------------------------------
Data component information:            Current allocation options:
Volume serial:        VSAM03           RACF protected          NO
Device Type:          3380             Write Check:            NO
Organization:         AIX              Buffer Space:       45568
KSDS key length:      7                Erase on delete:        NO
KSDS key location:    0                Imbedded index:        YES
Average record size:  160              Replicated index        NO
Maximum record size:  160              Reuse option:           NO
Allocated space: Unit  Primary  Secondary  Share option:      2-3
      Data  -   tracks    20        5      Spanned records:       NO
      Index -   tracks    1         1      MSS binding:       STAGED
Dataset information:                   MSS-destage wait:       NO
 Creation date:       11/10/90        Key ranges present:     NO
 Expiration date:     11/10/99        AIX-unique keys:        NO
 Modification date: 09/12/89          AIX-upgrade
 Modification time: 02:27 PM          Load option:
>>>>>>>>press ENTER to go to page 2; END key to return to utility menu<<<<<<<
```

10-9 File-AID VSAM INFORMATION

A third file is an Equipment Repair File that keeps track of all equipment repairs while monitoring equipment movement in and out of service. A repair record is shown in its physical expansion in lines 220 through 284 of FIG. 10-8. The concatenated key to that record is made up of the following elements: an equipment unit number denoting the equipment to be repaired, an equipment or problem code, and a specific service date telling you just when the above equipment was removed from active service. This record is unusual in the sense that it does not contain the carrier code in its qualifier. The reason is that a piece of equipment that physically belongs to Central, for example, can be transferred for the duration of a repair job to another carrier such as Northeastern Illinois. Thus, a carrier designator in this particular instance would not be very meaningful. A File-AID expansion of this VSAM record is further illustrated in FIG. 10-10. Finally, a repair table shown in lines 285 through 291 of FIG. 10-8 provides a description for a particular repair type. Key to this record is a single repair code.

```
---------------- File-AID VSAM INFORMATION - (PAGE 1 OF 2) -----------------
COMMAND  ===>
Catalog.. CATALOG.MVSICF1.VVSAM01
Cluster.. NIRVT.TOPS.REPAIR.KS                    +--------------+
Data..... NIRVT.TOPS.REPAIR.KS.DATA               |   owner-id   |
Index.... NIRVT.TOPS.REPAIR.INDX                  +--------------+
----------------------------------------------------------------------------
Data component information:              Current allocation options:
Volume serial:        VSAM03             RACF protected          NO
Device Type:          3380               Write Check:            NO
Organization:         KSDS               Buffer Space:           10240
KSDS key length:       12                Erase on delete:        NO
KSDS key location:      0                Imbedded index:         YES
Average record size:  260                Replicated index        NO
Maximum record size:  260                Reuse option:           NO
Allocated space: Unit  Primary  Secondary  Share option          1-3
     Data  -   tracks     20        5     Spanned records:        NO
     Index -   tracks      3        1     MSS binding:        STAGED
Dataset information:                     MSS-destage wait:       NO
  Creation date:      11/10/90           Key ranges present:     NO
  Expiration date:    11/10/99           AIX-unique keys:
  Modification date:  09/12/89           AIX-upgrade
  Modification time:  02:28 PM           Load option:         SPEED
  >>>>>>>>press ENTER to go to page 2; END key to return to utility menu<<<<<<<
```

10-10 File-AID VSAM INFORMATION

There are two additional expansions by the compiler. The first one is presented in lines 294 through 339. Another table, the so-called Execute Interface Block is expanded in the LINKAGE SECTION of this program, shown in lines 341 through 372.

Glossary

ACF2 A software package to provide additional user security for CICS transactions. It is a product of the CA corporation.

ADD program Transaction or program that is the result of a NOTFND condition detected during a read operation which is a prerequisite of adding a record to a file.

Attributes Allow the programmer to refer to a data field through various characteristics (i.e., protection, color, modified data tag, etc.).

BAL Basic Assembler Language—a product of the IBM Corporation.

BMS Basic Mapping Support is an IBM productivity tool for creating a screen layout.

CHANGE program Refers to a CICS transaction whose sole purpose is to modify the contents of an existing record on file. Since the premise "existing record" is defined relative to a record key, it is assumed that no such record key can be modified without deleting and reading it to the file.

CHARATR A record layout or format placed into the copy library to give other programmers access. CHARATR provides clarity and some added flexibility in developing a program.

CICS Customer Information Control System is a telecommunications-monitor software developed by the IBM Corporation.

CICS task Synonymous with a transaction (see transaction).

COMMAREA COMMUNICATIONS AREA is part of the LINKAGE SECTION and facilitates the continuous transfer of messages between one or more transactions.

Concatenated key The use of a record key that is made up of at least two or more data fields.

Copy Library: Used for storing standardized record layouts for common reference. Also referred to as COPYLIB.

Cursor sensitivity Refers to attaining HELP or reference based on the particular location of the cursor. For example, HELP can be invoked to highlight the requirements of the EMPLOYEE I.D. field, showing edit rules and format requirements.

Customer Master One of the files used in the case studies to provide demographic data for some of the problems in reference.

Data omission Refers to a validation process, especially during the ADD transaction cycle, designed to detect missing yet mandatory data fields.

DATONLY Command used in conjunction with a HANDLE CONDITION in which only the data portion of a map is being sent.

DELETE transaction Where the programmer defines logic for deleting a record from the file.

DCT Destination Control Table needs to be defined when sequentially processing and printing a report through a transient queue. DCT defines for the programmer where or at what location a particular report is to be printed, its trigger level (how many records), etc.

DEQ Used to dequeue or release a resource.

Diagnostics A process to check the accuracy of code and how such code conforms to established rules.

DFHAID block A copy-statement-generated set of instructions to provide program reference to the keyboard.

DFHBMSCA A block presented in the compiled version of a CICS (command-level) program so that the programmer can maintain reference to a comprehensive attribute scheme.

DFHCOMMAREA A communications area that is part of the LINKAGE SECTION. Facilitates the continuous transfer of messages between one or more transactions.

EIB Execute interface block contains useful information such as that of message length, etc.

EIBAID Block that establishes reference to the keyboard: i.e., IF EIBAID = DHFPF4. . .

EIBCALEN This field is available so that the programmer can check the contents or the length of the COMMUNICATIONS AREA.

EDIT Rules required to test certain processing requirements in a program.

ENDBR Denotes the ending of a BROWSE operation.

ENQ Used to single thread a resource or enque it. It is synonymous with suspending a resource.

ERROR CONDITION A condition for which there is a defined set of procedures in your program, normally resulting from failure to meet certain EDIT requirements.

Extra points Used to allow program linkage to other programs, messages or subroutines (see XCTL).

Extended attributes Refers to the use of special attribute features normally not part of a conventional environment, i.e., reversed video, underscoring, extended color display capabilities, etc.

External module Used to access an external program, file or procedure during the processing of a transaction.

FCT File Control Table, which is designed for the definition of key data characteristics such as a dataset name, access method, record format, the type of service requested, etc.

HANDLE CONDITION A command that allows the programmer to refer to a certain path in case of an ERROR CONDITION.

Hard copy Refers to a programmer-defined record layout in the body of an application program, rather than providing for such a program through a copy statement.

IBM International Business Machines Corp.

INDDEST An indirect destination defined in your DCT.

Item number Used when building a temporary storage (queue). Item key is similar in concept to a record key, which identifies a particular item in temporary storage.

Inquiry Accessed data that is normally kept in a protected mode to avoid modification by the user. Inquiry keys must be stated fully unless using a generic option.

Inquiry key Also referred to as a search key. Necessary to locate a particular record.

Inquiry program A program that handles fully defined inquiries.

JCL Job control language. Required when compiling or submitting an online program for processing.

KSDS Key Sequenced Dataset, which is a type of VSAM file that enables the programmer to access data in a direct mode.

Line/statement(s) Used interchangeably in reference to a line in a source program.

Main directory A main menu representing high-level functional areas of a particular system.

Map Refers to a particular screen layout part of a mapset.

MAPFAIL An ERROR CONDITION caused by failure to properly transmit a map.

Menu See subdirectory.

Menu-driven A term used to simplify a particular task through a series of selections. This process enables the user or a group of users to access a small functional area in an otherwise complex application.

Menu program   A CICS program that displays a set of selections to the user.

MCRA   Metropolitan Commuter Railways Agency. Represents the parent company in some of the case studies presented in this book.

Modified data tag   Modification of certain data elements to show recent reference by the user.

Monitor (TP)   Teleprocessing software that enables the user to utilize remote and/or local interactive systems.

Multiline BROWSE   The display of a predefined number of lines per page in BROWSE/INQUIRY mode.

NOTFND   A command issued during a HANDLE CONDITION to determine a logical path in case a record does not exist on file.

PF keys   Programmed function keys used to trigger a specific action, such as the updating of a file, deleting a record, etc.

Prototype   To simulate a real production environment during the requirements study or detail design phase. This type of "live" simulation does not require any programming effort.

Pseudoconversational processing   Refers to a type of processing that enables the computer to efficiently execute only the active transactions, while suspending those awaiting an operator's response.

READNEXT   Used during a BROWSE operation to receive the next sequential record on file. This mechanism applies to forward processing.

READPREV   Used during a BROWSE operation to receive the next sequential record on file. This mechanism applies to backward processing.

RECEIVE MAP   Reads a map or screen display as soon as it appears.

Record key   Enables the user to reference a particular record or dataset, either in sequential or direct processing mode.

Reinvocation   A technique used in command-level (pseudoconversational) programming to reexecute a program after performing a particular task.

RETURN   A command in CICS used to reinvoke a transaction.

REWRITE   A command used to update a record during a CHANGE transaction.

Security   READ ONLY, meaning the user's ability to read a file without being able to CHANGE or UPDATE such a file (i.e., BROWSE, INQUIRY).

READ AND UPDATE enables the user to ADD, CHANGE and DELETE both data fields and record types. It enables the user to have full control over a file, regardless of the date element contained on such a file.

DATA FIELD LEVEL SECURITY refers to the user's ability to have access to a certain number of fields on a particular panel, while no access to others in UPDATE mode.

Additional security definitions can also include security on the following levels: Transaction, File, Record, Terminal, and Location.

Send/receive flag An indicator using a single position to differentiate between the send and the receive map cycle, thus monitoring the pseudoconversational sequences.

Search key An inquiry key used to locate a record on file and retrieve information from it.

Search—nongeneric Type of search used to find an exact match to an inquiry.

SEND MAP Sends or writes a screen layout, as defined in the program.

Shells Refers to the development of a generalized program that can be either modified or enhanced to do a specific job. For example, you can develop a CHANGE program based on an ADD program, which can be used as an initial driver.

SINGLE RECORD BROWSE Displaying one record per page in BROWSE mode.

STARBR Denotes the beginning of a BROWSE operation.

Subdirectory Refers to a submenu, which is a secondary system menu presenting the user with a number of detail-oriented options.

Subscripting A method used, for example, in defining a multiple line map to save substantial coding time.

Suffixes Generated during the assembly process of the symbolic map. Each suffix (i.e., A, L, F, I, O) enables you to refer to attributes or characteristics of a given field.

Symbolic map A translated version of the BMS or Basic Mapping Support. Translated by the compiler or by the assembly process.

Temporary datasets CICS uses temporary, transient queues to satisfy some minimum printing requirements during online processing (also see Destination Control Table or DCT).

Temporary storage Referred to as TS queues. CICS allows the programmer to create, update, delete and maintain reference to internally created small VSAM files, which do not have to be defined in the File Control Table.

Terminal operator Synonymous with the user of the system. One who either uses or owns the particular application.

Top down Each program relies on a previous hierarchical logic. The concept normally subdivides a program into main and subroutine logic.

TRANSID A four-position (or less) transaction identifier field through which a user can initially invoke a particular program or transaction.

Transaction Refers to a single task performed by a CICS program, such as deleting or adding a record to a file, etc.

Transient A temporary holding area in CICS to build print images for an online report.

Tutorials One or a series of screens providing the user with assistance in defining computational requirements, edit rules, error messages, etc.

VSAM Virtual Storage Access Method is a type of record structure (cluster) that can be organized three different ways. CICS utilizes the KSDS technique (see KSDS).

WRITE A command used to add a record to a file.

XCTL EXIT CONTROL, a command used in CICS causing the termination of the current transaction, followed by a branch to a predefined program.

Index

Other Bestsellers of Related Interest

APPLIED ADA® —Gerald L. Mohnkern, Ph.D. and Beverly Mohnkern
With this book as your guide you'll actually build an Ada vocabulary and develop a feel for the "sentence structure" of the Ada language . . . not just memorize a variety of topics or "parts of speech." Each chapter states the problem which the program is to solve, then lists and discusses the program, emphasizing the Ada features which are introduced in that program. Plus, sample programs can easily be converted to your own application needs. 320 pages, 94 illustrations. Book No. 2736, $25.00 hardcover only

HANDBOOK OF DECISION SUPPORT SYSTEMS—Stephen J. Andriole
This practical, working text outlines design strategies that will help your organization perform real-world tasks such as forecasting budgets and planning sales promotions more quickly and efficiently. Andriole deals directly with evaluation questions in helping you set up a realistic, requirements-driven system that will be adaptable to, but not dependent on, future technologies. With this book, you'll be able to select software and hardware that suit your needs. 256 pages, Illustrated. Book No. 3240, $29.95 hardcover only

MODULA-2: Programmer's Resource Book—Don Etling
Make Modula-2 more productive and easier to use! This book presents a series of procedures, modules, and utility programs that make programming in Modula-2 easier and more productive. It deals specifically with using Modula-2 to develop commercial applications on IBM PCs and compatibles, and defines specific modules that give Modula-2 access to the full power of the hardware. 380 pages, 114 illustrations. Book No. 2741, $19.95 paperback only

MICROCOMPUTER APPLICATIONS DEVELOPMENT: Techniques for
Evaluation and Implementation—Michael Simon Bodner, Ph.D.,
and Pamela Kay Hutchins
Learn the secrets of making your applications programs exactly fill the needs and wants of today's business professional. This comprehensive guide offers an overview of the process of applications development in the microcomputer environment from both a technical methodology and a business issues point of view. The authors also offer shortcuts and development tips based on their experience as professional consultants. 256 pages, 69 illustrations. Book No. 2840, $24.95 hardcover only

COMPUTER TOOLS, MODELS AND TECHNIQUES FOR PROJECT
MANAGEMENT—Dr. Adedeji B. Badiru and Dr. Gary E. Whitehouse
Badiru and Whitehouse provide you with practical, down-to-earth guidance on the use of project management tools, models, and techniques. You'll find this book filled with helpful tips and advice. You'll also discover ways to use your current computer hardware and software resources to more effectively enhance project management functions. 320 pages, 112 illustrations. Book No. 3200, $32.95 hardcover only

SYSTEMS DESIGN UNDER CICS® COMMAND AND VSAM® —Alex Varsegi

Here is a comprehensive summary of CICS functions, design considerations, and related software products to acquaint you with the concept of on-line data processing and its established role in current computer design. You'll cover system design, screen painting techniques using SDF to create input/output maps, the use of CECI, VSAM (virtual storage access method), and all the CICS commands and how they relate to system design. 272 pages, 204 illustrations. Book No. 2843, $28.95 hardcover only

OFFICE AUTOMATION SYSTEMS HANDBOOK
—Kenniston W. Lord, Jr., CDP, CSP, COAP

Here is the perfect introduction to all aspects of the computerized office environment. The basic principles of system design, decision support, and ergonomics are presented, as well as a discussion of the most commonly used types of software. Concepts are presented on a practical, nontheoretical level with detailed line drawings, tables, and examples to demonstrate how systems work. Lord also includes a case study to illustrate the principles of office automation. 352 pages, 150 illustrations. Book No. 2899, $39.95 hardcover only

DATA ACQUISITION AND CONTROL: Microcomputer Applications for Scientists and Engineers—Joseph J. Carr

This comprehensive overview of automated data systems for research and industrial applications describes the professional applications of transducers and components and covers the spectrum of measurable input. The author describes in detail the peripheral components essential to data transference and signal processing including op amps, electronic integrator and differentiator circuits, and more. 430 pages, 150 illustrations. Book No. 2956, $34.95 hardcover only

COMPUTER INTEGRATED MANUFACTURING: Techniques and Applications
—Michael Hordeski

Keep in step with current strategies—learn to use computer integrated manufacturing (CIM) systems to tie together all segments of your manufacturing operation. This examination of today's strategies for planning CIM systems, standards, and protocols such as MRP, MRPII, CAD, CAM, and MAP will help you plan every phase of CIM implementation, from cost justification through choosing the best system for your needs. 480 pages, 145 illustrations. Book No. 2988, $44.95 hardcover only

THE PICK® PERSPECTIVE—Ian Jeffrey Sandler

"This is the first book on the PICK environment that a software developer absolutely must buy. It tells what PICK does, and how it does it."
—John Treankler, Chairman
PICK Software Developers Association

"I heartily recommend it."
—Theodore M. Sabarese
President and CEO, The Ultimate Corporation

This book examines the unique PICK environment. In it you'll discover professional methods of performing such operations as word processing, asynchronous communication, creating spreadsheets, and more. 304 pages, Illustrated. Book No. 3123, $34.95 hardcover only

PICK® FOR THE IBM® PC AND COMPATIBLES—John W. Winters, Ph.D. and Dale E. Winters

This essential guide to creating business applications with PICK/OS in the IBM environment leads you step by step through the multi-user business applications that are possible in PICK/OS. It also gives you hands-on experience using PICK's tightly integrated set of statements and commands. Topics covered include: PICK file structures, PROC, PICK/BASIC, PICK ASSEMBLER, ACCESS, PICK SPOOLER, floppy disk and tape control, RUNOFF, and more. 352 pages, 245 illustrations. Book No. 3152, $29.95 hardcover only

Prices Subject to Change Without Notice.

Look for These and Other TAB Books at Your Local Bookstore

To Order Call Toll Free 1-800-822-8158
(in PA, AK, and Canada call 717-794-2191)

or write to TAB Books, Blue Ridge Summit, PA 17294-0840.

Title	Product No.	Quantity	Price

☐ Check or money order made payable to TAB Books

Charge my ☐ VISA ☐ MasterCard ☐ American Express

Acct. No. _____ Exp. _____

Signature: _____

Name: _____

Address: _____

City: _____

State: _____ Zip: _____

TAB Books catalog free with purchase; otherwise send $1.00 in check or money order and receive $1.00 credit on your next purchase.

Orders outside U.S. must pay with international money order in U.S. dollars.

TAB Guarantee: If for any reason you are not satisfied with the book(s) you order, simply return it (them) within 15 days and receive a full refund.   BC

Subtotal $ _____

Postage and Handling
($3.00 in U.S.,
$5.00 outside U.S.) $ _____

Add applicable state
and local sales tax $ _____

TOTAL $ _____